THE FILIPINO MIGRATION EXPERIENCE

THE FILIPINO MIGRATION EXPERIENCE

GLOBAL AGENTS OF CHANGE

MINA ROCES

CORNELL UNIVERSITY PRESS
Ithaca and London

Copyright © 2021 by Cornell University

All rights reserved. Except for brief quotations in a review, this book, or parts thereof, must not be reproduced in any form without permission in writing from the publisher. For information, address Cornell University Press, Sage House, 512 East State Street, Ithaca, New York 14850. Visit our website at cornellpress.cornell.edu.

First published 2021 by Cornell University Press

Library of Congress Cataloging-in-Publication Data

Names: Roces, Mina, 1959– author.
Title: The Filipino migration experience: global agents of change / Mina Roces.
Description: Ithaca [New York]: Cornell University Press, 2021. | Includes bibliographical references and index.
Identifiers: LCCN 2020058210 (print) | LCCN 2020058211 (ebook) | ISBN 9781501760402 (hardcover) | ISBN 9781501760419 (epub) | ISBN 9781501760426 (pdf)
Subjects: LCSH: Filipinos—Foreign countries—Social conditions—20th century. | Filipinos—Foreign countries—Social conditions—21st century. | Return migrants—Philippines—Social conditions—20th century. | Return migrants—Philippines—Social conditions—21st century. | Social change—Philippines. | Philippines—Emigration and immigration—Social aspects.
Classification: LCC JV8685.R63 2021 (print) | LCC JV8685 (ebook) | DDC 305.899/21—dc23
LC record available at https://lccn.loc.gov/2020058210
LC ebook record available at https://lccn.loc.gov/2020058211

The Australian section of chapter 6 was published as Mina Roces, "Changing Migration Policy from the Margins: Filipino Activism on Behalf of Victims of Domestic Violence in Australia, 1980s–2000," in *History, Historians and the Immigration Debate: Going Back to Where We Came From*, ed. Eureka Henrich and Julian M. Simpson (Palgrave Macmillan, 2019), 71–90.

ISBN: 978-1-5017-8504-7 (pbk.)

Contents

Acknowledgments vii

Introduction: Toward a History of the Filipino Migrant as Agent of Change, 1970s–2018 — 1

Part One: Breaking Taboos: Family and Gender

1. Migration and the Rethinking of the Filipino Family, 1970s–2018 — 21

2. Challenging Constructions of Gender and Sexuality, 1980s–2018 — 39

Part Two: Changing Social Mores and Economic Landscapes: Filipino Migrants as Consumers

3. Consumption and Social Change, 1980s–2018 — 57

4. The Impact of Consumption on Businesses, 1990s–2018 — 76

Part Three: Changing the Homeland and the Host Country: Activism and Philanthropy

5. Filipina/o/x Americans as Community Historians, 1980s–2018 — 89

6. Advocacy and Its Impacts, 1970s to circa 2000 — 114

7. Migrants and the Homeland, 1986–2018   148

Conclusion: Refusing to Be Marginal   173

Notes   183
Bibliography   227
Index   247

Acknowledgments

I have benefited from the generosity of many individuals and institutions in the research and writing process for this book. The research was funded by an Australian Research Council Discovery Grant (DP120100791), for 2012–2014, a school grant from the School of Humanities and Languages, University of New South Wales, and a small grant from the United States Studies Centre, University of Sydney. Visiting fellowships at the Southeast Asian Studies Centre at the University of Freiburg (2013) and the Center for Asian Studies, Lund University, gave me the opportunity to write, present early drafts to colleagues, and receive feedback. I am grateful to Monica Lindberg Falk for arranging my fellowship at Lund University that enabled me to write the chapter on Filipino migrants and the homeland and to Judith Schlehe and Jürgen Rüland for giving me written comments on the chapter on migrants as historians and for publishing it in their working paper series. I appreciate Jonathan Okamura, Maruja M. B. Asis, and Roli Talampas for sharing their sources with me and for many helpful discussions on the topics of Filipino migration. I thank Eureka Henrich for important feedback for the Australian case study that formed part of chapter 6, published in *Historians, History and the Immigration Debate: Going Back to Where We Came From*, edited by Eureka Henrich and Julian M. Simpson (Palgrave Macmillan, 2019).

Most of the archives I used were personal papers or collections. For their generosity in sharing their private collections, I acknowledge Deborah Wall, Rosa Droescher, Joan Dicka, Cecilia Silva, Amefil Agbayani, Clement Bautista (Operation Manong [OM] archives), Dee Dicen Hunt (*Kasama*), Mona Lisa Yuchengco (Philippine International Aid [AID] archives), Pio de Cano Jr., Mao and Ophee de Vera, Cora Francisco, Estrella "Lilia" McKinnon, and Rogelia Pe-Pua. Nicki Saroca invited me to her home in Newcastle, New South Wales, Australia so that I could avail of her excellent personal archive of Filipinos in Australia, and Joan Dicka also welcomed me into her home in Adelaide. Sonia Soosot Nisa Zerrudo gave me privileged access to the written journals of the members of Lakbay Dangal in Hong Kong. For providing much needed rare material on migrant life stories I am indebted to Vivienne Angeles, Nicole

Constable, Charito Basa, Luz Campos Mesenas (for copies of *OFW Pinoy Star* magazine [Singapore]), and to Roli Talampas, who lent me his hard-copy issues of *Tinig ng Marino*.

I appreciate the help of Dorothy Cordova and the late Fred Cordova, founders of the Filipino American National Historical Society (FANHS), for welcoming me in the National Pinoy Archives and for arranging interviews with Filipino Americans. I thank the late Robert Santos for sharing his story with me and for showing me around the International District in Seattle. I am indebted to the late Dawn Mabalon—the premier historian of Filipinos in Stockton, California, for personally giving me a tour of Filipinos in Stockton, for sharing her photo archive with me, and for introducing me to the FANHS-Stockton group. Terri Torres and Linda Claramo past president and president of FANHS-Stockton regularly sent me their newsletters by email since I joined their organization in 2013 and responded to my queries for more information. I want to extend a very special thank you to those who helped me with organizing interviews: Maruja M. B. Asis, Mona Lisa Yuchengco, Joy and Arnel Baradas, Charito Basa, Verma Villanueva, Precy Villanueva, Sally Rousset, Maya Jezewksi, Benjie de Ubago, Melinda Kerkvliet, Amefil Agbayani, Clement Bautista, Jacinta Carlos, Marian Laarni Silva, Rowel Valdez Tugas, John Nobelo Reyes, Masaaki Satake, Cecilia Silva, Cedie Lopez Vargas, Marianna Lopez Vargas, Andrea Rubio, Luz and Clem Mesenas, Gemma Nemenzo, Jonathan Okamura, Lita Patricio, Nina "Cute" Rotelo, Gilda Malaluan, Cristina Santos, Edna Aquino, Emil de Guzman, Sonia Soosot Nisa Zerrudo, Alpha Grace Vicente, Dee Dicen Hunt, and the Philippine Consulate General in Milan. MC Canlas took me on a personalized Filipino American tour of San Francisco, Ramon Virata took me to the PIA archives in San Francisco, Lisa Monteroso Mayor welcomed me in the PinoyWISE (Worldwide Initiative for Investment Savings and Entrepreneurship) financial literacy seminar in Singapore in 2016, and Mai Añonuevo arranged my participation in the PinoyWISE financial literacy seminar in Malolos, Bulacan province, in 2019. Precy Villanueva and Marian Laarni Silva arranged my participation at the debut celebrations in Padova in 2018, and Verma Villanueva took me to Andrew Templo Avecilla's fiftieth birthday in 2015 also in Padova.

I have had the good fortune to be able to enlist the aid of several excellent librarians in the task of hunting for sources: Susi Yamaguchi and Anna Rutkowska, University of New South Wales Outreach librarians, Mitchell Yangson, librarian, Filipino American Center, San Francisco Public Library, Mercy Servida of the Lopez Museum and Library, Metro-Manila, who provided consistent outstanding service in pursuit of rare materials, and Barbara Quek from the National Library of Singapore.

Anita Navalta Bautista not only shared her life story with me as a second-generation Filipina American, she also arranged interviews with first-generation Filipino Americans in Stockton, took me to the Stockton cemetery and the Daguhoy Lodge, and sent me valuable sources, including photographs. Elena Mangahas invited me to come as a guest of the Filipina Women's Network to the PIA fundraising event, took me on the Filipino American tour of Stockton, posted to me her copies of *Filipinas* magazine, and arranged several interviews in San Francisco and Manila. Maruja M. B. Asis arranged interviews for me in Santa Rosa, Laguna, and accompanied me there for fieldwork.

For corrections to early drafts of this book, I thank Mao de Vera, Mona Lisa Yuchengco, Anita Navalta Bautista, M C Canlas, Clement Bautista, Amefil Agbayani, and Debbie Wall. For his invaluable help in Manila, taking me to archives and interviews, I thank Jun Dulay. Raina Ann Bernardez and Esther Ann S. Gov transcribed most of the interviews for this book. And lastly, I thank Martyn Lyons, who translated all the Italian material for me, accompanied me to Rome, Rotterdam, Hong Kong, and Padova, and gave me feedback and support in the writing process. To all those who gave me their valuable time and to all the interviewees, *maraming salamat po*.

Introduction
Toward a History of the Filipino Migrant as Agent of Change, 1970s–2018

In the popular blockbuster Tagalog film *It Takes a Man and a Woman* (2013), the character of Laida Magtalas (played by actress Sarah Geronimo) returned to Manila after a two-year stint in Canada. The film was part of the typical romance genre ubiquitous in Tagalog cinema. Laida claimed to have undergone a personal transformation from her experience abroad, presenting the new and improved version of herself to her work colleagues as Laida 2.0, adopting the linguistic marker for updated computer software.

Change was at the epicenter of the lives of Filipino migrants from the day they decided to leave the homeland. Like Laida, they reinvented themselves as new subjects. The following short biographies from the migrant archives illustrate the magnitude of the personal metamorphoses. Zita Cabais (formerly Obra) was born in Pangasinan, the second of nine children born to a poor farming family. She was compelled to stop her schooling after completing sixth grade in 1976 because her parents needed her to work to help support her siblings. She worked as a *katulong* (helper or maid) in Manila from the age of thirteen and later as a clerk in a pharmacy in Santa Mesa, Manila. She married and had two children. In 1994 she went to France as an undocumented migrant to earn a living as a domestic worker. After working as a babysitter for eleven months, she found employment as a nanny for two boys, but after two years she received only 1,500–2,000 francs (out of her monthly salary of 6,000 francs) because her employers claimed that the deductions were to pay for the lawyers who were working on her papers. When she discovered that nothing had been done to process her case for legal residence, she confronted her employers and demanded her passport and the money due her. When nothing happened, she took legal action, becoming the first Filipina in France to file a case against her employer on the grounds of "modern slavery" and exploitation. She took her case to the trade union Confédération française démocratique du travail (CFDT), which provided her with a lawyer. On May 14, 2001, the court decided in her favor, and she was awarded 45,000 francs. Rather than take the money (she was asked to "name her price"), she took it up with the Court of Appeal, where she was awarded her due salary including legal interest. Her efforts made her a celebrity in both France and the Philippines. She was featured in the magazine *Témoignage Chrétien*, and a French television company accompanied her to the Philippines when she visited her family.[1] Although she claimed that the Philippine Embassy did not help her (blaming her troubles on her undocumented status), the first lady of France at the time, Bernadette Chirac, responded to her letter. After her victory, she was offered a position with the CFDT helping migrant workers encountering similar cases. The union paid for private French lessons so she could master the language she needed to use to write letters to employers. In my interview with her, Zita told her life story with an enormous amount of pride and a clear self-awareness of her own metamorphosis from a domestic worker with primary school qualifications to a union advocate for the rights of all exploited workers in Paris and its environs.[2]

Would Zita have been able to acquire a professional job and gain celebrity status if she had stayed in the Philippines? Zita's story shows that she made the most of the opportunities available in her host country. She reinvented herself from domestic worker to professional union advocate. There were many parallels to Zita's account. Nina "Cute" Rotelo, a domestic worker in Singapore, joined the Humanitarian Organization for Migration Economics (HOME), a Singaporean nongovernmental organization (NGO), in 2008–2009 as a volunteer on her Sundays off. In 2010, she was invited by HOME founder Bridget Tan to accompany her to Geneva, Switzerland, to give testimony for a closed-door session for the convention on decent work for domestic workers for the International Labour Organization's Convention 189. At that venue, Rotelo shared stories of the way the Singapore government treated the domestic workers there. In 2017 when I last interviewed her, she had become president of HOME Roses, the organization's arm that deals with migrant health issues.[3] She became an international delegate—a role she would not have had the chance to perform if she had stayed in the Philippines.

I gave two brief examples here to demonstrate the dramatic personal transformations experienced by some migrants who empowered themselves and discovered their leadership potential. Each individual migrant who left the Philippines from the 1970s experienced his/her own version of Laida's Filipino migrant 2.0 upgrade. These personal stories revealed that migration was not just an economic project. Although financial opportunities were probably the most important motivations for the decision to migrate, in reality the circumstances of mobility had an impact beyond the person's economic status. The migration context—away from the family, the kinship group, and the prying eyes of the village and the community, coupled with the novel environment complete with its new norms, values, and ways of seeing and interpreting the world—provided the impetus and nourishment for these migrant makeovers. Filipino migrants embraced these new opportunities and discovered the advantages that came with living mobile lives: learning languages, customs, and food practices, becoming leaders representing their ethnic community, and rising to middle-class status. Since Filipino migrants numbered about ten million, or 10 percent of the total population of the Philippines, their combined transformations had the potential to alter aspects of Filipino culture. This book is a history of these transformations *outside* the sphere of labor, written from the perspective of the migrants themselves. How did migrants alter Filipino social institutions and norms? Did they also influence the host countries where they lived and worked?

I argue that after almost half a century of history, migrants became agents of change, able to challenge fundamental social institutions and well-entrenched traditional norms as well as altering the business, economic, and cultural landscapes of both the homeland and the host country. By telling these stories, I hope to add a novel dimension to the usual depiction of migrants as disenfranchised workers or marginal ethnic groups. Instead, I suggest alternative ways of conceptualizing Filipino migrants—as critics of social institutions and cultural constructions of gender and sexuality, as consumers and investors, as philanthropists, and, finally, as historians.

Migrants were able to break major cultural taboos about the most fundamental social institution of the family and cultural constructions of gender and sexuality. They became philanthropists who did the civic work normally expected of politicians by bringing free health care to the poorest, providing scholarships to needy children, and coming to the rescue when disaster struck the homeland. As activists, they also lobbied to improve the status of marginal groups in the host countries; and as consumers, they influenced the growth of business ventures and altered social norms on reciprocity. This book will analyze some of the areas where Filipino migrants have forever altered the status quo.

This study used a historical approach, investigating the history of Filipino migration in the period from the 1970s to circa 2018. Migrants' life stories alert readers to the way their migration changed family dynamics no matter the length of time spent overseas. The autobiography of Nenita, the forty-four-year-old wife of a carpenter (who mended fishing boats) and mother of four from Malabon City in Metropolitan Manila, who went to Saudi Arabia for two and a half years as a seamstress, records her astonishment at the changes she encountered on her return:

> They all seemed to change, not like the time before I left. All of them drink [alcohol]. Jay drinks. Luis drinks. Romy [her husband] is the worst one, he drinks every day. He didn't do that when I was around because I stop him from doing it. But maybe because I'm away he succumbs. [Romy claimed that he drank because he was very anxious that Nenita might find a boyfriend in Saudi Arabia.] They used to listen to me then. I didn't observe that they were like that. The changes are so great that it seems like I don't know them anymore, not like before. I was shocked because I was only away for two years, imagine that, and yet the changes have been so huge! I said: "I just left and all of you now have vices!"[4]

The memoir concludes with Nenita barely able to pay for improvements on her house or the tuition of her children, all of whom had to drop out of school and earn a living as salespersons or cooks in the fast food retail business. But the postscript tells readers that Nenita was considering returning to Saudi Arabia.[5]

Many migrants spent much longer than two years abroad. After twenty years working as a nanny in Hong Kong, Juanita was so disappointed with the cold reception she received from her children on her return to the Philippines for a holiday that she decided to go back to Hong Kong where she felt most needed as a volunteer with an organization that promoted the rights and welfare of all domestic workers there. She reflected on the change:

> It's also true that I hoped and dreamt that I will leave Hong Kong for good. And home, I went with all the expectations and I came to realize that to be lovingly welcomed by my family after twenty years of not being with them was an illusion. I thought my children would be happy to be with me. I dreamt of going out with them, playing with my grand children [sic], just doing things together as a family. I guess I spent too long in Hong Kong, I failed to realize that I really don't know them at all. And they don't know me at all, too. For them, I was just the mother that sent them their allowances without fail every month.[6]

Juanita's account documents the pain she felt when her children took her for granted. Her daughter Raphaela did not meet her at the airport and was too busy to spend time with her, so she spent her holiday alone. Her own children's lack of affection for her contrasted greatly with that of her ward in Hong Kong who told her she was very welcome to return there because her cooking was much missed. She recalls how, in despair, she addressed her children: "'I came home to see my kids, I didn't find them here! I went to Hong Kong to give you a future. I think you already had one. I am going back to Hong Kong so I will have one too!' I cried. I meant every word I said. 'Raphaela, you don't need me to fit in with your schedule, I will find my own way to the airport.'"[7] Juanita's story ended with her decision to return to Hong Kong to build her own life there, which included volunteering her free time assisting migrants in distress. This was a difficult decision for her because she knew that it was transgressing social expectations of motherhood. "I felt so guilty afterwards," she admitted, "but Mary [her friend] assured me it was nobody's fault. My children had found a life of their own without me. I need to find one, too."[8] Sadly, Juanita's story was not unique. Some of the consequences of prolonged separation from family have been analyzed in the scholarship on Filipino migration.[9] But here I wanted to draw attention to Juanita's decision to embark on a life of her own, *separate* from her children and family. The project of pursuing her own individual dream unattached to the family was a radical move. Juanita rejected the cultural construction of the ideal mother as the suffering martyr mother who lives only for her offspring.[10] She redefined "family" when she chose to transfer her affection to her ward in Hong Kong who missed her rather than attempt to win back the love and affection of her own biological children. Rejecting the role of mother so intrinsic to Filipino cultural constructions of the feminine was at the very least controversial and at most a shocking act. And finally, she found fulfillment as an active member of the mission or the NGO devoted to the care of other migrant workers in Hong Kong. Juanita challenged the connections between gender and motherhood and altered the definition of the family. These were all revolutionary changes to Filipino traditional cultural constructs of gender and the family. The above radical changes had not yet been investigated in the scholarship on Filipino migration.

The changes experienced by Juanita and Nenita are just the tip of the iceberg. This book is the first step in analyzing the migrant as agent of change over almost half a century of history. It is the unique context of migration that allows migrants to be self-reflexive about their own culture. The new environment relatively free of kinship ties and the pressures to conform to traditional practices makes it possible for these mobile individuals to imagine an alternative present and future.

The popular construction of the Filipino migrant as suffering martyr— enduring the challenges of living in a foreign environment, vulnerable to exploitation and abuse, and experiencing periodic bouts of loneliness due to separation from family—remains entrenched and unchanged despite more than a century of labor migration history. The Philippine government's pronouncement since 1988 that Filipino overseas workers are *bagong bayani*, or "new heroes," is inextricably linked to this mental representation as self-sacrificing subjects. The journey undertaken by the migrant is equated with the passion of Jesus Christ—a road to Calvary that climaxed with the crucifixion rather than the resurrection. Even though some tales circulate underscoring that for some the migration project is a successful one, the authorial voice reminds the audience of the social costs or heavy price paid for the migrant's new affluent lifestyle. Popular film representations in Tagalog movies such as *Anak, Milan, Dubai, The Flor Contemplacion Story, Transit,* and *Caregiver,* to name some of the blockbusters, propagate this stereotype, conflating the Filipino migrant story with the genre of tearjerker, highlighting the drama of family separation, estrangement, and the harsh reality of living on the fringes.[11] NGOs dedicated to lobbying for migrants' human rights deliberately reproduce this trope when they criticize the Philippine government and global neoliberal policies that they blamed for the migrant exodus.

Filipino migrants are imagined to be liminal subjects—belonging neither to the homeland they left behind nor to the host country—driven to leave because of their marginal position and becoming a member of an ethnic minority in their new destination. Even though Filipino migrants are acknowledged to have "revolutionized the Philippines" due to their large numbers and massive remittances (totaling US$33.5 billion in 2019), the discursive emphasis on what Filomeno Aguilar Jr. labels "double liminality" meant that in the public perception they remain relegated to the periphery of both the homeland and the host countries.[12] Aguilar is writing about migration from the perspective of the Philippine nation.[13] This study aims to shift the perspective to the opposite direction. Is it possible to tell an alternative story with the migrant at the center of analysis? What new insights can be gleaned about migration if the narrative is written from the migrant's point of view? Are the migrants themselves keen to tell their version of the story, and if so, what is it?

Most studies on the post-1970s migration wave focus on migrant's working lives, activism, social integration (in the case of marriage migration, for example), or evolving new hybrid identities. Social scientists focusing on the post-1970s migration wave have been able to capture the experiences of migrants in specific sectors, especially domestic workers in Hong Kong, Singapore, Taiwan, Rome, Bologna, Los Angeles, caregivers in Canada and Israel, nurses in the United States and the United Kingdom, entertainers in Japan, seafarers, construction workers in the Middle East, and migrants for marriage in Japan and Australia.[14] These studies—most of them excellent—each focus on the conditions of work and leisure experienced by one particular sector of Filipino migrant workers. The studies dealing with marriage migrants emphasize the challenges faced by intercultural marriages particularly in the contexts of migration to rural or remote areas of the host countries.[15] There have also been a series of studies on migration and the role of technologies such as the media, mobile phones, the Internet, and Facebook in the project of keeping migrants connected with families in the homeland.[16] They have analyzed work, labor exploitation, as well as everyday forms of resistance and creative ways of connecting to home. The concern with what NGOs have called "the social costs of migration" also inspired studies on the impact on families left behind, particularly those separated by overseas contract work.[17]

My book differs from the published scholarship in the field because it offers new categories to understand the migrant experience beyond that of disenfranchised laborer. While the popular and scholarly discourse focuses on Filipino migrants as de-professionalized, underclassed, or precarious laborers from the global South, this book will demonstrate that migrants have also become agents of change in several arenas. Migrants have critiqued a fundamental social institution such as the family and challenged constructions of gender and sexuality. As consumers of goods, real estate, and telecommunications, migrants have had an enormous impact on the businesses they chose to patronize. As activists they influenced the conditions of their minority ethnic group in the host country, and as philanthropists they have improved the lives of the poorest in the homeland. And finally, as historians they have ensured that their contributions will be acknowledged in the social memory of the host countries as well as their homeland. This resulting portrait of global migration is complex but very rich in data and insights. The time frame encompasses more than four decades—beginning from 1974 when President Ferdinand Marcos signed the labor code that propelled the massive global migration to all parts of the world, a time period that overlaps with a major wave of Filipino migration to the United States after 1965, up until 2018. This viewpoint from the historical perspective shifts the perception of the migrant as a victim of poverty and circumstances and promises to stop provincializing the migrant as peripheral to the center (read the Philippine or overseas metropole), giving credit to the contribution this unique group has brought to the homeland and internationally. I am not downplaying the circumstances of exploitation or experiences of violence and discrimination, but I am suggesting that the time frame of almost half a century allows us historians to make a contribution to the social science–dominated scholarship on Filipino migration by giving credit to the way the migrants have been at the very center of social change and acknowledging their potential for altering not just the homeland but also the host countries where they reside. For example, Filipino migrants have been able to alter major legislation in one host country—Australia—making it abundantly clear that policy can be shaped from what Australians perceived to be the marginal minority ethnic group of Filipino *women* (see chapter 6). While the role of nationalists and activists as instigators of social and political change have long been acknowledged, I suggest here that Filipino migrants have also become radical revolutionaries in the project of breaking cultural taboos and introducing new practices and attitudes over time.[18]

While most scholars also tend to focus on either one sector (domestic workers, entertainers, seafarers, and so on), or one geographical area (Filipinos in the United States, Filipinos in Japan, and so on), this book goes beyond these usual parameters and takes a very big picture approach to the topic. It includes all Filipino migrants—whether temporary migrants such as overseas contract workers or seafarers or those who have permanent residency overseas (or indeed foreign citizenship papers)—and embraces all geographical locations. It also blends hitherto separate fields together: Filipina/o/x American studies and Philippine migration studies. Hence, the examples in each chapter cover more than one geographical area and more than one sector of migrants.

What unites this broad spectrum is the focus on migrants as agents of change and the use of primary sources that I will call the "migrant archives": data collected, published, and disseminated by migrants themselves. Migrants have been meticulously compiling, preserving, and telling their stories in the public domain. This project of telling and retelling this heroic narrative of migration is very important to them especially because they feel that their version of history—that they struggled and survived despite the terrible odds of discrimination they faced—is not acknowledged or appreciated in the host countries and in the homeland. They want their voices heard, they want their stories of challenges and successes to be visible and publicly validated. They refuse to remain invisible. They are so committed to this project that they continue to invest an enormous amount of time and resources to the project of writing their life stories and publishing or presenting them in as many platforms as possible (including self-publication, visual arts, radio, film, the Internet, migrant newspapers, and NGO outputs, performances, and so on). These accounts are multilingual: many are written in English, Tagalog, and colloquial Taglish (a mixture of Tagalog and English), while a smattering are in other languages, such as the collection of children's stories published in the Italian version (though interviews with children were originally conducted in Tagalog) by the Turin organization ACFIL (Associazione Culturale Filippina del Piemonte).[19] All the translations from the Tagalog original to English in this book are mine unless otherwise specified. Some of the stories are published in Filipino diasporic newspapers and anthologies and cover the wide geographical spread of the migration—Europe, the Middle East, Asia, Australia, and North America in particular. Migrant magazines, such as the online *Positively Filipino* (published in the United States), for example, encourage readers to send in their immigration story, and NGOs, such as Lakbay Dangal Hong Kong founded to train Filipino domestic workers into travel guides doing a "Philippine Historical Tour of Hong Kong," require their members to keep a journal with the aim of future publication. Even migrants' children have published their stories of reuniting with migrant parents in the Middle East through text and paintings in a splendidly illustrated coffee-table book.[20] Filipina/o/x American second- and third-generation migrants are the most prolific of the group, producing their stories and histories in print form, oral performance, visual art (street murals in California, for example), and cultural performances by college students in Pilipino Cultural Nights on campuses particularly on the West Coast.[21] The Filipino American National Historical Society (FANHS) has its own physical archive, the National Pinoy Archives in Seattle, and its Stockton chapter opened its own museum in October 2016. (FANHS claims to have thirty-eight chapters organized all over the United States.)

The migrant archives document the migrants' voices, including their agendas, achievements, and aspirations, as well as their own critiques of the homeland and its social institutions. The continuous publication of migrant life stories and anthologies, which one FANHS member has referred to as the making of "perpetual anthologies," is testament to their intense desire to present their own version of their history/histories.[22] These histories present the Filipino migrants' own unique interpretation of events in which they are *the* major characters. Their stories are a classic example of the new history from below because the authors are no longer an anonymous mass (since most publish with their own names), and they are written by autodidacts who taught themselves how to write their own histories (see chapter 5).[23] But by and large these archives have been untapped by scholars of Filipino migration. Although migrants have embraced the project of telling and retelling their heroic narrative of migration, they are silent about the role that they played in launching major evolutionary changes. This book uses detailed case studies from the migrant archives to analyze how migrants have enacted change in both the host countries and the homeland in making a plea for a reconsideration of migrants as revolutionary actors outside the sphere of labor. Migrants also need to be analyzed as consumers and investors, as philanthropists, and, finally, also as historians (a category that has been completely ignored in the scholarship).

This global approach to the history of the post-1970s Filipino migration requires a multisited analysis of several sectors, types, generations, and classes of migrant cohorts. I have selected the areas where I have found evidence for the most revolutionary changes. I wanted to cover changes in a wide gamut of areas, including challenges to the foundations of Filipino culture and traditions, as well as changes to the economy and social conditions in the homeland. Hence, part 1 of this book analyzes the way migrants have contested cultural constructions of the family and gender and sexuality. Part 2 makes a case for viewing migrants as influential consumers and investors hoping to confound the usual narratives of migrant laborers as the source of care or service for the global North or as sources of remittances sent home to the Philippines. I argue that shifting the focus from the migrant as laborer or breadwinner to the migrant as consumer demonstrates the way migrants alter social values of reciprocity also considered by anthropologists as foundational to Filipino "smooth interpersonal relations." This section also demonstrates the impact consumption has had on the businesses that they patronized both overseas and in the homeland. Finally, part 3 discusses how migrants have been proactive in advocacy and philanthropic endeavors and the impacts of these time-consuming activities. In this section I also introduce the new category of migrants as community historians and custodians of their own historical past.

There are class differences in the migrant cohorts. Filipina/o/x American second and third (and plus) generations (from the post-1965 migration waves), many of whom are permanent residents or citizens of the United States, are largely a middle-class cohort (with the exception of Hawaii; see chapter 6). The motley of migrants around the world ranges from permanent residents and citizens of Italy to marriage migrants in Australia and elsewhere, and those on overseas contract work in places such as the Middle East, Singapore, and Hong Kong, seafarers, and undocumented migrants occupy an entire range of class categories. In addition, as I shall demonstrate in the chapter on consumption, the transnational context of migration also unsettles categories of class, as domestic workers in Italy, for example, are classified as lower class or working class in the host country, but their spending power in the Philippines locates them as part of the rising middle class there. Hence, the migration context where they earn money in one country but spend it in another enables them to straddle two class categories simultaneously—an innovative situation in itself. Each chapter will discuss these class positions in more detail in relation to the case studies.

The Heroic Narrative

The myriad migrant accounts tell and retell a familiar story: a heroic narrative of struggle, survival, and sacrifice amid a hostile and lonely alien environment. This tale of epic proportions usually ends in triumph rather than tragedy. The hero or heroine of the story is not a martyr but a phoenix who rises from the ashes of a metaphoric trial by fire transformed into an improved version of the original person: a Filipino migrant 2.0. In this sense, the migrant perspective differs from the popular construction of the migrant as suffering subject: as martyr, or as *bagong bayani*. If there are any similarities to the passion of Christ, it departs from the popular discourses by ending with the resurrection rather than the crucifixion. These narratives also demand to be heard, entreating the readers to acknowledge and appreciate the hard work and contribution migrants make to the Philippine nation and to the host countries where they live and work. Filipino migrants also use the heroic narrative to legitimize pleas for inclusion in the host countries and recognition in the homeland (see chapter 5). Activists for example, mine the history of migration in order to make certain claims for "space," human rights, better employment conditions, and citizenship status. The development and dissemination of the heroic narrative in the migrant-generated publications also attests to the emergence of Filipino migrants as community historians motivated to have their voices heard and their version of events recorded for all time (see chapter 5).

Is this heroic narrative a celebratory one? Of course it is, but at this particular point in time when they are minorities in their host countries, in order to have a visible presence and to get noticed for their contributions, they need to present a particular migration story that underscores and celebrates their positive achievements. The main rationale for the magazine *Filipinas* (published between 1992 and 2010) was precisely to find a space in which to celebrate Filipina/o/x American achievements in order to build ethnic pride: "Our common dream was a fine magazine that would honor the country we came from, and celebrate our presence as Filipinos."[24] Greg Macabenta, the publisher and editor of *Filipinas* magazine from 1992 to 2010, wrote in his editorial that "even among us, there is a tendency to think lightly of our capabilities as a people. It is not unusual for fellow Filipinos to express surprise that there are so many in our community who excel in the U.S. mainstream and internationally. This is the *raison d'etre*—the reason for existence—of *Filipinas* magazine. It is the only publication whose pages consistently and proudly showcase the achievers among us."[25] In 2000 the magazine produced a list of "Filipino American Faces of the Century," giving tribute to those who have contributed to the United States, "assuring us a place in the history of the nation."[26]

In addition to the magazine's regular features of Filipina/o/x American achievers, the magazine also bestowed its own achievement awards from 1998. These awards were to honor "Filipino Americans whose achievements in their respective areas of endeavor make them exemplars, not only for members of our community in the United States but also for Filipinos worldwide."[27] *Filipinas* ceased publication in 2010 and was succeeded by the online community newspaper *Positively Filipino* (first published in November 2012) whose raison d'être was the same: "*Positively Filipino* celebrates our people's heritage and achievements and is a proud promoter of role models and achievers."[28] Thus, the heroic narrative that migrants proclaimed in public was deliberately a celebratory one in order to counter negative stereotypes produced by the host countries and to build ethnic pride.

I would add that the celebratory angle of the heroic narrative was also important because it sent migrants the comforting message that their decision to leave the homeland was the right one at the time. And finally, the heroic narrative was also used to demand appreciation for the support they have given to the homeland—some of which was made at the cost of tremendous personal sacrifice. What did the migrant deployment of the heroic narrative tell us? First of all, it revealed the contrast in representations between the dominant popular discourse that depicted them as *bagong bayani*, or the suffering migrant martyr, and their own stories where they viewed themselves as heroes and heroines who triumphed over adversaries. In other words, they did not see themselves as pitiful subjects. Second, migrants continued to feel that their contribution to the host countries and the homeland has not yet been acknowledged and appreciated. Hence, the collection, publication, and dissemination of the heroic narrative demonstrated that migrants were embroiled in a history project committed to the view that their migration history needed to be told in their voices, from their perspective.

In this book, the word "migrant" also refers to the descendants of migrants even though some of their migrant identities have morphed into the hyphenated or compound identity of Filipina/o/x American or Filipina/o/x Australian. I apply a very elastic and flexible use of the term "migrant," preferring to refer to the subjects moving away from the geographical borders of the Philippine islands and their descendants. I use the term "Filipina/o/x Americans" to refer to those who use this term as a self-referent—mainly second-generation American-born children of Filipino parents as well as Filipinos in the United States more generally.

The term "Filipina/o/x American" has undergone several permutations. Scholar Oscar Campomanes objects to the word "migrant" to refer to the Filipino "nationals" who arrived in the United States (between 1906 and 1945) because as citizens of an American colony they could not be technically seen as migrants.[29] Scholars Rick Bonus and Maria Root claim the label "Filipino American" is a work in progress,[30] while Campomanes maintains that the term "is a redundancy (and not just an apparent oxymoron)" because "to be Filipino is already, whether you move to the United States or remain where you are, to be American," highlighting the connections between imperial America and colonial Philippines.[31] Feminist scholars have preferred to use "Filipina/o American" rather than "Filipino American" or "Filipino/American" or "Filipino-American" to "call attention to the gendered nature of the Filipina/o experience," particularly since they were writing "women" into the history of the pioneer generation at a time when perceptions of their past were dominated by the mistaken view of a "bachelor society."[32] A group at the University of California, Berkeley, coined the term "Pin@y" in order to engender the slang "Pinoy," the word Filipino Americans used to describe themselves before World War II. I will use the term "Filipina/o/x American" because it is rapidly becoming the preferred choice used by scholars; the *x* was added by them very recently to be more gender inclusive. Filipina/o/x Americans writing about their identity are very inclusive in the way they define the term.[33] When I asked FANHS cofounder, the late Fred Cordova, who he considered to be Filipina/o/x American, he responded facetiously with: "one drop of *bagong* [shrimp paste] and they are ours!"[34] However, I use the term "Filipino American" (without the a/o) when that is the actual label used by the group I am referring to—for example, the Filipino American National Historical Society. I also use "Filipinos" (for men and women) and "Filipinas" (when only referring to women) to refer to those migrating to countries other than the United States.

I am a Filipina who was born in Manila, Philippines, and migrated to Sydney, Australia, as a teenager in the late 1970s, making me what social scientists label a "1.5 generation" immigrant.[35] I have led a mobile life—finishing my undergraduate degree at the University of Sydney and my postgraduate degrees at the University of Michigan. My first academic job was at Central Queensland University (CQU) in a town (Rockhampton) classified by Australia as "rural and remote." It was there that I first collected stories of Filipino women migrants for marriage who composed the majority of the Filipino community in that area. I worked at CQU for seven years in the 1990s, and I transferred to the University of New South Wales in Sydney where I have taught since 1999. I am a historian who has published on twentieth-century Filipino women's history, and my own life experience as a mobile person has given me an empathy for the way the migrant archives interpret the past, while my Filipino upbringing and my annual sojourns to the Philippines have enabled me to appreciate the difference between the migration experience of the diaspora and the viewpoint of the nation left behind.

Sources: The Migrant Archives

I coined the term "migrant archives" to refer to the group of sources written and produced by the migrants themselves. Some were published works such as memoirs, autobiographies, diaries, short life stories (including jokes and poems) that were either published separately or in collected anthologies (some of them self-published). I have read the community histories written by migrants who taught themselves how to write local histories and watched the documentaries on the history of Filipina/o/x America and on the myriad experiences of Filipinos in several countries including Israel, Hong Kong, and Singapore. Newsletters and magazines produced by migrants and NGOs were examined in connection with the case studies discussed in the chapters of this book. Government reports and twelve episodes of a radio program were also used for the case study on Filipino activism on behalf of victims of violence in Australia (chapter 6). In addition to published sources, I conducted more than seventy interviews with Filipino migrants in Hawaii, Australia, Manila, Athens, Milan, Padova, Hong Kong, Paris, and Singapore; with members of the Filipina/o/x American "bridge generation," or the second generation born in the United States who came of age in the 1940s and 1950s; with Filipinos in the United States involved with the Filipino migrant community either as activists, newspaper publishers, or members of the local Filipino American historical societies; and with Filipino shop owners at Lucky Plaza, Singapore. I had permission to read the personal papers of Filipino migrant activists, scrapbooks and journals of migrants, and the private archives of the organizations discussed in the case studies—sources not yet mined by scholars. Finally, I also conducted ethnographic work. This included participant observation of two PinoyWISE financial literacy seminars, one in Singapore in 2017 for overseas migrants and one in Malolos in the province of Bulacan in the Philippines for migrants' families left behind in 2019. In addition, I have attended fundraisers, walking ethnotours, performances, events such as the anniversary of the Philippine National Bank in Singapore and the graduation ceremony of Filipino domestic workers who enrolled in short-term courses from the organization HOME. The research and fieldwork for a project such as this were clearly multisited. I spent about eight to nine months in the Philippines, about seven months in the United States (Hawaii, San Francisco, and Seattle), three weeks in Singapore, a week each in Athens, Milan, and Hong Kong, and five weeks in Padova, Italy. In Australia, I conducted interviews in Sydney, Wollongong, Adelaide, and Melbourne. A more detailed discussion of the primary sources appears in the relevant chapters that follow.

Short History of Filipino Migration

The history of Filipino mass labor migration began in 1906 when Filipino agricultural workers were recruited by the Hawaiian Sugar Planters Association (HSPA) to work in the plantations of Hawaii. Filipino migration to the United States was a product of the entangled histories of the American empire and its colony. The Philippines became an American colony at the turn of the twentieth century, and from 1906 until the 1930s many young Filipino men provided the mobile labor force that worked in the sugar plantations of Hawaii, the Alaskan salmon canneries, and the agricultural fields of California. More than 100,000 Filipinas/os/x went to Hawaii from 1906 to 1935.[36] This pioneer generation (mostly from the Ilocos provinces in the Philippines) was later called the *manong* generation since *manong* was an Ilocano term of respect for male elders. From 1903 to 1911 around 289 Filipinos also arrived as *pensionados* (government scholars) to study in tertiary institutions all over the United States. The US Navy also began recruiting Filipinos as stewards and mess boys from 1903 (nine persons), reaching a peak of six thousand in World War I, remaining at an average of four thousand, or 5 percent of the total navy manpower, during the 1920s and 1930s.[37] Filipino women were not excluded from entry into the United States, and Filipina nurses were an important group of professionals who began to migrate to North America soon after they graduated from the nursing schools established by Americans in the colony.[38] By 1930 there were more than thirty thousand Filipinas/os/x in California alone.[39]

The next major wave of Filipino migration to the United States happened after 1965 when professionals such as doctors, nurses, and teachers moved to the United States. By the 1960s and 1970s too, the second generation of Filipinos born in the United States joined the civil rights movement and began to use the term "Filipino American" as a self-referent. By the 1980s there were two types of Filipinos in the United States: those who were born there and were second- or third-generation descendants of immigrants and those who had just arrived "fresh off the boat" (called FOBs). While the two groups experienced conflict in the 1990s, this tension may have abated.[40] Filipinos continued to migrate to the United States in huge numbers (the Philippines currently sends more immigrants to the United States than any country other than Mexico and China), so that a decade into the twenty-first century the newcomers outnumbered the generations born in the United States. The continuous migration could be partially explained also by the colonial past. The impact of the American educational system, the English language, American media, and postcolonial ties (major US military bases remained in the Philippines until 1991) nurtured an image of America as the ideal country to visit, study, or live in. (The United States is still the most popular destination for Filipinos wanting to study or migrate permanently.) Currently there are about 3.4 million Filipinos in the United States.[41] In contrast to the first generation of mostly working-class laborers, the majority of the post-1965 migrants who came as professionals quickly became part of America's middle classes. The median income for them in 2010 was $51,668, with 7.3 percent living below the poverty line and 37.9 percent holding at least a bachelor's degree.[42] Hence, the stories of this most recent migration contrasted with the first wave of migrants because of vast class differences. With an estimated disposable income that was higher than the average American this most recent group lived a much more privileged life than the *manong* generation, many of whom died poor.[43]

President Ferdinand Marcos's Labor Code of 1974 launched the great contemporary labor diaspora Filipinos all over the globe in a myriad of occupations. The post-1970s diaspora to countries outside the United States includes both overseas contract workers, and those who acquire permanent residence overseas (such as migrants for marriage or family reunion). In 2013, some eight million Filipinos participated in the overseas employment program, 10 percent of the country's overall population.[44] According to Stephen McKay, 275,000 Filipino seafarers made up 28.1 percent of the global seafaring workforce in circa 2007.[45] Filipinas began working in Japanese bars from the mid-1970s but those on entertainer visas increased in numbers dramatically from 8,500 in 1980 to 57,000 in 1991, peaking at 80,000 in 2003 and 2004.[46] In 1995, out of the 150,000 foreign workers in Hong Kong, 130,000 were from the Philippines, making Filipinos the largest non-Chinese ethnic group there.[47] In the Kingdom of Saudi Arabia alone there were 1,018,220 Filipinos workers in 2009.[48] Since the government-led outsourcing of Filipino labor began in the 1970s, the diaspora has grown to become one of the largest in the world with around eleven million, or one-fifth of all working-age individuals, living in more than 140 countries.[49] These include workers in Italy, Greece, Spain, Hong Kong, Singapore, the Middle East, Taiwan, caregivers and nannies in Canada and Israel, professionals including hospitality workers in Dubai, undocumented construction workers in Japan, entertainers in Japan (which reached a peak in the 1990s but has slowed to a halt since 2005), to name a few of the more obvious examples. There are also migrants for marriage in Australia, Germany,

Switzerland, Canada, and the United States. In 2013, of the more than ten million Filipinos of the diaspora, about three million were migrants for marriage who left the homeland permanently, compared to 8.5 million overseas Filipino workers (OFWs).[50] Each day more than three thousand Filipinos leave the country.

In 2006, 23.3 percent of households received remittances from abroad, with 9 percent of families dependent on them for their main source of livelihood and 60 percent of the population benefiting in some form from the salaries of their relatives toiling overseas.[51] By 2012 the Philippines had tied with Mexico in third place among the top five remittance-receiving countries with an inflow of US$24 billion, 8.5 percent of its gross domestic product (GDP).[52] The scale and sustained history of migration has made it part of the routine of Philippine life, but the impact of this culture of mobility can be seen not just in the growth of the middle class and in the real-estate boom and the stimulation of the consumer economy but also in the growth of educational institutions such as the proliferation of nursing programs (491 at its peak in the first decade of the twenty-first century) and maritime colleges.[53]

This is just a quick overview of the history of Filipino migration. Since the chapters particularly in parts 2 and 3 present substantial case studies, I have provided more in-depth discussions of the historical contexts of the relevant places there. The post-1970s migration has already had almost half a century of history and it makes sense to reflect at this point on the impact this global migration to the United States and the rest of the world has had on the host countries and the homeland. After almost five decades of labor migration, it is about time we also think about migrants as more than just laborers and workers but also as proactive subjects whose overseas experiences have inspired them to change not just their financial circumstances but also Filipino society, social mores, and cultural practices. Expanding our view of Filipino migrants as consumers, investors, activists, philanthropists, and historians also alters the way we locate them—away from the periphery toward the center—and credits their contribution to the homeland and the many host countries they inhabit.

Part One

Breaking Taboos
Family and Gender

CHAPTER 1

Migration and the Rethinking of the Filipino Family, 1970s–2018

Migration has been justified in the public and private discourses with the view that it must be done for the preservation of "the family." "The family"—its survival, its continuity, its improvement, its status—has been the rationale for all the struggles and sacrifices that migrants endured abroad. Sociologist Maruja M. B. Asis has observed that "in the Philippines, migrating for the sake of the family runs through the script of migrants, men and women alike."[1] Hardship was expected to be the price one paid to improve the status of "the family," making it almost impossible to divorce the heroic narrative of migration (as a struggle and sacrifice) from its core—"the family." The survival of the family was the narrative trope that gave meaning to the saga of migration.

Public discourses affirmed "the happy Filipino family" as an unchanging ideal. The Filipino family—both nuclear and extended—was imagined as almost unchanging and resilient to modernity and its challenges. The absence of a divorce law in the Philippines upheld this myth of the close-knit happy family, idealized as a nurturing and supportive institution where children practiced filial piety and respect for parents who made constant sacrifices for the future of their offspring. The centrality of the family was such that it was often cited as a major social cost of migration.[2] Despite the de facto physical separation of families of the overseas contract workers (almost 10 percent of the population) who remained divided physically and temporally, the traditional "happy family" continued to be idealized and reaffirmed in official discourses.

For example, the Overseas Workers Welfare Administration (hereafter OWWA), the Philippine government's premier bureaucratic institution assigned to oversee the welfare of overseas workers whose mandate included the promotion of their general well-being, distributed annual "Model OFW [overseas Filipino worker] Family of the Year" awards.[3] The 2005 and 2006 awardees from all regions of the country were memorialized in two anthologies.[4] The titles of the books—*Mga waging kuwento ng OFW* (Stories of triumph of overseas Filipino workers)—articulated the Philippine government's perspective that the ideal migrants were those whose families remained whole (read "were still together") unscathed by the migration experience. In these two volumes, there was hardly a mention of the social costs of migration on the family. Set up as stories meant to inspire even more people to migrate (since the government policy was to send at least a million overseas workers a year from 2007 onward), the publications emphasized the financial benefits of working abroad on improving the status of the family particularly through the education of children. From the OWWA-endorsed memoirs (written much like official political hagiographies), one might be led to the conclusion that migration had no revolutionary social effect on the family except in improving its financial status.

Official discourses like the OWWA awards produced by the Philippine government were reluctant to problematize "the Filipino family." On the other hand, NGOs were quick to point out that whittling away at the traditional family structure was too big a cost for migration.[5] Rhacel Parreñas's pioneering research on the impact of migration on children revealed that public discourses viewed the "transnational family" as a "bad family."[6] Thus, despite almost half a century of overseas contract migration, which involved the separation of family members, transnational families remain invisible or judged to be morally dubious in the national psyche. Social scientists have analyzed migration and the transnational family from the perspective of children and the kinship network left behind, focusing on the way long-distance relationships have impacted on the marriage and quality of family life.[7] Scholars have also acknowledged the complex ways that migration has impacted on the institution of marriage, including the introduction of the new concept of transnational motherhood and the trauma of separation and reunification. The desire to maintain intimacy, part of the project of keeping the family together, also inspired a plethora of studies on the use of media and technologies (cell phones, the Internet, Facebook, Twitter, the World Wide Web, Skype, webcam, phone cards, electronic remittances, telegraphic bank transfers, and so on) as a way of communicating from afar in as close to real time as possible.[8] This perspective perceived the Filipino family (imagined as the heteronormative family of father, mother, and children and the extended family that includes elders) as the ideal, interested primarily in how migrants have deployed strategies to keep the family "whole" or maintain the traditional dynamics and ties of the family. The dominant approach of these social scientists is best encapsulated by Filomena Aguilar Jr.'s research question for a book on the impact of migration on those left behind: "What does it mean for families with members who are overseas migrant workers to remain as a family?"[9] I am shifting the analytical lens to the opposite direction. Instead of examining how migrants and their families who remained behind struggled to maintain the official narrative and traditional ideals of the family despite the temporal and physical separation, I want to analyze how migrants have broken the taboos regarding the Filipino family and prompted a rethinking of this highly mythologized institution. The sources for this chapter include published memoirs, private journals of Filipina domestic workers in Hong Kong who are members of the NGO Lakbay Dangal, published jokes, poems, and stories of Filipino migrants, issues of *Tinig ng Marino*, the newspaper of the United Filipino Seafarers union, interviews with Filipino domestic workers and NGOs in Hong Kong (Lakbay Dangal), Singapore (PinoyWISE–Atikha), and the Philippines (Center for Migrant Advocacy and Atikha), and ethnographic work in Hong Kong and Singapore. These sources all come from the cohort of migrants who left to go to Japan, the Middle East, Singapore, Hong Kong, and Europe, as well as seafarers. This cohort comes from a working-class background, although some of them have become part of the rising middle classes at least with regard to their consumption practices (discussed in chapter 3). The selection of this particular migrant group is linked to my intention to focus specifically on migrants who are separated from their families in order to highlight the way this relatively new phenomenon of physical and temporal separation has had an impact on cultural constructions of the Filipino family over almost half a century.

Hegemonic Discourses on the Ideal Filipino Family as Constituted since 1986

In Philippine hegemonic discourses, the ideal Filipino family, according to scholar Belen Medina, is defined as "basically the nuclear or elementary group of husband, wife and unmarried children—natural-born or adopted."[10] Odine de Guzman, writing about gender, migration, and the romance of the

"Filipino family," further explains that it could be "functionally extended in form: it is still understood to adhere to a core group or basic unit—the nuclear configuration—from which it extends to include grandparents, aunts, uncles, cousins, and in-laws."[11] In these hegemonic discourses, the family was usually imagined as heteronormative. The composition of the family was described as a nuclear-based unit with a strong extended kinship base, a Catholic marriage accompanied by "the script of cohabitation, women's maternity, men's authority and familism, including filial piety."[12] The strong Catholic influence in the culture of marriage explained why divorce continued to be illegal in the Philippines and spouses who have separated (whether they did so legally or not) were considered to have failed to achieve normative ideals. Single moms were not accepted as a type of family in the Philippines.

The household was also important in the conceptualization of family life where members shared a common residence. Household members could include domestic help, godchildren, or adopted children.[13] According to ethnographer Naomi Hosoda, the practice of eating together, or sharing daily meals, was one of the symbolic activities that confirmed one's membership in the family.[14]

The circumstances of migration threatened these hegemonic definitions of the family. Migration unsettled the traditional family ideals and has shaken some of concepts of the "Filipino family."[15] Away from the Philippines and far from the censure of society and social mores, migrant accounts reveal that they have not just been proactive in refashioning the structure of the family, they have also broken cultural taboos by launching arguably the first major critique of this imagined ideal. These initiatives were radical in the context of a culture that is conservatively Catholic in orientation and where the 1986 constitution identified the Filipino family as the foundation of the nation.[16]

Refashioning the Filipino Family
The NGO as Family

The membership of the heteronormative Filipino family, which included the father, the mother, the children, the grandparents, and kin, including the household, has always been assumed to be the standard, and those falling short of it are seen as below the norm. Migrants introduced new criteria for family membership. Who was family was no longer defined by relations based on blood or kinship ties but on who provided emotional and material support during times of crisis. The rise of NGOs as the new imagined families began to happen only after the 1970s, particularly for overseas contract workers. While social scientists have argued that migration "inhibits the right to family life of the migrant domestic worker/care worker,"[17] they also acknowledge the way migrants have been able to create "quasi-familial networks" or "communities of care."[18]

From the 1970s onward, Filipino overseas contract workers who composed a significant pool of the migration demographic found themselves physically separated from their spouses and children as well as their extended kinship group. NGOs became the substitute families for many migrants abroad, including overseas contract workers who returned to the Philippines. The plethora of NGOs that blossomed in defense of migrants' rights or to address migrants' concerns adopted their clients and members as part of the larger transnational NGO "family." Odine de Guzman's doctoral dissertation mined the many letters migrants wrote to one NGO. Migrants complained that their own families in the Philippines broke the epistolary pact by neglecting to write their overseas-based relatives. One poignant but telling example came from May Jane Flores: "Thank you very much for answering my letter. I wrote to all (my family) but no one even answered, considering that letters are our only comfort from homesickness and from all the challenges we face."[19] NGOs were the ones who provided support services (legal advice, counseling, housing, emergency assistance, and emotional support), performing the duties normally executed by the kinship group. Migrants sent almost their entire salaries home, extending financial aid particularly during emergency situations, providing funds for health care or for rebuilding a house devastated by a typhoon. But who looked after the migrants? NGO activists were the first ones who came to the rescue when migrants encountered trauma, abuse, exploitation, violence, and sundry emergencies. Since NGOs deliver the help and emotional support needed in a crisis, these organizations have come to be imagined as the migrants' new family.

Mary Joy E. Barcelona, who completed a six-month contract as an entertainer in Japan in 1995, encountered ridicule in her hometown when she returned, while her family ruined the small business she set up from her earnings saved during her short stint overseas. In 1999, she found refuge in the Development Action Women's Network (DAWN), the NGO that helped distressed former entertainers who had been sent to Japan. DAWN provided her with skills training, employment, and a role in amateur theater. Eventually she was appointed coordinator of the organization's alternative livelihood project after graduating with a bachelor's degree in entrepreneurial management in

2006. Mary Joy published her life story in two separate anthologies where she acknowledged DAWN as her new family: "In DAWN, I have found a new family—one that taught me my rights and how to stand up on my own"; "in my search for new direction, I found my new family—DAWN. They became my guide towards my simple dream."[20]

Lakbay Dangal is an organization founded by Father Robert Reyes, a Filipino Hong Kong–based Catholic priest, with the aim of training domestic workers to become tourist guides on their Sundays off so that they could give visitors a historical trail of Filipino presence in that city. I had the privilege of participating in this tour on April 24, 2011, and was given the rare opportunity to read members' journals, which they hoped to publish one day as an anthology. The Lakbay Dangal tour, advertised as "a Philippine trail in Hong Kong," had as its tagline the phrase "Journey of Dignity"—a literal translation of "Lakbay Dangal." Marites Mapa's journal included a section entitled "Lakbay Dangal Family Tree" (Figure 1.1), where she strategically placed photographs of Father Reyes in the trunk of the tree, her history teachers (Sonia Zerrudo and Professor Vim) in the main branches, and the rest of the members in the subsidiary branches and leaves. Mapa wrote: "Like a tree having branches spreading from a single stem, Lakbay Dangal is a group that was formed from a passionate priest that wishes to help every overseas Filipino worker here in Hong Kong. . . . Although at times there are incident [sic] that made others leave this group because of some problems encountered, still it's good to know that we as a group stays [sic] strong and intact like a tree that even though branches are falling here and there is still stand [sic] strong and proud."[21]

The physical absence of blood relatives inspired migrants to rethink the criteria for family membership. The case of Mary Joy Barcelona was an extreme example of an individual whose natal family betrayed her trust, while her own village ostracized her because she was considered a "Japayuki" (the pejorative term for entertainers in Japan that made reference to *karayuki-san*, Japanese prostitutes to Southeast Asia in the prewar period). Mary Joy chose to embrace the NGO as her new family. This NGO helped her recover from the trauma of her overseas contract work and was instrumental in her metamorphosis from entertainer into businesswoman, amateur actor, and feminist activist. Here migrants have changed the rules for defining *who* was part of a family unit. The criterion for family membership was emotional support. The people who were physically there with you to celebrate your birthday and the many rituals of life and who could be counted on for financial aid, empathy, and unconditional support during times of crisis were now considered de facto members of the migrant's family.

FIGURE 1.1. A page from the journal of Marites Mapa representing the NGO Lakbay Dangal's founder, leaders, and members all as part of one family tree.

Transnational Families

Since the 1970s, the transnational family (defined as a family in which one or more parent is working overseas while their children remained in the Philippines) has become the reality for many children whose mothers or fathers worked abroad especially as domestic workers, seafarers, construction workers, nurses, teachers, and caregivers. Sociologists Rhacel Parreñas and Filomeno Aguilar Jr. have noted that no evidence indicates that children of migrant parents suffer the negative consequences such as increased juvenile delinquency imagined by society.[22] Yet the memoirs and stories of children left behind especially by mothers express sadness and feelings of abandonment.[23] Children's memoirs reveal a poignant yearning for a "complete" family: "nothing is better than the warmth of a complete family to go home to."[24] Parreñas's findings show that children of "father-away families" experienced a "gap" with the absent father that continued even when he returned home; they felt "uncomfortable" having him around.[25] This emotional distance, what one memoir referred to as an "emptiness I feel inside," was connected to the physical separation: "I miss my dad and no amount of material wealth will ever suffice as substitute."[26]

Children were often oblivious to the economic problems their parents experienced trying to support their families at home. Perhaps that explains why the longing for a complete family was very much romanticized: "If I would be given the chance to rearrange my life again, I would choose us living together as one complete family above anything else. Dad's income might not be as high as what he is earning overseas but I am sure we would be happy and content just the same."[27] Children clung to the normative ideal of a complete family despite their migrant parents' tacit acceptance of the transnational family unit as the new model for them. Instead, they longed for the ultimate reunification of the family even though this might happen many years later when they would already be adults with their own families. The life stories and artistic works written by children who reunited with their parents in the Middle East all repeated the same refrain: joining their parents abroad made them happier as a family and helped them adjust to their new environment.[28] Even so, Geraldine Pratt's important study of Filipino domestic labor in Canada reveals that such reunions were not always "happy endings." Once reunited, children continued to process the trauma of being separated from their caregivers not just once but twice (first when their mothers immigrated to Canada and the second time when they left their primary caregivers in the Philippines to join their mothers), struggling with the challenges of reconnecting with mothers who were almost strangers to them, in addition to the trials posed by new environments.[29]

The story of Romy and Nenita and their four children is a poignant example of the effect of a mother's absence on the daily life of the household. The title of the memoir—*Pamilya, Migrasyon, Disintegrasyon* (Family, migration, disintegration)—gives more than a hint of the interpretation to come, but the format, in which each member of the family has a separate space to narrate his or her own feelings and experiences, produces unique intersecting perspectives. In this particular family, Nenita's absence due to her job as a seamstress in Saudi Arabia resulted in her husband Romy's growing paranoia about his wife's possible infidelity. This constant unease, which Nenita described as "jealousy," became an excuse for him to drown his sorrows in alcohol. Unfortunately, his drinking habit had a tragic effect on his children who became victims of his violent beatings.[30]

Rey Ventura's two-volume memoirs of the one year he spent as an undocumented day worker in Japan unveils the dark secrets of life in Kotobuki, the area considered Filipino territory in the outskirts of Tokyo. What is shocking in Ventura's work is the candid depiction of Filipino married men with second families in Japan and their wives in the Philippines who tacitly accepted the situation as long as remittances continued to arrive.[31] Ventura recalls the words of one of these practically minded wives: "I had met his wife in Manila. She was fat and unglamorous. When I asked her what she wanted me to tell Dante (one of the Filipino illegal day laborers) when I met him again in Kotobuki, she said: 'Tell him that I don't mind his girls. He can have as many women as he wants provided he isn't remiss in his remittances.'"[32] Apart from the wife and family in the Philippines, most of the men had girlfriends in Japan, fathering several children they proudly boasted were "made in Japan." Ventura's prose captures the unique, poignant, and troubling situation:

> In the meantime, every married man I knew, apart from one old man, was unfaithful one way or another to his wife, and some of the wives knew this and understood it. And sometimes in their letters the wives made the rules explicit: the husband might have a girlfriend, but he must never have a child by her. That was the One Commandment.
>
> But that understanding attitude only lasted as long as the benefits lasted, the remittances came and the money accumulated in the bank, or the house was built or improved, or the mortgage paid. But when the advantages ceased the letters would turn bitter and the wives would beg their husbands to come home. And the husbands might be faced with the knowledge that they had got used to Koto, with their live-in companion, no family, no relatives, none of the restrictions of barrio life. They had become addicted to their exile. Unfree by the rules of Japan, they had nevertheless found freedom from their own morality and culture. This was the charm of Koto, the lure.[33]

In these memoirs the Filipinos "underground in Japan" were not depicted as victims or individuals to be pitied. Instead, Ventura makes two important points: (1) that both the migrant and the wife remaining in the Philippines were practical about their separations, privileging the economic sustenance over the emotional preservation of the "family unit" or marriage, and (2) that the physical absence of "family" in the migrant's life generated a certain freedom from obligations and rules. Ventura does not paint a pretty picture of the life of an undocumented migrant who has to avoid the radar of the police and settle for substandard living conditions. The migrant workers in Ventura's account were callous about personal relationships. The men, however, were good providers for their families and genuinely loved their children more than they loved their wives or girlfriends.[34] The undocumented migrants' subject position was indeed incredibly free of social mores since they were not bound by their home culture or their host country's culture as illegal persons living on the fringes of society. The motivation for living such a clandestine existence was not merely to improve their financial situation but also to escape from the shackles of the social conventions of both the home country and the host countries. Nevertheless, Ventura was bothered by the ethical question: should one live a life completely free of moral standards, a situation that means any sort of behavior is legitimate? "What am I supposed to do with my dick?" Dante asked. "Pickle it? Then shred it into little bits and cast them to the chickens for it to become useful?"[35] Ventura then concluded:

> An overworked *tachinbō* [day laborer], a pining OCW, an exile, a migrant worker—he is Dante, he is Rudy, he is Ernesto, he is Dado, he is Jesus, he is Gabriel, she is Aurora, she is Alma. Could they be faulted for yielding to temptation, for responding to the call of nature? Could they be blamed for acknowledging human frailties?
>
> "Am I not entitled to some pleasure?" Dante said. "I gave my best to my family; I sent them millions of yen; my children were able to go to college; they could buy anything they wanted; I built them a house. Isn't it only natural for me to make myself happy?"
>
> But where is the boundary between a morally permissible life and promiscuity? Who draws the line and what are the wages of those who cross this moral line? Where is the beginning, where is the end? A migrant worker in a foreign land: who defines his vices? Who appreciates his virtues?[36]

In Dante's view the remittances he sent home regularly—money that came at the price of his suffering—legitimized his sexual dalliances. The book's authorial voice disclosed that in Kotobuki all but one old man was unfaithful to his wife. Some men formed "second families" with their new loves.

According to Atikha founder Mai Añonuevo, when wives left behind in the Philippines were asked "Where is your husband?," some responded by saying, "Wala, sumakabilang bahay na" (Not here, he has moved to another house). The joke was a play on the expression *sumakabilang buhay*—a euphemism for death that says someone has simply moved on to the next life. Instead of passing to the next life, the witty women were saying that their husbands had simply moved on to the next house.[37] It was not uncommon for Filipino men to keep mistresses in the Philippines and have children with them; this was tolerated though frowned upon, especially by the Catholic Church. But usually the men still lived with their "legitimate" family. According to Añonuevo, these responses reveal the extent to which these women were resigned to their fates—brought upon by the prolonged separation.[38] In 1999, the Philippine Overseas Employment Agency (POEA) recorded 1,439 "abandoned families."[39] Ellene Sana, executive director of the NGO Center for Migrant Advocacy, admitted that although "the figures have not yet reached alarming levels," the fact that over 1,000 families had officially complained to the POEA pointed to "an emerging problem."[40] The open discussion of extramarital affairs and abandonment of wives and children in the migrant archives broke a social taboo because it demythologized the public discourse of the sanctity of the Filipino family.

Critiquing the Family

Official discourses from the OWWA and migrants' accounts considered migration as a "family project."[41] The migrant was supposed to be prepared to endure hardship and separation in order to send the remittances needed to sustain both the nuclear and extended family and, in some cases, even the village. Mothers who lived apart from their children legitimized their absence with the discourse that they were martyr moms—enduring long hours of work and missing their children in order to the build the family home and pay the tuition for the education of their children.[42] Few mothers would represent migration in terms of self-fulfillment or careers. One rare exception was the seafarers (mostly male) who viewed their overseas deployment as essential to the advancement of their professional careers.[43] Although a small number of migrant stories mentioned the desire for adventure or the need to escape from an unhappy marriage as an important motivation to migrate, the majority of migrants' accounts acknowledged the need to support their families, both nuclear and extended, as the primary reason for leaving the Philippines.

In this sense, the migrant as family breadwinner endorsed the traditional belief of placing the family's interest above the individual one. Migrants' stories exuded pride in sending siblings and children to school, building and furnishing the family home, and providing not just basic necessities but also luxury items for the day-to-day expenses of the family back in the homeland. Malu Padilla spoke for her fellow Filipino migrants in Europe:

> We keep enough of the euros, pounds, francs, and kroners for the essentials of living, and send the rest to the Philippines. In this way, we have raised and educated our children and the children of relations who cannot otherwise afford to. We have built homes for our families, who

are also fed and clothed by our efforts. Driven to leave our homeland by an economy that has been battered by recession and political instability, we struggle not just to alleviate the poverty of our own insecure social status abroad, but the poverty of our families in the Philippines.[44]

Daisy, a domestic worker in Singapore for eighteen years on a salary of between $400 and $600 a month, helped three of her siblings through university in the Philippines. This included a brother who qualified as a marine engineer, a sister who qualified as a nurse, and another sister who became a computer programmer.[45]

But the enormous self-esteem arising from the ability to improve the family's financial status did not come without a price. The narrative of sacrifice that dominated the script of migrants' accounts underscored the point that every bit of money sent was an act of self-denial. One priest in Kiso, Japan, "complained that Filipina migrants in Japan denied themselves necessities—sometimes eating only instant noodles for weeks on end—so that they could send money to the Philippines."[46]

The price paid for these remittances became the main focus of the migrants' autobiographical metanarrative that equated their lives with the passion of Jesus Christ. In their life stories, migration was described as their "calvary" (*kalbaryo*), where they endured a litany of sacrifices in order to provide for the family. A Tagalog poem written by Let-let A. Sulit, a domestic worker in Hong Kong, explained her journey abroad as *magsasakripisyo* (sacrificing) to be able to give her parents "kahit konting ligaya at kaginhawanhan" (even just a small amount of happiness and wealth).[47] The two-volume *Migrants' Stories, Migrants' Voices*, published by the Philippine Migrants Rights Watch NGO, was described as "a tribute to all the migrants and their families who have sacrificed for a better life."[48] Collections of migrant short autobiographies are bound to include a story with "sacrifice" in the title or one that calls attention to the "pains" of toiling abroad.[49]

One witty but poignant poem by a domestic worker in Hong Kong entitled "Mag-abroad ay di biro" (Going abroad is not a joke, sometimes it can be translated as Going abroad is never fun), where the author makes a reference to the traditional folk song "Magtanim ay di biro" (Planting [rice] is not a joke, an English translation of the song is Planting [rice] is never fun), captures this narrative of sacrifice and hardship where the meager salaries earned were quickly absorbed by debts and expenses.

> You get your salary but your pockets have no silver
> Because all your money is on its way to remittances

> If you have a mortgage it is completely finished
> And on top of this were the debts you had to pay the agency [placement fees]
>
> How many mothers are here bowed down with work
> Because they want their children to get an education
> Alone they endure their own Calvary
> Bad luck if your husband had thought about finding a mistress.[50]

The poem captured the way remittances disappeared so quickly, preventing migrant workers from accumulating savings or capital. It also raised the specter of infidelity that haunted the long-distance marital relationships.

An intrinsic component of the narrative of sacrifice was the emotional distress resulting from the absence of families. Many poems in Tagalog written by domestic workers in Hong Kong and seafarers (published in the United Seafarer's *Tinig ng Marino* [Voice of the Seafarer] newsletter) are about the pain of separation from families and the yearning for the end of their work contracts so that they can reunite with them. For example, in a Tagalog poem *Pagtitiis at kinabukasan* (Enduring and the future) published in *Tinig ng Marino*, authors Miss Thee and Abrico expressed the dangers of life at sea and confided that the thought of their beloved families inspired them to stay strong for a future:

> The beloved family is always in my thoughts,
> Spouse and children. . . .
>
> And this acts as the strong defense
> Against the sadness of life at sea
> And inspiration to keep my will strong
> In order to have a beautiful future.[51]

Other poems reveal a poignant acceptance of the risk that separation could result in broken homes or broken hearts.[52] In Arnel Pura's poem published in *Tinig ng Marino* he confesses that he felt like a typhoon suddenly hit the boat at sea when he found out that his love had abandoned him.[53] In the heroic narratives of their exile, migrants talk about a life of struggle and hard work that they were prepared to endure for the benefit of their families. On face value, these dutiful sons and daughters, mothers, fathers, wives, and husbands who sent remittances and goods home by denying themselves a few pleasures (or a future, since some did not have a retirement plan) appeared to be interested only in maintaining the dynamics of the traditional family. But these very same migrants' accounts also contained the first serious critiques of the traditional family dynamics. This public censure of the family's relentless exploitation of migrant labor violated social taboos that prevented individuals from tarnishing the image of the Filipino family as a nurturing and loving institution.

One common topic of the conversations in remittance agencies in Canada was the "seemingly never-ending financial obligations to the family" and the financial drain that prevented migrants from achieving middle-class status: "that's why we remain poor because we have to send money back home regularly."[54] In Ventura's second book of fictionalized stories about Filipino migrant labor in Japan, one of the workers, Dante, tells the author that his wife's letters were all about money problems and proposals to buy appliances and furniture: "'Even before I open my wife's letter,' he said, 'I already know its contents. A letter from her is always about *a problem*. I never want to open it.' So, when letters from home arrived, Dante would read Laura's [his daughter] first and his other children's next, his wife's last. Sometimes, he only opened his wife's letter when he was ready to remit some amount to her."[55]

In the collective autobiographies of migrant domestic workers entitled *The Path to Remittance*, the twenty-one informants whose individual stories make up the book have two main targets for complaints: (1) the unscrupulous agents who required them to pay exorbitant job placement or job transfer fees that often cost them almost their entire salaries, sometimes for six months; and (2) their own families in the Philippines whose incessant demands for money drained them of their entire savings and reduced them to cash cows.[56] According to Daisy: "Because we are working overseas our families think we are ATMs (Automatic Teller Machines). Many girls don't want to say they don't have money," she explained. "They usually send money on the last Sunday of the week [*sic*] and two weeks later they start getting requests for more."[57] The same Daisy who put her three siblings through university in the Philippines declared in her life story that she resented the way many families in the Philippines treated their children as cash cows. She gave examples from the experiences of her friends who were helpless to control how the money was spent in the end:

> Often I hear from friends who are married that the husband asks for money one week and get [*sic*] the sons to ask the next week. The money sent to the husband often ends up with another family, or that he has another family, or that he has another woman . . . kids in college or secondary school often ask the mommy for money to buy things for projects. The truth is they buy drugs or sex, and if it's the daughter she goes shopping with the mom's hard earned money. . . .

Only a few kids tell the truth.... Now they have hand phones (mobiles) and they SMS [text] mom asking "please send money your uncle's son has died" or the uncle's son had a new born child and need [sic] to buy a present. Or it will be your neighbour getting married and need [sic] to buy a present.[58]

Addressing the receiving families on behalf of all migrants, Papias Generale Banados writes: "And those from our families back home, who may read this book, I hope they will stop making unrealistic demands on us to send money home, and also use the money we sent home wisely and usefully, when they understand from these stories how much we have to go through to earn the money we remit. I hope they take a note that it is not easy to find money outside of the country."[59]

The family's insatiable appetite for more, more, and more of the migrant's hard-earned money was a source of frustration for many migrants who, like Cora, a Filipina in Japan, lamented: "Hanggang kailan?"—when will it end?[60]

At a birthday party I attended for Julie (pseudonym) in Singapore on a Saturday evening in September 2011, all the guests who were domestic workers on their night off complained to me that they were perpetually bombarded by text messages from their family members in the Philippines with demands for money. Once they sent the money however, they never received so much as a "thank you" and had to call their families to check that the money had arrived safely. Eventually, they realized that it was better not to get any news at all from families than to be continually harassed by a family that would never be satisfied. In despair, Lisa (pseudonym), a domestic worker who had been working in Singapore since she was nineteen years old, told me tearfully: "I just want my family to ring up just once to ask me how I am without asking for any money!" Lisa's statement captured the hurt, anger, and disappointment in the family—which was no longer imagined as a loving one. Instead, she accused the family of being self-centered and callous. In anthropologist Deirdre McKay's recent study an entire village competed with each other to claim financial dole-outs from one migrant couple. Such exploitative behavior was explained by the assumption made by those left behind that they were entitled to some of the salary and benefits of life overseas.[61] Some of the tactless remarks made by family members claiming to show "concern" for the migrant's welfare painted a picture of the family locked in a narcissistic world distanced from the life of their relatives living overseas. Leo Sicat, who had a career as a steward in the United States Navy showed a candid acceptance of his one-sided, purely financial relationship with his family in the Philippines in his life story: "The only time you receive a letter from home is when they need money. They are not going to write you a letter just to see how you are doing."[62]

Migrants resorted to a number of strategies to show resistance to the pressures from families. One tactic was to cease all forms of communication and to stop sending remittances temporarily.[63] This line of defense unfortunately could result in social ostracism or being branded ungrateful or shameless (*walang hiya*).[64] Relatives, including immediate family members such as brothers and sisters, would either speak ill of them or refuse to see them when they returned to the Philippines to visit.[65] In Raquel Delfin Padilla's personal reflections, she admonished family members for greeting their migrant members with "Where are your gifts?" (*Nasaan na ang padala mo?*). She chastised relatives who communicated only when they wanted something from them and who destroyed the reputations of those who did not cede to their requests.[66] Robert de Guzman's personal message to families of overseas workers was not to sulk (*huwag magtampu*) or ostracize them when their requests for money or gifts were turned down. Instead he appealed for some empathy for the hardship these migrants endured.[67] Another strategy observed by anthropologist Elisabeth Zontini among Filipina workers in Bologna and Barcelona was to petition another family member (usually another female) to join them in order to share the financial burden of providing for the families in the homeland.[68]

Hence, it was in the public telling and retelling of their stories that migrants exhibited the most radical form of resistance—by exposing the family's excessive financial demands and venting their anger at the family for taking them for granted, they revealed the Filipino family also as an exploitative institution. Daisy, the domestic worker from Singapore discussed above, ended her life story accusing her family of taking her for granted: "They don't realize that we get a meagre income, even though in pesos it may seem a lot. The other day, just a week after I sent most of my salary to my mother, she rang and said that their roof needed repairs and she don't [sic] have money. . . . I asked her do you want me to go out to the street and do prostitution?"[69] The publication of their stories was not just motivated by the desire to be acknowledged and appreciated for their contribution to the family's financial status; these same accounts violated social taboos that forbid and frowned upon finding fault with the family. The traditional way of coping with family secrets, wrongs, or weaknesses was to sweep them under the rug, not to air complaints in public. But through the public exposé of their families' excessive financial demands they had collectively debunked the myth of the Filipino "happy family" and "family values." Hence, the "migrant archives" become not just a record of the lives of migrants; they also communicate what cannot be articulated directly to their own families. The only way they could break the taboo is to tell their collective stories. This critique of the most sacred institution was extremely radical. Such a critique was also legitimized by the migrants' impeccable track record for sending remittances and supporting the family.

The Filipino Family and Ethnic Identity

Earlier I described my experience attending Julie's birthday party in Singapore when guests told me their grievances about their families' lack of appreciation of the hard-earned money they sent to their families regularly and lack of empathy from their families for their individual feelings. I was moved by their pain and could not stop myself from trying to offer some suggestions or solutions. For me, the most logical proposition was for them to send less remittance and to save money for themselves, a solution proposed by NGOs such as Atikha in its PinoyWISE financial literacy seminars (see chapter 3). This suggestion, however, was met with loud protests from the women, who claimed they could not possibly discontinue their current practice because "we are Filipino!" What struck me most by the response was that they constructed Filipino identity, their very Filipino-ness, as being inextricably connected to their performance as dutiful and obedient daughters and to their subservient roles in the Filipino family.

In this concluding section, I want to show that although migrants have been willing to dismantle traditional concepts of who the family is and what the family does, even so far as to critique its exploitative nature, they still cling to the image of the idealized "Filipino family" when they want to distinguish themselves as an ethnic group. In their memoirs and life stories, Filipino migrants mark difference from the Western Other by claiming that they are family oriented; that they are closely attached to the extended family, which *must* be imagined as a nurturing one.

In the Philippines, children of liaisons between Japanese men and Filipina entertainers (from the 1970s onward) have suffered enormous discrimination and taunts, driving many to seek refuge in NGOs such as DAWN (Development Action Women's Network).[70] A poignant tale of a Japanese Filipino child raised in the Philippines, entitled "The Stranger" because he was treated like one all his life, begins: "Many say I am not an ordinary kid. Some even say that kids like me have no place in this cruel world."[71] In his story, Tzitza (a pseudonym) confided that he believed that it was only his Filipino grandfather who loved him because his Filipino grandmother and aunts subjected him to continuous beatings: "for every mistake I commit, they would punch me, slap me, or throw things at me."[72] At school he was anxious; he explained: "I was afraid they would shoo me away. What if they find out I'm half-Japanese? Would they treat me in the same way my family is treating me?"[73] Tzitza constantly felt unwanted by his Filipino family ("I do not really know but somehow it is as if the entire house did not want me"), and it was only when he joined DAWN where he met other children like himself and performed with their theater group that he "soon realized that I am not alone."[74] Transethnic families were almost completely absent in the discourse on the Filipino family. My reading of the evidence was that the transethnic family threatened the way migrants conflated the Filipino family with their unique identity as an ethnic group distinct from the host society. The presence of mestizo children unsettled their fixed notions of the Filipino family and national identity. If Filipino families were what distinguished the Filipino ethnic group from the mainstream host country, was there a place for families who were of mixed ethnicities?

Migrants invested heavily in the family—it was the institution that benefited the most from the financial fruits of their hard work and sacrifices. And yet, they were willing to dismantle the traditional composition of the family and fashion new types of families. In addition, they did not hesitate to critique the family and its relentless demands for remittances. But despite the radical way in which they broke cultural taboos, they referred to a romanticized notion of the "traditional Filipino family" in order to distinguish themselves from the Western Other. Migrants had the acute sense that they were pioneers in the project of rethinking the family from afar. This project was extremely radical. It was very difficult to alter established notions of the family in a country where it was considered a cultural taboo to tinker with such a sacred institution. Perhaps that partly explains why the intervention had to come from abroad. The Filipino family was not the only social institution that Filipino migrants dared to change. In the next chapter, we shall examine the ways Filipino migrants have challenged cultural constructions of gender and sexuality, revealing that social activists were not the only actors who initiated changes in gender politics.

Chapter 2

Challenging Constructions of Gender and Sexuality, 1980s–2018

The Philippines is arguably one of the tiny handful of countries in the world where absolute divorce is not legally possible. If divorce was not an option, what happened to migrants who found themselves physically and emotionally estranged from their partners over a number of years? Did they remain chaste? And if not, how did this affect their marriage? How did they respond to the unique challenge of being married to an absent spouse? How did migration affect sexualities?

The topic of infidelity was very much taboo, particularly if it was the woman who was guilty of adultery. As a result, it is extremely difficult to find informants willing to talk about their own sexual liaisons outside marriage. One would expect that the migrant archives would be silent on the subject of sexuality and infidelity. But, to my surprise, there were accounts discussing the topic both from migrants whose partners cheated on them as well as those who had sexual affairs while away from the homeland. Given the sensitive nature of the topic, the first-person accounts were published using pseudonyms. Others revealed their observations about the romance and sexual infidelity of their acquaintances and friends in published stories and in my personal interviews with them.

Sexual affairs outside marriage were frowned upon socially in the Philippines. But far from the prying eyes of the village, the migrant discovered that it was possible to break the rules and get away with it. One memoir suggests that extramarital affairs by overseas Filipino workers were so common that it could be labeled a "trendy" practice: "The OFW [overseas Filipino worker] who is older sister or older brother, has two spouses. When s/he is in the Philippines s/he is with his/her original spouse but when s/he is in a different country, his/her second spouse is the partner. Ooh la la."[1] The use of the French expression "ooh la la" captured the author's admiration for the sheer audacity of the actions while communicating the message that the behavior referred to broke social rules. In Nenita's story, she confides that sexual affairs occurred even in Saudi Arabia where the society was conservative and strict concerning sex outside marriage: "Many Filipinos in Saudi Arabia, large numbers of them, many have spouses here [in the Philippines] as well as spouses there [in Saudi Arabia]. It is true, over there, there is temptation."[2] Jessica Flores Napat makes a similar observation about Dubai in her migration story, in which she claims that infidelity was commonly practiced by Filipino migrants there where love affairs were considered "pandandalian or sideline nga lamang" (just a quick or sideline activity only), since "ditto lang naman kami, pag-uwi ay kanya-kanya ng uwian sa pamilya" (we are together here only, when we return we go to our own families).[3] However, Napat is critical of these romantic liaisons, imploring migrants to think about the hurt they cause by betraying their spouses and their families in the Philippines.[4]

Napat's reaction reflected the dominant Filipino cultural view on extramarital affairs. However, while men's infidelity was tolerated, the specter of married women working abroad and having sexual liaisons with more than one partner was considered particularly shocking and radical in the homeland where the chaste wife was still the feminine ideal. Women who committed adultery were the object of salacious gossip and disparaged for transgressing gender norms. And yet, the story of Glenda, published in Papias Generale Banados's anthology of stories of Filipina domestic workers in Singapore, shows that multiple boyfriends from different racial mixes in Singapore was no longer considered rare:

> Through the influence of her Filipino friends and introductions through them Glenda began to communicate with men, not only Filipinos working in or passing through (i.e. seamen) Singapore, but also with Bangladeshis, Indians, Malaysians, local Chinese and Caucasians. If you really need a boyfriend it is not difficult to find one here, but if you are looking for a husband it is a different matter.
>
> One of the first men she dated was a Bangladeshi construction worker. He had every Sunday off, he was very kind and respectful, but he earned only $800 a month and had to send back money to help his

family—parents and sisters. Thus, he did not have that much money to spend on her. She then found a Filipino seaman who was regularly taking shore leave in Singapore. After she had dated him for a few months, they had a big fight when he found out that she had a Bangladeshi boyfriend. As a result she broke off with both of them, since both found out about the other.

Glenda was then introduced by one of her Filipino girl friends to a local Chinese businessman, after two meetings he brought her a mobile phone. It is very common for Filipino maids here to ask their boyfriends for "handphones" (this is what a mobile phone is called in Singapore) and after that for some of them to "top it up" whenever the credit there runs out. While the Chinese guy bought the handphone, her other male friends from Bangladesh and Malaysia top up the credit. With a handphone in hand, it was easy for her to communicate with, more than one man at a time without the other knowing about it.

The Chinese guy preferred to meet her on weekday mornings because he was married and had to spend time with the family on Sundays. He used to come and pick her up and drive to a Hotel 81 [hotels that rent by the hour, or a euphemism for a sexual tryst] to spend a couple of hours, and then have lunch at a hotel and return. She returns home just about the time when she needs to serve the children their lunch at 2:00 p.m.[5]

Glenda's lifestyle in Singapore, entertaining several lovers including a married man, was frowned on in the conservatively Catholic Philippines. She would be branded as immoral and ostracized. But the memoir carries no such censure. Glenda was introduced by her friends to potential lovers including a married man. She kept her liaisons secret from her employer but obviously not from her friends. Although the narrator shows some empathy for Glenda, the practice of exploiting other lonely migrant men (Bangladeshi contract workers, for example) for economic benefit (free mobile phones, text load, gifts, and so on) represented Glenda and her coterie as materialistic and opportunistic in their pursuit of romantic partners. Glenda's actions violated the Filipino ideal of the "good" woman. She had sex regularly with a Chinese "boyfriend" whom she did not love, and since he was married, she was aware that her liaison would not end in marriage. A woman's sexual encounter described here is no longer connected with romantic love or marriage. This migrant account where Glenda and her friends are represented as sexual subjects or agents capable of sexual desire completely transgresses Filipino cultural constructions of gender and sexuality where women are supposed to be devoid of sexual desire. It also contradicts the Virgin Mary as the role model for women touted by the Catholic Church in the Philippines.[6]

This chapter analyzes the way migrants have begun the process of rethinking and reimagining gender and sexuality since the 1980s. It examines the way migrants have broken taboos about women's sexual agency using the migrant archives written by domestic workers in Singapore and the Middle East. In addition to the memoirs written by migrants, I also read issues of *Manila Press* in the 1990s (the magazine that targeted Filipino domestic workers in Singapore as their readership), conducted interviews in Singapore, and did ethnographic fieldwork at Singapore's Lucky Plaza. The migrant cohort analyzed here are the working-class migrants who are on contract work and are separated from their families. The selection of sites for this chapter was solely determined by the availability of archival material on sexuality since the topic is a very sensitive one. I was not able to find material in the migrant archives on this topic written by the middle-class professionals or the Filipina/o/x Americans for the time period covered in this book.

There are two classic pioneering studies on how Filipino migration has challenged gender norms of motherhood and the male breadwinning role.[7] In addition, there is excellent work on Filipina/o/x American studies and the literature on migration and intimate labors.[8] Scholarship on gender and sexuality in Filipina/o/x America and Filipina/o/x Canada also focuses on the links between sexual and ethnic identities in the diasporic contexts, while the body of work on Filipina entertainers in Japan discuss sexualities in the workplace.[9] There is also work on the policing of the sexuality of Filipino overseas domestic workers by employers who fear that the presence of the "beautiful maid" stereotyped as a "potential seductress" might tempt their husbands to indulge in a romantic affair.[10] The literature published so far is concerned with the way sexualities are connected to migrants' performance of labor or ethnic identities.[11] This chapter looks away from these perspectives and focuses instead on the way migrants have challenged enduring cultural constructions of gender and sexuality. I acknowledge that the scholarship gives us a very nuanced interpretation of the way sexuality was linked to the performance of good and valuable workers and as model ethnic groups in the host countries. I would like to add another dimension to the discussion by introducing the concept of migrants as radical revolutionaries capable of challenging some of the most conservative and entrenched Filipino constructions of gender and sexuality, an angle that is still unexplored in the oeuvre. In doing so, I show how migrants have been able to challenge long-held views on gender and sexualities in the homeland. Contesting traditional gender constructs is a radical act that also alters the dominant view that migrants are marginal actors. Their stories reveal that migrants defy social conventions and cultural norms in the most intimate of spaces. In the process, they not only break taboos about sexual behavior, they also dismantle the connections between romantic love, sex, marriage, and the family, while forging new links between love and race in the form of interracial romance.

Filipino Cultural Constructions of Gender and Sexuality

One of the lasting impacts of the Spanish colonization of the Philippines was the introduction of Roman Catholicism. This enduring religion has shaped constructions of gender all the way until the present writing. The Spanish colonizers defined the "feminine" as convent bred, religious, charitable, demure, chaste, and strictly located in the domestic sphere. Such a definition was an elite ideal since lower-class women continued to dominate the markets and were already in factory work in the nineteenth century.[12] Maria Clara, a character in the novels of Jose Rizal (the Filipino national hero whose writings inspired the revolution against Spain) epitomized this ideal Filipina in the nineteenth century. A shy, reticent (almost vapid) character, she was naive and obedient to her parents. She was convent bred and deeply religious and spent most of her teen years secluded from the vicissitudes of the real world, including misery and poverty. The daughter of a native mother and a Spanish friar, the mestiza was extremely beautiful, described as looking like the Virgin Mary. On her first encounter with a leper, surprised that there was misery in the world, she was moved to give him her precious locket because she had nothing else to give him. Maria Clara, though a fictional character in a novel, could be read as the Spanish construction of the Filipino woman: isolated from knowledge of politics and kept in the domestic sphere. She was a beauty in form and a Catholic saint in action.[13] This feminine ideal that denied women's sexuality continued to be held up as a model for Filipino womanhood all the way until the latter half of the twentieth century and was one of the stereotypes that Filipina feminists hoped to dismantle.[14]

Although the Americans replaced the Spanish colonizers from 1898 until 1946 (interrupted by the Japanese occupation from 1941 to 1945), Maria Clara, the chaste and subservient dutiful daughter, continued to be touted as the ideal woman that Filipinas of all classes should aspire to become. The American colonial period did alter definitions of the feminine by transforming women into university graduates, heralding their entrance into the professions and, by 1937, politics. While the popular press frowned upon the appearance of the "Modern Girl" (epitomized by "the coed"), because of her autonomy, the image of the chaste Maria Clara continued to haunt Filipino women.[15] As recently as 2002, Filipina feminist psychologist Sylvia Estrada-Claudio noted that a woman's right to sexuality was not sanctioned by Filipino culture and that the suppression of sexuality was an intrinsic part of the cultural construction of being female.[16] Women were expected to be chaste until married and to be faithful wives, while men's sexual dalliances even after marriage were tolerated. If women were imagined to be incapable of performing desire, men, on the other hand, were imagined to be naturally lustful.[17] There is a dearth of scholarly material on the topic of male sexuality in the Spanish colonial period in the Philippines, but Raquel Reyes's book on sexuality and the Filipino nationalists in Europe between 1882 and 1892 argues convincingly that Filipino male expatriates who demanded reforms in the colony distinguished between the Western women they desired and the Filipino women who were idealized as chaste, pure, and devoid of sexual desire.[18] In her study of this small unique group of expatriate men, sexual promiscuity was not encouraged, even though they were equally fascinated and repelled by European women.[19] Between 1902 and 1946, the American colonizer's policy of democratic tutelage encouraged the growth of the Filipino politician and patron. The Americanized Filipino male spoke English, had a university education, and had political aspirations.[20] Among elites and politicians, the man as patron, who could provide jobs and distribute largesse to his followers, became a masculine ideal.

After the Philippines gained independence in 1946, the sex life of male politicians, which became the focus of scandal and gossip, endorsed the connections between virility and power, disclosing the way masculine sexuality had evolved into the polar opposite of women's sexuality. This conflation of virility with masculinity seemed to cut across class barriers (though, presumably, richer men could more likely afford to support mistresses), judging from the findings of social scientists. According to sociologist Elizabeth Eviota, while sex was a source of masculine self-esteem, women were supposed to deny themselves the pleasure of sex.[21] The subjects of Amaryllis Torres's study of sexuality in a rural community in the province of Zambales show that men believe that sexuality is part of their nature and "therefore, they can appropriate it whenever they need sexual gratification, even if they have to pay for it."[22] While parents of daughters wooed by these men might prefer that they be successful breadwinners, and while the ability to provide is often attached to the perceived sexual potency of Filipino men, the pursuit and winning of women is intrinsic to the macho ideal. The man without girlfriends or the bachelor who is uninterested in pursuing women is not viewed as normative.

Men's virility is very much linked to images of male power and potency, evidenced by the fact that male politicians with mistresses won election contests, and scandals involving sexual dalliances with mistresses did not harm the political careers of Philippine politicians in the postwar era unless these women benefited from corruption.

Although Filipino migrants brought these beliefs about sexuality with them when they went abroad, the physical distance that cut them off from the dominant social conventions and protected them from the prying eyes of family, relatives, neighbors, the village, the church, and critics allowed flexibility and potential radical change. Even though migrants themselves attempted to police the sexual practices of both men and women, they were not always successful.

The Overseas Contexts

What was the nature of the new environments? The majority of the migrant memoirs used for this chapter were written by Filipino migrants who worked in Singapore and the Middle East. Both Singapore and the Middle East were described by scholars as conservative on matters of sexuality. Laurence Wai-Teng Leong argued that "there is an official discourse of sexuality that similarly essentializes West versus East (Asian), and this discourse has long served as the rationale or alibi for repressive sexual policies."[23] Calling it "Singapore exceptionalism," Leong argued that the conservative sexual politics there was characterized by prudishness, epitomized by the orthodox view that sex was confined only to procreative vaginal intercourse (no oral sex, for example).[24] If Singapore politicians were role models, the lack of sexual scandals among members of Parliament mirrored the straight-laced and high moral caliber expected of them in public. This behavior was also expected of all Singaporeans, as "sexuality falls into that aspect of life of which the state wants to be the final arbiter."[25] Writing about criminal law, women, and sexuality in the Middle East, Sherifa Zuhur underscored that sex was only sanctioned within marriage with *zina* (adultery/fornication) identified as one of the seven serious crimes in sharia.[26] In Iran, sodomy was punishable by death (or, if confessed fewer than four times, by flogging) and lesbianism by one hundred lashes.[27] Women were pressured to become bearers of constructed national or religious identities. Customary practices that controlled their sexuality were considered Islamic, while the polar opposite—the portrayal of sexual autonomy or homosexuality—was identified as "Western" and thus a threat to Muslim practices.[28] The feminist movements that appeared in the 1990s had to face the double challenge of traditional taboos regarding sexual preferences and the conservative religious policies and politics of contemporary governments who needed support from the religious fundamentalist movements to maintain legitimacy. In this tension, issues of gender equality and sexual autonomy were ones most "easily compromised."[29] But being far away from the prying eyes of the village allowed some Filipino women migrants to break traditional mores. Their subject position as "outsiders" in the Middle East and Singapore probably gave them a little bit more freedom to transgress the dominant sexual mores in the host country.

Sex, Sexuality, Celibacy, and Infidelity

The post-1970s Filipino global migration outside the United States had very different effects on feminine constructions of sexuality. Migrant memoirs (some of them published under pseudonyms) illustrate the ways women have broken social taboos and succeeded in claiming sexual rights clandestinely. Filipino migrant women dismantled one of the very foundational blocks in constructions of the feminine by taking in lovers (including lovers from different nationalities or who are not Filipino) or indulging in adultery.

Moral Surveillance

Filipina domestic workers in Asia, especially those who lived with their employers, found their physical appearance and moral behavior heavily policed by their female bosses who regarded them as a "potential seductresses" and therefore a possible threat to their marriage.[30] This anxiety caused female employers to impose strict dress codes with the sole intention of making their maids less physically attractive—including rules banning lipstick, nail polish, sleeveless shirts, tight pants, spaghetti straps, skirts above the knee, shorts, perfume, jewelry, and makeup.[31] This attempt to reduce the sexual appeal of maids, however, could only be enforced in the employer's home.

Outside the employer's home, Filipina domestic workers were subject to the moral surveillance of the local Catholic church if they chose to be part of the religious community. Irregular Filipina migrants in Paris who attended Saint Bernadette Chapel and who were active in the chaplaincy practiced sexual abstinence and participated in church activities to avoid temptations, while the fear of gossip acted as a way of policing moral behavior, since popular topics for discussion include "marital infidelity, conjugal separation and juvenile delinquency."³² The lack of a divorce law in the Philippines was a strong incentive to keep them from straying since they knew that it was impossible to change partners if they wanted to be welcome in the Catholic Church. Despite this rigid atmosphere of surveillance, there was greater freedom and opportunity for women to find romantic partners. Scholars analyzed the impact of the cell phone and the Internet in maintaining connections between spouse, family members, and the village separated in time and space.³³ But what scholars have not yet investigated is how this same technology could also be used to find new romances and break marriage vows. The accounts of migrants reveal that a number of them found sweethearts through Facebook.³⁴ According to one memoir of a domestic worker in Singapore, "nowadays, many Filipina maids here go on the Internet to hook up with men, whom they meet on Sundays."³⁵ The website FilipinoHearts was a popular Internet dating site visited by Filipina domestic workers in Singapore, and "Hotel 81" became the code name (or euphemism) for love nests or trysts, meaning they would visit a hotel that rented rooms by the hour.³⁶ In Taiwan "love hotels" offered discounts on Sunday afternoons—evidence that businesses competed for the migrant clientele and that they were willing to launch promotional strategies directed at migrant couples.³⁷ The mobile phone became a tool for phone sex with men who were not their husbands.³⁸ Lucky Plaza, the mall on Orchard Road at the center of Singapore's shopping district, was not only a Sunday gathering place for Filipinos, it also functioned as a "pick-up point" for potential lovers.³⁹ On the one hand, Filipina domestic workers in Singapore complained that the specter of loneliness was a great challenge they had to overcome while overseas, but, on the other hand, they also admitted that it was relatively easy to find boyfriends because many men of different nationalities (but especially South Asian men) followed Filipinas around on their Sundays off.⁴⁰

Resistance and Transgressions

Filipina domestic workers found ways to resist some of the rules intended to police their moral behavior. In Paris, those who did not want to comply with the Catholic Church's advice to remain chaste but who also wanted to escape the censure of gossip simply refrained from joining Filipino church gatherings and kept their romantic liaisons secret from friends and family.⁴¹ Domestic workers shed their identities as "maids" by donning fashionable attire and transforming themselves into chic and sexy ladies on their days off. One domestic worker in the Middle East entitled her personal story "My Maid's Uniform" (Damit ko na pangkatulong). Poking fun at her maid's uniform, which her male employers claimed made her look like a tablecloth or flower vase, she narrated how wearing this attire made her invisible to Arab society because it hid her individual identity and personal beauty and underscored the lowly position of her work. However, on her day off her usual ritual was to model all her fashionable clothes while striking provocative poses and taking selfies on the makeshift "catwalk" inside her private room.[42] Yet, she ended her narrative with the words: "I am proud of my maid's uniform because through wearing it, my brother/sister completed school and it has been part of my life here in a foreign land."[43] The Sunday sartorial transformations allowed the domestic workers not just to shed their working identities but also to reclaim their sexual selves artificially suppressed on weekdays by their employers sumptuary laws. Stepping out in full makeup, painted nails, short shorts, off-the-shoulder blouses, or spaghetti straps, it was no longer possible to distinguish them from their female employers as they frequented similar public spaces—visiting the zoo, eating at restaurants, and shopping at the mall. As one memoir put it: "Skinny Ako, pero sexy!" (I am skinny, but I'm sexy).[44] In fact, an article published in the *Manila Press*, a magazine that targeted domestic workers in Singapore, disclosed that it was easy to spot the Filipino woman having a sexual affair because of her "sexy" attire of miniskirt or denim shorts, black stockings, high heels, and permed hair.[45]

When I did field research at Lucky Plaza in July 2017, Filipinos told me they mistakenly thought I was Singaporean not just because of my relatively fair skin and almond eyes but because of my dress choices: I was told that Filipinas were attired in sexy, fashionable clothes, whereas Singaporeans dressed simply and elegantly. And the chic ladies promenading in Lucky Plaza on Sundays looked as if they just stepped out of the many beauty parlors in that mall: with their hair newly "rebonded," dyed, and styled, wearing short shorts and off-the-shoulder blouses and stilettos, they all looked dressed to impress. This weekend look was also for the benefit of a wider audience than Singapore since many took selfies that were subsequently posted on their Facebook pages to let their relatives in the Philippines know that they were successful women.

The most radical way women transgressed gender ideals was by having sexual affairs or indulging in adultery. The candid way that Filipino domestic workers in Singapore recounted their sex lives abroad (albeit using pseudonyms) broke a social taboo. Women's open discussions about sexual matters would be considered shocking. Furthermore, the disclosure that women had not just one but several lovers revealed that they were behaving more like the masculine ideal rather than the feminine one. The title of one of these migrant stories—"A Childless 'Single Wife' Overseas"—meant that they even invented a new category to describe themselves—the single wife—to explain their romantic lifestyles.⁴⁶ These women had left behind troubling marriages or husbands who had abandoned them in the Philippines. The unusual demographic of one Filipino man to one hundred Filipino women (from 1970s to the present writing) enhanced the value of Filipino men (the running joke in Hong Kong was "As long as a guy is Filipino, it does not matter whether he is cross-eyed or has three nostrils he will be in demand"), but this did not prevent women from finding lovers from other nationalities.⁴⁷ In Paris some married Filipino women had French, Sri Lankan, and Pakistani lovers.⁴⁸

In their life stories, Filipina domestic workers in Singapore openly admitted to having boyfriends (and sexual relationships) with Chinese, Bangladeshi, Sri Lankan, Indian, and American men. Most of these boyfriends were married men.⁴⁹ For example, in Rita's story her boyfriend Sanjay was an Indian who worked as a computer science lecturer at a local polytechnic, but his Indian wife was a doctor in Canada. Sanjay took Rita on overseas holiday trips to Bintan Resorts and Bali in Indonesia, Bangkok and Pattaya in Thailand, and Penang and Cameron Highlands in Malaysia.⁵⁰ Since neither partner was single and since Filipinas could not obtain absolute divorce in the Philippines, the result was that they formed short-term relationships, including one-day stands (since their day off from work was normally from nine to five only and did not include the evenings).

In these published autobiographical accounts, women were candid about their sexual encounters with boyfriends during their days off. Daisy addressed the reader in a very matter of fact way:

> I'm closing in on my 52nd birthday now. If I remained in the Philippines with my husband, I may be a grandmother by now. I haven't been a saintly nun here in Singapore either. Like many Filipino women here, I have had a few boyfriends on the way, especially after I got the Sundays off. It is easy to find a boyfriend here. Many come behind us, especially on Sundays if you go to Orchard Street, you find men of many colours and many shapes looking to hook up with a Filipina—sometimes just one day (not night) stands. . . .
>
> I have had Bangladeshi, Malay, Chinese and *angmoh* [white] boyfriends and got on well with them. But they were all married and were not planning to divorce their wives nor did I want to break up any marriages. It is taken for granted these were only flings on our day off.⁵¹

Singapore's tough immigration laws prohibited marriage between overseas workers and Singaporean nationals. Since the demographic showed a clear majority of up to a hundred Filipinas to one Filipino male, potential boyfriends came from the pool of foreign men from different nationalities, many of whom were also working in Singapore on temporary contracts and who did not have permanent residency. Since a number of these men were already married (with their spouses located overseas), they were unavailable as potential life partners. Filipina domestic workers knew that the solace they found in another man's arms was ephemeral.

The advice column, or Agony Aunt column ("Dear Tita Lily"), of a magazine directed at Filipina domestic workers in Singapore around the 1990s featured several letters from women who were having illicit relationships with "boyfriends" who were not their husbands, appealing for wise counsel over anxieties over sexual health and sexually transmitted diseases, dilemmas involving several suitors or affairs with their employers.[52] According to Michael, who owned a jewelry shop at Lucky Plaza the Filipino mall in Orchard Road: "On Sundays it's very common to see Filipinas cuddling up to guys who obviously are married and are not their husbands. They are happy."[53] Filipinas were spotted holding hands with their boyfriends in the MRT (underground metro train), Lucky Plaza, or botanical garden[54] The ubiquity of illicit romances between "single wives" and South Asian construction workers in Singapore inspired a special feature article in this same magazine (*Manila Press*), which attempted to explain "the mystery of the romance between Filipinas and Singaporeans."[55] Explanations put forward by the women interviewed included loneliness, sexual excitement, revenge against cheating husbands in the Philippines, and financial gain since boyfriends lavished them with gifts of mobile phones, jewelry, clothes, and cash, which they could remit to their families.[56]

These women broke taboos in two radical ways. First, while men's infidelity was tolerated in Filipino society, women's adultery was not. Thus, in publicly confessing their sexual affairs (albeit using pseudonyms), they asserted women's sexuality and sexual agency outside of marriage. The married woman with a lover was considered extremely rare in official representations of women. Thus, Filipina overseas workers' stories debunked the myth of the chaste wife. Were they aware that they were breaking taboos? One poem by a Filipina overseas worker in Hong Kong (and who appears to be using her real name) clearly showed migrant agency:

> We fell in love, it went strong
> Though we knew it was wrong
> We became captives of our heart's desires
> So we took the risk and broke the rules
>
> It was all right to love you
> But I couldn't have a hold on you

Long before, you belonged to someone
And, I believed, you wouldn't give her to anyone.

Over and again, my heart breaks
When I think of you
Because I can't deny it, I still love you.[57]

The poem's author, who confessed her illicit affair, clearly asserted that she knew it was wrong and that she was aware that the lovers had broken the rules.

Second, women knew that their liaisons were not going to lead to forming new families. They did not intend to divorce their husbands (which was not legal in the Philippines) or form new families with the new partners. The stories of these women migrants who openly discussed their relationships with many men illustrate the ways women migrants celebrated their sexuality and reveal that women's sexual relations or emotional attachments were no longer connected with ideals of creating "families." Since the normative behavior in the Philippines was that Filipino women were expected to form romantic relationships with the intention of marrying and starting families, this behavior of domestic workers in Singapore challenged traditional constructions of the feminine and the primordial instinct to form "happy families." Nevertheless, this did not mean that Filipina domestic workers did not yearn for romance and remarriage. Most of the short stories written by Filipina domestic workers in Hong Kong that were first published in the NGO newsletter *Tinig* (Voice) and later published in an anthology had one overarching main plot and theme: romance in which the Filipina protagonist met and married a white foreigner.[58] Hence, those who wanted a second chance to conform to the happy family ideal hoped to do so with a non-Filipino partner, challenging the ethnic ideal of pure-Filipino families.

Finally, women began to take other women as lovers. Given that sexuality was sublimated in hegemonic cultural constructions of women as incapable of experiencing desire but who were in themselves objects of male desire, most Filipinos in the Philippines found the concept of lesbianism—as women who desired other women—unfathomable.[59] Lesbianism as a feminist issue only entered the public sphere in the early 1990s.[60] When the topic of lesbianism was raised in a 1988 Sisterhood Is Global conference in Manila, Aida Santos briefly mentioned that it was practiced as an alternative sexual preference for women by overseas migrant workers, however, she ended further discussion with the words: "We don't want to talk about it because it is a taboo issue."[61] In a television news program, one Filipina estimated that a quarter of domestic workers in Hong Kong were lesbians.[62] Writing on lesbianism among

Indonesian domestic workers in Hong Kong, Amy Sim noted: "Other Indonesians expressed shock that Indonesian women in Hong Kong had become lesbians. They found this to be unbelievable and attributed it to the 'bad' influence of Filipina domestic workers."[63] The NGO Atikha has pointed out that "a growing number of women in Hong Kong and Italy are also engaged in extramarital affairs or lesbian relationships."[64] One story published in *Manila Press* in the genre of "true confessions" was about a two-year lesbian affair in Hong Kong written by a woman who claimed she entered the relationship because she was upset with her husband.[65] How did they discuss this taboo of all taboo topics with regard to female sexualities? One memoir of Filipina workers in Paris was very revealing:

> Gay Paree is *très* sexy! But in French Philippines, most Filipinas are "sexless." Married women (with husbands in the Philippines) have no sexual partners while in France. This remains one of the unexpressed strains on the very human nerves of our super-heroines. Due to isolation, fear of men and unequivocal devotion to family, the practice of sexual abstinence is very high in the Philippine community. To protect themselves, women frequent religious rites and encounters, keep to themselves (among women) or simply stay at home after work, intensifying isolation and solitude. Now and then, one hears of a heterosexual woman shacking up with a *tomboy*. Filipinas with their wavering sexuality do not seem to consider this a deviance. "I am not lesbian," somebody told me, "but the men here are not good for me. My partner is caring and tender. I prefer her...." A married woman living with a lesbian says: "It is not like being with a man. I do not feel unfaithful to my husband!"[66]

In the above examples, one woman claimed she was not a lesbian although she had a female partner, while another did not consider sex with a woman a sign of unfaithfulness (underscoring traditional beliefs that sex is imagined to be only heterosexual sex).[67] Yet, all the migrant women who rejected the ideals of the chaste wife became pioneers in dismantling traditional constructions of the feminine. By having sexual liaisons, heterosexual or not, and especially because these relationships were not imagined to be permanent, these women were proclaiming that women had the right to sexual desire and rejected the Catholic Church's teachings that sex should be confined solely to the marriage bed.

Despite the surveillance and heavy policing of migrants (by the host country and migrants themselves), women were able to break the cultural taboos on sex outside of marriage and included sexual identity as part of the new constructions of the feminine. Filipinas in post-1970s Singapore, Hong Kong, Paris, the Middle East, and Taiwan were able to enjoy sexual relationships in a way that was not possible in the Philippines.

While I discuss here the sensitive issue of extra-marital affairs and sexual liaisons which these migrants have described in their own memoirs as "one-day stands" (as opposed to "one-night stands" since they only have the day-off and not the full 24-hour day off), I do not interpret these in a negative light.[68] As a feminist historian who has written about the women's movements in the Philippines and activists' struggles to alter how the Filipina is defined by religion, the state, and cultural traditions, I see their actions as empowering particularly given the limits placed on Filipino constructions of sexuality. After all, men's infidelity is tolerated in the homeland. While conservative Filipinos and Singaporeans might dismiss these actions as evidence of immorality, I take the perspective from the sources I use and the interviews I have had where these actions are not judged but instead presented as a new norm. In the accounts of Filipino workers in Singapore where authors speak candidly about their sexual affairs, this behavior is not condemned.[69] In the independent feature film *Remittance* (about Filipina domestic workers in Singapore with real-life domestic workers as part of the cast), the heroine, who is a domestic worker in Singapore, has a South Asian boyfriend.[70] But since the story is told from her perspective, the audience is sympathetic to her plight as the film discloses that her Filipino husband has taken a mistress in the Philippines, and at the end of the film he not only steals her hard-earned money, he almost physically assaults her. Meanwhile, the South Asian boyfriend is represented as kind and caring. A Filipino former overseas contract worker who was stationed in Iraq for five years in the 1980s confided to me that, based on his observation of his batch of workers, infidelity happens when migrants feel unappreciated for the remittances they send back home.[71] I am of course writing about migration from the migrant's point of view (and not that of the nation left behind) and this allows me to be empathetic to their particular situation.

The migrant archives reveal the many ways Filipino migrant women have broken taboos and radically altered established constructs of women's sexuality and desire. Their new status as breadwinners has given them the disposable income that can be used to transform themselves into fashionable cosmopolitan ladies. Women whose husbands remained in the Philippines might find themselves pressured to remain celibate, especially by church groups or through peer pressure and gossip, while others found that the freedom from village social mores gave them unprecedented opportunities to form sexual liaisons outside marriage. Finally, the demographic context also influenced the pool of potential lovers. In Singapore and Hong Kong where there were approximately one hundred Filipino women to one Filipino man, Filipino women formed romantic attachments with other ethnicities—Bangladeshi or South Indian contract workers, or Chinese locals and white expatriates. Writing on the "mystery" of Filipina romances with Singaporeans, Deney Rue warned the reader [assumed to be Filipinos all over the world] not to be shocked ("huwag kang mabibigla") to see a Filipina cuddling up to a Tamil man as if she was his wife.[72] The observation that it was commonplace to see Filipinas on Sundays holding hands with Tamils, riding motorbikes with Malays, going to discos with Chinese, and going on holidays with expatriates (presumably whites) revealed that Filipinas in Singapore were breaking taboos not just about sexuality (since readers were warned not to be shocked) but also about interracial romance.[73]

PART TWO

Changing Social Mores and Economic Landscapes

Filipino Migrants as Consumers

Chapter 3

Consumption and Social Change, 1980s–2018

In his chronicle of Filipino male undocumented workers in Japan, Rey Ventura shares the story of the eighteenth birthday celebration of Dante's daughter Laura.

The party was held at a five-star hotel in Manila. There were around a hundred guests. There were eighteen boys who presented her with eighteen roses. She danced with them plus a few old men. She was like a princess in her pink gown. She looked innocent and virginal. She also starred in a fashion show in which she was the only model: as the evening wore on she sashayed in several dresses especially made for her. As the youngest of three children and the only one left in school and not married, she was special. While her escorts took turns dancing with Laura, Dante rang from Japan; his call was hooked up to the public address system. This was the climax of the party—a father-daughter long-distance dialogue. Everybody froze to attention and listened to a private conversation. Around Laura were gathered her elder sister, her brother, and her fat mother:
 "Hello! Daddy!"
 "Hello, my daughter. Happy Birthday!"
 "Thank you, Daddy. I miss you!"
 "I miss you, too. I love you! I miss you!"

> "I love you, Daddy. I miss you."
>
> "I love you! I miss you."
>
> Dante's voice was cracking and the members of his family were all teary-eyed. Their relatives and friends, too, were on the verge of tears. The line was taken off the PA system and Laura passed the phone to her elder sister. She wiped her tears.
>
> For this two-hour party, Dante had set aside US$7,000—a year's savings."[1]

This poignant tale of conspicuous consumption underscores the amount of savings Filipino migrants were prepared to spend to mimic the practices of the elites in the Philippines who host a lavish debutante ball for their daughter's eighteenth birthday in a five star hotel. Dante hoped to taste what it felt like, if even for a moment, to be an upper-class family on show—the envy of all his guests. The irony of the situation where Dante was not able to enjoy the party he paid for and bask in the high social status of the venue seemed to be lost on all participants. The climax of the celebration—Dante's international phone call where father and daughter's intimate conversation about their love for each other was broadcast publicly to the audience of guests—also underscores the connection between a father's material gift of a grand party and his love for his daughter in the context of his physical absence. Dante's story demonstrates a new cultural norm born out of the great labor migration of the post-1980s, where material gifts are interpreted as signs of love.

The US$7,000 that Dante spent that night, however, would have allowed him to finally return home. Dante, a forty-six-year-old grandfather of three who worked as a scaffold builder for twelve years, suffered lingering back pain. He lamented that if he only had savings of $5,000 he would go home. More than a decade later he still was not able to fulfill his dreams for return. Instead, his daughter, whom he had hoped would work in a hospital, followed him to Japan to work in the "pleasure districts" as a bar hostess.[2] Dante's decision to have an extravagant celebration for his daughter's debutante ball had tragic consequences for him and his family. While Ventura's account does not discuss whether Dante's splurge plunged him into debt, migrant debt has been identified as an important issue in a study conducted by the Filipino Women's Council among Filipinos in Italy.[3]

This chapter investigates the underresearched topic of migrant spending habits and the way these consumption patterns express changes in class and social norms. The very notion of migrants as consumers is still largely absent and remarkably underresearched in the scholarship on Filipino migration since the 1970s. Perhaps it is because most scholars are interested in migrants as laborers rather than as consumers. While the social science literature has interpreted the practice of building "remittance houses" (houses built in the homeland funded by migrant remittances) and sending *"balikbayan* [returning Filipino migrant] boxes," or regular shipments of gifts (sometimes translated as "the tea-chest cargo"[4]) to the homeland as one way migrants connect to the family and the village and fulfill the values of filial piety, I would like to move beyond these excellent studies that privilege consumption as a way of connecting kin and community to suggest that these very consumption practices, including sending these boxes, have radically altered norms and values while expressing new class and cosmopolitan identities.[5] This perspective underscores migrant agency and sees them as radical actors changing foundational norms of reciprocity and introducing the possibilities of imagining class in a transnational context. Focusing primarily on Filipino migrant domestic workers in Europe (especially Italy) and contract workers in the Middle East, as well as seafarers, this chapter highlights the unique transnational location of migrant consumption—straddling two class positions because they are considered lower classes in the host country, but their salaries when converted to pesos and their spending habits in the Philippines locate them among the ranks of the rising middle classes there. Seafarers who are not officers are classified as low-rating seamen in the shipping industry, but their high salaries paid in US dollars enable them to build houses in gated communities and send their children to private schools, indicators that they are among the ranks of the social middle class in the Philippines

In addition, this chapter also analyzes the way migration has altered the social values, attitudes, and norms associated with reciprocity since the 1980s. Changing long-held cultural beliefs takes time. A historical perspective enables us to identify the transformations that over four decades of labor migration have made to the practices of gift giving and the meanings associated with this custom. Today it seems to be a normal practice, or a "tradition," for migrants all over the world to ship *balikbayan* boxes, or huge cartons full of gifts and food, to the family and the village in the Philippines. But this is an invented tradition that dates back only to the 1980s.

What were the dramatic alterations in recent years in cultural norms associated with gift giving and reciprocity? First, the belief that migrants *must* send gifts in *balikbayan* boxes to the homeland in regular shipments throughout the year has become entrenched. This gift giving that was only one way, that is, that those who benefited were not expected to reciprocate, was a revolutionary change to Filipino values of reciprocity, normally seen as the cornerstone of Filipino social values.[6] Whereas, traditionally, recipients were obliged to reciprocate gifts and favors with interest in keeping with the values of *utang ng loob* (debt of gratitude), this is no longer the case. The social perception that migrants were wealthy because their salaries when converted to pesos are much higher than local wages encouraged a sense of entitlement to some of their earnings by those who remained in the Philippines. Hence, while migrants were now expected to give gifts, the recipients were no longer expected to give anything back. These new rules of etiquette seen today as "normal" actually shook one of the very foundations of Filipino cultural values. Second, migrants' gifts were now seen to be the barometer for the giver's love and affection for the receiver. Because of this semiotic connection migrants felt enormous pressure to give away their hard-earned money to family, relatives, and the village even though they could not afford it. Third, the need to demonstrate that the migration was a success story motivated migrants to show off their new status as middle class through the purchase of real estate or branded goods and to become patrons of the community by paying for relatives' education and donating to the village church, for example. Fourth, all these demands prevented migrants from saving for their future. The fear of losing future remittances (which in 2017 reached US$28 billion, or 10% of the GDP) is one reason why the Philippine government, Philippine banks, and NGOs now offer free financial literacy seminars (since circa 2005) to try to direct migrants away from spending and toward saving and investing. While it is still too soon to evaluate the impact of these seminars, I can, however, point out after having attended two myself that these modules propose revolutionary changes in Filipino norms and attitudes not only because they advise migrants to think about their retirement, investments, and their financial future, but also because they encourage participants to say no to financial requests from the family, the kin group, and the village. The consequence of denying the many pleas for money and gifts is social ostracism, and, thus, this advice though prudent will increase the anxieties that migrants already experience in their new position as breadwinners and patrons of the family and village left behind. To address this problem the NGO Atikha now runs financial literacy seminars for families left behind by migrants.

Consumption was as important to migrants as working for a living. It was the reward for all the hard work they endured overseas.[7] Although the experiences of Filipino migrants all over the world were varied and cannot be homogenized, the one common denominator was that consumption symbolized the affirmation of the success of the migration project and the migrant's new status as middle class. The lifestyle that included eating out in trendy restaurants, the purchase of the latest electronic gadgets, and travel tourism was now an intrinsic part of the migrant's new identity as a cosmopolitan subject.

Consumption fulfilled an important vacuum in the migrants' life. Gunnar Lamvik entitled his dissertation on Filipino seafarers "The Filipino Seafarer: A Life between Sacrifice and Shopping," capturing succinctly the contrast between the male seafarer's monotonous life aboard the ship and his arrival home as a nouveau riche.[8] Lamvik discusses the seafarers' preoccupation with gift giving to fulfill social expectations: "months of absence and months of aggregated expectation are expressed through an exhibitionistic, though planned dispersal of material things within the social surroundings."[9] They spent a considerable amount for these gifts (seen as necessary to display their status), some up to 25 percent of their salary, with one informant confiding that he spent $2,000 on gifts annually.[10] Seafarers spent their dollars on expensive watches, Ray-Ban sunglasses, golden rings and necklaces, branded sneakers, food such as coffee and chocolate, and liquor such as whisky, as well as an entire gamut of souvenirs from their travels to distribute as gifts.[11] Lorna Vea Munnecom, a Filipina who owns a travel agency in Paris, confided to me in an interview that it was difficult to sell a package tour to Filipinos in France unless it included a shopping expedition (preferably in Andorra where things are duty free).[12] Many indulged in spending sprees of branded goods such as handbags from Louis Vuitton, Prada, and Hermès, scarves from Burberry, clothes from expensive international designers such Prada and Armani, and the latest technological gadgets including laptop computers, iPads, mobile phones, and smart phones.[13] Children whose parents worked overseas were notorious for demanding expensive gifts, especially the latest computers and mobile or smart phones.[14]

When the migrant returned home for the holidays, the spending intensified. Returning overseas Filipino workers to Baguio City treated their friends and relatives to the newest trendy restaurants in town, such as gourmet coffee at Amadeus Café, dinner and wine at Luisa's Café, and "compulsory food binges at Jollibee with our nephews and nieces."[15] Among those who benefited from their generosity, one confessed: "We feel like movie stars each time my sisters would come home from Saudi. Hordes of visiting relatives and neighbors would drop by, hoping of course for some *pasalubong* (gift)."[16] In a collection of overseas Filipino workers' stories, Sherald Salamat remembered how happy he was as a child when his father returned for his holiday because he knew they would have a lot of money and they would spend it on shopping at the mall, eating at restaurants, and going on vacations.[17]

Migrants in Italy even coined a phrase to refer to the binge spending especially on holidays and special occasions. The term *ubos biyaya* (literally meaning to pour out all the blessings until they ran out) described the lavish lifestyle of returning migrants who borrowed money and spent it all in one month's holiday. One migrant described the experience of many: "We behave as if we are rich. That is the problem. In 1995, I went home with ₱100,000, part of which was borrowed. Would you believe that in one and a half month's time I spent all the money?"[18] Eating out daily in fast-food places such as Chow King (a Chinese fast-food chain) and Jollibee (the Filipino version of McDonald's) and spending ₱18,000 on dog food and enormous grocery bills took their toll even on the highest earners, such as the seafarers who earned a very good salary of US$5,000 a month.[19]

For some, their transnational location allowed them to live the double life of a domestic worker in Europe and a rich person in the Philippines.[20] An essay from the migrant archives by Maria Thelma Novel-Jezewski, entitled "Maria Is Poor in Paris," where Maria is representative of the Filipina woman, tells the touching story of a self-sacrificing domestic worker who dwelled in tiny room without a bathroom located in a Parisian attic but whose family lived in a mansion in the Philippines. Filipinos in France had a saying to refer to these martyr migrants: "enduring life like a cockroach in France in order to be able to buy a mansion in the Philippines."[21] These stories underscore the unusual transnational class location of some Filipino overseas workers, particularly domestic workers who were classified as working class or lower class by the host country, but who earned money in euros, dollars, riyals, and other currencies that, when converted to pesos, enabled their families to experience the lifestyle of the middle class in the Philippines.

Filipino migrants spent their remittances mainly for housing (including maintenance), for the education of their children, family members, or relatives, and to pay for health and day-to-day grocery bills, either through cash advances or through the sending of *balikbayan* boxes. Budgets were also set aside for phone calls and the equipment necessary for communication, such as mobile phones, iPads, smart phones, and computers, including laptops.[22] Children left behind by migrant parents were sent to private schools, so tuition fees, interpreted positively as investment for the children's future employment, are a major expense for families. Remittances also cover the health-care expenses of elderly parents.[23] My focus here is on consumer practices rather than on remittances, although the line between remittances and consumption was often blurred when remittances were sent in the form of goods—such as the ubiquitous *balikbayan* boxes. Remittances in the form of cash were also used to purchase land or set up businesses.

I used archival material on Filipino domestic workers in Italy and Singapore, as well as seafarers. A signed agreement between the Philippines and Italy allowed Filipino migrants to work as domestic helpers in Italy from 1977.[24]

By 1995 more than 200,000 Filipinos had settled there, with slightly half of them in Rome.[25] In 2003 official records showed 74,030 Filipino legal residents, 64 percent of them women working in the service sectors as domestic helpers, caretakers, and babysitters, primarily in big cities such as Rome, Florence, Milan, Turin, Naples, Parma, Bologna, and Messina.[26] Eldercare and childcare were identified as sectors of high demand for immigrant women's labor, and Filipinos as well as other immigrant groups such as Moroccans performed this much-needed work.[27]

In Rome, those working part-time received an average monthly wage of US$1,229, while live-in workers earned US$722, and those who cared for the elderly took home an average of US$778 prior to 2001.[28] Live-in domestic workers in Rome earned a minimum of €600 a month according to a 2008 study. There were, however, great disparities in incomes among the domestic workers and care workers from the spectrum of €500 to €1,700. The majority of those interviewed by scholars Charito Basa, Violeta de Guzman, and Sabrina Marchetti earned between €700 and €1,400.[29] The differences could be partially explained by the living arrangements.[30] Some workers lived with their employers and received lower salaries. However, my interviews with Filipino domestic workers in Padova and Milan revealed that those in this situation were able to save more money since accommodations and most living expenses were provided by their employers and some of the workers were given separate apartments (sometimes in the basement of the buildings where their employers lived).[31] Women send roughly half of their wages as remittances plus what some scholars have termed "random" remittances such as cash and gifts (toys, clothing, cellular phones, and computers).[32] Included in my cohort of interviews in Padova was a group of four siblings who each sent €50 a month in cash to their elderly parents in Santa Rosa in the province of Laguna in the Philippines.

There are about 70,000 Filipino domestic workers in Singapore (as of June 2014).[33] In Singapore about one in five households employs or is dependent on overseas foreign workers for housekeeping and care for the young and elderly.[34] The total number of all foreign domestic workers in Singapore is 218,300 (or 16 percent of the total foreign workforce) with Filipinos composing more than a third of this niche group. Domestic workers in Singapore earned an average monthly salary of S$515 in 2015.[35] My own interviews with Filipina domestic workers divulges a slightly higher average wage of about S$600, with the highest paid person (working for a foreign embassy) receiving S$2,000 a month. Many Singaporean families were highly dependent on them for doing practically all the domestic and caring duties in their everyday life.

If domestic workers were one end of the earning spectrum, occupying the lowest class rung in their host countries, seafarers were among the highest paid dollar earnings in the group of overseas Filipino workers. By 2001 their numbers increased to over 255,000 or around 28.1 percent of the global labor market.[36] According to *Ahoy Magazine* (the Apostleship of the Sea–Philippines newsmagazine), in 1997 the pay of a Filipino able seaman or oiler averaged US$1,000 a month, with officers earning many times more and a master mariner receiving US$3,000 a month. The magazine's conservative estimate for a Filipino able seaman was about US$13,000 a year, including vacation pay of one month.[37] According to a 2009 news report, the salary for an ordinary seaman (a rank below the able seaman) was US$500–US$800 a month, while an officer like a ship captain earned as much as US$8,000–US$12,000 a month.[38] By law Filipino seamen were required to remit 80 percent of their salaries to the Philippines (and in 1997 that amounted to US$10,000 per seaman as a conservative estimate).[39] This overwhelmingly male group of consumers also spent a huge percentage of their earnings on gifts. Gunnar Lamvik interviewed a chief mate who disclosed that he spent around US$2,000 on gifts each year, while an officer told him that he spent nearly 25 percent of his salary on gifts.[40] Since their earning power (especially when translated into pesos) placed them at the top end of the social hierarchy in their own rural communities, they were often invited to become godparents or sponsors; while this gave them high social status, this role required them to be generous beneficiaries who shared their economic capital through gift giving, including cash donations. Some of this can be a huge economic burden on the individual concerned.[41] Nevertheless, Lamvik argues, the act of shopping was essential as a coping strategy for the seaman while on board ship as it helped him remember his absent family and demonstrated his status as nouveau riche when he returned.[42] Seafarers sometimes spent millions of pesos for wedding receptions held at five-star hotels in Manila with a plethora of godparents, on par with those of the top elite families in the Philippines.[43]

Sources for this chapter include materials from the "migrant archives," including memoirs, autobiographies, migrant magazines and newsletters such *Filipinas* (San Francisco, 1992–2010), *Planet Philippines* (London issues, 2007–2008, 2011–2012, January–June 2013), *Tinig ng Marino* (the newsletter of the union of Filipino seafarers, 1999–2010), interviews with a Filipino travel agent in Paris and owners of stores in Lucky Plaza, including employees and managers of shipping companies that sent boxes of goods to the Philippines, and Filipino migrants in Singapore, Padova, Paris, Santa Rosa and San Roque, Laguna, and fieldwork in Santa Rosa and Padova, Italy, as well as Lucky Plaza, Singapore. Finally, I also attended two financial literacy seminars run by

PinoyWISE (a subsidiary of Atikha)—one directed at migrants in Singapore on July 16, 2017, and another targeting the family left behind, in Malolos, Bulacan Province, Philippines, on February 27, 2019.

Living in a Material World: Consumption as Love

Consumption connected migrants to the homeland and enabled them to fulfill the social expectations of contributing to the family and the village/community. The establishment of door-to-door courier businesses made it possible for migrants to send gifts to the Philippines on a regular basis. These shipments of *"balikbayan* boxes" became a regular practice—an invented tradition. The origins of this could be traced to the custom of buying *pasalubongs* (souvenirs and gifts) that travelers brought back to their family in the Philippines to give to friends and relatives as a token to show that they had thought about them while they were away and to share their overseas experience with them. But the *pasalubong* was meant to be a small inexpensive one-off gift. The *balikbayan* box custom magnified the *pasalubong* tradition into an expensive time-consuming exercise, with senders filling gigantic sized boxes with gifts (the "super jumbo" box of Alsomavic Cargo Ltd from the United Kingdom is 34″ × 27″ × 23″) and shipping them several times a year.[44] The goods that filled the boxes ranged from daily grocery items, such as canned goods like Spam and sardines, laundry detergent, beauty products like shampoo and soap, chocolates, and clothing (new, branded, or secondhand), to secondhand appliances (including air conditioners) and even an entire kitchen.[45] The boxes they sent varied in size but the larger boxes were the most popular.[46] According to courier LBC, domestic workers in Singapore sent home boxes year round but particularly during Christmas and New Year (to send Christmas gifts), Chinese New Year (since employers gave their helpers cash and secondhand items as part of the "spring cleaning" for the New Year), and at the start of the school year (to send school supplies, including notebooks, shoes, and socks).[47] Rey Ventura's autobiographical account of the lives of undocumented Filipino workers in Japan describes the dwellings of these intrepid construction workers as crowded with items destined for their families in the Philippines—from secondhand clothing to knickknacks picked up at outdoor markets.[48] The undocumented Filipinos in London also cluttered their houses with toys and canned goods, many of them bought religiously from weekend car boot sales (*karbut*).[49]

Sending these boxes was an expensive enterprise. In Singapore, the boxes cost S$100 to send a large box of 24 × 24 × 30 inches to Manila (it cost S$115 to send the same size box to Mindanao) in 2017.[50] The steep prices endowed the sender with the status of generous benefactor or patron, especially if the gifts were distributed beyond the family to the rest of the community.[51]

Since some of the goods sent were actually available in the Philippines, the popularity of this custom defied economic logic. If the practice was not really about the tightly packed contents, then it was more likely about the meaning of the contents that were so carefully chosen for each family member. Hence, Filipino journalists labeled it "love in a box," concluding that "albeit materialistic in nature, it's living proof of our thoughtfulness, a tangible expression of care and concern across the miles."[52] Deirdre McKay argued that through the sending of groceries and household items "migrants remind their households of their long-distance affections and demonstrate, in a material way, how they continue to participate in these households."[53] According to Clement Camposano and Jade Alburo, another reason migrants were prepared to send these items was because they wanted to have some control over the household expenses.[54]

Migrant memoirs claimed that these boxes were symbolic of the love and sacrifices they made for their relatives. A male nurse in Kuwait described the *balikbayan* box as the symbol of overseas Filipino workers' love for their family ("Iyan daw ang sumisimbolo sa pagmamahal ng isang OFW sa kaniyang pamilya").[55] In Sherald Salamat's story, he remembered how much he looked forward to the big boxes that accompanied his father's return because he was sure to receive a number of gifts that included expensive toys, electronic robots, remote control toy cars, new clothes, and chocolate.[56] Another migrant named Dahlia confided: "You have your love in that box for people back home because you purchased something for them. . . . It symbolizes . . . love for people back home."[57] Mothers working abroad confessed that they deprived themselves of luxuries in order to send expensive items, including chocolates they have never themselves tasted: "Ako nga di kumakain ng Ferrero Roche [sic] dito pero pinapadala ko iyan sa Pilipinas" (I don't even eat Ferrero Roche[r] here but I send them to the Philippines).[58] Deirdre McKay's informants lived a life of austerity and abstained from health care, haircuts, new clothes, and vacations just to be able to afford to send gifts and fulfill their filial as well as community expectations.[59] The recipients of the imported gifts interpreted these as a sign that they were in the thoughts and memories of their kin despite the physical separation.

I discovered that this connection between the sending of material gifts and the migrant's affection was not lost on savvy businesses, which benefited from this practice. Entrepreneurs responsible for shipping further endorsed the view that "what is inside the boxes would not be as important as the idea of them: keeping the family close even over great distances."[60] Advertisements perpetuated this constructed connection between the material gift and the abstract affection migrants felt for their family and friends. For example, an advertisement for LBC International Freight Company at Lucky Plaza Singapore in August 2017 included a handwritten imaginary letter from a mother to her child:

Hello Anak,
   Sana maramdaman mo lalo ang pagmamahal ko habang binubuksan mo ang padala ko. Wala naman ako dyan sa Kaarawan mo alam mong nandito lg ako parati para sa 'yo. Nanay [surrounded by heart emojis]

(Dear Son/Daughter,
   I wish that you would feel my love while you open the presents I have sent you. I am not there for your birthday but you know that I am always here for you.
Mom)

Another one (also in August 2017) stated:

Dear Baby Chloe,
   Your favorite toy is inside na. Mahal na mahal ka ni Mommy. Mommy Olga [with emoji love hearts]

(Dear Baby Chloe,
   Your favorite toy is inside this box. Mommy loves you very much.
Mommy Olga)

If indeed the sending of gifts was a symbolic gesture of one's love, no wonder the custom became so entrenched. The mother who felt guilty about leaving her child, the seaman father who felt obliged to provide for his community, or the dutiful eldest daughter who felt responsible for her younger siblings kept the tradition going despite its negative affect on migrant savings. This mix plus the family and community's perception that all migrants were wealthy pressured many to agree to handing out cash gifts and loans that they could not afford. There was the story of a seafarer's astute wife who had forbidden him from seeing anybody in the village when he returned home for vacations for fear that he would be inundated with requests for loans from the neighborhood—hoping to protect his hard-earned salary from disappearing rapidly.[61] This example reveals the extreme measures that may be required to challenge this well-established expectation that migrants must share their earnings with the family and the community left behind.

If sending a *balikbayan* box was a symbol of love, its opposite—not sending one—implied that the migrant had forgotten his obligations. Gunnar Lamvik's interviews with seafarers explained that not giving anything caused a deterioration of friendships: "Sometimes they who did not receive a gift from you have a hard feeling for you," or "if you do not give them, they have a hard feeling, they do not love you anymore."[62] A column written by Frederick Arceo, a Saudi-based OFW, complained that the consequence of forgetting to give one person a gift was social ostracism since the offended party would sulk and then ruin the migrant's reputation (presumably through spreading gossip that the migrant was "shameless" [*walang hiya*]).[63] Lamvik also noted that gift giving enabled seafarers to perform *pakikisama*, or the Filipino social value of getting along with the group.[64] If the buying and sending of gifts was a symbol of love, this made the sending of gift boxes compulsory. According to anthropologist Deirdre McKay, writing on Filipino undocumented migrants from the Cordillera who work in London: "Sending goods was such a fundamental obligation for Kankanaey migrants that locating, selecting, and acquiring these goods formed a big part of their leisure activity in London. . . . Making up these boxes diverted value, time, and space from their United Kingdom–based activities and relationships, crowding non-Filipino partners and visitors out."[65]

At the same time, *not* sending gifts also sent the tragic message that the migration project was a failure. Divine Villanueva, an overseas domestic worker in Jordan, entitled her life story "Bagahe" (Baggage), confessing that her migration narrative was one of "bad luck" because she returned home without gifts for her family.[66]

Migrants hoped that their thoughtful gift giving would be cherished. A domestic worker in Hong Kong wrote a poem about door-to-door boxes, ending it with the hope that the recipients would acknowledge the hardship she endured.[67] Raquel Delfin Padilla, who has compiled at least two anthologies of migrants' stories, complained that the "abusive family" was one that took these presents for granted. According to her:

> Some family members do not think that the expensive gadgets they are using are the result of the OFW's frugal lifestyle adopted in order to give the family their desire for luxurious items. Older sister is now popular with her branded clothes, bags and shoes. Elder brother has a car now. Younger sibling has the latest expensive gadgets. Mother has become a gambler and father who now has lots of friends because he goes drinking with them and treats them. . . . What can she [the overseas worker] do if she has already spoken of her hardship but her family takes it for granted?[68]

Not all recipients appreciated the acts of self-denial that made the shipment possible.

Directing Migrant Consumption Practices

The story of Dante's debutante party for his daughter that opened this chapter was a grim reminder of how spending could sabotage the overseas worker's dream of returning to the Philippines to retire or of building a nest egg for the family. The story of Eloina Reyes Rebollos, whose earnings over nine years as a domestic worker in Riyadh and Kuwait paid singlehandedly for the education of countless nieces and nephews who owed their careers in engineering, nursing, and social work to this one selfless relative, is all too familiar. Her remittances also enabled them to build their own homes. But unfortunately, when she returned to the Philippines, no one was there to meet her at the airport, and she had no money at all and had to be housed temporarily by activists of Kakammpi, an NGO dedicated to overseas workers' rights.[69] The mother of a returning entertainer from Japan coined the term "one-day millionaires" in an effort to warn her daughter from spending all her hard-earned money from her six-month stint in Tokyo. Unfortunately, even before she started unpacking, siblings asked her for iPods and new clothes. Relatives begged for money for investment in low-cost housing or to start businesses, and they demanded to be treated to restaurants, while two of them joked about asking for a loan. Despite her plans to go back to school to give her daughter a better life, a few months later she was dead broke, her ₱250,000 savings all gone.[70] She was not unique. Other "one-day millionaires" checked into five-star hotels and spent their money shopping and eating at bars and restaurants.[71]

The conspicuous consumption indulged in by Filipino overseas workers has been criticized by some who were concerned that the inability to save would not put an end to the cycle of migration, especially for those who wanted to reunite with the families they had left behind.[72] Their anxiety was connected to the fear that such profligate spending did not foster development in the home country and encouraged a culture of dependence.[73] The positive impact of remittance spending in improving the quality of life of many families, including investment in the education of children, has been acknowledged.[74] However, studies have revealed that many migrants were unable to save enough money in order to return home permanently, and the lavish spending on birthdays, graduations, fiestas, as well as the money given to relatives for health care and emergencies, constantly drained disposable income, preventing migrants from saving and driving them into debt.[75] The NGO Atikha's interviews with Filipino migrant women in Rome reveal that even after many years working overseas and despite their relatively high salaries, 80 percent of the women were unable to save and invest their hard-earned money for their future return to the homeland or for their eventual retirement.[76] In his study of Filipino migrants in the Gulf region, published in 1991, F. R. Arcinas found that few had invested in productive assets (7 percent on machineries and 18 percent on vehicles for the transportation sector), with only 10 percent of respondents making business investments, 40 percent of which were in small-scale retail (*sari sari*) stores.[77] Habits of conspicuous consumption were partly to blame for this inability to accumulate sufficient savings, especially among those who had children left behind since migrant mothers pampered their loved ones with expensive gifts, afraid to deny them anything they asked in order to assuage the guilt feelings engendered by their prolonged physical absence.[78] In addition, in places such as Hong Kong, for example, it was relatively easy for Filipino women to acquire loans.[79] Half of those interviewed by Joy Tadios in her pioneering study on migrants and loans had borrowed money to buy technological gadgets such as laptops and smartphones for themselves or their children, items identified by others as luxury products rather than essential goods.[80]

Since the middle of first decade of this century, the Philippine government (through the Overseas Workers Welfare Administration and the Commission on Filipinos Overseas, for example), banks, and migrant-focused NGOs embraced the task of encouraging migrants to save and invest their money in projects perceived to be more "development oriented."[81] Government, banks, and NGOs produced the mantra "we must force overseas Filipinos and their families to learn financial education," which scholar Kathleen Weekley has argued was yet another way of "disciplining" migrant workers "for the greater good," defined in the literature as "investment for development."[82] Banks and NGOs launched initiatives to direct migrants away from spending toward investing and saving. For example, they taught short courses on financial literacy to help families budget their disposable income and invest their savings. The Bangko Sentral ng Pilipinas (Central Bank of the Philippines) started the Financial Literacy Campaign (FLC) in 2005 in collaboration with the Overseas Workers Welfare Administration (OWWA).[83] It extended its partnerships to include government agencies, NGOs, and private entities running half-day activities.[84] The FLC aimed to "cultivate financial education among OFs [overseas Filipinos] and their families by informing them of alternative opportunities for the use of remittances, such as savings, investments in financial instruments and other microbusiness ventures. The thrust towards promoting financial literacy is to promote a culture of savings and investments among OFs and their beneficiaries."[85] These initiatives were radical moves that challenged Filipino families to resist the urge to express social status through conspicuous consumption and to reverse the view that material goods—including gifts posted to the family—was the only way to measure family love or migrant success.

One NGO that embraced this challenge was Atikha Overseas Workers and Initiative Inc. Atikha's target group was Filipino overseas contract workers who left their immediate family in the Philippines and viewed migration as only a temporary labor strategy. In 1995, a women's resource center study found that many migrant women returned home without savings to a situation no different from that when they first migrated. Mai Dizon-Añonuevo, together with other migrant returnees from Hong Kong and the Middle East and some religious leaders from Laguna Province, founded Atikha Inc. as an NGO aimed at addressing the issues of migrant returns by conducting seminars and skills training for alternative livelihoods.[86] Eventually, Atikha focused on the social problems faced by children and families of overseas migrants in the Calabarzon area (acronym referring to the provinces of Calamba, Laguna, Batangas, Rizal, and Quezon provinces in northern Luzon) with offices in San Pablo City, Laguna, and Mabini, Batangas. In 1998, they formed Balikabayani, an organization of OFWs focusing on the socioeconomic component of reintegration with a focus on financial planning and investment.[87] They developed financial education modules aimed at teaching migrants how to save and invest their money. In 2012, they launched the PinoyWISE (Worldwide Initiative for Investment Savings and Entrepreneurship) International movement. This initiative was a financial education and investment mobilization program among whose objectives were "to provide financial education and encourage the overseas Filipinos and their families in sending province and receiving country to save and invest to enable successful integration" and "to link overseas Filipinos (OFs) and families to business opportunities, business advisor services and concrete savings and investment programs of selected cooperatives, microfinance institutions, social enterprises, banks and other financial institutions in their provinces of origin."[88] Atikha and Balikabayani conducted financial literacy seminars and provided financial counseling to families. Members in Hong Kong were offered concrete packages such as time deposits and trust funds to real-estate investments.[89] PinoyWISE ran forums to promote agribusiness and investment opportunities in goat raising, organic farming, rice and corn production, hog raising, cassava production and processing and linked the migrants to farm business schools, agriculture training institutes, and private corporations or cooperatives involved in the business (such as the forum on "Investment and Business Opportunities"). Atikha and Balikabayani also formed Koop Balikabayani International to focus on "consumers cooperatives for migrants' families in the Philippines, savings and credit cooperatives for the migrants abroad, housing cooperatives, and business development services for its members."[90] These NGOs ran education modules in places where there were huge concentrations of Filipino overseas workers, such as Italy, Hong Kong, Singapore, and Dubai.

I attended two PinoyWISE seminars. One, entitled "Family and Income Management Training Module," was held on Sunday, July 16, 2017, at the Church of St. Bernadette in Singapore for migrants there, and the other was a one-day workshop for the families of migrants left behind in Malolos, Bulacan Province, Philippines, on February 27, 2019. In Singapore, there were about fourteen to sixteen all-Filipina participants as well as a larger number of PinoyWISE trainers (composed of both men and women). The lectures, delivered in Tagalog, informed participants about the need to have health insurance. They recommended that the participants invest their savings at a rate higher than inflation (4%) and suggested that all of them keep an emergency fund of six times more than their monthly expenses. The second half of the program focused on "borrowing and getting out of debt."

The Singapore seminar devoted an entire module to "how to say no" to repeated financial requests from relatives for financial support or material gifts because "no one was abroad forever" (walang forever sa abroad).[91] Lectures at that seminar alerted participants to rethink the way two emotions—guilt and pride—manipulated them into spending more money. Instead, participants were encouraged to involve their families in making a budget. This way any requests that were not in the budget could be declined. Some strategies for saying no to requests from relatives for money for birthday celebrations and treats (including eating out at restaurants) included letting them know that they only could not afford to exceed their predetermined budget. This module on "how to say no" was absent in the workshop for migrants' families left behind held in Malolos, Bulacan province.

Atikha's Mai Añonuevo was also well aware that the intimate connection between conspicuous consumption and "love" had to be dismantled because it drained savings and sabotaged the migrant's future plans to return home.[92] To address this, Atikha ran "family interventions seminars" in the Philippines to replace the notion of "consumption = love" with an alternative one that stressed that "love = family reunification." Instead of according symbolic capital to the material goods they received from the parent working overseas, children left behind were told that they needed to work together toward the migrant's eventual return, suggesting that "love" meant bringing the family together after years of separation.[93] Atikha included a "values formation component" where families were told to change the meanings and importance assigned to material goods and to shift their priority toward the future of the family instead of the usual "instant gratification."[94]

The Bulacan seminar I attended in 2019 began with an exercise that contrasted "a day in in your life" with "a day in the life of a migrant." The aim of the two-hour activity was to allow Atikha to reveal to the participants the long hours their migrant family member spent at work, contrasted sharply with the much shorter work hours experienced by the family left behind. The challenging work conditions and minimal free time that migrants endured everyday was underscored because Atikha was aware that migrants seldom tell their families the true circumstances of their day-to-day life because they did not want their families to worry about them.[95]

This advocacy was revolutionary for several reasons. First, it was going to be extremely difficult for migrants to say no to continued family requests for money because in traditional culture saying no resulted in a loss of face for the person making the request and could result in social ostracism. Second, such advocacy went against the migrants' need to spend to express their rise in status as middle class (what Atikha referred to as "pride"). According to Atikha founder Mai Añonuevo, the seminars that were run for families left behind also had an impact. Children of migrants who participated in these seminars confided to their caregivers that they should be more prudent in spending their mothers' remittances.[96]

My interviews with those who completed these seminars in Singapore and Padova, Italy, revealed that some of them had become successful and assertive investors, buying apartments in the Philippines and homes in Europe.[97] Jesme (pseudonym), a single domestic worker in Singapore admitted that before she joined PinoyWISE she paid for the debut celebration of her niece in the Philippines, funded the roast pig and cake/sweets for various birthday celebrations in the village, and never thought of rejecting requests for gifts. These gifts were in addition to the weekly cash remittances she sent to her parents and the hospital bills of her siblings. Jesme acceded to all the requests because she felt she had a salary coming every month and so she should share this with her family. She did not think about saving for her future retirement or for an emergency. Lisa confided that she sent money for the funeral expenses of many people in her village. Both women claimed that after they completed the PinoyWISE modules they no longer sent money for luxuries, and they focused on saving and investing for their future retirement.[98] The Filipinos I interviewed in Padova who completed the Atikha seminars that were offered in Milan used the skills they learned to invest in properties in the Philippines and in Italy.[99]

These examples may illustrate the success of the Atikha interventions, but they may also show that there are a good number of judicious consumers who have now become successful investors.

Consumption has proved to be a double-edged sword for Filipino migrants since the 1970s. On the one hand, it proclaimed their new status as members of the growing middle classes in the Philippines, and it gave them enormous satisfaction as benefactors if they helped the family build or remodel a house and fill it with white goods and furniture, or if they sent siblings and relatives to school and university. Sending goods and presents to the Philippines regularly also maintained their emotional connections to the family and the village and gave them some control over the daily grocery budget. But on the other hand, the family's relentless demands for goods and money undermined their capacity to save for their retirement and often landed them in serious debt.

In order to curb the tendency toward conspicuous consumption, the Bangko Sentral ng Pilipinas and NGOs like Atikha tried to alter the semiotics of spending by dismantling the imagined link between consumption and "love." Migrants were also advised to discipline spending practices by adhering strictly to a family budget and to resist the urge to splurge. These were challenging tasks. They also went against the fashioning of the migrants' identities as middle class and against the social values of *pakikisama* that pressured migrants to share their new wealth with everybody.

This chapter demonstrated that consumption was critical to social relationships in the family, kinship group, and community—since all three were beneficiaries of migrant spending and patronage. It also underscored the migrant's role as agent of radical change, altering social mores and values and unsettling notions of class. They were introducing novel positionalities and complex identities. They straddled two classes simultaneously: they were classified as working-class laborers in the host country, but in mimicking their employers' tastes in spending habits, which included the purchase of branded items (such as Louis Vuitton bags, which one informant confided to me in Padova was "every girl's dream"), they were transformed into middle-class cosmopolitan Filipinos. This new ultramodern, westernized, and cosmopolitan Filipino was evident from his or her newly acquired consumption tastes in fashion, food (preferring pasta to rice), wine (prior to leaving the Philippines, they did not drink wine), and outlook based on foreign travel. But the migration context also introduced new meanings to consumption, some of which were detrimental to a migrant's financial situation. If gift giving was increasingly interpreted as a material expression of a migrant's affection for the those left behind, migrants were pressured to buy presents in order to fulfill their duties as good parents, filial children, and good citizens, even if they could not afford it. Those left behind did not see the migrant's perspective and may have been oblivious to the migrants' real financial situation or the hardship migrants endured while making a living overseas. Perhaps this ignorance of the work migrants did may partially explain why cultural mores changed so much that family members absolved themselves from reciprocating even in a small way or even appreciating in a big way the gifts and material goods that they were given often at great sacrifice. Banks and NGOs advised migrants through financial education seminars to say no to repeated requests for things that would sabotage their ability to save for their retirement. Yet, the consequences for denying these requests was social ostracism, an outcome that caused profound emotional pain for many migrants.

CHAPTER 4

The Impact of Consumption on Businesses, 1990s–2018

Since shopping and spending were important rituals in the day-to-day affirmation of migrants' status, their purchasing power had a tremendous impact—transforming the Philippine business landscape and generating enormous profits for the lucky businesses that migrants chose to patronize. Savvy businesses repackaged their products and services in order to tap this very lucrative market. Those who were successful in attracting the patronage of migrant sectors reaped spectacular profits. For example, Filipina overseas domestic workers' addiction to romance novels in Tagalog catapulted this genre to best-seller status, forever transforming the history of the book and publishing in the Philippines.[1] Filipina/o/x American appetite and nostalgia for Filipino food has enabled the family of Ramon Quesada and Maria Serapio, founders of Ramar Foods International in Pittsburg, California, to build a business empire selling packaged foods from Magnolia ice cream to meat products (in four different labels—Orientex, Pampanga's Best, Turo Turo Gourmet, and Kusina ni Maria) catering to Filipinas/os/x in North America.[2]

I will discuss two examples in this chapter—the Filipino Channel (hereafter TFC) and Philippines-based real-estate companies—to illustrate the impact of Filipino migrant consumer power and introduce the concept of migrants as investors. I have chosen these two different types of businesses because not only do these disparate case studies demonstrate the breadth of migrant consumer interest, these two business sectors (media and real estate) have reinvented themselves several times in response to consumer demand. Their consumer cohort also comes from the Filipino global diaspora not just the United States but also seafarers, Filipino domestic workers in Europe, Asia, and the Middle East, and permanent residents of countries such as Australia. Anywhere in the world where there are critical masses of Filipinos there are TFC subscribers and potential real-estate buyers and investors. The way consumers have influenced the histories of these two business sectors provides evidence of the impact of migrant consumer choices. Thus, while part 1 of this book discussed the way migrants have altered social institutions such as gender and the family, this chapter investigates the way they have altered the economic landscape of the homeland.

The history of TFC demonstrates the way that migrant consumption behavior collectively transformed Filipino businesses—a topic that has so far been ignored in the existing scholarship, which to date has focused only on the way TFC fashioned a "global Filipino identity," on how the programs connected viewers overseas to the homeland, or on specific TFC television shows and films produced by Star Cinema.[3] While scholars, mostly from the media discipline, alerted us to TFC's important role in bringing migrants into a global community and the way its content is evidence of the performance of migrant identities, they did not yet consider the way audiences were also consumers who by their purchasing power had an enormous impact on the business side of TFC, transforming it from a small company installing home satellite dishes in the 1990s to a global brand with overseas subsidiaries and able to generate 40 percent of the profits of its homeland mother ship. TFC's continuing reinvention of its products, shows, content, and delivery were a result of consumer demands and desires. The story of the rise of the Filipino Channel was evidence of the transformative power of Filipino migrant consumption.

Real-estate companies benefited from seeing migrants as investors. This was a view that has yet to be embraced by the scholarship on Filipino migration. Why would overseas Filipinos buy real estate in the homeland? According to Filomeno Aguilar Jr. and Lieba Faier, the house was the migrants' prize or trophy for their hard work overseas, proclaiming to all and sundry that they had "made it"—that they had become upper middle class.[4] How else could one explain the fact that houses built in the provinces that cannot be resold or rented (and therefore cannot be interpreted as assets for investment) mostly remain empty all year round waiting for the migrants' eventual return?[5] Eric Pido distinguished between the houses in the gated communities observed by Aguilar and those built by *balikbayans* (defined by the Department of Tourism as "Philippine nationals who are temporarily residing abroad" or Philippine citizens who return to the homeland on visits) because the latter held US or overseas permanent residency or citizenship and therefore already had status.[6] Pido argued that since *balikbayans* were "already perceived as economically privileged, their performance of class distinctions, paramount to the structure of Philippine society, is much subtler. Rather than relying on their homes to communicate their status outwardly, balikbayans convey their success through throwing large parties, shopping in malls, and treating family members and friends to meals."[7]

Condominiums, I suggest, fall into another type of purchase since these were used as investment property due to their potential for high rental income and because these units could be resold. Some buyers also consider them as a retirement property.[8] I do agree with the scholarship that the purchase of a house is considered the "prize" or "memorial" to migration. However, in this chapter where I examine the impact of consumer agency, I also present a novel view of the migrant as investor.

My interviews with a Filipina domestic worker in Padova first alerted me to the category of the migrant as assertive investor since apart from owning a Mediterranean-style house in Laguna she also owned an apartment in Tagaytay, which she rented out. Another example is that of fifty-five-year-old merchant seaman Rodolfo Oliverio who bought two small houses in the heart of Manila for his wife and children and purchased a third south of Manila, costing over ₱1.5 million.[9] Interviews with three real-estate company sales representatives clearly reveal that Filipino migrants are important investors in the condominium market.

The migrant consumers whose collective buying power has transformed the savvy real-estate companies and ABS-CBN enterprises into wealthy business empires come from the middle professional classes in the United States, as well as those who straddle the transnational location of lower-class domestic workers in Italy, for example, and middle-class spender in the Philippines. I also include here the seafarers whose salaries are earned in US dollars and who are definitely part of the rising middle class in the Philippines.

Sources for this chapter include the archives of ABS-CBN (the mother company of TFC) kept at the Benpres building Pasig City, Metro-Manila, materials from the "migrant archives," including memoirs, autobiographies, migrant magazines and newsletters such as *Filipinas* (San Francisco, 1992–2010), *Planet Philippines* (2007–2008, 2011–2013), *Tinig ng Marino* (the newsletter of the union of Filipino seafarers, incomplete issues from 1999 to 2006 and 2009–2010), interviews with the CEO of the Filipino Channel, representatives from Rockwell Land, Century Properties Inc., and Filinvest Properties, owners of stores in Lucky Plaza, including employees and managers of shipping companies that sent boxes of goods to the Philippines, and Filipino migrants in the

United States, Singapore, Padova, Milan, Athens, Hong Kong, Santa Rosa, Laguna, and San Roque, Laguna.

The Story of the Filipino Channel (ABS-CBN Global)

The Filipino Channel was the brainchild of Eugenio "Geny" Lopez Jr., who was the prime mover of ABS-CBN television, a major player in the Lopez family media empire that was nipped in the bud by the martial law period. The Lopez family became a victim of the Marcos dictatorship when Geny became a political prisoner used as a "hostage" to pressure his father, Eugenio Lopez Sr., to sign over the Lopez-owned Manila Electric Company, the *Manila Chronicle* newspaper, and the television channels 2 and 4 (ABS-CBN) to the Marcos family.[10] After his escape from political detention, Geny and his immediate family lived in exile in the United States, where he set up a small business importing Filipino food. He discovered that in the United States there was a great demand for Filipino products.[11] After Marcos was ousted in 1986, Geny Lopez returned to the Philippines. The Lopez family reclaimed ABS-CBN, Channel 2, with Geny at the helm, becoming "the largest entertainment media corporation in the Philippines."[12] In 1992 Geny and eldest son, Eugenio Lopez III, "Gabby," decided to launch ABS-CBN programs in the United States.[13] Geny persuaded his younger son Rafael L. "Raffy" Lopez, who was then working for the American company Bell Atlantic as an engineer, to quit his job and focus on tapping the US market.[14] In 1994, Raffy Lopez began his new job as information technology head of ABS-CBN International in North America.[15] Starting with Betamax tapes from their ABS-CBN local shows such as *TV Patrol* (broadcast news) that were flown into California by Philippine Airlines stewardesses, they launched an eight-hour program and then a 24/7 channel. In 1994 they offered to sell and install home satellite dishes to access the Filipino Channel (TFC). From then onward, Lopez confided, "the business really took off."[16] The purchase of this equipment was a huge investment for families who had to pay US$1,000 to set up the satellite dish in order to access the channel followed by a $10 a month subscription.[17] According to Lopez, "Some people, if they didn't have the money would borrow or really save for it. It was that important to them. It was almost like as important for them as their grocery budget. A thousand dollars in that day was a lot of money."[18] Clearly, Filipina/o/x Americans, in particular the post-1965 migrants, had the disposable income to purchase an expensive luxury item. Thus, part of TFC's success was the rise of the Filipina/o/x American middle class in the late twentieth century.[19] Filipina/o/x Americans were obviously hungry for news of the homeland. TFC fulfilled this need. Lopez exclaimed: "They were, wow, this is the best thing since *adobo* [the Filipino national dish]."[20] After its US success, TFC immediately expanded to the Middle East, Japan, and Australia. Europe was the last frontier.[21]

When TFC was launched in 1994, offering eight hours of programming on cable, it charged US$8.95 a month. In 1995, it was available to subscribers for the price of US$8.95 to US$13.95 a month.[22] Less than a year after its launch, it was able to deliver twenty-four-hour service on satellite.[23] It introduced the TFC "bundle," charging $22.95 for six channels of ABS-CBN (including popular telenovelas) plus twenty minutes of free phone calls (to the Philippines) a month in 2004.[24] By 1999, ABS-CBN International (TFC) had generated ₱839.2 million in revenues and held a total subscriber base of more than 58,000 (37,000 on cable and 20,100 on direct-to-home [DTH] units) in the United States, and more than 15,800 DTH customers in the Middle East, and 800 cable clients in Australia.[25] In 2003 it posted a net income of US$2.7 million exclusively from its North American operations on gross revenues of $47 million, contributing 20 percent of the income of its mother ship ABS-CBN.[26] That same year it reached 250,000 households worldwide, 200,000 of which were in North America alone.[27] By the end of 2003 it had a total of 1.3 million subscribers (a 24% increase from the previous year and with about 53% located in North America).[28] Ten years later, close to its twenty-year anniversary, Raffy Lopez confided to me in an interview that ABS-CBN International accounted for 40 percent of the revenue of ABS-CBN, raking in over $100 million.[29] Lopez dreamt that one day it would "be big enough by then to absorb our mother company."[30]

The meteoric rise of TFC could be explained by the fact that the ABS-CBN leadership had its fingers on the pulse of migrant consumer desires. Aware that its market was genuinely global (ABS-CBN's motto is "in the service of Filipinos worldwide"), it made sure that the content of the programs was relevant to the subscribers. The company did not merely distribute Philippine news, sports, and entertainment; it also produced shows that would directly appeal to the Filipino migrant group. Just a few years after its launch, ABS-CBN International set up its own "back lot" studio complex in San Francisco, patterned after the Universal and Fox studios in the United States.[31] In the late 1990s it produced a community news program about Filipina/o/x Americans called *Balitang America* (*balita* means "news"). This expanded to *Balitang Middle East*, *Balitang Australia*, and *Balitang Japan*, until each region had its own program.[32] ABS-CBN also established offices in cities all over the world where there was a significant population of Filipino subscribers.[33] It developed programs that were directed specifically at migrants, which were advertised as "programs tailor made for overseas Filipinos."[34] For example, it produced a regular series called *Mabuhay OFW* (Long live overseas Filipino workers) that included a "Job Market" segment that advertised overseas jobs.[35] When ABS-CBN produced its own movies under the banner of "Star Cinema" (considered the largest film studio in the country),[36] movie scripts included migrants' stories.[37] The award-winning blockbuster hit *Anak* (Child), considered in 2000 to be the highest grossing film in the history of Philippine cinema (and that year's Philippine entry in the Best Foreign Language Film category of the Academy Awards), was and is still regarded as the film that poignantly and accurately portrayed the experiences of Filipino migration.[38] Star Cinema produced films with titles like *Dubai* (2005), *Milan* (2004), *Caregiver* (2008), *American Adobo* (2002) that showcased the life and dramas of Filipino lives overseas. But ABS-CBN became even more than just a producer and distributor of Filipino television programs and films. The empire expanded to include the motley of products patronized by Filipino migrants abroad: phone cards to make overseas calls (Maalaala Mo Kaya calling plan through ABS-CBN telecom),[39] remittance services, and cargo delivery (for *balikbayan* boxes). The aim was to make ABS-CBN a "one-stop shop" for Filipino migrants to purchase their needs. For example, overseas-based Filipinos could pay the electricity bills of their families in the Philippines through ABS-CBN.[40] They advertised these services in migrant print media such as *Filipinas* magazine (San Francisco) and *Planet Philippines* (London, Vancouver, and Melbourne).[41] They even sponsored a Filipino talent search that offered the winner a recording contract with TFC's sister company Star Records.[42] Filipino domestic workers in Milan forked out twenty-five euros a month in 2015, while those in the United Kingdom paid nineteen pounds a month to access TFC.[43]

Migrants and the Real-Estate Boom in the Philippines

The real-estate boom in Metro Manila and surrounding areas has been attributed to the demand for housing by overseas Filipinos.[44] According to Manuel Serrano, head of the Chamber of Real Estate and Builders Association of the Philippines: "overseas workers have revitalized the condominium market."[45] Another factor contributing to the interest in purchasing real estate in the homeland was the government incentives for encouraging *balikbayans* to retire there by "selling the American Dream in the Philippines."[46] The trend of Filipina/o/x American investments in Philippine property took off only in the early 1990s.⁴⁷ According to Eric Pido's pioneering study of *balikbayan* returns, the 2007 financial crisis that precipitated home foreclosures in the United States compelled some to think about returning to the homeland, where they could afford a house or a condominium in a gated community and live a middle-class lifestyle complete with domestic servants.⁴⁸ Filinvest Land Inc. disclosed that overseas Filipino workers accounted for half of its sales in 2007, a trend the company anticipated would continue.⁴⁹ According to Phyllis Theresa Cruz of Century Properties, this property boom peaked in the years 2005–2010, then hit a plateau by 2016.⁵⁰

Real-estate companies in the Philippines immediately responded to this demand for houses and condominiums by expanding their services and thinking transnationally from around 2000 onward when OFW purchases started to have an impact on the real-estate boom.⁵¹ Ayala Land launched Ayala Land International Sales Inc. in early 2005 precisely to target OFWs, Filipino professionals who have emigrated, as well as Filipinos residing in the United States and Europe who might be thinking of retiring in the Philippines.⁵² According to Arnisson Andre Ortega, Camella Homes pioneered this by enlisting OFW sales agents in cities overseas with a sizable Filipino community.⁵³ Companies such as Rockwell (a subsidiary of the Lopez family business empire), Century Properties Inc., Filinvest, and Ayala Land sent teams of sales representatives overseas, targeting Filipinos in the United States, Canada, the United Kingdom, Dubai, and Singapore.⁵⁴ Between 2004 and 2005 Rockwell's sales representative Mika Bautista traveled to the United States four to five times a year to sell condominiums to Filipina/o/x Americans.⁵⁵ In the United Kingdom, real-estate companies capitalized on events such as Filipino barrio fiestas (for example, Rockwell at the Birmingham Barrio Fiesta in 2012 and Ayala Land at the London Barrio Fiesta in 2013) to give their presentations.⁵⁶ Century Properties ran a "Mega Europe Tour" in 2011, promising a meet and greet with movie star Sharon Cuneta.⁵⁷ These foreign road shows were sometimes organized by the Philippine government, but companies reoriented their sales pitch to target potential overseas buyers.⁵⁸ I saw a Century Properties booth at a Filipino fiesta in Sydney in 2011 and at a fundraising event in 2013 in San Francisco for Philippine International Aid (PIA; see chapter 7). Real-estate companies also established office spaces in places with big Filipino communities.⁵⁹ Ayala Land had international offices in Rome, San Francisco, London, Dubai, Singapore, and Hong Kong.⁶⁰ Robinsons Land Corporation (RLC), the real-estate arm of the Gokongwei group of companies, had an office in Earls Court, London.⁶¹ CDC Holdings stationed 140 marketing representatives in various "global offices."⁶² There was a Filinvest office, for example, in Lucky Plaza, the Filipino mall on Orchard Road, Singapore, when I did fieldwork there in 2017.

Companies advertised aggressively in Filipino international media such as the Filipino Channel (for Rockwell) and magazines such as *Planet Philippines* (London, Canada, and Australia) and *Filipinas* (United States).[63] They ran attractive promotions. For example, in 2002 Rockwell president Nestor Padilla offered Filipina/o/x Americans a free night's stay in a Rockwell property for every studio apartment that was presold.[64] Century Properties invited interested buyers a chance to meet popular actor Piolo Pascual, who was given the title of "Century's Global Ambassador."[65] At their Mega Europe Tour in 2011, Century Properties also offered prospective buyers a chance to win tickets to a Sharon Cuneta concert or a meet and greet with the singer-actress if they visited their booth at the Hounslow Barrio Fiesta.[66]

The strategies yielded enormous profits. In 2007, 31 percent of unit sales of Ayala Land and between 40 and 50 percent, or half, of Filinvest Land Inc.'s unit and house and lot sales were bought by OFWs.[67] Megaworld, known to focus on overseas Filipino clients, reported a profit increase of 92 percent in 2006 of $US30.2 million.[68] Ayala earned ₱5.2 billion from US-based overseas Filipino workers in 2007.[69] Even the design plan and allocation of condominiums or houses were influenced by the overall strategy of attracting overseas Filipino buyers. Philippine law restricted ownership of private property to Philippine citizens only and allowed a margin of 60 percent Filipino owned and 40 percent foreign owned for residential buildings.[70] With this in mind, Century made a calculated decision to relegate 60–70 percent of the apartments as studios or one-bedroom apartments.[71] A typical Century complex building houses about 1,400 apartments with overseas Filipinos owning 40 percent of the market.[72] Their clientele included Filipino overseas workers in the hospitality or hotel industries, nurses and doctors, engineers (in Saudi Arabia), and seafarers (whose wives in the homeland look after the payments).[73]

The different property-developing companies sold condominiums (apartments) as well as houses, with some of them branching out into socialized housing projects.[74] The development of real estate was not limited to the Metro Manila area; new homes and high rises were built in Tagaytay (a trendy area an hour south of Metro Manila), in provincial capitals like Cebu, and in booming rural towns like Las Piñas and Angeles, and homes and townhouses were constructed in rural areas in places like Laguna, Bulacan, Davao, Pampanga, Tarlac, and Zamboanga.[75]

The costs for these condominiums were in the millions of pesos. For example, a studio apartment in Rockwell cost ₱3–4 million in 2014, and the cheapest brand-new studio unit in Century Makati was ₱3.5 million if presold in 2010. By 2016 the average price per square meter was ₱170,000–180,000.[76] Prospective buyers needed to pay up front a 10 percent deposit, as well as monthly upkeep fees.[77] According to one real-estate profile, most overseas Filipino buyers could afford up to ₱2 million for a housing package with professionals (like nurses and seafarers) able to buy up to the ₱4 million range.[78] Filipina/o/x Americans bought either in the ₱300,000 to ₱2 million range or in the even higher range of ₱2.5 million to ₱40 million.[79] Condominiums were classified as the higher end of the real-estate market, especially if they were located in the Metro Manila area. Due to these steep prices, OFWs who earned money in foreign currency were seen as ideal candidates as clients and investors. Three real-estate company sales representatives I talked to clearly viewed Filipino migrants as important investors in the condominium market.[80]

Advertisements from real-estate companies revealed that they were selling more than just land, concrete, and mortar. Both Ortega and Pido have explained how real-estate advertisements sold the "Filipino dream" of owning a home or, for *balikbayans*, exporting the American dream to the Philippines.[81] My own view is that migrants who purchased condominiums were also buying an ultramodern upper-middle-class *lifestyle* close to modern conveniences in a building where there was twenty-four-hour security and a swimming pool. Property developers intended the new apartment buildings to function as independent "cities" within walking distance of the grocery, banks, gym, hospital, schools, cinemas, shopping malls, restaurants, pharmacies, and a chapel for Sunday mass. In one Century property in Parañaque, white sand was flown in from the famous Boracay to create an artificial beach next to the swimming pool—a luxury enjoyed by the entire extended family on weekends.[82] Advertisements promised this rosy lifestyle of modern convenience and comfort where every necessity was accessible.[83] An advertisement for SM Residences claimed that "all condominiums are conveniently located near transportation hubs and will feature Wi-Fi in common areas. Select projects will have an SM Mini-Mall with Savemore Market, BDO [Banco de Oro] branch and other commercial establishments."[84] A full-page advertisement for GA Sky Suites proclaimed: "We're Not Selling a Space. You're Buying a Lifestyle."[85] SM Residences told prospective buyers to "look forward to a pampered lifestyle as SM Residences offers hotel-like property management services."[86]

The new lifestyle also had visual markers broadcasting the foreign connections of the owners. Mediterranean-themed exteriors were popular—for example Pila Townhomes in Laguna claimed that they had a "Mediterranean environment,"[87] and Filinvest Citti di Mare in Cebu created one piazza patterned after Piazza Duomo in Milan, Italy,[88] and another one designed by Versace.[89] In the provinces, several towns were dubbed "little Italy" because of their Italian-style architecture, and there is a "Hong Kong Village" where the houses had a Chinese-theme and a majority of the residents were domestic workers in Hong Kong.[90] Houses owned by seafarers displayed naval themes of portholes and anchors, linking their homes with their professional overseas occupations.[91] Hence, these visual designs reflect the migrants' new cosmopolitan identities shaped by their overseas work and travel experiences.

Filipino migrants' collective consumption practices transformed Filipino businesses in the homeland and overseas. The enormous flow of remittances was influential in transforming the history of banking and banking services in the Philippines. Philippine banks now have branches in parts of the world where there are significant Filipino populations, making sure to locate themselves strategically in designated "Filipino spaces" or "Filipinotowns" and adjusting their opening hours to suit the working schedules of their valuable clientele. For example, in Lucky Plaza, Singapore, Philippine National Bank is open on Sundays in order capture the domestic-worker market who only have Sundays off to send remittances. In addition, banks now provide a whole gamut of new product services catering to the needs of overseas Filipinos—for example, Banco de Oro (BDO) offers an Asenso Kabayan Program, allowing customers to link their savings account to home, car, and personal loans. BDO partnered with Max's Restaurant to provide a food remittance service to deliver the famous Filipino fried chicken to relatives in the homeland paid for by the overseas worker.[92] Hence, banks have reinvented themselves, expanding their role from simply providing remittance services to facilitating the transnational consumption of goods. They have also encouraged savings and investment, offering free financial literacy seminars for overseas Filipino workers. Interestingly, Filipino products and businesses have benefited from the loyal patronage of Filipino migrants. From TFC cable television to Filipino fast-food outlets, Filipino food products, and Filipino real estate, the purchasing power of the migrant has altered Filipino economic history.

Filipino migrants' power as both consumer and investor has been acknowledged by top business corporations like ABS-CBN (TFC) and the growing number of real-estate companies and property developers. These companies transformed their business practices in order to attract Filipino migrant customers to buy their products. They became transnational operators. The pages of *Planet Philippines* were replete with real-estate advertisements—all competing for the migrant dollar. The story of TFC and the transnational real-estate operators reveals that the migrant market is an extremely lucrative one. The impact has been enormous—from the media profits to the visual transformation of urban Manila and its peri-urban fringes into a vast concrete condominium jungle and funding rural building makeovers. The perception that migrants are not just consumers but also worthy and reliable investors alters the dominant view that migrants are liminal subjects and extends their image beyond laboring subjects. As consumers and assertive investors, Filipino migrants are clearly not marginal actors; they have transformed business and physical landscapes, and they have become the purveyors of the new ultramodern lifestyle—inflected with a foreign cosmopolitan flavor from their sojourns—that is rapidly being introduced to every corner of the country.

Part Three

Changing the Homeland and the Host Country

Activism and Philanthropy

CHAPTER 5

Filipina/o/x Americans as Community Historians, 1980s–2018

In section 42 of the Stockton Rural Cemetery in Stockton, California, the descendants of Policarpio Pete de la Cruz (1904–1994) of the Rubianes family inscribed the following words on their father's gravestone: "Rest dear Daddy, your journey is over. You left the Philippines at age 17 in search of riches and adventure, but discovered a lifetime of backbreaking poverty and prejudice instead. In other people's fields you trudged, pausing only long enough to love and nu[r]ture the family you started so late in your quest" (Figure 5.1).

The brief poignant biography of the deceased told the sad story of a Filipino male migrant who came to the United States, probably as one of the first wave of labor migrants that arrived in the early twentieth century to work in the agricultural fields of California. The life story on the tombstone made reference to several of the well-worn themes depicted in the plethora of community histories published by Filipina/o/x Americans: the hard physical labor that their ancestors performed as "stoop labor," the migrant mobile labor force that was the backbone of the US West Coast's agricultural industry, the discrimination endured by these young men who were marginalized in the white communities who made sure that "no Filipinos were allowed" in their public spaces, while anti-miscegenation laws deprived these men of having families until after the war, and finally the continuing poverty that haunted these intrepid migrants whose struggle for survival continued until death. That the

CHAPTER 5

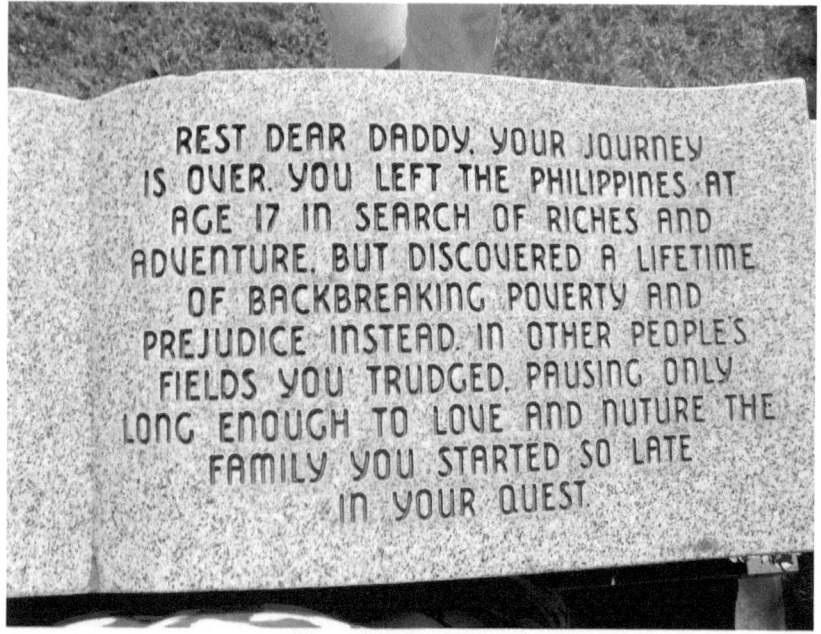

FIGURE 5.1. The engraving on the gravestone of Policarpio Pete de la Cruz (1904–1994) at the Stockton Rural Cemetery in Stockton, California. The engraving, written by his descendants, narrates his heroic narrative of survival.

children of the deceased felt the need to inscribe this story publicly in their father's tombstone illustrates the intense desire to commemorate this particular interpretation of the Filipino migrant's early history (1906–1946) in the United States.

Policarpio Pete de la Cruz's experience of hard work, struggle, and survival—the heroic narrative—defined the Filipina/o/x American story. The project of publicizing this heroic narrative has been an important enterprise for Filipina/o/x American migrants and their descendants who wanted their contributions to both the host society and the Philippines acknowledged and appreciated. This campaign for a space in social memory—for a place in the national, transnational, and international histories—was much more than cultural activism. As chroniclers of their own past, Filipino migrants and their descendants used this history of struggle, survival, and contribution—this heroic narrative—both as a powerful legitimizing discourse for social inclusion and as an important rite in performing migrant identities.

This chapter focuses on the Filipina/o/x American activists' crusade to have their own histories included in the mainstream white American historical accounts. It argues that Filipina/o/x American migrants and their descendants have taught themselves to become historians and custodians of their particular past as part of an overall project to make themselves visible as an important ethnic group that has made a significant contribution to American society. Given the activist agenda of these histories from below, the story of Filipina/o/x America that is presented by these migrants as historians proposes a particular interpretation. This interpretation, what I label the "heroic narrative," represents Filipinos in the United States as hardworking laborers who suffered terrible racial discrimination, relentless exploitation, and extremely harsh environments, including physical violence. My reading of these histories, written from the perspective of the migrants and their descendants, is that their ancestors had struggled and yet survived against the odds, but that their hard work has not been adequately acknowledged by the host society or the homeland. Therefore, the writing of these specific histories is a unique form of social activism to call attention to their own ethnic group, which in their view has so far been ignored, and to empower this group by giving them a place in social memory.

This chapter has a very specific focus—the migrant as community historian. The migrant archives are particularly rich on this topic with a plethora of autobiographies, memoirs, essays, poetry, art, documentary films, conference papers, and community and family histories produced by Filipina/o/x Americans. I deliberately do not include fiction writing due to my emphasis on migrant historiography. But representations of past histories have also been reproduced in "ethnotours," which are historic tours of migrant sites for tourists and students, as well as in lectures given by second-generation Filipina/o/x Americans. I visited the Filipino American National Historical Society (FANHS) archive in Seattle (National Pinoy Archives) twice in three weeks, each time to read their collections, including the programs of the FANHS annual conferences. I mined the archives of the Wing Luke Asian Museum including its permanent exhibit of Alaskeros (Filipinos who worked in the Alaskan canneries in the 1920s and 1930s). I also read the complete set of transcripts of fifty-five interviews conducted by the Demonstration Project for Asian Americans in 1977–1978. I participated in two ethnotours (one in San Francisco and one in Stockton) and had the privilege of hearing second-generation Robert "Uncle Bob" Santos talk about his life experiences at a lecture series sponsored by the Manilatown Heritage Foundation in San Francisco. I joined FANHS-Stockton chapter in 2013 and read all the newsletters they assiduously sent to me by email, from that date until the present writing (2021). In addition, I have interviewed seven second-generation Filipina/o/x Americans (who were in their eighties at the time of the interview; sadly, two have passed away since then) and two Filipina/o/x Americans who were civil rights activists in the 1960s in Seattle, Stockton, and San Francisco.

It is not only academic historians who have been writing about the history of Filipina/o/x migration to the United States. Migrants and their descendants have trained themselves to become community historians (they are autodidacts in this sense; they do not enroll in postgraduate or undergraduate history or oral history courses; while one or two academics often are consultants, it is the migrants themselves who document, research, and write their own histories). The body of work they produce can be considered an example of a history from below. Since the production of migrant community histories is fast becoming an industry, it is important to analyze why Filipina/o/x Americans are preoccupied with the documentation, preservation, and dissemination of their usable past.

The community historians here comprise several generations of Filipina/o/x Americans, although the founding members of FANHS were second generation American born. In addition, first-generation migrants from the post-1965 migration wave are also extremely active in cultural advocacy, and FANHS membership included these different cohorts and generations. This motley group of intergenerational cultural activists was mostly from the middle class of highly educated professionals. The members of FANHS could afford to publish their community histories, pay membership fees, and travel to the biannual FANHS conferences. While the stories from the domestic workers I analyzed in previous chapters were in Tagalog and English, the accounts by Filipina/o/x Americans were solely in English. Despite their middle-class location, the second- and third-generation Filipina/o/x Americans were extremely proud of their ancestors—the first-generation migrants who were working-class agricultural laborers and Alaskan cannery workers. Part of their mission was to pay homage to the contributions of these men and women who had made it possible for them to have a better life in the United States.

I also wish to make an artificial distinction between the work of academic historians (professionals) and community historians. By "community histories" I refer to the cohort of publications, performances, films, and documentaries produced by Filipinos in the United States. I use the term "community histories" because a majority of these texts (and I include as "texts" performances, dress, festivals, historic tours, calendars, films, and street murals) focus on local histories or the history of the Filipino community in one particular geographical location or the life stories of migrants. For example, a number of FANHS local chapters published a number of these histories, some under the Arcadia Images of America series. In reality, the line between these two groups (academic historians versus community historians) is blurred since academics in the field of Filipina/o/x American studies, many of them anthropologists and historians, have maintained close links with the Filipina/o/x American communities they study, and they collaborate with them in the project of documenting the history and preserving and/or performing cultural practices. For example, some academics are active members in the various chapters of the Filipino American National Historical Society (FANHS), and others are involved in heritage projects such as the Manilatown Heritage Foundation or Stockton's Little Manila Foundation.

Much of the scholarship on Filipina/o/x American studies/history has been published quite recently and is excellent. The body of work is interdisciplinary, theoretically sophisticated, and reflexive. The scholarly literature is rich on the topic of Filipina/o/x identities, histories, performance, gender, and activism (unions, NGOs, and the civil rights movement in particular).[1] This chapter makes a modest contribution to this growing scholarship by analyzing the historiography of works produced by historians outside the academe. In addition, this chapter marries two areas that have not yet been discussed together in the scholarly literature: the topic of social and cultural activism and the writing of community histories. In doing so, it gives prominence to the Filipina/o/x community itself as proactive in telling the stories of Filipina/o/x Americans in their own voices and on their own terms. It also then underscores the importance of writing and performing the past in the project of empowering a minority group. Sociologist Theodore S. Gonzalves has argued that Pilipino Cultural Nights on college campuses are part of the performance of Filipina/o/x American identities.[2] The evidence from this chapter supports this view and suggests that the production of community histories has an even more ambitious aim. They are all part of an activist project to claim a space in mainstream white America's social memory—and to proclaim that Filipina/o/x Americans have made an important contribution to American histories.

The Filipina/o/x American Story

The civil rights movement in the 1960s started the process of fashioning the new identity Filipina/o/x American. The descendants of the pioneer generation of Filipino migrants caught up in the "heady times" joined the Asian American movement and participated in the rallies and demonstrations demanding affirmative action for minority groups and the university students' demands for the teaching of ethnic studies and minority histories in the college curriculum.[3]

Scholar Leny Strobel traced the origins of the sudden interest in all things Filipino to the "Born Again Filipino Movement" and the process of mental decolonization that critically reflected on the "colonial mentality" that deemed Filipino culture inferior to all that was American.[4] Strobel's research informants were post-1965 immigrants from the Philippines and their children. But the process of decolonization she described, including the rediscovery of one's Filipino roots, could apply also to the second and third generation of American-born Filipinos. N. V. M. Gonzalez, a fiction writer, observed that Filipinos (whether or not they were migrants) were inflicted with "cultural Alzheimer's disease," meaning they had virtually no knowledge of their past.[5] To become a "born-again Filipino" meant understanding the colonial heritage and rediscovering one's cultural and historical past. Leonard Andaya, who grew up on a Hawaiian plantation, the son of Ilocano immigrant parents, captured this sentiment when he reflected on his metamorphosis from "American Filipino" to "Filipino American": "Those aspects of my identity linked to Hawai'i and America were ones that I believed to offer future promise because they were my home. Filipino culture, on the other hand, I saw as the culture of my parents and their friends."[6] Determined to embrace their "Filipino-ness," a select group of Filipina/o/x Americans from both post-1965 immigrants and second and third generation American born embarked on a project of remembering the past and learning Filipino cultural traditions. Filipina/o/x Americans learned the ancient precolonial writing called *baybayin* (now almost forgotten in the Philippines), practiced the indigenous martial arts of *arnis* (also known as *escrima* or *kali*), wore ethnic jewelry, sported tattoos from the Cordillera, while the young teenagers danced the *tinikling* (bamboo dance) and the *pandango sa ilaw* (a folk dance that required the delicate balancing of glasses with lighted candles inside). Pilipino Cultural Nights (PCNs), which depicted Philippine and Filipina/o/x American history in theater, song, music, and dance annually at college campuses in California, became institutionalized in the 1980s.[7] In 1957, Dorothy and Fred Cordova founded the Filipino Youth Activities (FYA), a Seattle-based drill team that used Filipino Muslim costume and responded to commands in Philippine languages.[8] The FYA is still active today (I saw them perform in Muslim costume to a loud cheering audience at Seattle Space Needle's center stage during Filipino Week in June 2010).

The writing of Filipina/o/x American history became a critical project for these migrants and descendants of migrants. Researching, documenting, and writing their histories became a collective project for this ethnic group. The first historical association founded was the Filipino American Historical Society of Hawaii (FAHSOH), formed in 1980 and incorporated in 1982 as a nonprofit organization under the name Filipino Historical Society of Hawaii.[9] The organization's aims were to initiate and sponsor "various activities such as community forums, workshops, exhibits, audio-visual presentations, performing arts, research and documentation, and the publications of books and manuscripts."[10] When Dorothy and Fred Cordova founded the Filipino American National Historical Society (FANHS) in 1982 (although it was not incorporated until 1985), they found fertile ground for it to prosper, and by 2015 FANHS had thirty-three chapters throughout the country, each with its own local community history projects.[11] The society's raison d'être was "to preserve, document and present Filipino American history and to support scholarly research and artistic works which reflect that rich past,"[12] Since 1987 FANHS has sponsored biannual conferences nurturing a plethora of research topics with panels on "growing up brown in America" and roundtables on "who/what is a Filipino American." Conferences were also venues for training future historians with seminars on "how to write journals" and "how to create an archive without money." A lecture series labeled "TGIF: Thank God I'm Filipino," a play on the American colloquial expression "Thank God It's Friday," celebrated ethnic pride.[13] Local chapters became proactive in publishing their own local history books and videos and launching heritage projects, such as "Little Manila" in Stockton, for example.

A tidal wave of publications began to appear, including reflections on "growing up brown," community histories about the Filipina/o/x American presence in Vallejo, Stockton, Los Angeles, San Diego, Puget Sound, Chicago, Alaska, East Bay, San Francisco, and Hawaii. By 2012 there were fourteen histories of Filipina/o/x Americans in various parts of the country published under the Images of America series alone. The time, resources, and effort put into the research, production, and publication and/or performance of these various types of community histories was enormous. Theodore Gonzalves called attention to the hours and hours of time devoted to the rehearsals for the annual Pilipino Cultural Night (PCN) held at several California college and university campuses every year.[14] There apparently was no such thing as a "small" PCN night—casts of hundreds entertained audiences in spectacles that lasted more than six hours.[15] Over twenty-five years an estimated sixty thousand college youths across two dozen campuses each invested more than a hundred hours of their time for rehearsals.[16] Similarly, the number of individuals participating in the production of the oral histories published by the FANHS chapters was staggering. Teams of volunteers conducted interviews and transcribed them. For example, the book *In Our Uncles' Words* had an oral history team of around forty-eight volunteers and a transcribing team of about thirty-one people. There were video committees, technical staff, and even a "glossary committee."[17] Even after publishing the book of oral histories of women in Hampton Roads, the team of high school interviewers dramatized these oral histories on stage for the Virginia Beach Contemporary Arts Center.[18] A two-volume syllabus designed by the group calling itself Pin@y Education Partnerships, for use in teaching Filipina/o/x American studies in high schools, was put together by a team of no less than fifty-eight teachers.[19] Around four hundred to five hundred FANHS members met every other year at their own expense in a different American city to present papers on their local histories or share their skills about preserving and documenting the past or tell their stories.[20] The Museum Team of the Stockton Chapter of FANHS (organized to bring about the FANHS Museum, see below) conducted more than fifty planning meetings after FANHS acquired its museum space in April 2015 (for the opening on October 8, 2016).[21] The telling and retelling of the history of Filipina/o/x America had become such an enterprise that one of the books in this genre described the voluminous publications of community histories as a "perpetual anthology."[22]

Why did Filipina/o/x American migrants invest (and continue to invest) an enormous amount of time and resources toward the reproduction of their own past? Theodore Gonzalves suggested one possible answer when he argued that Pilipino Cultural Nights were part of the sacraments of Filipina/o/x American identity.[23] A shared history was definitely critical to the process of fashioning new identities as Filipina/o/x Americans. But community histories also had higher goals: Filipina/o/x Americans aspired to have their histories included in mainstream American history textbooks. This was a highly ambitious objective. In his presentation to the FANHS Fifth National Biennial Conference in 1994, Fred Cordova confessed that he was still "smarting" from a 1981 pronouncement of the Academic Senate of the University of California at Berkeley that denied accreditation of Filipina/o/x American history as a fulfillment to the US history requirement because "Filipinos have not made enough major contributions in building this nation."[24] One of the reasons for writing Filipina/o/x American histories was to dismantle this assumption. At the opening credits of the seminal documentary produced by FANHS on the history of Filipina/o/x America, Fred Cordova asked the audience, "What do the average Americans know about the Filipinos who have been here for over four hundred years and who have helped in the advancement of this nation? Men, women and children, it is a story that has never been told and a story that should be told."[25]

A sense of urgency about the need to document the past was fueled by a crisis discourse about the threatened "disappearance" of their ethnic group. Two seminal books written by "bridge generation" (second-generation American-born) authors were entitled *Filipinos: Forgotten Asian Americans* and

Vanishing Filipino Americans.[26] Dorothy Cordova, one of the cofounders of FANHS, has written that Filipinos were "a minority within a minority," while Lily Mendoza reminded us that Filipina/o/x Americans were designated as "the invisible minority."[27] Scholars also appropriated this crisis discourse, with Oscar Campomanes speaking about "the new Empire's forgetful and forgotten citizens" subject to all kinds of "institutional invisibility."[28] Canadian-based scholars published an anthology in 2012 entitled *Filipinos in Canada: Disturbing Invisibility*.[29]

Even though Filipina/o/x Americans succeeded in writing their histories in their own voices, the history that they wanted to be included in mainstream American histories was a very specific interpretation of the past. It was a story that underscored the migrants' tenacity to survive against the odds and to make the best of their challenging situation. In the historical accounts, Filipina/o/x Americans were not victims but agents who worked hard and overcame these great odds to survive. While the pioneers in these community histories were admired for their tenacity, the heroes in this historical narrative were clearly people like Pablo Manlapit, who led the sugar strikes in Hawaii; Philip Vera Cruz, Pete Velasco, and Larry Itliong, who were pivotal in the United Farm Workers movement on the West Coast; and Virgil Duyugan, Gene Viernes, and Silme Domingo, who were important leaders in the Alaskan cannery union.

Published accounts describe the first generation of migrants as "hard workers." Plantation workers in the sugarcane fields of Hawaii worked long hours for very little pay and were subject to the harsh rules of the managers and the racial segregation of the workers. Agricultural workers in California were described as enduring the hot sun, the peat dust (for asparagus workers), the difficult manual labor, and the long hours, all for a dollar a day.[30] The experiences of Alaskan cannery workers focused on the substandard conditions of their housing and food and the big difference in wages between Filipino migrant workers and white workers.[31] According to one account: "Working to survive was real hard work in the Alaskan cannery. At the time there was no machinery and much of the hauling was done by pure manual labor. Ours was the work of a mule. The work schedule was indefinite and hours were long. You need will and strength to keep up with the work in those early days."[32] Social exclusion was epitomized by the signs outside restaurants and public places that declared "Positively no Filipinos allowed" and the anti-miscegenation laws that prevented the mostly male population of Filipino migrants from having families. Narratives stressed the great disillusionment pioneers experienced when they felt betrayed by American ideals of democracy and equality they learned at school taught by American teachers in the Philippines and the reality of racial discrimination. Carlos Bulosan's succinct statement, "In America it is a crime to be Filipino" was a constant theme permeating the oral history accounts of the daily traumas of work, leisure life, and the poverty that made every day a challenge to survive.[33]

In these accounts, Filipino labor was isolated as making an important positive and unique contribution to American society and history. The prologue to Virgilio Menor Felipe's "talk-story history" of Filipino contract worker Lilo Bonipasyo quotes him saying: "With my bare hands I helped build Hawai'i. I plowed lands for the canefields with mules, I cut cane, I *hapaiko*, carried cane and watered sugarcane."[34] Fred Cordova stated in John Wehman's documentary *Filipino Americans: Discovering Their Past for Their Future*, produced by FANHS: "All throughout Filipinos have always cleaned America, cooked for America, and they've always harvested for America. And that to me is a tremendous contribution. It may not be so dramatic, it may not sound so world shaking but nevertheless that is how America survived."[35] The message was that although Filipinos were relegated to the underclass, their labor was an important yet unacknowledged contribution to America's prosperity in the twentieth century.

This history of struggle and triumph—what I call the "heroic narrative"— defined the Filipina/o/x American story. I deliberately used the singular (read: "story" rather than "stories") because this metanarrative was firmly embedded in the popular histories and was very difficult to challenge. The lack of debates between community historians further entrenched this single narrative. A potentially controversial issue—the actual date when Filipina/o/x American history "began"—managed to avoid contentious debate when FANHS succeeded in its lobby to have October proclaimed "Filipino American History Month" by no less than United States Congress House Resolution 780 (in concurrence with Senate Resolution 298) in 2009.[36] The month was chosen in recognition of October 18, 1587, the day a landing party from the Manila-built galleon *Nuestra Señora de Esperanza* sent a group of Spaniards and *indios* (the name Spaniards used to refer to natives of the Philippines) on shore at Morro Bay near San Luis Obispo.[37] Thus, the proclamation endorsed 1587 as the "starting date" of Filipino American history. Alternative dates could have been 1763 when the first Filipino settlement was founded in New Orleans, Louisiana, or 1906 when the first workers landed in Hawaii to work on the sugar plantations, or 1903 when the first Filipino *pensionados* (government scholars) went to the United States to study. Scholar Oscar Campomanes critiqued the way this starting date was never problematized or even posed.[38] But in choosing the earlier date, Filipina/o/x Americans could claim that the long history of migration legitimized claims for recognition in the mainstream society (read: Filipinos were in North America even before the Plymouth landing).

This lack of debate has not gone unnoticed by the Filipina/o/x American community itself. Tongue in a Mood, a theater group, has satirized the PCN's historical presentations as "predictable" and "ossified,"[39] with scholar Theodore Gonzalves observing that "critics have argued that the PCN genre reinforces static constructions of Filipina/o American identities and that the origins of the folk forms need to be more concretely historicized or subjected to experimentation and play," with some even going to the extent of labeling it "Orientalizing."[40]

Performances of the Filipina/o/x American story succeeded in the aim of making the ethnic group visible. The community histories began with America's colonial empire in the Philippines and highlighted the importance of the Philippine-American War. The production of these histories called attention to the entangled histories between the Philippines and the United States.

With the small exception of the memoirs of those who became successful in political publics like former governor of Hawaii Ben Cayetano or Bob Santos or those who intermarried white Americans, I rarely saw a white face appear.[41] The FANHS-sponsored publications, the documentary films, the street murals, the PCN performances, all tell the story of a Filipino American community sans white Americans. The stories were all contextualized in the world of white exclusion and white oppression. In the memoirs of Philip Vera Cruz, Pablo Manlapit, and Peter Jamero, in Angeles Monrayo's diary, and in the community histories, the few white Americans that are mentioned are one-dimensional characters. Perhaps this was due to the fact that Filipina/o/x Americans were ostracized from white society for most of the twentieth century, compelled to socialize only with each other and barred from being accepted as equal members of white society. This exclusion from white society extended to second-generation Filipina/o/x Americans, labeled the "bridge generation" by FANHS founder Fred Cordova because they were sandwiched between the pioneer generation, who migrated between 1906 and the 1930s, and the post-1965 migration wave. Peter Jamero's seminal account of the bridge generation revealed that as young teenagers in the 1940s and 1950s they were more or less compelled to socialize with each other since they were not included in mainstream white society. In his memoirs he confessed that as a small boy growing up in an agricultural camp, he thought that the world was composed of Filipinos and anything outside that world was foreign.[42]

These community histories had a significant impact because they began the process of revising popular perceptions of Filipino history in the United States. Led by FANHS founders Dorothy Cordova and the late Fred Cordova, community historians challenged the androcentric representation of the migrant group in the 1920s and 1930s as a "bachelor society," emphasizing the important role of the few Filipino women in the first half of the twentieth century. Beginning with Fred Cordova's seminal book *Filipinos: Forgotten Asian Americans*, the community histories underscored the impact of the Filipino women of the pioneering generation. For example, FANHS Hampton Roads Chapter published the book *In Our Aunties' Words*, and Dr. Patricia Brown (FANHS–Hawaii Chapter) collected and edited stories about women in Hawaii's plantation era from their descendants.[43] Both books were conceived to engender the previously male-centered accounts of early Filipino history in Hawaii and the mainland. Local histories also challenged the stereotype that all Filipino migrants of the pioneer generation were agricultural workers, janitors, busboys, waiters, or Alaskan cannery workers. FANHS publications called attention to the fact that these migrants were also part-time students, many of whom were working in order to finance their education only to discover that even with a college degree racial discrimination and their accents prevented them from gaining professional employment.[44] As one informant put it, "I don't think there were opportunities. I only recall that when I graduated from UCLA, the dean of women called me and said that if I wanted a job, a professional job commensurate to my education, I could go to Hawaii. . . . Why is that America would educate the minority and not give them an opportunity to use this education? Why is it that they need a college education to be a dishwasher?"[45]

Finally, although these "community histories" became predictable, they began the project of staking the Filipino *place* in the locations they wrote about. The volumes produced proclaimed that Filipinos were, are, and will continue to be living all over the United States—from San Francisco, San Diego, Los Angeles, East Bay, Vallejo in California, to Chicago, Louisiana, Hawaii, and Alaska. Filipinos of both sexes and a variety of occupational sectors were honored—as Alaskeros, farmworkers, sugar plantation workers, union activists, nurses, doctors, navy men, and politicians. Robert Santos, a prominent Filipino American whose involvement in civil rights activism for the restoration of the International District in Seattle earned him the nickname of "unofficial mayor of the International District," used to deliver lectures about growing up there. The lectures formed the basis for the script of a play entitled *Uncle Bob's Neighborhood*, which Santos performed in 1994 to raise funds for Inter*Im, the organization responsible for nonprofit agencies of the International District.[46] The title of the play staked the International District as Uncle Bob's "home." I had the good fortune to hear excerpts of this from Uncle Bob himself when he shared his story at one of the regular "talk story" features sponsored by the Manilatown Heritage Foundation in San Francisco in July 2009 (sadly, Robert Santos passed away in 2016). The audience, mostly composed of young Filipina/o/x Americans, was regaled with the stories of a successful second-generation Filipino American who could claim the International District as *his* neighborhood. The next stage in the project of staking a place in social memory was to have actual physical heritage sites. The struggle for heritage sites will be discussed in a section below.

This training to become historians and custodians of the past is an excellent example of a history from below. In this case, migrants who are perceived to be marginalized actors (invisible) in mainstream history undertake to write their own histories—doing their own training, research, and documentation.[47] Not only do they produce new narratives or alternative histories with themselves at the center of the story, but they do this with an autonomous voice of their own, independent from the academy of professional historians. This new history from below differs from the previous "old" history from below in that actual members of the lower classes are no longer an anonymous mass of people. Instead, it reevaluates individual experience, it lets us hear the personal and private voices of the common or ordinary people (unmediated), and it sees these community historians as active agents of change.[48]

The Struggle for Heritage Sites

Accompanying the Filipina/o/x American activist aims to have their histories included in the mainstream history of white America was the struggle to preserve Filipinotowns, especially in California. There was a real fear that these ethnic enclaves would completely disappear, as the Filipino population was pushed out because of redevelopment projects in the 1970s, and pressured to move out of sections of the cities where they once lived as a community. Filipina/o/x American cultural activists lobbied to preserve the remaining physical sites to pay homage to their ancestors who once made the buildings their homes, a major challenge when some of the physical sites no longer existed and the community was no longer the dominant ethnic group there.

I discuss two historic tours run by Filipina/o/x Americans in recent years. These projects reinvent the trope of historic tours—by "marking" sites where the Filipino community was quite literally disappearing and through commentary revising mainstream histories and inviting audiences to join in their crusade of remembrance. The two tours are nonprofit ventures run by volunteers who had activist agendas: to lobby for markers to be placed on streets or sites that were important in Filipino migrant history, to reclaim Filipino heritage sites, and/or to preserve and remember Filipinotowns that have disappeared or are in danger of vanishing. The tours I analyze are MC Canlas's ethnotour of the South of Market (or SoMa) district in San Francisco and Little Manila Foundation's tour of Little Manila, Stockton.

SoMa Pilipinas

Since 1999 Mamerto Calalang "MC" Canlas has been running two Filipino ethnotours of the SoMa district in San Francisco.[49] A SoMa Pilipinas Ethnotour was developed in partnership with San Francisco Architectural Heritage and the National Trust for Historic Preservation, producing a brochure for a self-guided tour of various sites in the district that were associated with Filipino heritage.[50] By 2012 the Filipino American Development Foundation received funding to publish the SoMa Pilipinas Ethnotour Guide Book from the National Trust for Historic Preservation and the San Francisco Architectural Heritage.[51] The tour was concentrated between Mission Street and Harrison Street between Third and Seventh Streets.[52] The evolution of this ethnotour was inextricably linked to social and cultural activism by Filipinos who were afraid that the redevelopment projects and resulting demographic movements out of the area might erase the once vibrant presence of the Filipina/o/x American community that had a long history there from the 1920s until the 1970s.

Filipinos living in San Francisco before World War II congregated in Manilatown, adjacent to Chinatown and the South of Market area.[53] From the 1940s to the early 1960s, Manilatown and Japantown continued to be the two most important neighborhoods for Filipinos in San Francisco. Manilatown boasted a number of Filipino-owned businesses, including barbershops, photo studios, food outlets, and pool halls, most of them located along Kearny Street.[54] The neighborhood around the International Hotel (known as the I-Hotel) provided shelter to the first Filipino community in San Francisco. During the period of social exclusion (1920s and 1930s) only certain hotels in Manilatown, San Francisco allowed Filipinos to become their tenants. According to Estella Habal, at its heyday, up to 30,000 Filipino workers lived in hotels in Manilatown, San Francisco.[55] In June 1968, the owner of the I-Hotel applied for permission to demolish it. The eviction notices affected a number of Filipino elderly tenants living there. Filipina/o/x American youth, and activists such as the KDP (Katipunan ng mag Demokratikong Pilipino, or Union of Democratic Filipinos) allied with the retired pioneer generation migrants to form an anti-eviction movement hoping to save the hotel from demolition.[56] Although the movement did not prevent the hotel from being demolished in 1977, it succeeded in winning a Filipino space in the new structure that was built in 2005. The building that replaced the I-Hotel included a Manilatown Heritage Center, which has an archive and a physical space for Filipina/o/x Americans to run events, exhibits, and lectures.[57] The Manilatown Heritage Foundation website advertised tours of Manilatown in 2019, but there were no ethnotours when I did research there in 2010.[58]

The postwar Filipino migration to the United States also resulted in the formation of a Filipino neighborhood enclave in the South of Market district. The urban renewal projects, including the demolition of the I-Hotel, compelled Filipinos to relocate to other districts such as SoMa due to its relatively inexpensive rents and proximity to jobs in the service industry.[59] Hence, the I-Hotel eviction coincided with and encouraged the movement of Filipinos to the SoMa district.[60] In the 1970s, out of an estimated population of 17,000 in SoMa, 5,000 were Filipinos mostly of the working class.[61]

The Filipino population in San Francisco doubled from 12,300 in 1960 to 30,000 by 1976 (overall 665,000 Filipinos entered the United States between 1964 and 1984, many of whom were professionals, including a large number of doctors and nurses).[62] By the end of the twentieth century the Filipino population moved to the suburb of Daly City, where they are the fastest growing ethnic minority, making up 32 percent of the population. (In 2009 there were 32,720 Filipinos among Daly City's total population of 103,621,[63] making it arguably "home to the largest concentration of Filipinos outside of Manila.")[64] In Serramonte Center, Daly City's premier shopping mall, one in three persons were of Philippine descent, with one half of Target (retail store) employees of Filipino ancestry and where Philippine-based businesses such as Bench (an apparel store) and Filipino fast food can be found in the court.[65] But, according to Canlas, Daly City lacked "the Filipino character," thus forfeiting the possibility of claiming it as a designated Filipinotown in the same way as there was a Nihonmachi (Japantown) and Chinatown.[66] On the other hand, despite the growing exodus of Filipinos out of the area, SoMa remained "a center of gravity for the Filipino people living throughout the San Francisco Bay Area."[67] In the 1970s, SoMa was home to many Filipino businesses, including two Mission District movie houses specializing in Filipino movies, the Mint Mall (a mixed-use building with apartments occupied by newly arrived Filipino families), several Filipino grocery stores, food outlets, hair salons, and laundry establishments.[68]

Unfortunately, the Yerba Buena Redevelopment Project resulted in the demolition of a number of businesses in the SoMa area. In the absence of legislation that ensured that every Filipino cultural resource (including Filipino-owned businesses) would be sustained and preserved, Canlas feared that "we might vanish from the neighborhood."[69] Activists who mobilized to fight against the Yerba Buena Redevelopment scheme therefore founded the Tenants and Owners in Opposition to Redevelopment (TOOR) organization, which then gave birth to the Tenants and Owners Development Corporation (TODCO) in 1971.[70] TODCO built a series of low-income housing buildings to replace those demolished by the Yerba Buena Corporation, of which one was specifically geared to Filipinos.[71] A year later the Pilipino Organizing Committee (POC) was formed with an operating facility called Gusaling Pilipino, or "Pilipino people's space."[72] POC worked with TOOR. One of TOOR's aims was to "save the neighborhood" from "redevelopment without planning," and one strategy the organization used to do this was to put forward the concept of "social heritage" in its plea for the preservation of important landmarks relevant to particular communities who lived in the SoMa district.[73] Since there was a shortage of actual physical structures that they could target as heritage structures, activists coined the term "cultural preservation districts" and "social heritage sites" as legitimizing discourses for reclaiming (and marking) sections of the city as "Filipino spaces."[74] According to Canlas, the San Francisco Planning Department generally used the term "historical district" to refer to architectural structures. Due to the lack of Filipino buildings, the use of the term "cultural preservation area" allowed activists to expand the concept of heritage sites to include places that once were important to Filipinos even though Filipino presence was slowly disappearing. The San Francisco Board of Supervisors (the legislative body of the city and county of San Francisco) was familiar with the term "honorific designation" allowing banners to be placed to mark "Little Saigon," for example, in the place where Vietnamese restaurants abound. However, activists were afraid that this label might not protect the assets of the buildings.[75]

What were these spaces or buildings that Filipina/o/x American activists wanted to reclaim and preserve? The SoMa Filipino Cultural District had a clearly designated area from Second Street to the east, Eleventh Street to the west, Market Street to the north, and Brannan Street to the south.[76] It consisted of actual buildings, historical markers (such as the one in the Palace Hotel to point out that Philippine national hero Jose Rizal stayed there in the nineteenth century in his only visit to the United States), street murals, a park, churches, a theater, and a school. There was the Dimasalang House at 50 Rizal Street, which was a low-income housing project joint venture between TODCO and Caballeros de Dimas-Alang (one of the fraternal lodges established by the pioneer generation of Filipino migrants). The building was renamed the San Lorenzo Ruiz Center in honor of the first Filipino saint. There was the Delta Hotel, which was purchased in 1976 by Dr. Mario Borja and was transformed into affordable housing for Filipino World War II veterans. Caballeros de Dimas-Alang also campaigned to rename the streets surrounding San Lorenzo Ruiz Center to be named after prominent Filipinos. The Gran Oriente, a building purchased in the 1930s by another fraternal organization of the same name, was also an important landmark for the community.[77] For Canlas, the most important landmarks for Filipinos in SoMa were St. Patrick Church and Bayanihan Community Center (on the site of the former Delta Hotel) where Filipinos congregated.[78] The lobby to reclaim Filipino spaces by renaming streets was a successful one. In 1979 O'Doul Lane became Lapu-Lapu Street, Shipley Street was renamed Bonifacio Street, and Alice Street changed to Mabini Street—all names referring to Filipinos who resisted Spanish and/or American rule.[79] Two other streets in the same location were given Filipino names—Rizal Street and Tandang Sora Street (Jose Rizal is the Philippine national hero whose novels inspired the revolution against Spain, and Tandang Sora is the nickname of Melchora Aquino, the female elder who looked after Filipino revolutionaries in the 1896–1898 revolution against Spain).[80] In 2005, Filipino university students presented testimonies urging the mayor and board of supervisors to support the initiative to name the former Bessie Carmichael Elementary School site as Victoria Manalo Draves Park. Filipina American youth were looking for role models and they found one in Draves, who, as they learned in their Asian American and/or ethnic studies courses, was a Filipina American who had earned the distinction of being the first female diver to win gold medals in both springboard and platform diving at a single Olympics.[81] The campaign was successful, and the Victoria Manalo Draves Park was opened in 2006.[82]

The two ethnotours of the Filipino SoMa neighborhood were originally designed by Canlas to get fundraisers to view SoMa as a social heritage district (dubbed "Munting Pilipinas" [miniature Philippines] in the plans to redevelop the area).[83] Canlas used the Tagalog framework of *tabi tabi po* (the phrase one says to ask spirits permission to walk past their area), he said, because this told all and sundry that Filipinos had ancestors who lived there for a long time.[84] The effort to mark the SoMa neighborhood as Filipino/Pilipino space was an attempt to underscore the point that Filipinos were there a long time ago, as well as to keep the memory of it alive for generations to come. Canlas concluded:

> Amidst gentrification in South of Market, there is metamorphosis going on in our community—consolidation and integration of the Filipino community into a SoMa Pilipinas. SoMa Pilipinas is a community work in progress. A vertical integration is taking deeper roots, connecting our current generation of Filipinos and contemporary history in

the making with our past and rich heritage, both here and in the Philippines. At the same time we are horizontally linking Filipino families, organizations and communities into webs of plaza-barangay, of hometowns and new found lands, in SoMa, in the Bay Area, in America and in the Philippines.[85]

I had the privilege of being taken on a personally designed tour that was a combination of two tours, the Neighborhood Heritage Tour and the Philippine-American Tour of History (PATH) in July 26, 2010, and I did a follow-up interview with Canlas in July 11, 2012. The itinerary of the tour sites showed a close connection between sightseeing and activism on behalf of reclaiming Filipino spaces in the district. The tour took audiences to see the renamed streets in the Philippine Heroes Square, the Victoria Draves Park, the Bessie Carmichael School (which has a significant number of Filipina/o/x students), the Tutubi Park (*tutubi* is the Tagalog word for "dragonfly"), at least one Filipino street mural in the area, the Gran Oriente Filipino Hotel and Masonic Lodge Temple, the Filipino Education Center, St. Patrick Church, and the San Lorenzo Ruiz Center.[86] The participants were briefed in the Bayanihan Community Center at Sixth and Mission Streets, once the site of the Delta Hotel where many World War II veteran Filipinos lived in the 1990s. Note that most of the sites (with the exception of the Gran Oriente Filipino and the San Lorenzo Ruiz Center) were reclaimed Filipino spaces. The tour brochure came with a map of streets and included the Bindlestiff Studio (formed in 1989; since 1997, a center dedicated to Filipino performing arts), and St. Joseph's Church.[87]

In 2016 SoMa Pilipinas was officially recognized as a Filipino Cultural Heritage District by the City and County of San Francisco as it resolved to "preserve and further develop SoMa Pilipinas as the regional center of Filipino culture and commerce, recognize the historical and present contributions of the community and neighborhood, to stabilize Filipino residents, business and community-serving institutions."[88] A year later, in July 2017, the California Arts Council selected SoMa Pilipinas as one of the fourteen cultural districts "that will serve as California's first state-designated Cultural Districts, highlighting thriving cultural diversity and unique artistic identities within local communities across California."[89] This was clear evidence that activists' strategy to combine history and memory with "cultural preservation" in a unique ethnotour worked well for TOOR and the POC. It also illustrated the success of the political uses of history from below.

The Philippine-American Tour of History (PATH) added a couple of monuments to the itinerary, but what distinguished it from the other tour was Canlas's commentary. In his own words, he hoped to begin a "counternarrative" by giving alternative interpretations to the texts that accompanied these monuments. For example, Dewey Monument in Union Square, which celebrated the American victory in the Spanish-American War, was reinterpreted on the tour as a symbol of the beginning of the American colonization of the Philippines. The visit to the Presidio army post to see the Spanish cannon brought to San Francisco by the American army from the Philippines as a war trophy allowed Canlas to relate how Filipinos in the United States successfully lobbied to change the accompanying text about the Philippine-American War of 1899–1902. Instead of depicting Filipinos who fought against Americans as "insurrectos," the term was changed to Filipino "nationalists." In addition, Filipinos insisted that the textual commentary next to the cannon should include statistics of Filipino casualties of war.[90] Canlas's PATH presented a version of American history from a Filipino perspective—a new narrative of the past that included a demand for social justice for Filipinos in America.[91] In many respects, SoMa Pilipinas epitomized the struggles and achievements of immigrants in their new homeland, while serving as a focal point for Filipinos seeking to connect with their social and cultural heritage.[92]

Stockton's Little Manila Tour

The city of Stockton became the hub for itinerant Filipino farmworkers in the 1920s to the 1970s.[93] Located between the Alaskan salmon canneries and the agricultural fields of California, including the San Joaquin Valley where Filipinos became the largest ethnic group in farm labor in the 1920s, Stockton was the ideal meeting point and the natural place for this group to congregate between the seasons.[94] Local statistics confirmed the importance of that small city for Filipina/o/x Americans since "by 1930 there were more than 30,000 Filipinas/os in California, and approximately 10,000 lived and worked in and near Stockton."[95]

By the 1970s the Filipino community moved out of the downtown area of Stockton. Only three dilapidated buildings remained where once a four-to-six-block area boasted a plethora of Filipino-owned businesses, ranging from restaurants and pool halls to barbershops. By the end of the twentieth century, it was difficult to spot any traces of the once-thriving ethnic community. The Little Manila Foundation of Stockton, California, was founded in 2002 by historian Dawn Mabalon and Dillon Delvo to advocate "for the historic preservation of the Little Manila Historical Site in Stockton, California," and to provide "education and leadership to revitalize our Filipino American community."[96] The late Dawn Mabalon (she passed away in 2018) taught at San Francisco State University and wrote *Little Manila Is in the Heart: The Making of the Filipina/o American Community in Stockton, California*, which was based on her dissertation. Inspired by their motto "to remember and reclaim," volunteers conducted educational tours of the site once inhabited by Filipino migrants before World War II. I had the privilege of participating in one of the tours especially organized for my visit by Dawn Mabalon, Jessica Hernandez, Elena Mangahas, and Anita Navalta Bautista in July 2012. The tour took me to downtown Stockton at the intersection of Lafayette and El Dorado Streets where once a four-to-six-block Filipino community thrived and where many Filipino farmworkers spent their leisure hours, and the Filipino Center, which was built in 1972 and featured low-income housing, social services, and retail space for displaced businesses that had to make way for the superhighway in the late 1960s. The tour included a visit to the Daguhoy Lodge of the fraternal organization of the Legionarios del Trabajo to view a little exhibit that recaptured the living quarters of Filipino farmworkers who worked in the asparagus fields in the 1920s and 1930s. (The Daguhoy Lodge was sold in 2015.)[97] With only three dilapidated buildings left of the original site, the tour was really a history lecture. Although one was presented with special computer-generated maps of the changing ethnic composition of Stockton's downtown over the years with a special emphasis on Filipino presence, visitors who were expecting a typical sightseeing extravaganza would have been greatly disappointed. But this shortage of heritage sites was precisely the rationale for such a tour. The Little Manila Foundation's raison d'être was to ensure that Filipino historic presence in downtown Stockton was commemorated and remembered despite the fact that hardly any physical remains could be seen today. One must not dissociate the historic tour of Little Manila with the foundation's activist arm. For example, together with FANHS–Stockton Chapter, the foundation successfully lobbied the Stockton City Council for historic site status for the Little Manila area in 2000 (the first city-designated Filipina/o/x American historic site).[98] Little Manila Foundation's aims included educating Filipina/o/x Americans about the history of Filipinos in Stockton. The foundation succeeded in placing official markers and photographic banners on the actual sites where important Filipino landmarks once stood. The markers, clearly visible in downtown Stockton, displayed Filipino presence and succeeded in reminding visitors and residents that the area was significant to that particular ethnic community.

The Stockton Little Manila tour was also about reminding Filipina/o/x Americans about the consequences of historical apathy. It reminded young Filipina/o/x Americans of the need to preserve their past or else risk becoming invisible as a minority group (the crisis discourse again). A clip of the tour included in Marissa Aroy's documentary *Little Manila* about Filipinos in Stockton captures this sentiment. It shows the tour conductor Dawn Mabalon addressing the audience of young Filipino/a/x Americans, then asking: "Do you want to bring your grandchildren into an empty lot and say 'this is where an important strike was planned'? Because what does that say about what we think about ourselves and how we value our long history? Because if we allow our historic places to become parking lots, what does that say about how we think about ourselves, of how we value our long history in the United States?"[99] Mabalon's comments communicated the message that pride in one's ethnic heritage was a barometer for how they valued themselves as a migrant group. The tour ended with a call to arms to join the campaign to claim a space in social memory. At its core, the Little Manila historic tour was about the sins of forgetting, inviting its audiences to participate in the ethnic group's project of remembering and preserving their past.

Every Migrant a Budding Historian?

I opened this chapter with an inscription on a gravestone. This inscription was an abridged version of the heroic narrative produced by migrants. The inscription broke migrants' public silence on the acknowledgment of their difficult past. But it also communicated the desire to possess the authorial voice. The late Terri Jamero, former FANHS president, declared in her presidential address (later reproduced verbatim in a FANHS community history of East Bay): "If we do not tell our own story, then others will tell it for us—as they interpret it—and we will risk losing the essence and the truth about the Filipino American experience. That history could fade from memory, and one day our children's children could be asking, Who were our ancestors? What were they like? What did they do? And there could be no one to answer and nowhere to look."[100] The titles of their publications—*Voices: A Filipino American Oral History, In Our Uncles' Words, In Our Aunties' Words, Filipinas! Voices from Daughters and Descendants of Hawaii's Plantation Era*—communicate their desire to control the way their own stories are told and interpreted after a long history of exclusion.[101] This project of making migrants visible transformed migrants into historians and underscored the importance of the discipline of history, especially oral history.

The project of calling attention to Filipina/o/x Americans' contributions to American history has been an astounding success. Filipina/o/x Americans, led by FANHS, were victorious in their lobby to have the month of October pronounced as "Filipino American History Month" in legislation passed by Congress in 2009.[102] In 2015, the White House Initiative on Asian Pacific Islander

Americans celebrated Filipino American History Month with an event on October 2. The White House released a message from President Barack Obama acknowledging the contributions made by Filipina/o/x Americans. Obama's message read: "I am honored to join in marking Filipino-American History Month and in reflecting on the struggles and victories of the many Filipino Americans who have helped shape our nation. Generations of Filipino Americans have lent their unique voices to the vibrant diversity of origins, cultures, and communities that make America what it is."[103] Every October, FANHS chapters and affiliates launch various activities celebrating and commemorating Filipina/o/x American history and culture, activities ranging from photograph exhibits to dances, Filipino food, book launches, film screenings, and lectures. FANHS as an organization continues to thrive and the minutes of the FANHS-Stockton meeting of June 27–June 28, 2015, reveal the possibility of expansion, as members pointed out that the term "Filipino American" "could include those countries of North and South America, not just the United States."[104] In 2021, the FANHS website declares that they now have thirty-eight chapters.[105]

Filipina/o/x Americans are visible in the sites of memory: a permanent exhibit of photographs of Alaskeros in the Wing Luke Asian Museum in Seattle's International District; two Smithsonian exhibits on Filipino American topics;[106] a one-room permanent exhibit honoring Carlos Bulosan in Seattle; and a special exhibit about Filipino farmworkers in the 1930s, exhibited in the National Steinbeck Museum in Salinas, California, in 2012. On October 8, 2016, FANHS opened its own national museum at the Newberry Building at 337 East Weber Avenue in Stockton. The museum was the fruit of more than fifty meetings and countless hours of volunteer work, particularly from the Stockton Chapter of FANHS.[107] That FANHS was able to raise funds and establish a Filipina/o/x American museum using its own resources was a remarkable achievement.

In 2015, John Sawyer, mayor of Santa Rosa, California, issued a proclamation declaring that "we acknowledge the impact Filipino Americans have had on our City through their valuable contributions to the social, cultural and economic fabric of the community. . . . The City of Santa Rosa is proud of its skilled, talented, and dedicated workforce, including members of the Filipino American community who serve in a wide variety of jobs providing service to the people of Santa Rosa."[108] The achievement could be attributed to the successful lobbying of the FANHS Sonoma County chapter.[109] In 2010, the city of Carson, California, issued a proclamation to dedicate a day to Larry Itliong, and this was followed in 2013 by a resolution to celebrate the day each October 25. In 2013, California governor Jerry Brown signed AB123 into law, which required state curriculum to include the contributions of Filipina/o/x Americans such as Itliong and Philip Vera Cruz to the farm labor movement in California.[110] A symposium on the life and work of Larry Itliong was held at San Joaquin Delta College during October (Filipino American history month) in 2013.[111] In 2015, a bill requiring California to observe Larry Itliong Day was passed unanimously; this bill also encouraged public schools to teach pupils about Itliong's life and contributions to California. It stated: "The accomplishments and contributions of Larry Itliong should be properly memorialized within the history and culture of the United States of America."[112] The list of legal victories continued to lengthen each year. In 2019 a historical marker was unveiled to mark the first Filipino settlement in the United States (in Morro Bay), and in that same year, after nine years of annual petitions, a bill (replacing the temporary yearly resolutions) was passed in Olympia, Washington, establishing a permanent Filipino American History Month in October.[113]

FANHS and the Stockton Little Manila Foundation produced two documentaries about Filipina/o/x American history and the history of Filipinos in Stockton, which were shown in high schools and universities.[114] This has inspired the production of a documentary focused solely on the Filipino labor strike in Delano.[115] The FANHS Sonoma County chapter produced *Remembering Our Manongs* in 2007.[116] A documentary on the specific Hawaii Filipino experience from 1906 to 2006 was produced in 2006 in time to celebrate the centennial of Filipino migration to the United States.[117] The above documentaries produced by the Filipina/o/x American community complemented other existing documentaries such as *A Dollar a Day and Ten Cents a Dance A Historic Portrait of Filipino Farmworkers in America* and *The Fall of the I-Hotel*.[118]

Some streets were renamed to acknowledge Filipino presence there and markers laid at important Filipino sites. The Little Manila Foundation and the FANHS–Stockton Chapter succeeded in having the area of Little Manila designated as a Filipina/o/x American historic site in 2000 even though Stockton's premier historian Dawn Bohulano Mabalon argued that "Little Manila exists only in the memories of the early immigrants and their descendants. It has literally disappeared from the physical landscape of Stockton."[119] In 2017, perhaps inspired by Little Manila Foundation's activism, a group of University of Pacific students and faculty recreated Little Manila for a virtual reality online game, thus preserving—at least digitally—the thriving Filipino community in Stockton before World War II.[120] As mentioned earlier, in 2016 SoMa in San Francisco was officially recognized as a Filipino historical district. SoMa to date was the only place in the United States where you could find streets named after Filipino national heroes.[121]

On August 20, 2013, the Little Manila Foundation and FANHS, the Inosanto Academy, and Bahala Na Filipino Martial Arts in partnership with San

Joaquin County named a new street the "Leo Giron Drive" to commemorate a veteran of the famous 978th Signal Service Company and the Allied Intelligence Bureau (AIB) who served as secret operatives for General Douglas MacArthur in World War II.[122] Manilatown Heritage Foundation in San Francisco, located in the site of the former International Hotel, sponsored regular activities about Filipina/o/x American culture and history, particularly the activism of the 1970s during the fall of the I-Hotel. I used the archive twice and attended two events—one in 2010 where the late Robert Santos spoke to young Filipina/o/x Americans about growing up in Seattle, and a panel discussion about Filipina/o/x Americans in 2013. The Filipino American Historical Society of Hawaii (FAHSOH) launched an eFIL project to digitize Filipina/o/x American newspapers and interview transcripts with Filipinos in Hawaii, and make them available on their website. These achievements documented the coming of age of the Filipina/o/x American migrant as community historian. But they also revealed that the strategic use of the heroic narrative to legitimize the demands for a space in social memory had been very effective. Filipina/o/x Americans' consistent contribution to white society in the long twentieth century has also been recognized by mainstream society. The inclusion of Filipino history in school textbooks has begun to happen. The first ever series of Filipina/o/x American history books for children was launched on October 20, 2016. The eight-book installment began with *Journey for Justice: The Life of Larry Itliong*, with the plan to follow these with books about Victoria Manalo Draves and Carlos Bulosan.[123]

The growing cohort of migrant community historians was testimony to the empowerment of this group. Filipina/o/x Americans showed great pride in their ancestral heritage with its origins in working-class labor. This was unheard of in the Philippines where the common reaction was to obscure one's humble origins. This was also a direct contrast to the shame some second and third generation Filipina/o/x Americans once felt about their parents and grandparents who spoke heavy accented English. Becoming a community historian—joining FANHS, publishing books, performing in PCNs, lobbying for historic sites, painting historic murals, or becoming tour guides—gave them transformative power as ordinary migrants became custodians of their own past in a project that filled them with pride, and self-esteem.

These remarkable achievements underscored the strategic importance of the heroic narrative. This heroic narrative was by definition a celebratory tale: a story of struggle and hardship but also a tale that ended in triumph while highlighting the positive contribution made by this particular ethnic group to the host country. This affirmative narrative was necessary in the groups' attempt to counter negative stereotypes by the dominant white society during the more than a century of Filipino migration to the United States of America. The name of the San Francisco emagazine that targeted Filipina/o/x Americans is: *Positively Filipino* (published since November 2012–present) emphasizing the continuing need to create counter-discourses affirming Filipina/o/x-American-ness. The magazine's rationale referred to the classic Filipino-exclusionary signage "Positively No Filipinos Allowed" displayed prominently on doors of hotels and businesses in California in the 1920s and 1930s. Scholar Antonio T. Tiongson writing in 2006 claimed that the phrase "positively no Filipinos allowed" "continues to resonate, a reminder of the anti-Filipino practices and sentiments the *manong* generation encountered at a particular historical moment in the United States."[124] This historical context explained why Filipina/o/x American activists had to produce a counter narrative that celebrated their ethnic groups achievements. Such a counter discourse fulfilled the dual aim of dismantling negative stereotypes in white society whilst creating pride for their ethnic group.

The blossoming of Filipina/o/x American studies in the United States, the success of FAHSOH and FANHS and its chapters, the continuing production of migrant memoirs and stories were all evidence of the fashioning of the Filipina/o/x American as historian. Beyond their role in documenting the past, they also supported the research and publishing of Philippine studies and Philippine migrant studies and are currently among the most enthusiastic patrons of Philippine culture and history. In their drive to be recognized and to have control over the representation of their past, Filipina/o/x Americans not only marked themselves as custodians of Philippine history and culture worldwide, they also rejected their status as marginal actors and replaced that narrative with one in which they clearly were the heroes and heroines.

Chapter 6

Advocacy and Its Impacts, 1970s to circa 2000

For Filipinos who acquire permanent residency or naturalized citizenship overseas, their status as an ethnic minority group offered a unique set of challenges. These challenges differ according to the context of the host country and the situation in which Filipinos find themselves there. This chapter will analyze two sites—one in Australia and one in the United States—to give readers an in-depth discussion of the different types of trials Filipinos have grappled with as a group. I chose Australia and the United States (Hawaii) because I wanted to target the difficulties faced by the most vulnerable demographic of Filipino migrants—the youth and women. Filipinos compose around one quarter of the population of the state of Hawaii, but, although they make up a greater percentage of the population there than on the mainland, their socioeconomic position is relatively lower than their mainland counterparts. This lower-class status, coupled with the negative stereotyping of their ethnic group, has meant that the youth were not encouraged to go to university, thus making it difficult for some of them to move up the class structure. Filipino migration to Australia is distinctive because of the demographic imbalance of more women than men (especially in the 1980s–1990s)—a ratio of almost two to one, a consequence of women's migration as marriage partners of white Australian men. The experience of domestic violence in a cross-cultural marriage in the context of migration posed unique challenges, particularly if the woman was a recent arrival and did not yet have permanent residency in the host country. The woman might not be fluent in the language of the host country; she might not easily gain employment because her educational credentials were not accredited; she might not have information on the laws and cultural practices of her new country; and she was separated from her family and friends and therefore did not have her usual group of supporters. This set of factors gave enormous power to the male sponsor over his wife or fiancée and made the women more vulnerable to abuse, especially if they were dependent on partners for their immigration status.[1] Presenting these two case studies—marriage migrants and youth—from two different countries not only matches the contemporary reach of Filipino migration, giving some indication of the breadth and variety of challenges presented by each context, but it also gives some indication of the range of issues experienced differently by diverse demographic and gender cohorts. The evidence from these case studies underscores the importance of class, gender, and interethnic relations including cross-cultural marriage.

While many of the vulnerable groups here were from the lower classes, it was highly educated middle-class Filipino activists who dedicated their time, energy, resources, and commitment to advocacy on behalf not just of their ethnic group but also of all other minorities experiencing the same problems. Here, the case studies reveal how Filipino migrant advocates understood intersectionality and were able to transcend their own class positions to address the issues faced by youth and women of Filipino ethnicities. I chose two organizations—Operation Manong in Hawaii and the Filipino Women's Working Party in Australia—because they were quiet achievers. Neither had global connections nor were they well known internationally. I also wanted to analyze two organizations that had a relatively long history and therefore would be able to demonstrate a track record of achievements. Finally, both groups were distinct from the more common Filipino community organizations of which many abound.

Data from the migrant archives illustrates the diversity, scope, and serious nature of the trials faced by Filipino migrants. Let us begin with Filipinas who came as fiancées or spouses to Australia between 1985 and 1995. For the first year after Linda arrived in South Australia, her husband did not allow her to eat Filipino food, claiming that it was "shit food." He locked her up in the house all day and constantly shouted at her, calling her a "lazy woman" or "worthless woman."[2] In Sydney, Lisa confided to her welfare worker that she was treated like a prisoner in her home and could not leave the house without her husband's permission. She had no money of her own. When her husband reported for work each day, he removed the telephone from the socket and locked it in the cupboard so she could not communicate with anybody.[3] Susan's story revealed that her husband's abuse began as early as two weeks after she had arrived in Australia. Her husband shouted at her regularly, hit her on the head when she did not understand his instructions, and beat her until she bled on the nights he got drunk. He regularly threatened to send her back to the Philippines. Finally, one night he physically threw her out of the house. Susan found refuge in a Migrant Resource Centre.[4]

Yet these narratives on victimization were only one part of the complex story. In Linda, Lisa, and Susan's stories above, the victims were helped by other Filipinas who worked in the Migrant Resource Centres that mushroomed all over Australia in the 1970s and 1980s. These Filipinas raised the issue with the relevant Australian government sectors and began to advocate for legislative changes that would stop "serial sponsorship," or "the practice of men sponsoring a succession of women to Australia as fiancées or spouses," and to amend the laws so that victims of domestic violence would not be deported if they left their husbands before the two-year residency requirement.[5]

In Hawaii in 1974, Operation Manong volunteer tutor and University of Hawaii student Stephanie Padilla (of Filipino descent) wrote several entries in her journal describing the progress of her two charges, Artemio Borayuga, a fourteen-year-old Filipino from Ilocos Norte, and Asuisui Pas, age twelve, a Samoan immigrant from Honolulu:

> **March 4, 1974** . . . 5th period. I gave Artemio an assignment to do. He was to defined [sic] words from chapter 8. I noticed he will do his assignments, but doesn't seem to get anything from it. It's like he'll just go through the motions because he has to. And not get anything from it. I'm going to speak to his teacher, and possibly change his textbook.
>
> **April 15, 1974.** Asuisui is very willing to read. I am still drilling and she has made such a tremendous improvement. As I keep working with her, I realize her Samoan accent does make a difference in the pronunciation.
>
> **April 26, 1974.** Asuisui, to my surprise has been reading her book at home. She really made me happy. I know she feels proud of herself that she is able to read. Artemio is now really [sic] to questions from the back of the book by himself. Usually he copies everything.
>
> **May 5, 1974.** Artemio social studies. He handed in his questions from the back of the book. I'm glad to say they were answered correctly. I asked him questions/ he said he understood them better now by drilling with "mix and match" cards.
>
> **May 6, 1974.** Asuisui Reading. I picked her up from class, her teacher confronted me. She was surprise [sic] Asui had done so well. Mrs. Hee told me she thought it was impossible to get Asui to read.[6]

Padilla's journal documented the challenges faced by immigrant children in Hawaii, which included the public school teachers' dismissal of their potential, as well as the massive improvement these youths had achieved in less than six months after receiving tutoring from a sympathetic volunteer. This rare journal of a student volunteer from the Operation Manong archives gave us a snapshot of the passion, enthusiasm, and commitment of young Filipina/o/x Americans to the project of empowering the youth of not just their minority group but of all minority groups. Coming from the optimism of youth, Padilla's entry for March 23–24, 1974 concluded with:

> the kids kept commenting that didn't want to go home [from the camping trip organized by Operation Manong]. This kept up until we drop them home. From this experience in which I have never went camping with 45 kids. I learned a lot—one thing that's kid's [sic] everywhere are the same. Second—there are good grapes and there are very bad grapes but then that's what keeps our worlds balanced. Fourth [sic]—no matter what we do we cannot change them—it's either we except them for what they are or get out. But "loving them" is the most important thing to me. . . . [March 25, 1974] Our group has so much love within the group and I'm very proud of that.[7]

Migrants documented both the challenges and their insights into providing solutions to the everyday problems faced by youth and women. In both case studies, advocates had close interaction with their target demographic and it was this "hands-on" experience that made them effective activists.

This chapter will focus on Filipino advocacy for social or legal change aimed at addressing a distinctive set of issues experienced by Filipino communities overseas. My examples here—Operation Manong (OM), a group that aimed to help recently arrived Filipino youth migrants to Hawaii adjust to the American public school system; and the Filipino Women's Working Party (FWWP), the Centre for Philippine Concerns–Australia (CPCA), and their allies (who aspired to protect Filipina marriage migrants to Australia who were victims of domestic violence)—were founded by Filipino women who were already permanent residents or citizens of the host countries. As permanent residents or citizens, these Filipina migrant advocates had the same rights as Australian or American nationals. This location as Filipina Australians or Filipina Americans gave them access to the host country's bureaucracy and opened the doors for working with American and Australian civil servants.

Filipino migrant activism has been a popular topic tackled by social scientists, especially those writing about the post-1970s migration. The literature has tended to focus on NGO activism on behalf of Filipino overseas contract workers primarily because of their particularly vulnerable situation as nonpermanent residents without citizenship rights and, in the case of domestic workers or entertainers, their living situation as highly susceptible to employer abuse and exploitation.[8] The scholarship has to its credit moved away from depicting the Filipina/o/x migrants as victims, showcasing instead the robust nature of their resistance, particularly as NGO activists and union leaders.[9] In this body of work, Filipino activists were positioned in direct conflict with the host countries in their task of empowering the marginalized Filipino ethnic group.[10] NGOs had the formidable task of compelling governments of host countries to protect the rights of their guest workers. Such an agenda required NGO activists to assume combative positions.

But defiance against the host country was not the only strategy deployed by Filipino activists to achieve their goals. Governments also provided funding for their ethnic communities from the 1970s to the 1990s, and the history of migrant activism was more complex than the suggestion of a dichotomy between the protagonists as "activists = good" and "governments = bad." This chapter shifts the way the fault lines of migrant activism have been imagined by the existing scholarship by analyzing how Filipino migrants *worked in partnership* with the governments of the host countries in the *joint* project of empowering the Filipino ethnic group. In doing so it will dismantle long-held views that legal and policy changes do not come "from below."

The practical side of working with governments was funding. From the 1970s to the early 2000s, the host countries showed openness toward addressing the needs of their minority populations, including hiring qualified social and community workers from ethnic communities themselves and providing seed grants targeted specifically at minority groups. Activists in Hawaii and Australia in this time frame were very successful in winning government grants, enabling them to initiate projects aimed at improving the situation of the Filipino community. Activists were extremely savvy about navigating the political corridors of the government bureaucracies. The track record of Filipino advocates in OM, the FWWP, and the CPCA illustrates how a marginal group was able to change Australian migration law and introduce multicultural student services at the University of Hawaii. Their success inspired them to extend their portfolio to address the problems faced by other migrant communities, speaking for the disadvantaged groups beyond the Filipino ethnic enclave.

The demographic, historical, social, and cultural context in each case—Hawaii in the 1970s, Australia in the late 1980s—produced different challenges for each group of activists and compelled them to be creative in their advocacy. In Hawaii Filipino activists focused on newly immigrated Filipino youth in the hope of improving their academic performance and their adjustment to the novel environment, while in Australia activists had to protect Filipina victims of domestic abuse. This chapter will analyze the aims, strategies, and achievements of OM, the FWWP, the CPCA, and their allies to underscore the ways Filipino migrants have been able to work with the bureaucracies of the host countries in the larger project of improving the status of the Filipino ethnic group there.

While there is a good amount of scholarship on Filipino migrants for marriage, these studies have been more preoccupied with the gendered and racial experience of migration, including discourses on Filipina brides rather than on advocacy on behalf of the Filipino ethnic group.[11] Social scientists writing specifically on Filipina marriage migration to Australia have tended to focus on analyses of the reasons for international marriage migration between the two countries,[12] Filipina "brides" as victims of domestic violence and homicide,[13] and the ways in which Filipinas have been subjected to Orientalist stereotyping as "mail-order brides," highly sexualized mercenaries.[14] This social science scholarship on Filipino international marriage migration delivered a powerful narrative of Filipina women's victimization in the hands of white male patriarchy. Some studies, including my previous work, have broadened the research questions in the field that tended to ossify representations of Filipino women migrants to Australia as "brides" by examining these women's roles as mothers, workers, and citizens who contributed to Australian society as laborers, civic workers, or volunteers and through participation in cultural life, for example, through folk dancing.[15] But there has been little attempt to date to document the activism that Filipinas initiated to address the problems of migrants for marriage who became victims of violence.[16] This chapter is a first step toward addressing this gap in the scholarship in order to write the first history of Filipino women's advocacy in Australia in the post-1980s. It will contribute to the historiography of Australian migration by showing that activism initiated by migrants themselves can alter migration laws. In this sense, it should initiate a rethinking of how migrants are positioned in Australia. Finally, by lifting the taboo on discussing the delicate issue of domestic violence, this case study also unsettles the usual heroic narrative of migration where stories of struggle end with triumph. It departs from the usual trope that either documented the contributions migrants made to the host country or celebrated the refashioning of migrant identities. Although the activism I discuss here has achieved legislative success, the topic of Filipina victims of domestic violence was and continues to be a sensitive issue for the Filipino community (and perhaps the Australian community as well) because of the "shame" attached to this extremely private form of abuse. The period I analyze here was unprecedented in the history of Australian immigration.

The choice of these two case studies was also influenced by the availability and accessibility of archival sources and interviews. These archives have hitherto not yet been examined by scholars. Operation Manong had archives at the University of Hawaii at Manoa, and Debbie Wall, one of the founders of the Filipino Women's Working Party (FWWP), and Rosa Droescher, formerly of the Ethnic Affairs Commission of New South Wales (EAC NSW), shared their personal archives with me and helped me arrange interviews. There was a critical mass of primary materials from the rich personal archives of Operation Manong, including incomplete copies of OM's two bimonthly newsletters (*Ads and Odds* and *O.M. Newsletter*), OM annual reports (produced from the 1988–1989 fiscal year),[17] flyers, project proposals, submissions to the state government of Hawaii, including funding applications, journals and diaries of volunteers, and testimonials from the Hawaii state government. Three OM directors (Amefil "Amy" Agbayani, Melinda Kerkvliet, and Clement Bautista) gave me several hours of their time for interviews, and they arranged interviews with one Filipina high school teacher (Ethel Ward) from Farrington High who worked with the tutors, and two volunteers (Charlene Cuaresma and Clement Bautista). In addition, I consulted the publications associated with OM's anniversary celebrations, including newspaper accounts and OM's own official histories, and the awards and citations given to the organization in the last forty years. The sources for the Australian case study included: (1) reports on immigrant issues of the Ethnic Affairs Commission, including annual reports from 1986 to 2009; (2) the personal papers of FWWP founder Debbie Wall, CPCA national coordinator Melba Marginson, Filipina social worker Joan Dicka, and Filipino community welfare worker Estrella "Lilia" McKinnon; (3) interviews with Filipino social workers and community workers in the Migrant Resource Centres who dealt with victims of domestic violence, interviews with the founders of the FWWP and with a Filipina who was employed in the Ethnic Affairs Commission (Chat Ramilo), several interviews with the project officer of the Ethnic Affairs Commission (Rosa Droescher) who worked with the FWWP, and with Melbourne activist Melba Marginson from the CPCA; (4) the CPCA archives, particularly its newsletter *Kasama*; (5) the complete episodes of the FWWP-sponsored radio program *Ngayong Aussie Ka na, Manay!* (Now that you are an Aussie) in the vernacular language (Tagalog); and (6) the video on marrying and migrating to Australia that was produced and shown to fiancées intending to migrate to Australia by the Australian Embassy in Manila and the Commission on Filipinos Overseas.

Affirmative Action in Practice: Operation Manong in Hawaii

Filipinos in Hawaii

Hawaii was the first American territory to play host to the initial wave of Filipino labor migrants in 1906, when they were recruited to work in the sugar plantations. By the end of 1919 there were 20,400 Filipinos in Hawaii, including 10,354 of whom were plantation workers, or 23 percent of the plantation labor force.[18] A second major wave of immigrants arrived after 1965. The majority of these migrants came as part of the family reunion scheme made possible by the passage of new immigration laws. They joined the families and descendants of the first generation of Filipinos. By the 1970s there were clearly two major cohorts of Filipinos in Hawaii—those born locally whose first language was English and those who arrived post–1965 who were born in the Philippines and whose first language was not English. The second group arrived in significant numbers (about four thousand a year since the late 1960s), eventually making that group the majority of immigrants to Hawaii.[19] The Hawaiian-born group identified themselves as "local"—"a pan-ethnic category with roots in plantation society" who did not have a positive image of the definition of "Filipino."[20] This group tended to reject their cultural roots and perceived the new cohort of migrants as Other in accent, dress, deportment, language, and values.[21] The youngsters of these two groups encountered each other in public schools, and the violent clashes that erupted between them highlighted the split between the local and immigrant Filipinos that continues until today.[22]

Filipinos were among the socioeconomically disadvantaged ethnic minorities in Hawaii.[23] According to the 2010 US Census, Filipinos were the country's second most populous group, composing 14.5 percent (in the single race category) and around one-fourth (if one included those who identified as mixed race) of the total population.[24] But while in the US mainland, Filipina/o/x Americans compared quite favorably with other Asian American groups and to whites in socioeconomic status and educational level (with 33.9% holding a baccalaureate degree and 7.8% holding a graduate degree), this was not the case in Hawaii. In the 1970s Filipinos made up only 3.9 percent of the college students at the University of Hawaii at Manoa (UHM), a small number relative to their population.[25] In Hawaii, Filipinos represented the highest percentage of those without a high school diploma (23.9%), and the lowest percentage with baccalaureate degrees (14.1%).[26] On the other hand, Filipinos were overrepresented in the community colleges.[27] Although in 1979 Filipino children made up 18.7 percent (30,704 children) of public school students, only 2.6 percent of the teachers were of Filipino ancestry.[28] These grim statistics were duplicated in the sphere of occupation and per capita income. Filipino men composed the highest percentage (69.8%) and Filipino women (45.2%) the second highest percentage in sales, construction, and service-related jobs compared to the national averages of 47.4 percent for men and 33.4 percent for women.[29] Filipinos in the Hawaii region had the lowest per capita income at $14,545 (the national average is $19,259).[30] This is a huge gap compared to Filipinos in the New York region who had the per capita income of $26,587.[31] Hence, although Filipinos formed a greater percentage of the population in Hawaii than in the US mainland, this did not translate to a better location in the overall socioeconomic hierarchy there.

The post-1965 Filipino migration of almost four thousand a year to Hawaii introduced many young immigrants into the public education system. These children had to cope with a different system of education in their second or third language. Filipino students also encountered negative stereotypes in the classroom. Some public school teachers discouraged Filipino students from going to college simply because they did not believe that Filipinos were capable of excelling at academic subjects.[32]

The Hawaii Department of Education (circa late 1960s–early 1970s) issued a report identifying four major problems faced by Filipino immigrant students. These were: (1) English language deficiencies, (2) difficulty in socializing with local students, (3) lack of relevant schooling in their native country, and (4) difficulty in understanding the value system of American society.[33] Amefil Agbayani, one of the founders of Operation Manong, suggested that one appropriate response would be to move the burden of adjusting from the immigrant student and compel the American school system to use an English-as-a-second-language approach.[34] One solution to the problem of English proficiency was to hire bilingual teachers who spoke the language of the Filipino student and were familiar with their culture.[35]

Operation Manong

Operation Manong was an outreach program developed to address the educational and cultural problems of Filipino immigrant schoolchildren with the emphasis on bilingual/bicultural education.[36] It was founded in 1972 by a group of Philippine-born graduate students, non-Filipino and Filipino faculty at the University of Hawaii at Manoa (UHM), Hawaiian-born Filipino undergraduate students in ethnic studies, and a Filipino government official working with immigrant communities.[37] The aims were to help the recently arrived immigrant children from the Philippines who had to adjust to the American public school system. In their project proposal they outlined their objectives for a requested amount of US$10,368:

1. To interact with governmental authorities and community resources related to education and to maximize learning opportunities for Filipinos.
2. To interact with governmental authorities and community resources related to employment to maximize job opportunities for Filipinos.
3. To seek financial and other resources to achieve its various goals.
4. To provide direct assistance to immigrants, particularly immigrant youths.[38]

The method they used to achieve their ambitious aims was to establish an outreach program where volunteers from the University of Hawaii's Filipino and Filipino American undergraduate students (given the name *manongs*) would be trained and then paired with immigrant Filipino children (called *adings*) in select high schools that had high numbers of Filipino enrollments.[39] The primary duty of the volunteers was to tutor the children in academic subjects. In addition, the volunteers were encouraged to organize extracurricular and social activities. The latter was one way of giving the children a supportive social network.[40] One key innovation was to ensure that the undergraduate students' volunteer work would be counted as university credit. This required collaboration, support, and approval from the faculty at UHM. The spouses of the core group of women who ran Operation Manong in its early years were all professors at UHM who were already teaching courses connected with ethnicity, Filipino politics, and linguistics. OM director Amefil "Amy" Agbayani (Phd in political science) was married to Bob Cahill, a professor in ethnic studies; Melinda Tria Kerkvliet (then a postgraduate student in history), who served as OM coordinator, is the wife of Benedict Kerkvliet, then a professor of political science; and Sheila Forman (Phd student in psychology), who was research supervisor dealing with the administration of the university credits that volunteers were to receive for their participation in the program, is married to Michael Forman, who taught linguistics. From its inception, OM collaborated with UHM, the TESOL (Teaching English to speakers of other languages) program of the Department of Education, and the Filipino student community.

The name "Operation Manong" was also a deliberate choice. *Manong* was a term of respect for an older person in the Ilocano language (the majority of Filipinos in Hawaii came from the Ilocos provinces in the Philippines). But in

Hawaii, it was a derogatory term used by non-Filipinos to denigrate the elderly Filipinos of the pioneer generation. Its connotations included the assumptions that these men were illiterate, ignorant, and stupid, and underscored that they were from poor backgrounds and had failed to assimilate.[41] Comments often heard in Hawaii included: "Isn't there already equal access to education—for those who want it? People in Hawai'i don't discriminate against each other; if some people don't succeed or do well, that's their problem. We should ship 'em all back to the Philippines!"[42] According to Melinda Kerkvliet: "We would like to change the way Filipinos are perceived by the system, including the public school teachers, and we think they were probably the ones who promoted the idea that Filipinos are not capable of going to college."[43] If the teachers themselves were prejudiced against Filipinos, Filipino children would not be encouraged to do well at school or aspire to go to university. The children, after all, came from a lower-class background and their parents were unable to go to college.[44] Influenced by the other minority group activists such as the Black Panthers and the Viva La Raza group of Mexican/Latino supporters of the farmworkers in California, who came up with slogans such as "Black is Beautiful" or "If you are brown, stick around," phrases used by civil rights activists in the 1970s and 1980s. OM founders wanted to bestow positive capital on the precise words used to put them down and restore the original positive meaning of the word.[45]

OM was attached to the College of Education at UHM and therefore was already a part of the state bureaucracy, since UHM was a state university.[46] The Social Science Research Institute of the UHM trained the volunteers, who committed for a year and were required to learn either Ilocano or Tagalog. Their participation counted for twelve university credits for each semester's fieldwork.[47] OM hoped to recruit volunteers to work along with TESOL teachers at Farrington High School, Kalakaua Intermediate School, and Dole Intermediate School, where there were large numbers of Filipino youth enrolled. The target number was eight volunteers per school.[48] Serving as mentors, the volunteers were supposed to provide individualized instruction in the English language.[49] The university student volunteers would be given training and were required to keep a journal and submit a monthly report. A memo of March 13, 1973, summarizing these reports, disclosed that there were at the time thirty-two volunteers who reported a total of 1,363 tutorial/academic hours or an average of 42.3 hours per month, including extracurricular activities. Extracurricular activities were given equal importance to academic hours, with volunteers organizing sports activities as well as social activities.[50] In addition, the volunteers spent twenty-four hours a month for in-service training and fourteen hours a month for research and special projects. The decision on which children should receive tutoring was based on those who scored below 110 in the TESOL class or Davis Test scores.[51]

OM received an initial funding of US$10,000 from the Hawaii United Presbyterian Church.[52] Federal funding from ACTION in the amount of US$325,000 for November 1972–December 1975 enabled the organization to hire three part-time staff members and pay around thirty volunteers a stipend of US$200 a month.[53] From 1976 onward, OM was funded by the state of Hawaii's general funds through the University of Hawaii. Two years after its inauguration, it received two awards: one from the House of Representatives of the State of Hawaii, which passed House Resolution No. 174, "congratulating Operation Manong for Receiving the Outstanding Service Award"; and the other from the Senate, which passed Senate Resolution No. 57, extending its congratulations to the project for its invaluable service to Filipino immigrants.[54] In 1974 volunteers assisted 250 children in English, math, and social studies and led weekend and afternoon activities and recreational field trips, including a camping trip to Kahana Bay.[55]

Very soon after OM began its outreach program, it modified its goals to include local-born Filipino youth, because tutors discovered that these children were also struggling in school, and other ethnic groups, such as Koreans, Chinese, and Japanese children, who found school a challenging experience.[56] In its first year, OM already included Pacific Islanders, Samoans, and refugees among its students.[57] At the same time, OM discovered that local-born Filipinos were "really lost as opposed to immigrant Filipinos who you can easily talk to about going to college. These guys had no inkling . . . much less ambition."[58] One of on-site leader Norma D. Sparks's journal entries in February 1972 noted that local-born Filipino students were the ones who needed the most help, followed by the Samoan children.[59] The discovery inspired OM to "to shift our focus beyond immigrants."[60]

For the first ten years, sending college students as bilingual tutors through Hawaii's Department of Education was OM's main task.[61] It was then transferred from UHM's Social Science Research Institute to the College of Education in 1976 with funds from the legislature, and finally to UHM's Office of Student Affairs in 1992.[62] In 1985 the Hawaii legislature authorized OM to conduct student service programs for the purpose of ensuring equal access to public higher education.[63] This gave the impetus for OM to expand its repertoire of services to include entrance to universities as one of its visions. Among its initiatives were: (1) sending TRCRs (tutors/recruiters/counselors/retentioners) into the community to disseminate information about higher education and to encourage pre-high-school students to think of college or university as a viable alternative and to expose elementary and intermediate high school students to the college experience through the OM "early intervention programs"; (2) offering orientation and "Buddy-Buddy" programs to assist new Filipino students enrolling at the UHM; (3) providing tuition waivers to select undergraduate and graduate students; (4) creating the Justice Menor Scholarship Fund in 1989, offering $500 scholarships for university students; (5) participating in the US Community College Manoa Transfer Project (begun in 1987), through which OM and the Center for Hawaiian Studies selected eleven new students from community colleges to enter the UHM to help those of Filipino and Hawaiian ancestry gain entry and graduate from UHM; (6) conducting workshops on Hawaiian and Filipino culture "to increase personal self-esteem and encourage an awareness of ethnic identity"; and (7) sponsoring the ninth annual Sariling Gawa (Our Own Work), a leadership conference for high school students aimed at allowing them to "gain a positive self-concept of being Filipino" (sixty high school students participated).[64]

In the 1980s, OM also contributed to curriculum development and pedagogy by offering courses on Filipinos in Hawaii or immigration to Hawaii and publishing research papers on Filipino history and culture.[65] As funding increased in the 1980s and 1990s OM expanded to Waipahu, Wahiawa, Waialua, Ewa Beach, Kunia, and downtown Honolulu. It also expanded its services to other immigrant students, including Koreans, Samoans, Vietnamese, Laotians, Pacific Islanders, and Chinese.[66] In 2000, OM moved from the UHM Department of Education and became incorporated into the UHM's bureaucracy in the Office of Student Affairs, changing its name to the Office of Multicultural Services.[67] It had evolved from a program specifically directed at the young Filipino ethnic group to a program that addressed the needs of *all* students from disadvantaged or marginalized backgrounds. The price to pay for this new identity was the erasure of its Operation Manong brand name.[68] Its expanded new role also meant that Filipinos were no longer the sole or priority target group. It currently addresses the underrepresentation of Native Hawaiians, Filipinos, African Americans, Samoans, and others.[69] On the other hand, the title change also came with an important advantage. OM no longer needed to apply for funding every year because it became a permanent section of the university's student services department. OM founder and former director Amefil Agbayani also became director of Student Equity, Excellence, and Diversity (SEED), the department where the Office of Multicultural Services is located.

Analysis and Impacts

How can one explain the success of OM as an organization that survived the budget cuts of the 1980s, expanded its program to include all marginalized ethnic groups, and eventually became co-opted as a university program? There is no doubt that the vision, passion, commitment, and hard work of OM's three directors—Amy Agbayani (1972–1986), Melinda Kerkvliet (1986–1992) and Clement Bautista (1992–2020)—were crucial.[70] The timing of its founding in the wake of the civil rights movement in the United States meant that the society was culturally prepared for an organization that functioned like an affirmative action for Filipinos. The rise of ethnic studies programs, a consequence of the Asian American movement,[71] provided a pool of civic-minded volunteers. A number of them were undergraduates in ethnic studies courses. Two ethnic studies UHM undergraduates, Emme Tomimbang and Johnny Verzon, were among OM's founders.[72] The Filipina/o/x American movement produced second- and third-generation Filipina/o/x Americans who discovered their Filipino-ness and were enthusiastic about researching, writing about, and performing Filipino culture (see chapter 5). These young men and women were hungry for anything Filipino and were highly motivated to join Filipino-themed activist or cultural organizations. These were the main cohort of volunteers. Agbayani's close ties with local politicians—including two governors of Hawaii, Ben Cayetano (governor, 1994–2002) and Neil Abercrombie (governor, 2010–2014)—helped protect OM from being a victim of budget considerations.[73]

Statistics on Filipino enrollments at UHM may be cited as evidence of OM's success. In the early 1970s, Filipinos made up less than 2 percent of the student body at UHM.[74] By 1994 they composed 20 percent of the total number in the University of Hawaii system.[75] Of course, it would be problematic to attribute the rising enrollment solely to the efforts of OM, but it is possible that the mentored students followed the footsteps of their tutors. OM's other activities, such as the Pre-Freshman Enrichment Project (PREP), bringing high school students to summer classes, and the sending of TRCRs to community colleges and the high schools, had some effect; studies showed that at University of Hawaii campuses where active recruitment of Filipinos had been weak, Filipino representation had no growth at all.[76] Unfortunately, this encouraging positive trend was reversed by the university's decision to increase tuition by 50 percent in 1996 and 23 percent in 1997.[77] The decline in Filipino enrollments at UHM from 20 percent to around 5 percent of students was a reminder that activists had to be vigilant.[78]

The sheer number of students served in a three-year cycle—2,501 high school students in 1989–1990, 3,956 in 1990–1991,[79] plus around 300–500 students at UHM campus in the same three years, 1989–1991[80]—when extrapolated would translate to a huge impact of thousands of students in OM's more-than-forty-year history. The number of tutors averaged about twenty-eight a year, and an OM document showed that after nine years four hundred OM alumni could be counted.[81]

In 1981 OM conducted a self-evaluation, using questionnaires distributed to tutors and former tutors (alumni), Department of Education teachers, and the immigrant children who were tutored.[82] A total of twenty-five tutors and twenty-five alumni completed the forms. The very positive comments from the teachers were testimony to the high quality of OM's contribution to the immigrant students' learning and revealed their appreciation for the tutors. The teachers praised the tutors for their initiative, dedication, and enthusiasm, and regarded them as excellent role models for the immigrant students.[83] The journal entries of tutors Stephanie Padilla and Norma Sparks written in 1974 documented both the teachers' prejudices against Filipino and Samoan children, who they concluded were incapable of reading because they had come from Samoa and the Philippine Islands, and the same teachers' surprise at the rapid improvement of the children who benefited from OM's tutoring.[84]

The biggest winners in the OM program were really the tutors, or the *manongs* and *manangs*, themselves, many of whom eventually became successful, powerful, or prominent individuals in Hawaii. Alumni wrote that the experience benefited their choice of careers and gave them confidence, new skills, and additional qualifications for a variety of jobs in the government bureaucracy, particularly those in the Department of Education.[85] Working for OM introduced them to top-level personnel from the university, state agencies, federal programs, and other private/public organizations, giving them the networks needed for careers in government, media, education, and the university bureaucracy. Many of volunteers chose to work with agencies that were concerned with the ethnic minorities or with marginalized groups. For example, Johnny T. M. Verzon and Arnold Managan became community service workers for the Kalihi-Palama Immigrant Service Center; Mariano Hernando found employment with the Catholic Youth Services; Amadeo Verzon became program director for the Kalihi YMCA; and Richard R. Umil became the Emergency School Aid Act (ESAA) project counselor at Castle High School.[86] Emme Tomimbang became a prominent television broadcaster and film producer. Charlene Cuaresma was appointed by the governor to the Hawaii Board of Education (on Agbayani's recommendation),[87] and she worked as a public educator in the Kalihi-Palama community mental health center with the Hawaiian State Department of Public Health.[88] She was on the advisory council for the Filipino Royal Project, a program of the domestic action center in Honolulu, between 1999 and 2001, when seven out of ten homicide victims related to domestic violence were Filipinas.[89] Colette Machado, a Hawaiian Portuguese 1973 OM alumna, became a counselor for the Honolulu Community College and rose to the position of head of the Office of Hawaiian Affairs, a major agency of the state of Hawaii.[90] Joey Manahan, an OM alumni, became vice speaker of the Hawaii House of Representatives in 2010 and in 2012 won a seat on the Honolulu City Council.[91] Amefil Agbayani became the first chairperson of the Hawaii Civil Rights Commission after the signing of the new civil rights law by Governor John D. Waihee III in 1988; she held the position for eight years.[92] Melinda Kerkvliet has referred to her as one of Hawaii's "national treasures" and as a political "kingmaker" due to her close connections with Hawaii's powerful politicians.[93] The pictorial book *Filipinos in Hawai'i* devotes an entire chapter to Amy's life.[94]

The almost five-decade history of OM (OM will celebrate its 50th anniversary in 2022) coincided with the Filipino Hawaiian community's own narrative of its rise up the social hierarchy.[95] On November 6, 1994, the local-born Benjamin J. Cayetano became the first Filipino American to be elected governor of an American state.[96] He was governor of Hawaii for two terms (1994–2002). In October 14, 2000, Angela Perez Baraquio, a Filipina American Miss Hawaii beauty queen won the Miss America contest. Finally, the erection of the Filipino Community Center in Waipahu, which occupied 50,000 square feet and for which US$14 million had been raised at the time of its opening on June 11, 2002, symbolized the Filipino community's "coming of age."[97] According to scholar Roderick Labrador, "the FilCom Center story of Filipinos finally 'making it' in Hawaii is about achieving social, political and economic parity with the other racial/ethnic groups."[98] Agbayani called it "the tangible symbol of the power of the Filipino community" since it cost US$17 million.[99] Although statistics above about Filipino educational attainment and per capita income and the persistence of negative stereotypes may challenge this symbolic statement (and indeed the FilCom Center still has an outstanding loan of US$3.5 million),[100] the center represents the Filipino community's public and confident aspiration. Their optimism is evident in their plans to build a Filipino community center on each of Hawaii's major islands. There is already one on Maui, and there are plans to build one on Kauai.[101]

The exponential growth of OM from a small organization run by three women sharing a part-time position to an essential part of UHM's student services, tackling the needs of all diversity groups, is phenomenal. Two alumni groups have been formed to supplement funding for OM activities and programs. The OM Alumni and Friends raise funds for the Justice Ben Menor Scholarship for entering UHM freshmen, and the Friends of PREP sponsors the PREP program. In 1994 these groups united to form the Friends of Operation Manong, focusing on fundraising activities.[102] OM's excellent track record for winning funding from the state coffers and from private philanthropists has been vital to its survival and metamorphosis.[103] But the political ties built by OM's directors, particularly Amefil Agbayani, were crucial, allowing the organization to escape the budget cuts over the years. OM received support from the highest officers of the UHM bureaucracy including Hugh Everly, dean of the College of Education, and Doris Ching, vice president for student affairs, was one of OM's biggest advocates, as she doubled OM's staff positions and placed the organization under SEED.[104] OM's political connections included two governors of Hawaii (the state's highest government official) and state legislators Akira Sakima, Rey Graulty, and Clayton Hee.[105] The timing of the organization's birth and development coincided with the country's recognition of its duty of care for its minority populations and the new global emphasis on the rights of women and people with disabilities. OM flourished in this environment of rights because it was a pioneer that provided a concrete practical solution for addressing the needs of those who have been marginalized. But the price to pay for this success was the expansion of its agendas beyond the Filipino minority ethnic group to help all disadvantaged groups reach their goals of acquiring higher education.

Filipina Activism on Behalf of Domestic Violence Victims in Australia, 1980s–2000

Between 1980 and 2011, forty-four Filipino women in cross-cultural marriages were killed by their husbands in Australia.[106] The murdered women were all sponsored as wives or fiancées of Australian nationals and a number of them were the second or third wives sponsored by the same individual. A study commissioned by the Centre for Philippine Concerns–Australia (CPCA) that was funded by the Human Rights and Equal Opportunity Commission delivered the shocking grim statistic that Filipino women in Australia were nearly six times more likely to be victims of spousal homicide than Australian women in general.[107] The timing of these stories and their locations across several states in New South Wales, Victoria, and South Australia underscored the point that it was a national issue and a serious concern for the Filipino and the Australian community.

Filipina Australians were the first to call attention to domestic violence as an issue facing the Filipino Australian community, and they were the driving force in the campaign to alter the laws and provide services to those who became victims of abuse. However, they did not do this alone. They found allies in the Australian government, which provided funding for research and organized forums to meet with fellow Filipinas to discuss possible solutions to the problem. I argue that the advocacy on behalf of Filipino victims of domestic violence in Australia was a *joint* project between Filipina Australian activists and the Australian government. It is an example of how a minority group was an agent of change, able to introduce new laws in the host country. Writing this history directly challenges the tendency to provincialize the woman migrant as peripheral to the center (read: Australia) and reveals the contribution this unique group has brought to the host country. These advocates are also pioneers in the area of transnational organizing for a feminist issue, since the practical side of the advocacy required navigating the Australian legal bureaucracy and liaising with the Australian Embassy in Manila and the Philippine government. I also suggest that the success of the advocacy could be explained not just by the relentless energy and robust actions of the Filipina Australians, particularly the Filipino Women's Working Party (FWWP) and the CPCA, but also because of the unique Australian historical context of the 1980s and 1990s.

I will focus on the strategies deployed by Filipina activists to address the issue of Filipina victims of domestic violence in Australia from the late 1980s until the end of the 1990s. These Filipina Good Samaritans—composed of community and welfare workers, psychologists, social workers, and educators who were permanent residents or Australian citizens—lobbied vigorously, demanding not just protection and services for the victims but a change in Australian perceptions of Filipino women. Almost all of these women were married to white Australian nationals and were Australian permanent residents or Australian citizens. Their location in a cross-cultural marriage gave them access to both the Filipino community and the Australian one. All were highly educated. Some were able to take courses in Australia, primarily in the fields of social work and welfare. Some of these women worked in the Migrant Resource Centres that mushroomed in this period, and it was through their positions as migrant settlement officers that they encountered the victims. Hence, while these Filipina advocates were not victims themselves, their educational background in social work or psychology (one of them was a former Catholic nun), or their previous involvement as activists protesting the martial law regime of President Ferdinand Marcos in the Philippines, meant that they had a track record as advocates for social justice.

The primary movers and shakers of the advocacy were Filipino women, first-generation migrants who had arrived in Australia in the 1970s and 1980s and were already Australian citizens or permanent residents. The period of openness toward ethnic communities that characterized the multicultural policies of Australia in the period from the 1980s to 2000 and the flowering of activity among the ethnic organizations (under the umbrella of the Ethnic Communities Council) and immigrant feminist organizations in this exceptional era were important in explaining the level of support given to Filipino advocates and the legislative victories that resulted.

"Domestic violence" has been defined as "the abuse, coercion and control of one or more persons over others and includes physical, emotional, verbal and sexual abuse, financial deprivation, social isolation and control of environment."[108] In the specific context of Filipina Australian marriages, Filipina Australian activists and scholars writing on its most extreme form—homicides of Filipina partners—pointed out that a fundamental factor in the abuse was "the relationship between Australian men and what they understand to be Filipino women."[109] In other words, the abuse occurred partly because the man "constructed their wives in particular ways and then resorted to violence when the women did not live up to their expectations."[110] Both Filipina activists and their Australian allies in government understood this context and the role of media in propagating Orientalist myths about Filipinas that touched two opposing ends of a spectrum: the gold digger or promiscuous highly sexualized prostitute and the docile, demure, obedient, religious, and accommodating wife who believed her destiny was to serve her husband. Thus, addressing the issue of domestic violence extended beyond the need to protect victims and provide services to help them to include the ambitious aim of altering Australian stereotypes of Filipino women.

The Australian Context

Filipina migrant activism followed a period of massive change in Australian government approaches to migrant settlement. In the 1950s and 1960s the policy of assimilation meant that non-Anglo immigrants were expected to discontinue the language and culture of their parents and absorb the Anglo-Australian culture. By the mid-1970s this shifted to a policy of "integration" wherein the non-Anglo immigrants were considered part of mainstream society but could keep their language and culture.[111] The policy of multiculturalism launched in the 1970s completely altered the way ethnic minorities were viewed. It became the responsibility of government to support (and this included funding) the language and culture of diverse groups and to provide special services and programs for all migrants.[112] In this perspective, the individuals had the right to their language and culture within the framework of the Australian legal system.[113] In May 1978 the Frank Galbally report made a number of recommendations that reflected this new attitude of openness and interest in working with ethnic communities.[114] The Galbally report self-consciously articulated in its brief that "it is now necessary for the Commonwealth Government to change the direction of its involvement in the provision of programs and services for migrants and to take further steps to encourage multiculturalism."[115] It recommended "a special program of multicultural resource centres phased over a three year period, involving the local communities to the greatest extent in their management and operation" and "an increase of ethnic welfare workers through an extension of the grant-in-aid scheme" from one to three years, as well as a special program to provide "once only" grants of up to A$5,000 to assist with special projects.[116] The same report also recommended extending ethnic (i.e., non-English) radio to all states and the establishment of ethnic television (this later gave birth to the television station SBS).[117] Furthermore, Galbally also recommended that the Department of Immigration and Ethnic Affairs should appoint more grant-in-aid coordinators.[118] The establishment of Migrant Resource Centres (from 1978) and the Ethnic Affairs Commission of New South Wales (from 1976)—both underresearched topics in Australian history—generated the need for seed grants specifically targeted at minority groups and the employment of social and community workers from ethnic communities. For the first time, Filipinas could apply for and be hired as community workers in Migrant Resource Centres and in the Ethnic Affairs Commission—entry points into the government bureaucracy that was once closed to them. Filipinas embraced these new opportunities for social inclusion. Filipino organizations applied for the funds, particularly state funds that were available for ethnic organizations.

The 1980s–2000 was also the period when ethnic organizations flowered in Australia (many of them run by the second-generation, or Australian-born children of immigrants). An umbrella organization called the Ethnic Communities Council of New South Wales was also established. The male-dominated leadership of that umbrella organization inspired the immigrant women to secure funding to establish their own lobby group to address gender-specific immigrant issues in their landmark conference: Immigrant Women Speak Out.[119] In the 1980s, Filipinas were still at the fringes of the ethnic community lobby groups.[120] But by the 1990s Filipinas had linked up with the Immigrant Women Speak Out group.[121]

Filipinos in Australia

The 1980s also coincided with the dramatic increase of Filipino migration to Australia, particularly that of spousal migration or women sponsored as fiancées. Filipino migration to Australia was unique because of the sex ratios favoring women. Australian Bureau of Statistics data revealed that in 2006, 42,680 Philippine-born residents were male, while 77,854 were female. The gender gap, with women outnumbering men by almost two to one, reflected the marriage migration pattern in which Filipinas arrived as wives or fiancées of Australian permanent residents, a trend that reached its apogee between 1974 and 1998. In 1991, for example, approximately 70 percent of Filipino women migrants in Australia were sponsored as fiancées of men who were Australian residents.[122] The profile of Filipinos in Australia showed that Filipino females outnumbered the males by a ratio of 2.2:1 and was more pronounced in the 20–29 and 30–54 age groups where difference increased to ratios of 3.5:1 and 2.9:1.4 respectively.[123] The 1991 census of New South Wales included the numbers of people born overseas residing in each town even if their total was less than fifty. An examination of these statistics reveals that Filipinas were scattered in small rural towns all over the state. For example, in Grafton there were no males but 24 females; in Lismore there were 14 males and 26 females; in Albury there were 28 males and 68 females; and in Shellharbour there were 38 males and 128 females.[124] (The 2014 statistics show that there were 225,110 Philippine-born persons living in Australia making them the fifth largest overseas-born group in the country.)[125]

Domestic Violence

The history of advocacy on behalf of Filipina victims of domestic violence was inextricably linked to the beginnings of the Australian government's establishment of Migrant Resource Centres. These centers offered one genuine opportunity for the employment of Filipino women in the fields of social work and welfare or community work. In 1985, Estrella "Lilia" McKinnon bested thirty-one other applicants to win the job of community welfare officer for migrant and refugee women at the then Illawarra Migrant Resource Centre, funded by the Department of Immigration. Born in the Philippines, McKinnon moved to Wollongong because she married a local Australian, and although she earned a bachelor's degree in library science from Far Eastern University in Manila and had worked for the Christ the King Seminary Library and the Columbian Father's Library there, her overseas qualifications were not recognized in Australia. In 1983 she took several short TAFE (technical and further education) courses, including one on financial and community management and administration, while volunteering as an officer of the Australian Filipino organization in Wollongong.[126] Her qualifications and links with the Filipino community in Wollongong worked in her favor when she applied for the newly created position. Della Ipong arrived in Sydney in the 1970s. A trained psychologist, in 1987 she was a welfare worker for the Filipino community in the Sydney area, filling a grant-in-aid position funded by the Department of Immigration.[127] Another Filipina, Dolly Bates, was hired as a grant-in-aid worker in Newcastle.[128] Joan Dicka, a social worker and former nun who obtained her qualifications in the Philippines with more than twenty years' experience working with the Catholic Church in southern Philippines, wrote a proposal to the Department of Immigration in 1983 to create a position of social worker to attend to the Filipinas married to Australian men. The department offered her a half-time position in Adelaide, South Australia (where she lived with her Australian husband).[129] Joan had worked in 1962 with the Jesuit missions in Bukidnon, Mindanao, in the southern Philippines, where she looked after the indigenous peoples in remote areas. Her tireless efforts earned her the label "the Joan of Arc of Mindanao." When she joined the order of the Oblates of Notre Dame as a Catholic nun, she worked with Bishop Gérard Mongeau, OMI, working with the homeless (both Muslim and Christian) in Cotobato City. When she left the religious order in 1972, she moved to Baguio Pelletier High School, which was run by the Good Shepherd nuns, where she was employed as a caseworker for troubled children, unwed mothers, and students with drug problems. She then moved to a job with the Department of Social Welfare, rising to the ranks of provincial social welfare officer and president of the Philippine Association of Social Workers. She migrated to Australia in January 1981 to join her husband Stefan Dicka whom she had married in 1980. Thus, even before her migration to Australia, Joan already had an impressive career in social welfare and a distinguished track record for helping society's marginalized sectors.[130] In 1990, Concepción "Chat" Ramilo was hired by the Ethnic Affairs Commission as a community liaison officer for the Asia Pacific Community. Ramilo had a degree in psychology from the University of the Philippines but left the country for Australia in 1986 because she was an activist against the Marcos dictatorship.[131] In the state of Western Australia, two Perth-based associations—the Filipino-Australian Cultural Exchange (FACE) and the Filipino Australian Association of Western Australia (FAAWA)—merged in 1985, and its Filipino Women's Group won support from key state government ministers, senior public servants, and the

Ethnic Communities Council to conduct interviews with Filipino marriage migrants with a view to investigating possible incidents of domestic violence among mixed couples.[132] A major outcome of this was that in 1989 the Department of Immigration and Ethnic Affairs hired a grant-in-aid Filipino social welfare worker, responsible to the Filipino Women's Club, to assist with the settlement needs of Filipino migrants in South Australia.[133] Deborah (Debbie) Ruiz Wall (one of the founders of the FWWP) was born in Manila and worked as a journalist with the Philippine Broadcasting Service in 1970. As a young undergraduate student at the University of the Philippines, pursuing a bachelor of arts degree in journalism at the Institute of Mass Communications, she worked for the campus newspaper, the *Philippine Collegian*.[134] She worked as press secretary for the opposition leader Matthias Toliman and his successor Sir Tei Abal in the Papua New Guinea House of Assembly in 1973. She moved to Sydney, Australia, when she married David Wall; there she taught communication and social sciences in the New South Wales Technical and Further Education (TAFE) system from 1975 to 2004.[135] She was involved in the advocacy for lifting martial law in the Philippines through regular contributions to *Solidaridad*, a newsletter based in Hong Kong established by Filipino political refugees from the Marcos regime, and she was one of the original members of the Philippine Action Support Group, a human rights organization that had a focus on the Philippines.[136] In 1985 she wrote a seminal article for the *Australian Journal of Social Issues* entitled "Filipino Brides: Slaves or Marriage Partners?—A Further Comment."[137] Hence, by the end of the 1980s, a small group of Filipino women, already trained as social workers, psychologists, and community workers, were working in the Migrant Resource Centres and the NSW Ethnic Affairs Commission to help Filipina/o/x migrants and provide information and services with regard to settlement issues, housing, language, and education—matters that were connected to life in the new country. In addition, there were Filipina former martial law activists like Debbie Wall and Melba Marginson (see below) who were experienced activists in the Philippines and in Australia.

What came as a huge surprise to these Filipino women was the number of cases of domestic violence brought to their attention. These took several forms—from physical harm to verbal abuse, emotional blackmail, withdrawal of financial support, and prohibition from speaking their own language.[138] The most extreme mental abuse included locking up the women in the house, preventing them from seeing friends, and not giving them enough food to eat.[139] While working as a case manager in the Migrant Women's Shelter Service in Adelaide between 1983 and 1989, Joan Dicka was inundated with cases involving Filipina victims of domestic violence.[140] In 1987 for example, fifty-five Filipino women sought help from women's shelters and the Migrant Women's Emergency Support Service in Adelaide. Considering that there were only nine hundred married Filipinas in South Australia, this was a significant percentage.[141]

Once the Filipina community workers and social workers became aware of the magnitude of the problem, those in the state of New South Wales took the issue up with the Ethnic Affairs Commission of NSW. Within the EAC NSW, they found allies in Filipina community liaison officer Chat Ramilo and then senior policy officer Rosa Droescher, whose roles were to develop interaction with the migrant communities themselves.[142] The EAC NSW sponsored a Filipino women's consultative meeting on November 28, 1989, which led to the formation of the Filipino Women's Working Party (FWWP) to carry out the recommendations that came out of that meeting. Filipino women working in Migrant Resource Centres or who were involved in Filipino community organizations attended the consultative meeting, including representatives from Newcastle, Wollongong, Broken Hill, and Wollongong. The workshop facilitators were all Filipino women: Sennie Masian (media), Deborah Wall (in education). and Della Ipong (welfare worker).[143] That same year (1989) Joan Dicka founded the Filipino Bride Working Party in Adelaide.[144] Dicka used her connections in the media to make the Australian public aware of the disproportionate number of Filipino victims of domestic violence in the state of South Australia, and in 1987 the minister of community welfare of South Australia formed a special review committee to investigate problems faced by Filipino brides.[145] The review, which took two years and cost the taxpayers A$96,000, involved the formation of a Domestic Violence Task Force with eighty members responsible for conducting the research and investigation.[146]

The formation of the FWWP launched the first serious advocacy for changes in legislation that were directly related to the issue of Filipina migrants for marriage who were victims of domestic violence. The twenty recommendations that emerged from the 1989 consultative meeting that was organized by the Ethnic Affairs Commission and co-convened by the New South Wales Immigrant Women's Coordinating Committee and the Women's Advisory Council set the agenda and priorities for the future. The first priority was to lobby for the changing of laws regarding "serial sponsorship" (defined as the practice of men sponsoring a succession of women to come to Australia as fiancées or spouses) and for an amendment to the domestic violence provisions to grant permanent residency to victims of domestic violence who came as spouses or fiancées but had not yet fulfilled the two-year permanent residency requirement.¹⁴⁷ The fear of deportation prevented women from asking for help or leaving abusive partners, thereby risking women's lives. They had to deal with the stigma associated with a failed marriage (divorce is not recognized in the Philippines) and the shame of an unsuccessful migration endeavor. McKinnon noted the poignant stories of Filipino women who were deported back to the Philippines because they had left violent husbands before their two-year residency requirement.¹⁴⁸ The issue of serial sponsorship was raised because the community workers and social workers noticed a pattern in which several victims of domestic violence all arrived as fiancées of one man. The other priorities included the need to address the negative representation of Filipinas in the Australian media, the need to provide support services for victims, and the need to disseminate information about services to the community.¹⁴⁹ Dicka, who had formed the Filipino Bride Working Party in 1989, as mentioned above, talked to the media to disseminate her findings about the domestic violence cases she handled.¹⁵⁰

In 1989 Charles Schembri strangled Generosa "Gene" Bongcodin in Newport, Victoria. Filipinos in Melbourne were outraged not only by the circumstances of her death but also by the relatively light sentence that the perpetrator received primarily due to representations of the victim in the media and at the trial as a "dangerous woman—a gold-digging opportunist who used Schembri as a passport for a better life in Australia."¹⁵¹ Schembri was sentenced to eight years imprisonment with a minimum of five and a half years; he was released July 11, 1993.¹⁵² The death of Gene, the light sentence bestowed on her murderer, and the misrepresentation of her character mobilized another group of Filipina activists in Melbourne who campaigned under the general theme of "Justice for Gene."¹⁵³ Melba Marginson led thirty Filipino Australians in a demonstration to denounce the decision of the Australian legal system for the verdict of manslaughter influenced by the image of the victim as "a loose woman" who "used him as a passport to Australia, and who was not morally fit to be a mother to their child."¹⁵⁴ An organization called the Collective of Filipinas for Empowerment and Development (CFED) was formed in the wake of the "Justice for Gene" campaign "to look for strategies to get Filipino women to engage in discussions of possible victimization."¹⁵⁵ The next step was to create a national organization, and in November 1991 the Centre for Philippine Concerns–Australia (CPCA) was formally established as "a national network of Filipino individuals in Australia committed to advancing the Filipino people's interests."¹⁵⁶ Its aims included addressing the issues of Filipino women in cross-cultural marriages and the negative public images of Filipinos in Australia.¹⁵⁷ Melba Marginson persuaded the CPCA to focus on violence against Filipino women in Australia in the early 1990s.¹⁵⁸ Marginson (then Melba de Guzman) was educated at the University of the Philippines in the early 1970s, at the height of student activism against Ferdinand Marcos. After she graduated, she taught at the Philippine Science High School while continuing to be actively involved in the Philippine national democratic movement.[159] In 1982 she became a member of the Alliance of Concerned Teachers, a militant teachers' union, and was elected secretary general in 1985. She married Simon Marginson and arrived in Australia in 1990.[160] Thus, Marginson already had an impressive track record as a militant activist at the time of the Marcos dictatorship, and she had experience leading a major union with a membership of 50,000, of which 85 percent were women.[161]

In 1994, the Australian government's Office of the Status of Women awarded a grant to CPCA to conduct a national conference on stopping violence against Filipino women. Held in Melbourne, October 6–7, 1994, it resulted in the formation of the Filipino Women's Network of Australia (FWNA).[162] CPCA also focused on accumulating data on the number of spousal homicides of Filipina victims in its crusade to promote greater public awareness of this pattern of extreme domestic violence experienced by the Filipino ethnic group in Australia.[163] In 1993, Marginson presented the grim statistics of twenty-three victims killed in the years 1987–1993 to Irene Moss, race discrimination commissioner, with the Australian Human Rights and Equal Opportunity Commission (HREOC).[164] Moss's response was to ask the Institute of Criminology, University of Sydney, to complete a research project on the topic, funded by the HREOC.[165] The findings that Filipino women in Australia were nearly six times more likely to be victims of spousal homicide than Australian women alarmed both the Filipino and Australian communities and caught the attention of the Australian media.[166] CPCA also raised the concerns that sponsored Filipina fiancées and brides need to have access to support services and be given information about their legal rights. In 1995, the *Sydney Morning Herald* published a leading story on the serial sponsorship of Filipinas.[167]

Strategies and Successes

The Filipina activists' crowning achievement was the passage of two crucial pieces of legislation. In chronological order they were the Immigration Law (ca. 1992), "which provides that women migrants will no longer be deported if they have left violent fiancées, defactos or husbands," even if they have not yet completed the two-year residency requirement,[168] and the Serial Sponsorship Law, which limits the number of potential fiancées that an individual can bring to Australia to two (Migration Regulations 1994-REG1.20J).[169] The two pieces of legislation had an impact on all women migrating to Australia as a spouse or fiancée of an Australian national. In addition, FWWP lobbied for increased services for Filipino women.[170] More funding was made available for Filipino grant-in-aid workers, and there was a focus on more culturally appropriate domestic violence services and programs.[171] In Adelaide, Joan Dicka was able to work with local police, giving them information on how they could be sensitive to Filipino cultural attitudes toward domestic violence.[172]

The advocacy also had a transnational dimension, involving the cooperation of the Australian Embassy in Manila and the Philippine government's Commission on Filipinos Overseas (CFO), the body tasked to assist Filipinos who are migrating permanently overseas or who are permanent residents and citizens of other countries. The Department of Immigration and Ethnic Affairs produced two short films intended to be compulsory viewing for all those who were going to migrate to Australia as a spouse or fiancée: *Marrying and Migrating to Australia: The Filipino Australian Experience* (1995) and *Marrying and Migrating . . . You Have to Work at It* (1996).[173] In the second film the emphasis of the script was the cultural differences in the migrant context and the need for both partners to discuss carefully their plans for the future, including where they would live and whether or not they plan to have children. The last segment of the video discusses the issue of domestic violence. It informed viewers that victims were eligible to apply for permanent residency even if they chose to leave their partners. Information on where to receive help and services were outlined in the video presentation.[174] These two videos were compulsory viewing for all those who attended the predeparture seminars conducted by both the Australian Embassy in Manila and the Commission on Filipinos Overseas (CFO).[175] Although by the time Filipinas watched the videos they would have more or less decided to migrate, about 5 percent of the women who had seen the video changed their minds about marrying and migrating to Australia.[176]

The Filipino advocacy on behalf of domestic violence went beyond the lobbying for legislative change. The Filipino women activists aspired to empower victims not only by informing them about the services available to them but also by altering the views about themselves, critiquing Filipino cultural expectations of women as subservient or obedient wives. Dawn House S.A. Inc. was a women's domestic violence service located in South Australia. It inspired the establishment of a survivor's theater group who called themselves Buklod (Buklod Kababaihang Filipina). Joan Dicka was appointed as the non-English-speaking background (NESB) worker in Dawn House, and she ran twenty-five hour workshops over a five-month period for Filipina survivors of domestic violence. The workshops helped increase women's confidence and self-esteem, and workshop participants took steps to empower themselves such as enrolling in full-time tertiary study, obtaining drivers' licenses, joining other community groups, and gaining part-time or full-time employment.[177] In 1997 Buklod produced and performed the play *For Better or Worse . . . Till Death Do Us Part . . . ?*, raising awareness of domestic violence as an issue experienced by Filipinas married to Australian nationals in South Australia.[178] The play was performed at the Adelaide Women's Community Health Centre, and a number of venues, including a national conference in Melbourne entitled "Stopping Violence against Filipino Women in Australia."[179] In the Illawarra region, a similar workshop was run in 2001, producing ten-minute radio stories in English and the Tagalog language. The workshop was conceived by the Australian Philippine association Illawarra Welfare Service, funded by the Wollongong City Council Small Grants Program, and facilitated by Merlinda Bobis, prize-winning Filipina fiction writer and academic from the University of Wollongong.[180] The aims were "to encourage self-expression of creative writing skills in a bilingual format, provide a medium to draw and examine story materials from their personal experiences, develop confidence and enhance cultural lifestyle through participation in community activities, and promote better understanding of women from different cultural and linguistic background."[181]

The FWWP also produced a radio program in the Filipino/Tagalog language. The twelve-episode radio series funded by the Department of Immigration and Ethnic Affairs (Migrant Access Projects Scheme) and the Department of Primary Industries and Energy (Rural Access Program) aimed to reach Filipinas rural areas "to increase the level of awareness of Filipino women in cross-cultural marriages about the community and welfare services available to them through a radio information campaign; and to evaluate the effectiveness of radio as a medium for the delivery of settlement information."[182] The show—*Ngayong Aussie Ka na, Manay!* (loosely translated as "Now that you are an Aussie!")—was aired on the SBS radio network in the major cities of Sydney, Melbourne, Adelaide, Brisbane, Perth, and Darwin, in the afternoon three times a week for four consecutive weeks on eleven stations from March 8 to July 18, 1994.[183] Cassette tapes of the series were also sent out to community stations in country towns that had no local community radio stations.[184] Resource persons used in for the programs included Filipino lawyers and community and welfare workers.

Ngayong Aussie Ka na, Manay! aspired to empower women listeners by encouraging them to assert themselves—a project that required them to transcend Filipino cultural constructions of the feminine that expected women to accept their suffering without complaint.[185] For example, in the episode on "cross-cultural marriage," a dramatic scene was reenacted where the Australian husband criticized his Filipina wife for cooking Filipino food, disapproved of her sending money to relatives in the Philippines, and told her that she was no longer allowed to socialize with "noisy Filipinas."[186] Psychologist Rogelia Pe-Pua, one of the program's resource persons, advised Filipina wives to learn how to assert themselves and explain cultural differences.[187] When the topic of domestic violence was introduced in episode 3, the audience was reminded that if they found themselves in this situation they should not endure it ("hindi ka kailangang magtiis").[188]

Filipina activists who were employed as settlement officers, migrant workers, social workers, or community welfare workers also conducted information seminars and workshops through the Migrant Resource Centres. These had a huge impact on attendees, some of whom only realized after attending that they were victims of psychological abuse.[189] The radio package and the workshops also encouraged women to reject the traditional ideals of the suffering wife. Thus, they were radical in the sense that they advised Filipino women to break away from their gender socialization as obedient wives and encouraged them to become strong, assertive women.[190]

The FWWP also aimed to change Australian perceptions of Filipina women by producing a "media kit" that would serve as a manual for community workers who were interviewed by the local media on topics involving Filipino marriage migration. Entitled *Dealing with the Media: Filipino Women in Cross Cultural Marriages; A Training Course Manual for Community Workers*, the "kit," funded by the Ethnic Affairs Commission of New South Wales, not only critically analyzed representations of Filipinas in print and television, it also placed Filipino women in their cultural and historical context of migration to Australia and gave practical advice on how to handle the media including "dos" and "don'ts."[191] In fact, it was so successful that it was adopted as a textbook in a class for undergraduate students at the University of Technology Sydney.[192] Royalties from the sales of the book funded a Philippine visit of Australian legislative council member Meredith Burgmann as part of the CPCA-led campaign against the sexual trafficking of Filipino women in 1995, illustrating the FWWP's transformation from a grant-receiving body to an organization capable of funding its projects.[193] This was quite a remarkable achievement.

The FWWP had its heyday in the mid-1990s at the time of its legislative victories. This time period also coincided with the peak time for cases of Filipinas reporting domestic violence.[194] By the end of the twentieth century FWWP had deregistered as an organization, but it occasionally sponsors activities such as inviting two speakers (descendants of Filipino pearl divers) from Broome to talk about the Liquefied National Gas (LNG) Precinct Development scheme.[195] The CPCA continues to raise issues relevant to the Filipino community in Australia.[196]

Eventually some of the core activists moved on to other issues that were transethnic rather than Filipino-centered. Chat Ramilo returned to the Philippines and began a new career working for an international organization.[197] In 1991 Debbie Wall became interested in issues that affected Aboriginal Australians, joining the Redfern Residents for Reconciliation, the Action for World Development (AWD), and the Women's Reconciliation Network.[198] In 1998 Melba Marginson became founding chairperson of the Victorian Immigrant and Refugee Women's Coalition. Her portfolio changed from advocacy for Filipino women to representing the needs of immigrant and refugee women from all over the world. In 2005 Estrella McKinnon lobbied to change the name of the Filipino Women's Group she founded in Wollongong to the Illawarra Filipino and Multicultural Women's Group Inc., to be more inclusive of migrants from Thailand, Vietnam, and Malaysia, in particular.[199] The name change was not just a political move since the organization adopted English as the lingua franca (instead of Filipino/Tagalog) even though 90 percent of its members were Filipino.[200] The organization has been very active, growing to a membership of three hundred and winning a major big government grant of A$300,000 enabling them to hire a full-time community worker and publish a book giving advice to new migrants on how to adapt to the Australian lifestyle.[201]

This core group of Filipina activists also received recognition from the Australian government, which awarded them with various honors: Deborah Ruiz Wall received an Order of Australia Medal in the 2004 Australia Day Honors list "for services to the community in the areas of Social Justice, Reconciliation and Multiculturalism."[202] McKinnon's slew of awards included the Law and Justice Award from the minister of women "in recognition of [her] outstanding achievements and contribution to [her] community" in 2010,[203] a University of Wollongong Vice-Chancellor's Award, and a New South Wales Premier's Award for her contribution to the prevention of domestic violence.[204] Marginson was appointed by the Victorian premier Steve Bracks as the first new commissioner of the Victorian Multicultural Commission in 2000 (serving for five years). She was the inaugural inductee into the Victorian Womens' Honor Roll and named one of the "100 women of influence" in Australia by Westpac bank and the Australian Financial Review in November 2014.[205] Joan Dicka was nominated for the 2009 South Australian Women's Honor Roll "for her role in disclosing abuses of Human Rights within cross-cultural relationships in the 1980s."[206]

Filipino women who were victims of abuse were empowered: they received information on how and where to seek help; survivors processed their trauma through finding their voice and performing in plays where they told their stories. In Joan Dicka's personal papers I discovered one statement and two letters written by three different survivors to the Department of Immigration and Citizenship and the Women's Shelter in Adelaide naming their husbands as abusers and imploring these agencies to do all that was possible to prevent the men from sponsoring more Filipina women as brides.[207] One of the statements declared that she was the seventh wife.[208] The sheer act of "writing upwards" whether or not they were coached by a Filipina activist, shows that they were no longer silenced victims but strong assertive survivors acting to prevent further abuse.[209] Others formed their own organizations for emotional and social support, running workshops and activities funded by grants they won from the Australian government. For example, the Illawarra Filipino Women's Group Incorporated ran a workshop series for Filipino women and their families funded by the Ethnic Affairs Commission of New South Wales from their 1997 community grants program and produced a profile of the Filipino community in Wollongong, Shellharbour, and Kiama funded by Planning New South Wales and supported by the local councils of the three areas.[210] The Australian Philippine association Illawarra Welfare Service produced a survey of Filipino youth in the area by Estrella McKinnon in her capacity as community settlement services scheme worker funded by the Department of Immigration, Multicultural and Indigenous Affairs (DIMIA) in 2004.[211]

A comparison of these two case studies presents rich insights for migration scholars and activists and shows the potential for ethnic collaboration with the host country's governments. First, none of the organizations I discuss were large Filipino community organizations. Perhaps by coincidence, the leaders were all highly educated middle-class women with relevant professional qualifications. The leadership also worked very closely with the host government. The deliberate strategy to use the language of human rights/citizenship rights was also very appropriate in that particular historical time where the context of the civil rights movement in the United States and the shift in policies toward migrants and multiculturalism in Australia meant that these states were open to advocacy for specific issues affecting ethnic groups. The funding received by these groups from the governments of their host countries was absolutely essential in explaining the success they achieved. And finally, the tenacity of the activists themselves revealed the necessary level of passion, dedication, and commitment (and bravery in the case of the Australian example) required to first make the issues visible to the dominant white society and then to motivate legislators and educators to act accordingly. The similarities will be discussed in detail below, demonstrating that advocates for issues as disparate as the youth and women marriage migrants have similar experiences and thus can possibly provide insights for future advocacy for a further myriad motley of issues.

The advocates discussed in the case studies for this chapter each composed a tiny group in terms of members. Operation Manong was administered by four people: Amy Agbayani, Melinda Kerkvliet, Sheila Forman, and later by Clem Bautista. Likewise, the active members of the FWWP were Debbie Wall, Della Ipong, Estrella McKinnon, the late Dolly Bates, Ning Alejo, and Emilie Rapinsky.[212] Among the most active personnel in the CPCA working on the issue of domestic violence were Melba Marginson and Dee Hunt. Joan Dicka was described by her political connections in Adelaide as an institution on her own.[213] They trusted the legal and political systems of Hawaii and Australia and lobbied parliamentarians, government bureaucracies, NGOs, and the media in order to reach their goals. They succeeded in getting their issues placed in the agendas for discussion and were able to get funding from the government bureaucracy for their initiatives. More important, they were able to find allies in the government bureaucracy and worked with them to ensure that their voices would be heard. OM had to continue to apply for funding from the state every year and the Filipina advocates in Australia wrote copious submissions to the race discrimination commissioner, to the Department of Immigration, and to the Ethnic Affairs Commission.

This handful of advocates were relentless and persistent in putting up grant and proposal submissions, devoting a lot of their time and energies to their campaigns. They were a unique coterie of assertive, feisty, strong, and tough women. Amy, Melinda and Sheila were called "the super-manangs," an invented term that combined the popular comic book hero Superman with the Ilocano language's term of respect for women.[214] These women were not shrinking violets. Amy Agbayani confided in an interview: "We were seen as very, very aggressive."[215] Filipina Australian welfare workers who rescued domestic violence victims had to brave the wrath of the victims' husbands who went to their homes and offices looking for "the bloody Filipina welfare worker" who facilitated their wives' escape.[216] Estrella McKinnon could not go from her office to the parking lot without a chaperone and had to hide under the table in her office when an irate husband stormed into the Migrant Resource Centre looking for her because he did not know the whereabouts of his wife who had been secretly taken to a women's refuge center.[217] One man broke into Joan Dicka's home when she was not there and stole her citizenship papers and her diploma. Dicka's husband and son were threatened, and even the neighbors received unwanted visits and phone calls by husbands of her clients.[218] Della Ipong was accosted by the furious husband of one Filipina woman who barged into in her office confronting her with: "Where is my wife? What did you do to her?"[219] Incidents such as these have happened more than once, prompting Ipong to admit: "Our work can be dangerous because we are dealing with angry men."[220]

It is worth mentioning that none of the advocates I discuss here were representing a Filipino community organization. This made applying for funding a challenge since in places like Australia during the 1970s and 1980s, governments usually preferred to give funding to the ethnic communities.[221] According to Rosa Droescher, who eventually became director of policy at the EAC, the availability of funding for non-English-speaking background groups was exceptional in the 1980s and 1990s, a fact not duplicated in later years.[222] In Australia, the practice was for the ethnic groups to approach the EAC with their issues.[223] Relationships between the Australian bureaucracy and the Filipina advocates, particularly those affiliated with the Migrant Resource Centres, were symbiotic: the Ethnic Affairs Commission did not have the legitimacy to speak on behalf of the Filipina community, so they needed those in the ethnic community, and the Filipinos needed the help of the bureaucracy to initiate legal change and to fund their projects.[224] According to Debbie Wall, "without the Ethnic Affairs Commission and the facilitation of the other agencies [such as the Migrant Resource Centres, for example], the FWWP would not have been founded and our work would have been in limbo."[225] This underscored that the time period provided a small window of opportunity and advocates had been able to have their voices heard.

One reason they had the ear of the government bureaucracies was that the advocates used human rights discourse, and this found resonance in the government chambers. OM reminded the public that everyone had the civil right to education, and Filipina advocates in Australia argued that women had the right to consent to a marriage, and they had the right to safety.[226] Melba Marginson took up the issue with the human rights commissioner Irene Moss.[227] Chat Ramilo confided that the use of the word 'overrepresented' as victims of violence and homicide immediately caught the attention of the EAC.[228] Both Justice Elizabeth Evatt and Sue Zelinka, speaking on behalf of the race discrimination commissioner Irene Moss in 1992, acknowledged that it was Australia's obligation to prevent and deal with the abuse and exploitation.[229] The concept that governments had a "duty of care" for the migrants they welcomed into their country was a very powerful narrative used by activists to gain empathy for their cause.[230] Even the survivors appropriated the vocabulary of rights. The final song in the Buklod play was entitled "Fight for Our Rights." Sung to the tune of "Blowing in the Wind," with lyrics written by the survivors of domestic violence, it asked a series of questions all answered by the refrain: "The answer my friends: We fight for our rights!"[231] Presenting their cases in the context of a fight for human rights received the attention and support of civil rights politicians in Hawaii and the Human Rights Commission in Australia.

I do not want to romanticize the alliance between the advocates and the government bureaucracies and parliamentarians of the host countries, but the personal and professional relationships that developed were crucial in facilitating the process of reform. Some of the personal ties were genuine and enduring. When I interviewed Rosa Droescher, she was a houseguest of Deborah Wall, since she was visiting Australia from Spain where she had moved after retirement. Amy Agbayani gave me a lift home on the way to attending a fund-raiser for Governor Neil Abercrombie in Waikiki.

The advantage of the small number of advocates was that there was little disunity within OM and the FWWP. The rifts occurred from within the Filipino community because some Filipinos did not want to be associated with the issue of "mail-order brides" and blamed the advocates for calling attention to what they saw as a source of great shame and embarrassment.[232] The Filipino community produced ambivalent responses to the issue, either blaming or pitying the victims.[233] Some members of the Filipino community accused Joan Dicka and Della Ipong of "airing Filipino dirty linen" or "shrimp paste" in the Australian media and therefore "painting a negative picture of our community."[234] In addition, members of the Filipino community were afraid that the Australian government would prevent Filipinos from migrating to Australia because of the problem.[235] Thus, from the very beginning the FWWP knew that it could not approach Filipino organizations for help.[236] In Hawaii, OM found itself servicing two types of Filipino communities often in conflict—the local-born and the new immigrants.

This chapter demonstrates that a handful of Filipino first-generation migrants can alter legislation in the host country or launch affirmative action initiatives. In illustrating the fruitful ways that migrants have been able to work jointly with the government bureaucracies of their host countries, it sets a powerful and optimistic precedent for the possibilities of migrant collaborations with the states of their host countries. Finally, it documents the way policies and university affirmative action initiatives can be changed from below—by an ethnic minority viewed as marginal or peripheral—proving that they can be at the very center of legislative and affirmative action history in Australia and Hawaii.

CHAPTER 7

Migrants and the Homeland, 1986–2018

On November 8, 2013, Typhoon Yolanda (international name Haiyan) completely devastated the town of Tacloban, Leyte, in central Philippines. It was the strongest typhoon to make landfall in recent history, resulting in more than six thousand deaths and inflicting damage on a million homes.[1] As soon as the magnitude of the disaster hit international television screens, Filipinos all over the world immediately mobilized their resources and their contacts to raise funds, collect relief goods, and send the much-needed aid to the area. All types of fundraising activities mushroomed—from selling tickets for culinary delights in Filipino restaurants in San Francisco to singing in the subways of Seoul, South Korea—to elicit donations. The response to this need to rescue the homeland in crisis was astonishing in its magnitude and generosity. Without even soliciting for aid, the Filipino Channel (TFC) received US$5 million from Filipina/o/x Americans in less than three months.[2] Filipino exchange students in Korea raised ₱32 million.[3] The relatively small organization of the Philippine Australian Medical Association (PAMA) raised A$23,000 and launched a special medical mission for Yolanda victims.[4] In just one week after the typhoon hit, Filipina/o/x Americans donated US$3 million. Filipina/o/x Americans under the banner of "Miami Heat" gave US$1 million.[5] The Commission on Filipinos Overseas (CFO) received a grand total (as of July 25, 2014) of ₱200 million from about thirty individuals and organizations donating from the Filipino diaspora.[6] The above account documents only the tip of the massive philanthropic campaign for Typhoon Yolanda victims by the Filipino diaspora, but it encapsulates the spirit of transnational giving that this group has been performing consistently, especially since the 1970s and 1980s. A history of philanthropic engagement with the Philippines underscores the deep connections Filipino migrants and their descendants have with the homeland.

Filipino migrants and their descendants (this includes the first, second, and third generations) have committed to philanthropic projects aimed at improving the lives of underprivileged groups in the Philippines. Filipinos abroad have invested an enormous amount of time and resources to these ventures. The homeland has been imagined as a developing country in need of rescue in times of natural disasters, a site where poverty is ubiquitous and where the state has been unable to help the poorest people access education, housing, and health care. As the migration experience gave them some distance from the homeland, it has provided them new insights, and armed with these novel perspectives they have been inspired to transform the homeland into the country they would like it to become. This action has been incredibly empowering, revealing that migrants do not see themselves as marginal persons at least in their relationship with their homeland.

This chapter examines the Filipino migrants' project of working toward social change in the Philippines from about the 1980s to 2015. It argues that Filipino migrants and their descendants committed to joint projects with Filipino partners based in the Philippines to address the needs of the poor and underprivileged sectors of society. I use the word "committed" deliberately because the projects were usually long-term ones and migrants invested an enormous amount of time and financial resources year after year. I will be focusing here on two types of diasporic philanthropic activities: fundraising for specific causes/underprivileged sectors of society and medical missions (which also inevitably involve fundraising in cash and kind). Both activities required transnational partners in the Philippines. Medical missions involved annual visits to the Philippines by medical teams of Filipino health professionals and their allies who, together with their Filipino-based doctors, nurses, and volunteers, provided free health care to the underprivileged in one particular rural or remote area for one week each year. In 2014, there were about fifty groups, mostly from the United States, that worked with the Commission on Filipinos Overseas (CFO) who sent medical missions to the Philippines.[7] This did not include the missions like the Australian medical ones that organized the trips independently of the CFO. (The Commission on Filipinos Overseas is the organization created in 1980 to serve overseas Filipinos who are permanent residents or citizens of other countries or who are migrants for marriage.)[8]

The long-term commitment of energy and capital (by donors and volunteers who continued their work year after year) testifies to the Filipino migrants' determination to change the social situation in the Philippines even though they were no longer living there. The Philippine Medical Society of Northern California (PMSNC), which has been sending medical missions to the Philippines since 1986, advertised on its website that "we are strongly committed to assisting the indigents who have little or no access to medical care in the Philippines."[9] Although the discourse of giving was articulated as the individual's way of "giving back" to the motherland, in practice these benefactors were actually doing the job of the politicians, and armed with their vision of what their homeland should become, they began the project of changing one hometown at a time. Although the migrants I discuss were permanent residents of the United States and Australia, the data here could also apply to temporary migrants or overseas contract workers who were also active in philanthropic projects, currently still an underresearched topic.

My time line begins in 1986 and continues to circa 2015. This period coincided with the end of martial law in the Philippines. The success of the "People Power Revolution" in removing a dictatorship through peaceful methods buoyed Filipino ethnic pride at home and abroad and inspired many to participate in rebuilding a nation and restoring democratic institutions. Donating money to charitable work in the Philippines carried with it concerns about whether the money would actually go to the needy and not be siphoned off by corrupt politicians/agents, but the immediate post-Marcos era was a time of great hope, inspiring many to help rebuild a nation recovering from the trauma of authoritarian rule. While Filipino migrants had been generous philanthropists before the 1980s, their donations were often sporadic, occurring in response to particular calamities or natural disasters. I am interested only in examining the interactions with the homeland that are outside the political sphere. The anti-Marcos struggle and the campaign for the overseas suffrage law and dual citizenship lie beyond the scope of this chapter.[10]

Scholars have only just begun to document the scope and impact of Filipino migrant philanthropic work.[11] This is remarkable given that, to quote Joyce Mariano, "support for philanthropic projects by Filipinos in the United States to the Philippines is an integral aspect of their identities as migrants."[12] The pioneering work on the topic has tended to link "diaspora philanthropy" with Philippine migration and development initiatives interested in examining the ways remittances, donations, or investments can be marshaled toward "developing" the Philippine economy.[13] The Commission on Filipinos Overseas (CFO), the Philippine government body whose portfolio is Filipino permanent migration overseas, has developed several initiatives designed to tap the potential for philanthropic work of its migrant cohort, including the Linkapil (Lingkod sa Kapwa Pilipino, which on its website is translated as Link for Philippine Development) with a focus on health and welfare, education, community building, and livelihood. The CFO and the Department of Foreign Affairs award prizes to "Filipino individuals and organizations overseas who have contributed materially—or in the form of selfless programs and endeavors—to our country's relief, rehabilitation, and development programs," including a Linkapil award.[14] Jeremiah Opiniano has compiled a list of philanthropic groups, including seventy hometown organizations in Hong Kong, alerting readers to what he saw as a potential entry point for civil society groups to work with migrant benefactors. He disclosed that Filipina/o/x Americans were the biggest donors, probably a reflection of their numerical clout but also that both temporary migrants (or overseas contract workers) and permanent residents of host countries outside the Philippines were all generous and proactive in charitable projects designed to assist their hometown, rebuild communities who suffered natural disasters, or simply to help improve the livelihood or health of rural Filipinos.[15] Shirlita Espinosa, writing on Filipino Australian diasporic philanthropy, interpreted the relationship as replicating the North-South, rich-poor, upper class–lower class or poor hierarchy.[16] This perspective sees migrant Filipinos in the privileged position of material donors, with the exchange moving in one direction—from the overseas-based Filipino to the Philippine-based recipient.

This chapter departs from the earlier scholarship because it views philanthropic endeavors as *joint* activities in which both Filipino migrants and Filipinos at home work together as partners (although unequal in the area of financial capital) in the project of addressing the problems of the underprivileged in the country. In interviews with Filipina Australian doctors who organized medical missions to the Philippines, they refer to their colleagues in the Philippines as "partners" in their annual projects.[17] Commission on Filipinos Overseas project officers likewise viewed the overseas medical team as "partners in development," because, as they explained, "we don't want them to think that they are like milking cows."[18] Filipino migrants' attempts to fashion the homeland involved the fostering of transnational relationships between expatriate Filipinos and volunteers based in the Philippines. Overseas philanthropic organizations relied on these Philippine-based partners who fulfilled a crucial role in the home territory. In this sense, the descriptive term "diasporic philanthropy" is problematic because it privileges the overseas actors and does not accurately capture the transnational partnership needed to carry out the project's goals.

I will be focusing on the overseas end of this partnership between Filipino volunteers separated by geographical space. I have chosen two types of philanthropic projects from two different countries. My choice was guided by my desire to showcase the unique projects that migrants from different parts of the world designed to address what they perceive to be the needs of the country they left behind and also to by the availability of archival material and personnel to interview. My preference was also for organizations that had a track record rather than those that mushroomed sporadically in knee-jerk response to natural disasters such as Typhoon Haiyan described earlier. In keeping with my focus on the migrant as agent of change, I wanted to study two organizations closely in order to be able to observe the impact of their philanthropy. In the end, I chose one organization in San Francisco that was dedicated to street children and one organization in Sydney, Australia, that was involved in medical missions. With three million Filipinos in the United States, most of whom occupy the middle and professional classes (see chapter 5 on the statistics of those with college degrees there) and who send the largest amount of yearly remittances, it is not surprising that they would also be major players in diasporic philanthropy. Australia's relatively closer location to the Philippines and what historian Anne O'Brien has called "the philanthropic disposition" also makes it an ideal choice for a case study on medical missions.[19] I live in Sydney and have ties with the Filipino community there. The philanthropists that founded and participated in these charitable projects came from the middle and upper classes of the United States and Australia. Medical missions required the proactive leadership and participation of doctors, nurses, and medical professionals, so by necessity, these actors were all highly educated Filipinos from the many waves of the post-1970s migration in the United States and Australia.

The physical distance presented a major challenge for donors who could not perform the civic work in poor communities for more than a few days/weeks during the year. One solution was for the overseas parties to act as fundraisers for a target group of NGOs. This did not mean, however, that the fundraisers had no control over the money raised. Philippine International Aid (PIA), discussed here, was not merely a money-raising machine. PIA was responsible for setting out the terms, agenda, and vision for its projects. NGOs who wished to avail of the funds were required to submit proposals to the board that decided which individual projects to support. PIA's chairperson conducted annual visits to the beneficiaries to ensure things were going well. All recipients needed to submit regular reports to the PIA board. Clearly, however, the organizations based in the Philippines did all the day-to-day charitable work. Although the primary role of the organization was fundraising, the philanthropic activity fostered personal connections between the donor and the recipient, between the PIA board and the NGO in the Philippines, and in the case of PIA, between the sponsor and the child who received a scholarship.

Medical missions were heavily dependent on the partnership with Philippine-based volunteers. Medicines had to be sent to a site, a makeshift hospital or area for consulting rooms had to be found and booked, accommodations needed to be made for the visiting medics, and patients had to be informed that a team was visiting. The overseas team was only going to spend one week in the Philippines, but the mere seven days required the logistical support of a team of Philippine-based medical staff.

Sources for this chapter include archival materials from Philippine International Aid (based in San Francisco), materials from medical missions from Australia, launched by the Philippine Australian Medical Association (PAMA), including a DVD short film of its sixth medical mission to Sasmuan, Pampanga, in 2013, a documentary film about the medical mission conducted by the Philippine Medical Society of Northern California (PMSNC) in 2003 entitled *Bloodlines*, and YouTube videos of its medical missions from 2010, 2011, 2012, and 2013 posted in its official website, memoirs from the "migrant archives," and interviews. The PIA was chosen as a case study because it is an organization that had been around for more than thirty years (at the time of this writing) and has a policy of transparency—publishing its revenues and beneficiaries. The organization has also given me permission to use its private archives in San Francisco. Archival materials from the PIA included the complete set of their newsletters from 1986 to 2013, applications and project proposals from NGOs requesting funds, minutes of the PIA board meetings, yearly financial statements, report cards from the scholarship beneficiaries in the Philippines, the PIA website, and letters from the children who were sponsored. I consulted issues of the monthly *Filipinas* magazine (1992–2010), the Filipino American cultural periodical that published advertisements for PIA. In addition, I conducted interviews with the PIA founder, two PAMA doctors, and two CFO project officers. I also attended the annual fundraising event run by the PIA in San Francisco in November 2014 and a fundraising event for a medical mission conducted by Filipina/o/x Australians in 2006.

Fundraising: Philippine International Aid

Philippine International Aid (PIA) was founded in April 1986 by a group of former classmates and coworkers from Manila who were residing in various cities in the United States.[20] The timing of its birth was significant—it was formed right after a popular revolt restored democratic institutions to the

Philippines after fifteen years of authoritarian rule under President Ferdinand Marcos. According to PIA chairperson Mona Lisa Yuchengco (formerly Abaya):

> This organization was the outgrowth of a shared belief that in order to preserve democracy in their Motherland, efforts must be made to uplift the social and economic situation faced by the majority of their countrymen. Although our efforts may seem miniscule compared to the enormous imbalances in our country today, we hope that whatever ripples we cause, may in turn, create a tidal wave of support, and lessen to that extent the work of the authorities and the Church, and even save a few lives. . . . The Philippines still has a long way to go in improving the living conditions of its people. As such, we shall continue to assist our less fortunate brothers by putting in more involvement and commitment.[21]

The success of the popular revolt in ousting a dictatorship promoted an enormous pride in "being Filipino," and the founders of PIA hoped to exercise their very own "people power" through philanthropic work.

In 1986, PIA published a set of guidelines for selecting beneficiaries. Nonprofit organizations could apply for a maximum grant of US$20,000 for local projects preferably with a livelihood or self-help platform.[22] A year later (1987), PIA decided to specialize in assisting the disadvantaged, abused, and malnourished children of the Philippines. The change in focus was reflected in the organization's name change to PIA–The Children's Fund.[23] Although it promised to continue supporting health care and feeding programs, it was going to dedicate itself primarily to the "rehabilitation of child prostitutes and street children" by giving scholarship grants for one hundred street children and sexually abused children.[24] Brandishing the slogan "Off the Streets—Off to School," PIA's scholarship program was initially administered by Caritas Manila under the supervision of Sister Myrna Tacardon, whose mission was working with child prostitutes. The children targeted by PIA were between the ages of two and fifteen years old. PIA's plan of action was to find a pool of donors willing to sponsor a child's education for one year (US$150), which would cover the child's tuition, clothes, transportation money, meal allowances, school supplies, and social workers to work with the child.[25] The donors were bestowed the honorific title of *ninong* or *ninang* (Tagalog for "godfather," or ritual godparent), a deliberate strategy by PIA: "very important because beyond money for school, the street children in our program needed to know that somewhere out there, there were people who cared."[26] The children were not chosen on the basis of scholastic achievements but on the child's desire to go to school. The child was required to continue attending school in order qualify for the scholarship.²⁷ PIA chairperson Mona Lisa Yuchengco was also publisher of *Filipinas* from 1992 to 2005, and the magazine ran a number of advertisements inviting its readers to sponsor a child for "only 44 cents a day" (making sponsorship affordable for many Filipina/o/x Americans). PIA also constructed a ritual kinship connection between donor and recipient, with patrons assuming the title of godparent to their sponsored child. Letters written by the children to their sponsors addressed them as *ninong* or *ninang*.²⁸ In creating this ritual kinship, PIA was actually suggesting that the patronage was going to be a long-term commitment since the ritual godparent relationship in Filipino culture was a lifetime relationship. Being a sponsor was not just a one-off donation—it was a long-term obligation in Filipino cultural terms. It connected the donor with someone from the homeland, a bond that was strengthened through correspondence from both ends. The children wrote their sponsors regularly and sent copies of their report cards. Some of the sponsors met with their "child/children" when they spent their vacations in the Philippines, and a number made an effort to attend their godchild's graduation ceremony.²⁹ A photo montage on the PIA homepage showed various sponsors visiting their young scholars in the Philippines, revealing that the relationship was personal and long term.³⁰ Many of them sponsored more than one child.

In its advertisement in *Filipinas*, PIA legitimized its aims with the slogan: "Education Is a Lifetime Gift," upholding the Filipino culture's value for education.³¹ It was also a strategic move, revealing that the organization did not believe in merely giving cash handouts to the poor as a one-off charitable act, proposing instead a long-term project of giving the youth the opportunity to obtain qualifications that would help them escape the cycle of poverty.

In its appeal for donors and sponsors, PIA represented the homeland as a place where "the government has failed in its duty to provide basic services to the poor."³² Statistics were trotted out to illustrate the serious consequences of this neglect. According to the PIA, more than 1.5 million children nationwide were begging in the streets, selling cigarettes, hassling drivers to look after their parked vehicles for a donation coins, or simply idly looking around for something to do but not attending school.³³ Sister Myrna Tacardon of Caritas Manila estimated that there were around 50,000 street children in Metro Manila alone.³⁴ Children under the age of twenty composed 55 percent of the Philippine population, where the mortality rate of children under six years of age was 54 percent.³⁵ Given these statistics PIA estimated that approximately twenty million children lived below the poverty line.³⁶ Some of the street children were abused or were sexually exploited. The PIA newsletter recounted the poignant story of Lilet, a suicidal twelve-year-old, who was only ten years old when she was trafficked for prostitution and beaten by sadistic partners who took her with them to holidays in Boracay, Cebu, and Puerto Azul.[37]

PIA decided to expand its outreach to other disadvantaged children, such as the deaf and hearing impaired, blind and visually impaired, autistic and mentally challenged children, sexually abused and commercially trafficked children, and the indigenous children like the Aetas and the T'bolis.[38] PIA claimed to have helped more than 2,400 children in 2013.[39]

This representation of the children of the homeland as innocent victims in need of rescue was a powerful discourse that touched the hearts of middle-class Filipina/o/x American audiences. At a fundraising event in November 2013, the PIA-produced short documentary about deaf children began with the heartrending words: "Metropolitan Manila, a place where silence is far from golden"; it ended with the success story of a scholar who had graduated and found suitable employment thanking (through sign language) PIA donors for their support.[40] Mona Lisa Yuchengco's speech at that event focused on the plight of the 140,000 deaf or hearing-impaired children in the Philippines who suffered from high levels of unemployment, low self-esteem, and lack of access to basic services. Virtually ignored and socially abandoned, even by their parents who presumed they were "useless," many of the children grew up illiterate and were compelled to survive through scavenging, vending, or doing laundry. Unable to receive an education and ostracized by society, deaf persons in the Philippines had an estimated income of between a dollar and a dollar and a half a day.[41] Hence, these children were condemned to a life of poverty and social exclusion.

PIA's website proclaimed that it served "homeless, orphaned and abandoned children. We find them living in the streets, under bridges and [in] cemeteries, deaf and hearing-impaired children, physically and sexually abused children, children rescued from trafficking rings, at-risk youth, young victims of typhoons and calamities, disadvantaged children eager to go to school, indigenous children like the Aetas, small NGOs like the Good Shepherd Convent and Mindanao Child Alert that take in orphaned, abandoned and abused children."[42] Ken Kashiwara, speaking on behalf of PIA in the organization's official YouTube advertisement, argued that the children had the right to an education.[43] By framing the advocacy in terms of "human rights," PIA called attention to the Philippine state's failure to attend to its most vulnerable citizens and offered Filipina/o/x Americans the opportunity to take on the role of patron or godparent, protector, and provider for those who have been deprived of their basic human rights.

PIA needed to have Philippine partners in order to carry out the day-to-day administration of the scholarships and to work with parents, teachers, and counselors. In its early years PIA's main partner was Caritas Manila, a nonprofit Catholic organization. In 1986 PIA established a rehabilitation center for child prostitutes. The Catholic nuns administered the scholarship for the youth. Caritas Manila had a Sagip Moral (Save Morality) program, "which provides alternatives to street children, thus keeping them away from the streets and the paths to child prostitution" through teaching the children "how to play games, make friends, discover their self-worth and relate positively to adults—guiding them back onto the childhood that they had been deprived of by their street existence."[44] The plan was to use the PIA scholarships to teach these children basic reading, writing and math skills. Eventually a PIA Manila office was established in 1987 by one of its board members, Robert Lopez, who shared the local administration of the sponsored children with Caritas Manila.[45] The Manila office was named Phil-Asia Assistance Foundation Inc., or PAAFI, which continues to be a PIA partner.[46] In addition, PIA worked with several NGO partners (the official website claims there are seventeen) based in the Philippines who focused on helping underprivileged children.[47] PIA chair Mona Lisa Yuchengco visited the NGO partners during her trips to the Philippines. When one visit proved that there were no children on the site, she recommended that the funding to that organization be terminated.[48] Since PIA prided itself for its transparency, assuring donors that their donations went directly to benefit struggling children, the NGO partner beneficiaries had to be credible organizations run by ethical volunteers. Given this concern, it was not surprising that a number of PIA's NGO partners were organizations founded and run by nuns or priests and social workers.[49] Some of these included the PREDA Foundation led by Father Shay Cullen, an organization that rescued children from sex trafficking or from illegal detention, Katilingban Para sa Kalambuan Inc. in Zamboanga City, an organization that helped victims and survivors of child trafficking by giving scholarships to children to attend high school, the Good Shepherd Sisters, Iligan Community, who funded the education of the children of prisoners, and Dangpanan, a temporary shelter for street girls in Cebu, that was jointly administered by the Reverend Faustino Paglinawan, the parish priest, and Sister Mary Marcia Antigua.[50]

On PIA's 2014 website a separate link separated the category "Filipinos" from that of "Filipino Americans." The Philippines was described as a country that ranked in the lowest 10 percent of countries on spending as a percentage of GDP, where 5.5 million school-age children worked to supplement the family income, making it difficult for them to complete their schooling. On the other hand, the category "Filipino Americans" was represented as having the second highest household income among Asian Americans and fourth in the lower half on college achievement. Hence as a group "they have great potential to take the lead in raising awareness and combating poverty in the Philippines."[51]

The PIA's major role was to be a fundraiser for its partners in the Philippines and in the San Francisco Bay area. I had the enormous privilege of participating in the annual fundraising luncheon for the PIA foundation held on Sunday, November 17, 2013, at the Hyatt Regency Hotel at Embarcadero in San Francisco. The event was a haute couture fashion show entitled "Holiday Haute Couture 12," featuring the Filipiniana clothing designs of Barge Ramos, who had been flown from the Philippines precisely for this fundraising show. Although the official part of the program did not start until lunch was served at noon, participants started arriving from ten o'clock in the morning to purchase items in a special bazaar composed of several stalls selling Filipiniana goods just outside the entrance of the hotel ballroom. ABS-CBN had its own stall promoting the Filipino Channel (TFC), and Philippine Airlines (a major sponsor of the event, donating business-class tickets for the auction, as well as airfare and excess baggage composed of the designer wear)[52] displayed its special airfare packages. Next to the bazaar was a room full of products and services donated by various individuals, hotels, and businesses that were available for a silent auction. At noon, everyone entered the ballroom where lunch was served. Although it was a cool November in San Francisco, some men were wearing barong tagalogs. The official program began right after the first course was served. Two emcees, Lloyd LaCuesta and Dianne Dwyer, welcomed the guests and introduced PIA chairperson Mona Lisa Yuchengco, who addressed the assembly with a speech summarizing the achievements of the organization and showcasing the impressive record of children sponsored who graduated from high school and university and who succeeded in gaining employment afterward. This was followed by the screening of a documentary of one of PIA's stellar missions—the education of deaf children. The touching video focused on the children's success stories told through their counselors and teachers.

After the video presentation, a Filipino American Wells Fargo executive congratulated the recipients of the PIA–Wells Fargo university scholarships for Filipina/o/x American youth. In 2010 PIA started to give scholarships to Filipina/o/x American youths to cover tuition fees, enabling them to attend various US universities. The primary donor was Wells Fargo Bank due to the support from a number of Filipina/o/x Americans who held executive positions in that company. The accomplishments of the previous year's winners were announced in a little PowerPoint presentation, paying particular attention to their grade point averages and their success in obtaining professional employment. PIA's decision to give scholarships to its own community was a response to criticism by some Filipina/o/x Americans that the organization should help the lesser privileged in its own communities in the United States and not just poor Filipinos in the homeland.⁵³ This was significant because it revealed that Filipina/o/x Americans admitted that their own community in the United State needed assistance. In this sense, they were breaking away from the belief that everyone in the United States was better off than those in the Philippines. It also revealed that the community was rethinking itself as not just an affluent middle-class group that was the wealthy benefactor to the poor of the "third world" Philippines. The PIA website called attention to statistics illustrating that Filipinos were underrepresented in American college enrollments and were a priority group for admissions at the University of California.⁵⁴ Thus, "while the needs children in the Philippines are very clear, especially to those who travel regularly, many Filipinos now firmly consider the US home and want to help there as well."⁵⁵ The PIA–Wells Fargo college scholarships (administered by PIA partner Asia Pacific Fund) were one attempt to help improve the profile of Filipina/o/x Americans attending tertiary schools in California. By 2014 PIA had distributed US$24,000 in scholarships for low-income Bay Area students of Filipino heritage for their college education (sponsored by Wells Fargo Bank) and disbursed US$38,000 to support Filipina/o/x American initiatives "covering cultural immersion, gang prevention, mental health education and technology training for veterans."⁵⁶

While technically the fashion show was meant to be the climax of the program, it was the public auction of eight lots that was the most anticipated segment, judging by the comments made by my informants and the sudden buzz followed by the hushed silence that enveloped the ballroom when the auctioneers took their places and the goods to be auctioned were flashed on the big screen. Suddenly the audience was drawn into a frenzied bidding for several holiday packages, Philippine Airlines business-class airfares to the Philippines that went for US$6,500, five hours of sailing around San Francisco that went for US$500, and even a dinner with the mayor of San Francisco, donated by the mayor's office. Handled by two Filipino American professional auctioneers, the feverish bidding elicited lots of cheering and laughter, particularly when emcee Lloyd LaCuesta (Mona Lisa Yuchengco's husband), carried away by the spirit of the moment, volunteered to auction literally the shirt off his back—the barong tagalog he wore, which had been designed by the event's featured designer Barge Ramos. His barong tagalog was quickly snapped up for US$600. LaCuesta offered to dry-clean the shirt before handing it over, but I noticed the winner proudly showing off his purchase to everybody as he left the ballroom, obviously not bothered at all by the fact that it was an unwashed secondhand article of clothing. While the bidding was all in good fun, the public auction could also be interpreted as a display of status in the Filipina/o/x American community. Seated at the table sponsored by the Filipina Women's Network, the premier organization of successful professional Filipina Americans, I could see that the gathering included the crème de la crème of Filipina/o/x American society in the San Francisco Bay Area. The guests included: the publisher of *Filipinas* (from 2005) Greg Macabenta; celebrities such as Joan Almedilla, who played Kim in the Broadway hit *Miss Saigon*, who sang a couple of songs; high-ranking executives from Wells Fargo Bank; and former civil rights activists including Emil de Guzman and his wife. The enthusiastic response to the bidding could be linked to individuals' aspirations for status in the community, as well as their genuine desire to become philanthropists.

The climax of the fundraising event was the fashion show. The models for the clothes were children of Filipina/o/x Americans in the audience. Children as young as four or five strutted the catwalk attired in contemporary haute couture barong tagalogs, and teenage girls pirouetted gracefully to show off the sleek line of the *ternos*. The event, held in one of San Francisco's exclusive hotels, was a huge departure from the usual run-of-the-mill beauty contests that were the trademark of Filipino diasporic events around the world.[57] Then, when the parade of couture ended, the couturier took his bows and everyone started going home, some carrying the prizes they had successfully won in the silent auction or in the public bid.

Fundraising was not just about the plight of the poor Filipino disadvantaged children but also about the generosity of the donors. The pages of the PIA newsletters regularly listed the names of donors, acknowledging individual patrons for their contribution. The public bidding not only made donors experience the joy in becoming patrons, it also gave them the opportunity to display their status as middle-class Filipina/o/x Americans with sufficient disposable income to make a donation to a credible, established charitable organization. Mona Lisa Yuchengco's speech ended by thanking the donors for their proactive role in giving the deaf children the opportunities to fulfill their dreams through acquiring education. At the conclusion of the fashion show, the name of each and every model that participated in the fashion show was announced and applauded. Although the audience was clearly composed of a majority of first-generation Filipina/o/x Americans who understandably still felt a strong attachment to the homeland, the catwalk models for the fashion show were their children, born in the United States, indicating that the event not only exposed their children to contemporary Filipiniana dress, but it also introduced them to the plight of disadvantaged children in the Philippines. Their involvement marked their initiation into the world of Filipino diasporic philanthropy. Some of these models were only about five or six years old, and the loud cheering they received from the crowd communicated the point that the event was not just about raising money for the Philippines but also about the status of the donors. The majority of the post-1965 migrants were professionals who quickly became part of America's middle classes. The median income for them in 2010 was $51,668, with only 7.3 percent living below the poverty line, and 37.9 percent holding at least a bachelor's degree.[58] The venue and show (haute couture) located it in the realm of middle-class professional Filipinos in the Bay Area of San Francisco, where the majority of the post–1965 professional migrants chose to live. Daly City is considered the "Pinoy capital" of the United States, with Filipinos numbering 32,720, or 32 percent of the total population of 103,621.[59] The day of the fashion show, the ballroom was set up with one hundred tables, each occupied by ten persons. A ticket to the event cost US$100, and there was barely an empty seat in the ballroom, indicating that the event was almost sold out. The fashion show raised a total of US$96,000.[60]

This once-a-year fundraising day required hours and hours of preparation. Tickets had to be sold at US$100 each, sponsors had to be found for the silent auction (which sold all sorts of sundry items from a roast pig, place mats and paintings, to spa treatments and dinners for two at fancy restaurants) and for the main public auction. Places in the bazaar had to be prearranged. The video documentary about the PIA support for the education of deaf children had to be shot in Manila and produced for its premiere presentation on the day of the fundraising. Each year a different couturier had to design and sew all the clothes. Rehearsals had to be scheduled, and amateur models had to be groomed for their day on the catwalk. One would be tempted to ask why would migrants invest so much of their valuable time and money? The hours of human capital devoted to this yearly fundraising event could be compared to the preparations for Pilipino Cultural Nights performed by a young Filipina/o/x American youth at college campuses all over the US West Coast (see chapter 5). Theodore Gonzalves argued convincingly that the Pilipino Culture Night was "itself a kind of sacrament . . . that invents a community against the larger backdrop of a culture that expects nation, ethnicity and identity to be the language of the past."[61] PIA's fundraising events, on the other hand, were important rituals that confirmed migrants' status as patrons vis-à-vis the homeland. This was incredibly important for migrants since the status of benefactor, patron, godfather/godmother legitimized their migration story. In chapter 5 I discussed the importance of the Filipina/o/x American heroic narrative in the migrant's project to alert the Philippines and the host countries to the sacrifices and contributions they had made. The ritual kinship as godparents to Philippine-based scholars placed Filipina/o/x Americans in the role of mentors. This position as benefactor affirmed the triumphant ending of the migrants' heroic narrative. The migrant's sacrifices and struggles have been rewarded with a position as godparent to children in the Philippines. At the same time, this allowed Filipina/o/x Americans to maintain a personal connection to the homeland.

Medical Missions

Medical missions were a more direct in-kind, hands-on form of philanthropic activity. Filipino medical specialists abroad visited the Philippines for one week each year in order to deliver health care and medicines to various underprivileged individuals in towns and villages usually in remote areas located far from the metropole. The sites were chosen because these were the places that did not have easy access to health care. The Filipino doctors and nurses based overseas contributed their own airfares to go to the Philippines, giving up about a week of their holiday time to dedicate to the medical missions. Sometimes the Philippine end succeeded in obtaining free accommodation for the overseas team, but this was not always possible.[62] Most missions ran from about five to seven days.[63]

Running a medical mission was a mammoth task that involved a year of planning, fundraising, and collaboration with a Philippine partner. Each mission was a well-coordinated event involving international organizations, professional associations, and local governments in the Philippines.[64] It was a combined effort between Filipinos overseas and those in the homeland who were united in their aim to provide medical treatment to those who could not afford it. Funds needed to be raised to buy medicines and equipment such as hospital beds and X-ray and EKG machines, and these had to be shipped to the site. Once the team of doctors, nurses, dentists, and volunteers arrived, they set up temporary rooms in school buildings. Patients were informed beforehand when the free medical team would be there, and they arrived by the hundreds. In the short time available, the team tried to see as many patients as possible, referring some of them to local hospitals for surgery when necessary (also paid for by the medical mission). From doing Pap smears to acute dental surgery, eye tests, cataract surgery, and other surgical operations, the medical team worked almost nonstop for a week.

The Philippine Australian Medical Association (PAMA) was founded in Sydney, Australia, in 1992 by Dr. Cora Francisco and a group of forty-one Filipino doctors who immigrated to New South Wales, Australia. Its purpose was to help other recently migrated Filipinos who had received their qualifications in the Philippines study for the Australian Medical Council examinations that would enable them to practice in Australia.[65] The goals of the association were:

1. To promote, maintain and uphold the standards of the medical profession in accordance with current trends.
2. To maintain professional relationships with local, national and international medical organizations.
3. To promote fellowship among its members and encourage the dissemination of knowledge.
4. To undertake charitable activities.[66]

By 2013, the organization had grown to about 140 members, all based in New South Wales.[67] From 1995 to 2006, small ad hoc mini–medical missions were conducted by one or two doctors who funded their trips to the Philippines to give free consultations and medicines. In the early years there were no major fundraising events, but the organization raised modest amounts of money and individual doctors like Francisco sent medicines to her home province of La Union.[68] In 2007 a major fundraising event raised A$17,000, enabling the organization to send its first serious medical mission in partnership with the Ugnayan ng Pahinungod Volunteer Corps, a team of volunteers composed of dentists, doctors, nurses, and surgeons from the University of the Philippines–Philippine General Hospital (UP-PGH).[69] The collaboration was particularly welcome because the PAMA team did not have surgeons.[70]

The first PAMA medical mission went to Polillo, Quezon, in 2008, followed by Gubat, Sorsogon, in 2009, Dumaguete City in 2010, Oroquieta City, Misamis Occidental, in 2011, Aurora and Pagadian City, Zamboanga, and El Nido, Palawan, in 2012, Sasmuan and Lubao, Pampanga, in 2013, Solana and Tuguegarao City, Cagayan, in 2014, and Tanauan, Tolosa, and Palo, Leyte, in 2015, La Union in 2016, and Paracelis, Mountain Province, in 2017.[71] Each mission cost on average about $25,000 a year (this amount did not include the medicines donated by pharmaceutical companies).[72] Around six Filipino doctors (PAMA members) and some nurses and nonmedical volunteers made the yearly trip together with around thirty to forty of their Filipino-based partners.[73] During the week they worked in the Philippines, each doctor saw between fifty and sixty patients daily. Eligible patients who had to be sent to surgery in the Philippine General Hospital (PGH) in Manila also had their hospital and medical expenses covered by PAMA. The usual medical procedures included hundreds of circumcisions, Pap smear tests, dental and eye checkups, including cataract surgery, and major surgeries like thyroidectomies, hysterectomies, cholecystectomies, cheiloplasties, ob-gyn cases, and many others.[74] PAMA was responsible for donating medicines and instruments such as dressings, bandages, operating beds and linens, X-ray and EKG equipment, operating tables, and so on, which it shipped in advance from Australia to the Philippine General Hospital in Manila and various hospitals in the provinces.

The Philippine Medical Society of Northern California (PMSNC) was founded in 1972 "to encourage fellowship and philanthropy amongst Filipino physicians."[75] Since 1986 it sent a team of physicians, dentists, optometrists, nurses, prosthetics, students, and other allied health professionals to a remote area in the Philippines to provide primary care, surgical specialties, ophthalmology, and dentistry. The volunteers, usually physicians, dentists, nurses, and support personnel, including premed students at the University of California at Berkeley, paid for their own airfare, while PMSNC raised funds for the medicines and medical supplies.[76] The presidents of PMSNC were the prominent Filipina/o/x American doctors, many of whom were involved in the Filipina/o/x American community even before they joined PMSNC.[77] The preparation for each year's medical mission included preliminary visits to the Philippines to meet with the local government and organizations in the target community, a huge investment of time and resources for the ten-day trip to the Philippines usually in January.[78] Their official website only advertises information on the most recent medical missions (since 2011) to Sarangani (2011), San Jose, Occidental Mindoro (2012), Tarlac (2014), Bohol (2015, chosen since this town was devastated by Typhoon Haiyan), and Laoag (2016). The statistics provided for this list of missions was only a tip of the iceberg that boasted thirty missions in thirty years.

The 2003 mission to Iloilo was filmed and made into a documentary entitled *Bloodlines*, while several other missions had short film clips available on PMSNC's website. These films provide a rich archive of the experience of the medical missions from the perspective of the volunteers rather than the patients.

The stories of the many patients are poignant tales of personal suffering. Dentist Edward Agyekum, who was part of the PMSNC mission in 2003, said that while dental practice in the United States was usually preventive dentistry, the patients who went to the mission had to be provided with a "very acute type of dental care."[79] Many patients suffered from tooth infections, particularly children who had never seen a dentist before, and dentists like Dr. Milagros Viernes spent most of her time performing tooth extractions and dispensing antibiotics.[80] A documentary of PMSNC's 2003 medical mission entitled *Bloodlines* includes scenes of many women with enormous thyroids and growths in the throat. With half a million Filipinos blinded by cataracts, ophthalmologists focused on removing cataracts and replacing them with clear lenses. Some of these elderly patients were only able to see their grandchildren for the first time when the bandages were removed.[81]

PAMA's Mao de Vera told the touching story of an elderly man in his sixties who was given a pair of nonprescription glasses bought for P200 or A$5.00 in Manila who was ecstatic that he could finally read again.[82] Many children needed surgery for cleft palates. The films documenting the medical missions run by PMSNC show images of many men, women, and children being fitted with artificial limbs, who had serious tumors, who had to have their teeth extracted, or who needed treatment for asthma and severe headaches. *Bloodlines* showed a young girl who was diagnosed with the terminal stages of cancer whose parents were told that the only thing they could do was give her morphine, while another woman with such an enormous growth on her face hoped to have the tumor removed.[83] One dental patient had to bear the trauma of two dentists chiseling out her tooth because the severe abscess that occurred meant that the crown of the tooth had almost disappeared.[84] All these images and stories deliver the powerful message that many poor people in the Philippines had to endure the pain or discomfort of illness because they could not afford to do anything about it. According to one of the dentists in the medical mission, it would have cost an average of three days' salary to have one tooth pulled, and therefore if one had several children, dental treatment was not a priority.[85]

The passion that these volunteers felt about their project was explained by a desire to "give back" to the homeland. According to PAMA regular volunteer Dr. Ophee de Vera, "it is time to give back ... because when you are stable financially, maybe it is time to help your countrymen ... yeah, because it is more like giving back what they have given to me. Like you studied there, you didn't do anything because after we studied, we just got married and then we went somewhere else and you really didn't do much."[86] Her words were echoed by a second-generation Filipino American pediatrician, who said, "The purpose of the medical mission is giving back to the homeland and actually being able to use the skills that you learned throughout the course of your life as a health-care professional and be able to serve the kind of undertreated and underserved of the Philippines. . . . Both my parents are from the Philippines, they were born and raised there and they came here, and that I am giving back means a lot to them."[87] In PAMA's official website the same narrative appeared as the rationale for its first mission. Dr. Grace Maano began her history of PAMA with: "In the spirit of 'giving service back to your own country' . . . the first-ever medical mission from 'down under' was held on April 6–9, 2008 at Polillo Island in Quezon Province, Philippines."[88]

This discourse of "giving back" became the institutionalized explanation for their mission, but the irony was that many of these doctors left the Philippines because that country was unable to give them the opportunities and the salaries that would have allowed them to remain in the homeland. More important than the feeling of "giving back," it was the appreciation they received from grateful patients that appealed to the volunteers who enjoyed the positive feelings generated from making a positive difference in one patient's life.[89] Dr. Cora Francisco confessed that she was motivated to volunteer year after year because of "the smile on their faces when they leave,"[90] and Dr. Ophee de Vera claimed that the patients in the medical missions appreciated them much more than their Australian clients: "It's a different feeling. Here [in Sydney] they are not so grateful. Here, some of them [their patients] are whingeing."[91] In a short YouTube film of the PMSNC 2011 medical mission to Sarangani Province, Governor Josephine Nene Sato's story of one boy who had to have two prosthetic arms captured the emotional experience felt by both the patients and the volunteers: "When he was asked to write something down [as an exercise to test his new limbs] we thought he was going to write his name but he wrote 'Thank you' and that made us all cry here, and that sums up everything that we feel for you [the medical mission]."[92] In the documentary *Bloodlines*, a middle-aged man who was about to have his leg amputated, was singing the Engelbert Humperdinck hit "Please Release Me, Let Me Go," which put the entire medical team at ease.[93] Dr. Paul Espinas enjoyed the work because he was able to devote 100 percent of his time to the patients unlike his practice in the United States, where he was required to set aside a significant amount of time to do paperwork (for example, for medical insurance).[94] The days went by quickly, with doctors encouraged by the knowledge that for many of the patients this was their only chance to see a doctor.[95]

Medical missions had clear limitations. The short time limit of one week for each medical mission per year meant that many patients were turned away.[96] In *Bloodlines*, a group of women burst into tears because they had traveled for over three hours only to be told they could not be accommodated.[97] One volunteer was clearly agitated when she observed: "We are running out of time and supplies. There are 120 patients and we can only do 50 so we have almost a riot here because they have been here since Monday but we have run out of supplies and we cannot do any more."[98] An African American volunteer doctor who was part of the PMSNC mission to Iloilo in 2003 summed up the strategy for dealing with the ones who missed out by saying that "your philosophy is that you don't look back, you finish what you can do and you leave, you don't try to think about whether you saw every patient or not."[99] The short time span of the medical mission trip prevented the team from seeing the recovery of some of those who had to have surgery. In a poignant scene from *Bloodlines*, a middle-aged woman who suffered from an enormous tumor attached to her face beamed at the camera, smiling radiantly after the surgery that appeared to have changed her life. But in the very next frame we were given the doctor's diagnosis that the removed tumor was cancerous.[100] The film ended without letting the audience know what became of the patient, mirroring the exact experience of the medical team. Local hospitals were saddled with the problems of dealing with complications from surgical procedures, and in this sense the patients themselves were "abandoned" by the doctors who had already left the Philippines and moved on.[101]

Other constraints included the timing of the missions themselves. Most medical missions from the United States happened only in the first quarter of the year, from January to March (when it was winter in the northern countries), resulting in a very uneven distribution of health care during the year.[102] Some areas such as Palawan and Aklan were overrepresented, and the Department of Health's preference that some missions go to underserved areas like Mindanao were ignored.[103]

It is difficult to assess the breadth of diasporic philanthropy across the entire Philippines. Migrant remittances are more easily traced because a significant portion of these cash transfers went through Philippine banks. Charitable donations, on the other hand, do not generally go through the banking sector and often went directly to the NGOs, or else donations arrived in the form of kind—schoolbooks, clothing, medicines, or free medical care. But some statistics provide us with some data for reflection.

PIA spent an average of about US$90,000 per year for thirty years, giving money to various NGOs and providing tuition and material support to underprivileged children. From 1986 to 2013, 30,000 children benefited from the program.[104] Since the 1990s, the organization distributed around $250–$287,000 in grants per year.[105] In 2012 alone, twenty-five NGOs received funding in cash.[106] Between 1992 and 2013 PIA paid for the education of 349 deaf children, of whom 98 completed grade school, 94 completed high school, 26 graduated from vocational or two-year colleges, and 16 finished with a bachelor's degree. After graduation 82.4 percent gained employment with 28 percent in the field of technology, 30 percent in education, over 15 percent in office work, and 3 percent in the hotel industry.[107] The PIA website's final tabulation of cumulative statistics since 1986 was impressive: over US$3 million in scholarships and grants distributed, and 38,000 children who benefited from a scholarship.[108]

Medical missions also produced an impressive record of patients who received free consultation, operations, and medicines. PMSNC claimed that the organization served over 60,000 patients in medical missions to parts of rural Philippines in the sixteen years leading up to 2003.[109] The *Bloodlines* documentary underscored the statistics of 2003: 6 days, 158 volunteers and 8,723 patients.[110] The medical mission to Sarangani Province, January 17–21, 2011, claimed that there were 140 volunteers who saw 11,278 patients, performed 208 surgeries, handed out 60 prosthetic arms, legs, and feet, and serviced 801 dental patients and 4,300 ophthalmology patients.[111] The 2012 mission to San Jose, Occidental Mindoro, had 146 volunteers treating 11,300 patients, with 107 receiving major surgeries, while the outpatient clinic attended 10,681 patients. The Bohol mission in 2015 treated 7,666 patients, including 269 who had surgery. The recent mission to Laoag, Ilocos Norte (2016) brought a team of 160 volunteers to help 6,597 patients.[112]

PAMA treated around 1,500 patients per medical mission.[113] On a few occasions, Dr. Ophee de Vera recalled seeing between fifty and sixty patients a day for four to five days with each volunteer doctor doing a minimum of fifty consultations per day.[114] The PAMA website trotted out the following statistics from 2008 to 2013: 2,000 dental checkups, 1,000 Pap smears, plus donations of hundreds of eyeglasses, an X-ray and an EKG machine. These did not include the number of medicines distributed. In 2013, for example, it sent 50,000 units of antibiotics and twenty-five beds donated by a hospital in Wyong, Australia (which had also donated fifty beds in 2012).[115] The sixth medical mission to Sasmuan, Pampanga, reported the following statistics: 774 consultations, 63 Pap smears, 67 ophthalmology cases, 136 patients in herbocautery, and 443 dental patients. In addition, this one mission conducted 222 minor surgeries and 26 major surgeries.[116]

One clear measure of success was the fact that local politicians were tempted to claim credit for the medical missions. Cooperation with local government officials was essential but sometimes problematic if medical missions were conducted before election time.[117] According to volunteer Mao de Vera, when the PAMA team arrived in one of the main government hospitals in Pagadian, Zamboaga Del Sur, the first thing they saw was a huge banner that proclaimed: "Welcome medical mission, joint program of the governor and the city mayor."[118] Of course, in this particular case the local politicians were not directly involved in the mission (their contribution was in offering the use of government venues and facilities), a fact noted even by one old man standing in line for a medical consultation who told De Vera: "The politicians are happy, because you are doing their job." De Vera was nonplussed: "We don't really care. We came here to help."[119] Other local politicians applauded the work of the medical volunteers.[120] Enrique J. Cabahug Jr., the municipal mayor of Aurora, Zamboanga del Sur, awarded PAMA with a certificate of recognition, and the organization was nominated for the 2014 presidential awards for Filipino individuals and organizations (Linkapil Awards, Lingkod ng Kapwa Pilipino).[121] Jerry Treñas, mayor of Iloilo, announced that he was very happy about hosting the medical mission from California in 2003,[122] and the governor of Panay Province nicknamed the medical mission as "the mission of love."[123] Local politicians often facilitated the administrative part of the mission but generally did not contribute any manpower or resources.[124] In this sense, the old man was correct. The medical missions actually performed the duties that politicians should have done if they genuinely wanted to address the needs of the underprivileged groups in their constituencies.

A comparison of the two case studies reveals that, despite the differences in advocacy and origin country, one striking similarity is the enormous amount of time and resources that Filipino migrants poured into these philanthropic activities to invest in the future of the homeland. They invested in the future of the children and in the health of the poor. According to John Silva, associate editor of PIA's newsletter, "In our own modest way, we have been keeping promises to children and providing them better opportunities for the future through the generous support of our donors and volunteers."[125] Mona Lisa Yuchengco's speech at the Unity Conference in 1987 linked PIA's goals with those of the homeland: "We mirror that country's [the Philippines] faith in its future—the children."[126] The word "investment" also implied a long-term commitment as opposed to a one-off contribution. As early as 1987 Mona Lisa Yuchengco wrote: "PIA is committed to the Philippines and its future. We invite you to join us in our efforts. Together we can make a difference."[127] Given the links of ritual kinship between the donor/godparent and the sponsored child, the sponsorship also committed donors to a long-term relationship in which they were responsible for nurturing the children's educational goals. PIA has been around for three decades and the success stories circulated were about former scholars who have graduated from universities and found meaningful employment. The letters of the sponsored children sent to their PIA benefactors document the way the scholarships enabled them to fulfill their dreams and ease the financial burden on their parents.[128] Among these were Jonathan Espana, who graduated from Philippine Christian University with a degree in social work and was (in 2003) working with Médecins Sans Frontières (Doctors Without Borders) as a street educator; Laarni Isanan, who graduated from Philippine Normal College with a bachelor of science degree in education, a consistent honor student who took the board exam for teachers on August 27, 2003; Jaypy De Juan (a PIA scholar ever since he was in the second grade), who at age twenty-five worked as a science research specialist, in the Food and Nutrition Research Institute at the Department of Science and

Technology after he graduated from the Polytechnic University of the Philippines with a bachelor of science degree in food technology in 2006; and Maria Dolores Almosara, twenty-two years old, who graduated from the City University of Pasay with a bachelor of science degree in secondary education and became a music and math teacher for Learn and Explore Montessori.[129] Since Laarni was a PIA scholar since she was in the sixth grade and Jaypy still wants to complete a master's degree, their sponsors—Milagros Vizcarra from Vallejo, California, and Fernando Lopez, Manuel de Leon, and Arthur Antonino from Manila—have supported their education for at least twelve years.[130] Clemen Pascao was a beneficiary of the "Off the Streets—Off to School" scholarship program in 1990 when she was only eleven years old and she graduated in 1997 with a bachelor of science degree in business administration, with a major in management, from the Southeastern College in Pasay City, Manila.[131] PIA solicited donors with the slogan "Education Is a Lifetime Gift," but in reality, sponsorship was also almost a lifetime *commitment*. Supporting each scholar until he or she could be self-sufficient illustrated the practical and fundamental way PIA made a difference in one individual's future. The organization was fashioning the youth into working citizens. Clemen Pascao, the fifth child in a family of eight was the first child to acquire a college degree.[132]

The energy and resources migrants contribute to philanthropic work in the homeland could just have been devoted to other causes closer to home, such as the homeless in San Francisco, or as one doctor put it, toward relief in Nicaragua.[133] In fact, both PIA and PAMA also extended their philanthropic work to Filipina/o/x American communities and Filipino Australian communities respectively. PAMA helped raise funds for the Australian bush fire victims, and PIA provided college scholarships for the Filipina/o/x American community. But the choice to focus on the homeland reinforced the personal and emotional connections with Filipinos back home. The philanthropic activities were also about connecting with the homeland. Godparent PIA sponsors were supposed to bond with their godchild, and doctors formed close friendships with their Philippine-based partners. Medical missions also allowed the second generation to touch base with their cultural heritage. As American-born Paul Espinas summed it: "It is really nice to be in touch with that sometimes those are kind of my cultural and ethnic roots in a way and going back to that was one of the joys of this medical mission."[134]

The hours of time and huge number of resources that Filipino migrants invested in the project of affecting social change has had an impact on the many individuals whose lives have been improved. Although it was difficult to ascertain quantitatively the exact social changes as a result of diasporic philanthropy, one can see physical evidence of improvements in the landscape of each little principality as government buildings and chapels were renovated, or in the decline in the numbers of street children in various neighborhoods. Another similar feature of diasporic philanthropic work whether it is run by Filipinos in the United States or in Australia is the psychic wages or the psychic income that donors earn from their charitable work. Overseas Filipinos were rewarded for their civic contributions with positive feelings about themselves. Philanthropic work has also been credited with making donors "feel good" because they helped someone less privileged than themselves. Doctors continued to volunteer every year because, as one explained: "You cannot really explain it. You can feel it in yourself. I did something good and I feel good."[135] A volunteer for the PMSNC medical mission to Sarangani in 2011 expressed a similar sentiment: "I know that we are doing something even though it is not much, but we are driven to come back every year so we can help some of our co-Filipinos."[136] Participants in medical missions confided that they got "addicted" ("you get the kick, it's addictive") to the endorphin rush that they experience from contributing to medical missions every year and the appreciation they received from patients.[137] PIA "fairy godmother" Coratec Jimenez claimed that "I felt good that day" when she attended the graduation ceremony of her young scholar Cynthia Batula.[138] She then promised to continue to sponsor Batula until she graduated from university.[139]

What insights can be gained about diasporic philanthropy from these two disparate case studies? Clearly, these philanthropists are committed to investing a lot of their time, energy, and financial resources to the project of saving, helping, and connecting with the homeland. This is a priority for them. Even if the United States or Australia is now their home, even if their passports proclaim their citizenship status as American or Australian, they still perform civic work in the Philippines. The connections with the homeland continue far and beyond the social and cultural ties of family and village since many of the people they help are mere strangers to them. At the same time, these projects are *joint projects* between migrants and Filipinos in the homeland. This chapter has examined these activities from the overseas end in keeping with this book's migrant perspective, but they must also be examined from the Philippine side. As the case study on medical missions shows, the Philippine side is often left to cope with problems on its own once the philanthropists have left the country. The civic work illustrates the potential of transnational philanthropic activity that crosses borders.

Finally, it must be underscored that the positive feelings migrants experience when they perform philanthropic work is intimately connected with the celebratory ending of their heroic narrative of migration. How does the heroic narrative end? Where are the hero and heroine at the end of the narrative? Are they in a better situation in the present? Is it a happy ending? Perhaps another reason why donors experienced a lot of satisfaction from performing good deeds was because the relationship between benefactor and recipient located the position of the migrant as a successful person who could share his or her wealth with the less fortunate. In this way, the heroic narrative is given its justification and ultimate legitimization. The heroic narrative is given not just a happy ending, it receives a triumphant one. At the end of the story, the migrant heroes and heroines are heralded as patrons whose selfless actions propose them to be alternative role models to the corrupt Philippine politicians who have neglected their duty of care toward the poor and disadvantaged groups.

Conclusion
Refusing to Be Marginal

With this book, I hope to have offered a fresh perspective on migrant influence beyond labor, using an approach from the discipline of history. What did the migrant archives tell us? What did they contribute to our understanding of global migration? What insights did the comparative contexts offer? How else should we imagine migrants apart from the usual role of breadwinner, laborer, or dutiful and filial family member? Could we rethink migrants separate from their labor sectors which categorized them as "domestic workers," "seafarers," "nurses," "caregivers," "construction workers," "entertainers," and so on? The case studies in this book illustrate that migrants were also influential consumers, astute investors, and important philanthropists. Migrants were historians documenting their own past through the publication of memoirs and community histories. The making of the migrant archives—the source base for this book—was very much a history project. Hence, this book also underscores the importance of the discipline of history in analyzing the migration experience. The suggestion that migrants are agents of change should motivate us to reconsider the way they are normally positioned in the dominant discourses as liminal subjects and instead appreciate their ability to introduce change.

Bagong Bayani or Bigong Bayani?

Ever since President Corazon Aquino conferred the title of "Bagong Bayani" on Filipino migrant workers in Hong Kong in 1988, the grand narrative of the overseas Filipino workers as "modern day heroes" became a reference point for discourses on migration in the Philippines. The deliberate use of the Tagalog word *bayani*, which prior to 1988 was only used to refer to heroes and heroines of the Philippine revolution against Spain and the Philippine-American War, suggested that the overseas worker's hard work and sacrifice in order to send much-needed remittances to the family was equal to the commitment and heroism of the martyrs of the Philippine nationalist movement and revolution. According to historians Reynaldo Ileto and Vicente Rafael, the construction of this new nationalist heroic discourse was founded on the passion of Christ as well as the martyrdom of Jose Rizal, the Philippine national hero whose books inspired the revolution against Spain and who was executed by the Spaniards in 1896.[1] The title *bagong bayani* was meant to elevate the status of overseas Filipino workers to that of noble (*dakila*) citizens, appropriating the adjective *dakila*, which until then had only been used to mark Filipino nineteenth-century eminent national heroes. The rationale for attributing the status of hero to these mobile individuals was the fact that their combined remittances (US$25 billion in 2015) played a major role in rescuing the Philippine economy.[2] President Gloria Macapagal's speech for the Bagong Bayani Awards in 2005 proclaimed that the OFWs were heroes because their remittances increased by 25 percent in the first three months of the year, thus raising the country's GNP by 3.6 percent.[3] As Jean Encinas-Franco and Vicente Rafael have demonstrated, the narrative of migrants as *bagong bayani* underscored the suffering and sacrifices migrants made living overseas (including exploitation, loneliness, separation from loved ones, ethnic discrimination, and isolation) and evoked the image of the migrants as poor "victims."[4] This *bagong bayani* discourse was inherently problematic not least because of its overemphasis on migrant victimhood (martyrdom does not only disempower them but results in the feminization of the migrant subjects), but also because it did not reflect migrants' own perspectives. The term, however, has become entrenched in discourses about migration.

In order to give some credibility to the rhetoric the government launched Bagong Bayani Awards and the awards for the Model OFW Family (discussed in chapter 1). The Bagong Bayani Awards, administered by the Philippine Overseas Employment Administration (POEA), honor outstanding overseas Filipino workers. Launched in 1984 and later sponsored by the Bagong

Bayani Foundation, the award "gives due recognition to the Filipino worker for his [or her] outstanding contribution both as a paradigm of national skills and talents and as ambassador of good will."[5] Since national heroes were remembered during prescribed national days, new traditions were invented to commemorate the migrant heroes. The week of the signing of the Magna Carta of Migrant Workers (June 7, 1995) was observed as "Migrant Heroes' Week,"[6] and the last Sunday of September was proclaimed "National Seafarers' Day" in 1996.[7] The latter's celebration included a memorial service and a grand parade.[8] A new ritual has been added to the state's annual Christmas tradition, with no less than the president giving a "heroes' welcome" at the Manila International Airport to the overseas Filipino workers (OFWs) returning to the homeland to spend the Christmas holidays with their families.[9]

Jean Encinas-Franco has argued convincingly that the Philippine government has used the *bagong bayani* discourse "as a discursive tool to manage and justify labor export," and that "the overemphasis on this discourse in political texts hides or de-emphasizes many aspects of labor out-migration."[10] In other words, the *bagong bayani* discourse was invoked by the government to legitimize its migration policies of sending out a million overseas workers a year, rather than as a genuine honor bestowed on the group. Even NGOs such as Migrante, known for its anti-statist advocacy and its campaign to end labor export, used this same discourse when they wanted to call attention to the plight of migrants as victims of exploitation.[11] Thus, Encinas-Franco concluded that there was a glaring absence of an emerging counterdiscourse to this well-entrenched grand narrative of migrant heroism in the Philippines.[12] Encinas-Franco was writing from the perspective of the nation-state, using primary sources from newspapers and legislative papers, as well as one NGO—Migrante.

If we shift the perspective to that of the migrants themselves, a slightly different picture emerges. I suggest that Filipino migrants have themselves critiqued this discourse, producing the beginnings of a counterhegemonic discourse that pokes fun at the label with poignant humor. Their responses reveal that they were not deceived by the honorific title and challenged the government with the query "Are we new heroes only in name?" Scholar Ma. Jovita Zarate hinted at this in her analysis of the concept of *bagong bayani* from the perspective of the narratives of overseas Filipino workers. In her article on the topic she quoted in full a blog entry by Jocelyn Ruiz who censured the Overseas Workers Welfare Administration for denying overseas worker Violeta Nicolas benefits because her membership card had expired. Nicolas died in Rome and her body had to be buried there because she had no funds or insurance money to pay for the transport of her corpse to the Philippines. The blog condemned the OWWA:

> Sino ang dabat sisihin sa pagakakaroon ng EXPIRATION? Tinatawag pa naming "BAGONG BAYANI" pero ganito walang nagawa kundi di ilibing sa dayuhang bansa. Kaya kung totoo na bayani tayo, bakit ganito? BAYANI LANG BA TAYO SA SALITA? At ILAN PANG VIOLETA ANG SUSUNOD NA HINDI MALILIBING SA SARILING BAYAN!?"[13]
>
> (Who should we blame for the expiration date? We are called "new heroes" but nothing was done except for her to be buried in a foreign country. If we are really heroes, why did it happen this way? ARE WE HEROES IN NAME ONLY? And HOW MANY MORE VIOLETAS WILL FOLLOW WHO CANNOT BE BURIED IN THEIR OWN COUNTRY?)

Jocelyn Ruiz's angry blog (evidenced by the use of all capital letters that had the double effect of sending emphasis and giving the impression of someone shouting) captured the feelings of many Filipino migrants.

Seafarers, who were among the biggest dollar earners and who were required by law to remit 80 percent of their salaries through Philippine banks, were cynical about the label. One of Steven McKay's informants was quite candid, saying: "Maybe they are projecting the sea men as saviors of this country because we bring in dollars, but . . . the government does not help us. They just flatter the sea men." Another expressed with characteristic Filipino wit: "We should be called *Gagong Bayani* [stupid heroes] because even if we contribute significantly to the country, the government fails to help unemployed sea men . . . I pity my fellow seafarers."[14] Raquel Delfin Padilla, in one of her edited anthologies on OFW life stories, addressed the readers with the rhetorical question: "Kami nga ba ay bagong bayani o bigong bayani?" (Are we new heroes or doomed heroes?).[15] By changing only one letter (the letter *i*) in the adjective *bagong* (new), she had transformed the meaning completely to mean "doomed [*bigong*] heroes." Padilla's essay produced a damning critique of the discourse from the perspective of the migrant. She claimed that migrants were unable to realize their dreams, their families were torn apart, foreign countries abused them, and the Philippine government did not value them.[16] Padilla's litany of accusations also blamed the family for taking for granted the money and gifts migrants sent to them regularly and for demanding more material things from an already overburdened overseas Filipino worker.[17] Although the alternative labels "Gagong Bayani" and "Bigong Bayani" have not yet made it to the realm of popular discourse, migrants have begun to disseminate their critiques of the label and are redefining the discourse in their own terms.

Filipino migrants however were not shy to use the label of *bagong bayani* to empower themselves or to legitimize migrant activism. I had the enormous privilege of meeting and interviewing one of the Bagong Bayani awardees. Cecilia Silva went to Padova in 1989 to work as a caregiver, and she immersed herself in civic work. From 1990 to 1997 she served as an officer of the Filipino community in Italy's Padova chapter. In 1994, she joined the Asociacion Unica Terra and was elected to its board of directors. This was an Italian organization formed to help immigrants in Padova. In addition, she acquired feminist credentials when she became an active member of the Equal Opportunities Commission of Padova (Colori di Donna), an organization composed of Italian women working toward equal rights for women. These activities show that Silva embraced civic and community work that was not limited to the Filipino community alone. In May 1997, she was elected to the Consigli della Comunità Straniere di Padova and was appointed president of the Equal Opportunities sector. In this capacity she acted as an interpreter for the police and the local court in cases where Filipinos were involved.[18] She also helped numerous Filipinos who were victims of illegal Filipino recruiters and Filipino nationals in Padova who were sick and needed hospitalization or who died and had to be repatriated.[19] Together with her sister Marian Laarni Silva, she cofounded Associazione Donne Filippine, which in 2017 had fourteen members, all of whom were Filipino women. The organization's aims included:

"a. To educate Filipino women about their rights and their value as members of Padua's society;
b. To promote Filipino culture in Italy;
c. To promote cultural exchanges between the Italian population and the Filipino community in the Paduan territory, through participation in various activities and events that may contribute to increasing mutual understanding between the two communities;
d. To make Filipino women aware of their economic and social situation in Italy and hence to provide the information needed to manage their acquired financial resources, in anticipation of their return to the Philippine [sic];
e. To inform the Filipino community on the various opportunities available within the Padovan territory in promoting the social and cultural empowerment of the Filipinos in Padova;
f. To develop initiatives and actions to support the Filipino community in their Homeland, with particular reference to cases of natural disasters, etc."[20]

Among its notable achievements were the sponsoring of financial literacy seminars for overseas Filipino workers, promoting Filipino food in the festival of Festa Dei Popoli, educating Italian-born Filipino children about Filipino culture, providing relief for victims of calamities, and helping indigenous children in the province of Mindoro in central Philippines by supporting the renovation of classrooms and donating instruction materials.[21] New fishing boats were provided to victims of typhoon Yolanda (international name Haiyan) in Leyte and the most recent project of helping the children of Mangyans (indigenous group in Mindoro) involved donating food, school materials and proper hygiene to 100 students in Bigaan Mangyan School in 2015, 140 students in Pagturian Elementary school in 2016 and 221 students of Safa Elementary School in Pinamalayan Mindoro Oriental in 2017.[22] In recognition of her achievements, Cecilia Silva was given the Bagong Bayani Award by the government of the Philippines in 2000. Being a Bagong Bayani awardee carried status. It gave legitimacy to the Associacione Donne Filippine, which she had cofounded. Her status as a Bagong Bayani Award recipient helped her succeed in her lobby to have a Philippine consul assigned to Milan and a Filipino pastor appointed to the Catholic Church in Padova. Hence, Cecilia's story from the migrant perspective reveals how these national awards were used to empower migrants in their own projects and advocacy abroad (some of which also had an impact on the homeland, for example, in diasporic philanthropic ventures).

The multisited approach this book has adopted produces a more complex portrait of migration than the national *bagong bayani* discourses. The figure of the "suffering migrant," while important to addressing the oppressive conditions experienced by many migrant laborers, is also bound to the concept of a migrant who longs for the nation. The multisited geography, then, also produces an analysis that is not determined by the professions that are recruiting the migrants to a particular location or the national accounts of migration. As stated above, Filipino migrants' own engagement with this discourse is different and complicated, ranging from critiquing and disparaging the semiotic import of the supposedly honorific label to using the prestige associated with the Bagong Bayani Award to promote their own diasporic projects. While the *bagong bayani* discourse is clearly a perspective of Filipino migration from the nation, what I hoped to achieve in this book was to reveal that the view from the multinational, global account of migration raises a more complex portrait of migration.

Proposing Their Own Role Models

Filipino migrants were extremely proactive in fashioning their own role models. By the late twentieth century, Filipino migrants created their own criteria for who should be their role models, and they began to hand out their own awards to these heroes and heroines. In defining their own role models, Filipino migrants did not duplicate the official discourse of the *bagong bayani*. For example, although they acknowledged the heroic narrative of migration (referring to the hard work, sacrifices, and struggle that they all experienced), they rejected the image of the migrant as suffering martyr or hapless victim as their role model. Instead, they put forward as heroes and heroines those individuals who have been able to compete with the mainstream society and excel. This criterion—the capacity to compete with the very best of the entire population of the host countries, as an equal, became a prerequisite for acquiring status. The benchmark for heroic status revealed the influence of the host countries' own yardstick for success. Recognizing that minority groups or new migrants do not have the advantages and personal connections of the hosts' mainstream societies, they naturally bestow the highest regard on those who have "made it" overseas by beating the odds.

Filipino migrants and their descendants initiated the discussion on what and who their role models should be. They celebrated the achievements of the men and women they held up as ideals. The Filipino American National Historical Society, for example, granted VIP (Very Important Pinoy) awards to those members of the Filipina/o/x American community who achieved distinguished careers or played important roles in the civil rights movement or in Asian American and Filipina/o/x American activism. In 2009 *Filipinas* magazine honored individuals in the categories of arts and culture, communication, community service, corporate leadership, entertainment, entrepreneurship, lifetime achievement, medicine, and public affairs.[23] During their 2007 leadership summit, the Filipina Women's Network (or FWN, the premiere organization of Filipina women professionals) in the United States started a tradition of handing out biannual awards for the one hundred most influential Filipinas. The stories of the awardees so far were published by FWN in three books in 2015, 2016, and 2018.[24] Mona Lisa Yuchengo, founder and publisher of *Positively Filipino* (which is entirely online), confided to me in an interview that the purpose of the magazine was to correct the mainstream white society's negative portrayals of the ethnic group by highlighting the positive contributions of Filipina/o/x Americans to mainstream society and creating a space for this group to celebrate their achievements.[25] This would act as a balance to the negative stereotyping of this ethnic group by the mainstream of the host societies. The circumstances of migration pressured migrants to change, and awards marked these alterations and sent the comforting message that the reforms were for the better. But more important, it affirmed publicly for the historical record that the migration story was a success—giving the heroic narrative its happy ending.

"We're Here, Get Used to it!"

One common theme that emerges from the archives is the huge amount of time and resources migrants devoted to migrant projects—whether it be creating an archive, writing their memoirs, campaigning for human rights, volunteering to help the less privileged, or buying goods for the *balikbayan* boxes destined for the homeland. Whether migrants were located in the United States or in the Middle East, Asia, Europe, or Australia, they invested time, resources, and money in the creative activities. They were conscious that the evolutionary changes they initiated would take time, and they were prepared to commit for the long term in order to sustain their goals. Perhaps this impressive devotion to their myriad projects and interests could be explained by their refusal to remain in the margins.

The history of Munting Nayon day-care center, established in 1994 by KASAPI-Hellas (Kaisahang Samahan ng mga Manggagawang Pilipino sa Gresya, or United Organization of Filipino Workers in Greece), an organization whose tagline is "Unity of Filipino Migrants in Greece," illustrates the remarkable resilience of an ethnic group determined to carve its own space in the center of the city.[26] The membership expressed a need for day-care centers.[27] The organization raised its own funds, and the center evolved into a primary school in 1996, teaching a Philippine syllabus because at that time many of the parents, the majority of whom were domestic workers, intended to return to the Philippines after a few years. Benedictine nun Mary John Mananzan sent them a teacher from of St. Scholastica's College (funded by KASAPI) who taught the college's curriculum for two years, with books ordered from the Philippines. Given that several Filipinas working in Greece had teaching qualifications, it was not hard to find instructors. The school thrived until the Philippine Embassy put up its own school.[28] KASAPI decided to close its school, not just because it could not compete with the new rival, but because the organization realized that "it is not fair to the children because we are creating a ghetto mentality . . . they should be in the Greek school already . . . there was some kind of a ghetto that we are not able to communicate in Greek language. It's very important."²⁹ After reflecting on their own experience with the school, KASAPI-Hellas founders Joe and Debbie Valencia confided in my interview, "we realized, we have to be part of the Greek society."³⁰

In 2006 after nine years of graduating four batches of children in primary school, Munting Nayon reverted back to functioning as a day-care facility.³¹ But it also reinvented itself. The day care began to accept non-Filipino children. At the time of my interview with its organizers in 2012, they had sixteen nationalities, including Albanian, Romanian, Ukrainian, Bulgarian, Senegalese, African, Nigerian, Ethiopian, Eritrean, Tunisian, Indian, Bangladeshi, Sri Lankan, and Chinese.³² The majority of children were no longer Filipino (of the twenty-five children in the group, ten were Filipino). When I visited the day care in September 2012, there was only one Filipino child. It was clearly a multicultural day-care facility, located right in the area of Athens where most migrants lived, with Filipinos only a tiny minority. The language of instruction was English.

The day care was popular with migrant communities because it was inexpensive, charging €150 a month (in 2012) for a ten-hour day including food. At the same time, the English language curriculum was attractive to migrant parents who wanted their children to learn that language. But Munting Nayon continued to struggle with the constant threat of closure by the police, who claimed that the structure of the building was not sound. KASAPI's response has been to get support from Greek organizations and members of Parliament. The Municipality of Athens, for example, donated food each day for the children's lunches. Hence, on the one hand, one part of Greek society was suspicious of them and threatened to close them down, while other Greeks gave them valuable support.³³

This case study of Munting Nayon (which literally means "little country" or "little nation") was a great example of how the Filipino migrant community overseas refused to be relegated to the margins. KASAPI, with a mere 1,200 members, put up a day care and a school on its own initiative. The day care struggled with a precarious existence due to constant threats to close it down. At its peak between 2008 and 2010, it had seventy children enrolled. In 2012 the enrollment had whittled down to twenty-five, but it was clear that they were not going to surrender. This tiny day-care facility has already been embraced by other migrant groups who appreciated the contribution the Filipinos made to Athens—by providing affordable day care for migrants who worked long hours and instructing them in the English language. Debbie Valencia recalled one African mother who was thrilled when her little girl waved goodbye to the teacher with the words "see you tomorrow." The mother exclaimed in Greek, "My daughter speaks English!"³⁴ Thus, Munting Nayon had an impact beyond the Filipino community to the greater multicultural population of Athens.

Munting Nayon's very existence was testament to the Filipino migrants' refusal to be a marginal community, content with living only in the shadows or only in places grudgingly conceded to them by the host country's elites. Instead, to quote from Filipino American scholar Dean Alegado, they declared: "We're here, get used to it!"[35] FANHS cofounder Fred Cordova coined the saying "the browning of America" in referring to the contribution Filipina/o/x Americans made to white society.[36]

Finally, what the case studies in this book have revealed is that the history of migration itself—the telling of the heroic narrative—was an important project for many Filipino migrants. They told their stories in order to become visible, they wrote their community histories to underscore the contribution they made to the host countries and the homeland, and they published their memoirs to lobby for change. By refusing to remain in the margins, Filipino migrants continue to remind audiences that they are not liminal subjects content to remain invisible in the margins.

NOTES

Introduction

1. Maruja M. B. Asis, "Women Migrants Who Make a Difference," *Asian Migrant* 15, nos. 1–2, (January–June 2002): 35–36; and Zita Cabais (formerly Obra), Paris, interview with author, March 4, 2008.

2. Zita Cabais (formerly Obra) interview.

3. Saturnina (Nina, or "Cute") de los Santos Rotelo, interview with author, Singapore, July 16, 2017.

4. My translation from the Tagalog original: "Parang lahat sila nagbago, hindi tulad noong bago ako umalis. Lahat sila umiinom. Si Jay umiinom. Si Luis umiinom. Lalo na si Romy, araw-araw umiinom. Na hindi niya dating ginagawa dahil pinipigilan ko siya noong narito pa ako. Siguro kasi, wala ako. Sa aking lang sila nakikinig noon. Hindi ko nasubaybayan ang ganyan-ganyan nila. Maraming pagbabago na parang hindo ko na sila kilala, hindi na katulad ng dati. Nagulat ako dahil dalawang taon lang akong Nawala, biro mo, ang laki na rin ang pagbabago. Sabi ko, 'Nawala lang ako, lahat na kayo nagkabisyo!'" Nenita's story, in Fanny A. Garcia, *Pamilya, migrasyon, disintegrasyon* (Manila: C & E Publishing for De La Salle University Press, 2012), 69.

5. Garcia, *Pamilya, migrasyon, disintegrasyon*, postscript, 228–232.

6. "Juanita," in Analyn D. Aryo, *Nanny Tales: Voices from the Diary of an Overseas Filipino Worker* (Benguet: ResearchMate, 2009), 43.

7. Aryo, *Nanny Tales*, 48.

8. Aryo, *Nanny Tales*, 49.

9. Rhacel Salazar Parreñas, *Children of Global Migration: Transnational Families and Gendered Woes* (Stanford, CA: Stanford University Press, 2005); Rhacel Salazar Parreñas, "Mothering from a Distance: Emotions, Gender and Intergenerational Relations in Filipino Transnational Families," *Feminist Studies* 27, no. 2 (2001): 361–390; Asuncion Fresnoza-Flot, "Migration Status and Transnational Mothering: The Case of Filipino Migrants in France," *Global Networks* 9, no. 2 (2009): 252–270; Cecilia Uy-Tioco, "Overseas Filipino Workers and Text Messaging: Reinventing Transnational Mothering," *Continuum* 21, no. 2 (2007): 253–265; Mirca Madianou and Daniel Miller, *Migration and New Media: Transnational Families and Polymedia* (London: Routledge, 2012); and Valerie Francisco-Menchavez, *The Labor of Care: Filipina Migrants and Transnational Families in the Digital Age* (Urbana: University of Illinois Press, 2018).

10. For an analysis on the ideal cultural constructions of the feminine, see Mina Roces, *Women's Movements and the Filipina, 1986–2008* (Honolulu: University of Hawaii Press, 2012).

11. For scholarly analysis of the Filipino diaspora in film, see Alice G. Guillermo, "The Filipino OCW in Extremis," in *Geopolitics of the Visible: Essays on Philippine Film Cultures*, ed. Rolando B. Tolentino (Quezon City: Ateneo de Manila University Press, 2000), 106–124; see also the following essays in Rolando B. Tolentino, ed., "Vaginal Economy: Cinema and Sexuality in the Post-Marcos, Post-Brocka Philippines," special issue, *Positions: East Asia Cultures Critique* 19, no. 2 (Fall 2011); Francisco Benitez, "Transnational Questing Desire in Star Cinema's *Kailangan kita* and *Milan*," 257–280; Elizabeth H. Pisares, "The Social-Invisibility Narrative in Filipino-American Feature Films," 421–437; Nobue Suzuki, "'Japayuki,' or Spectacles for the Transnational Middle Class," 439–462; Benjamin McKay, "The Politics of Mirrored Metaphors: Flor Contemplacion and *The Maid*," 463–498; and Sarah Raymundo, "In the Womb of the Global Economy: *Anak* and the Construction of Transnational Imaginaries," 551–579.

12. Daxim L. Lucas, "Remittances Hit All-Time High of $33.5B in 2019," *Philippine Daily Inquirer*, February 18, 2020, B1; Filomeno V. Aguilar Jr., *Migration Revolution: Philippine Nationhood and Class Relations in a Globalized Age* (Singapore and Kyoto: NUS Press in association with Kyoto University Press, 2014); see especially the introduction and chap. 4.

13. Aguilar, *Migration Revolution*, 10.

14. Rhacel Salazar Parreñas, *Servants of Globalization: Women, Migration, and Domestic Work* (Stanford, CA: Stanford University Press, 2001); Rhacel Salazar Parreñas, *The Force of Domesticity: Filipina Migrants and Globalization* (New York: New York University Press, 2008); Rhacel Salazar Parreñas, *Illicit Flirtations: Labor, Migration, and Sex Trafficking in Tokyo* (Stanford, CA: Stanford University Press, 2011); Nicole Constable, *Maid to Order in Hong Kong: Stories of Filipina Workers* (Ithaca, NY: Cornell University Press, 1997); Pei-Chia Lan, *Global Cinderellas: Migrant Domestics and Newly Rich Employers in Taiwan* (Durham, NC: Duke University Press, 2006); Elisabetta Zontini, *Transnational Families, Migration, and Gender: Moroccan and Filipino Women in Bologna and Barcelona* (New York: Berghahn Books, 2010); Kale Bantigue Fajardo, *Filipino Crosscurrents: Oceanographies of Seafaring, Masculinities, and Globalization* (Minneapolis: University of Minnesota Press, 2011); James Tyner, *The Philippines: Mobilities, Identities, Globalization* (London: Routledge, 2009); Robyn Emerton and Carole Petersen, "Filipino Nightclub Hostesses in Hong Kong: Vulnerability to Trafficking and Other Human Rights Abuses," in *Transnational Migration and Work in Asia*, ed. Kevin Hewison and Ken Young (London: Routledge, 2006), 126–143; Kathleen Weekley, "From Wage Labourers to Investors? Filipina Migrant Domestic Workers and Popular Capitalism," in Hewison and Young, *Transnational Migration*, 193–212; Shu-Ju Ada Cheng, *Serving the Household and the Nation: Filipina Domestics and the Politics of Identity in Taiwan* (Lanham, MD: Rowman & Littlefield, 2006); Megha Amrith, *Caring for Strangers: Filipino Medical Workers in Asia* (Copenhagen: NIAS Press, 2017); Deirdre McKay, *Global Filipinos: Migrants' Lives in the Virtual Village* (Bloomington: Indiana University Press, 2012); Deirdre McKay, *An Archipelago of Care: Filipino Migrants and Global Networks* (Bloomington: Indiana University Press, 2016); Robin Magalit Rodriguez, *Migrants for Export: How the Philippine State Brokers Labor to the World* (Minneapolis: University of Minnesota Press, 2010).

15. See especially Lieba Faier, *Intimate Encounters: Filipina Women and the Remaking of Rural Japan* (Berkeley: University of California Press, 2009); Nicole Constable, *Romance on a Global Stage: Pen Pals, Virtual Ethnography, and "Mail Order" Marriages* (Berke-

ley: University of California Press, 2004); Cleonicki Saroca, "Violence against Migrant Filipino Women in Australia: Making Men's Behavior Visible," *Review of Women's Studies* 15, no. 2 (2005): 113–139; Cleonicki Saroca, "Filipino Women, Migration and Violence in Australia: Lived Reality and Media Image," *Kasarinlan: Philippine Journal of Third World Studies* 1, no. 1 (2006): 75–110; Cleonicki Saroca, "Woman in Danger or Dangerous Woman? Contesting Images of Filipina Victims of Domestic Homicide in Australia," *Asian Journal of Women's Studies* 12, no. 2 (2006): 35–74; Cleonicki Saroca, "Representing Rosalina and Annabel: Filipino Women, Violence, Media Representation, and Contested Realities," *Kasarinlan* 22, no. 1 (2007): 32–60; Nobue Suzuki, "Transgressing 'Victims': Reading Narratives of 'Filipina Brides' in Japan," *Critical Asian Studies* 35, no. 3 (2003): 399–420; Nobue Suzuki, "Inside the Home: Power and Negotiation in Filipina-Japanese Marriages," *Women's Studies: An Interdisciplinary Journal* 33 no. 4 (2003): 481–506; Nobue Suzuki, "Filipina-Japanese Marriages: Intimate Relationships Located in the Space between the Colonial, Global and National," *Journal of Comparative Family History* 24 (2010): 1–19; Shirlita Espinosa, *Sexualized Citizenship: A Cultural History of Philippine-Australian Migration* (Singapore: Springer, 2017); and Johanna O. Zulueta, ed., *Thinking beyond the State: Migration, Integration, and Citizenship in Japan and the Philippines* (Brighton: Sussex Academic Press, 2018).

16. Madianou and Miller, *Migration and New Media*; Deirdre McKay, "On the Face of Facebook: Historical Images and Personhood in Filipino Social Networking," *History and Anthropology* 21, no. 4 (2010): 483–502; McKay, *An Archipelago of Care*; Mark Johnson and Deirdre McKay, eds., "Mediated Diasporas: Material Translations of the Philippines in a Globalized World," special issue, *Southeast Asia Research* 19, no. 2 (2011); Fernando Paragas, "Migrant Workers and Mobile Phones: Technological, Temporal and Spatial Simultaneity," in *The Reconstruction of Space and Time: Mobile Communication Practices*, ed. Rich Ling and Scott W. Campbell (New Brunswick, NJ: Transaction, 2010), 39–65; and Francisco-Menchavez, *The Labor of Care*.

17. Parreñas, *Children of Global Migration*; Filomeno Aguilar Jr. et al., *Maalwang Buhay: Family, Overseas Migration, and Cultures of Relatedness in Barangay Paraiso* (Quezon City: Ateneo de Manila University Press, 2009).

18. Filomeno Aguilar Jr. begins his book *Migration Revolution* with the sentence "Overseas migration has revolutionized the Philippines," 1.

19. The collection of Italian stories of Filipino children who migrated to Italy is called *Io e l'importanza della famiglia* [Me and the importance of the family] (Turin: ACFIL, ca. 2006).

20. *Art as Reality: The Transition of Filipino Migrant Children in the Middle East* (Muscat, Oman: Embassy of the Republic of the Philippines, Muscat, Sultanate of Oman, 2013).

21. Theodore S. Gonzlaves, "When the Walls Speak a Nation: Contemporary Murals and the Narration of Filipina/o America," *Journal of Asian American Studies* 1, no. 1 (February 1998): 31–63; Theodore S. Gonzalves, *The Day the Dancers Stayed: Performing in the Filipino/American Diaspora* (Philadelphia: Temple University Press, 2010).

22. A. L. Bergamo, "Prologue," in FANHS [Filipino American National Historical Society] Hampton Roads Chapter, *In Our Aunties' Words: The Filipino Spirit of Hampton Roads* (San Francisco: T'Boli, 2004), 9.

23. For a discussion of the new history from below, see Martyn Lyons, "A New History from Below? The Writing Culture of Ordinary People in Europe," *History Australia* 7, no. 3 (2010): 59.1–59.9.

24. Mona Lisa Yuchengco, editorial, premier issue, *Filipinas*, May 1992, 3.
25. Greg Macabenta, "Ignorance Breeds Contempt," *Filipinas*, November 2007, 7.
26. "Filipino American Faces of the Century," *Filipinas*, January 2000.
27. "Join Us in Honoring the Best and the Brightest! 12th Filipinas Achievement Awards, October 1, 2009, South San Francisco Conference Center," *Filipinas*, September 2009, 6.
28. "We Are Positively Filipino: The Premier Digital Native Magazine Celebrating Filipinos in the Diaspora of Nearly 13 Million Expatriates," *Positively Filipino*, accessed December 22, 2016, http://www.positivelyfilipino.com/editorial/.
29. Antonio T. Tiongson Jr., "On Filipinos, Filipino Americans, and U.S. Imperialism: Interview with Oscar V. Campomanes," in *Positively No Filipinos Allowed: Building Communities and Discourse*, ed. Antonio T. Tiongson Jr., Edgardo V. Gutierrez, and Ricardo V. Gutierrez (Philadelphia: Temple University Press, 2006), 26–42.
30. Maria P. P. Root, ed., *Filipino Americans: Transformation and Identity* (London: Sage, 1997), xiii–xiv; Rick Bonus in Antonio T. Tiongson Jr., "Reflections on the Trajectory of Filipino/a American Studies: Interview with Rick Bonus," in Tiongson, Gutierrez, and Gutierrez, *Positively No Filipinos Allowed*, 169.
31. Tiongson, "On Filipinos," 42.
32. Dawn Mabalon, personal communication with author, 2015; and Dawn Bohulano Mabalon, *Little Manila Is in the Heart: The Making of the Filipina/o American Community in Stockton California* (Durham, NC: Duke University Press, 2013), 19. Mabalon credits scholars Dorothy Fujita-Rony, Teresa Amott, and Julie Mattaei for pioneering this term. See Dorothy Fujita-Rony, *American Workers, Colonial Power: Philippine Seattle and the Transpacific West, 1919–1941* (Berkeley: University of California Press, 2003), xviii; and Teresa Amott and Julie Mataei, *Race, Gender and Work: A Multicultural Economic History of Women in the United States* (Boston: South End, 1991), 239–249.
33. Maria P. P. Root says, "As editor, I have taken the liberty of defining *Filipino American* in the most inclusive sense. We are immigrants-now-citizens, American born, immigrant spouses waiting eligibility for green cards, mixed-heritage Filipinos, students or workers on visa, *tago ng tago* (undocumented), and transnationals moving between the Philippines and the United States. Thus, *Filipino American* is a state of mind rather than of legality or geography" (*Filipino Americans*, xiv).
34. Fred Cordova, personal communication with author, Seattle, July 2009.
35. On the definition of "Filipino 1.5 generation" migrants, see Itaru Nagasaka and Asuncion Fresnoza-Flot, eds., *Mobile Childhoods in Filipino Transnational Families: Migrant Children with Similar Roots in Different Routes* (Houndmills, Basingstoke: Palgrave Macmillan, 2015), 1–19.
36. Mabalon, *Little Manila*, 49.
37. Yen Le Espiritu, *Filipino American Lives* (Philadelphia: Temple University Press, 1995), 15.
38. Catherine Ceniza Choy, *Empire of Care: Nursing and Migration in Filipino American History* (Durham, NC: Duke University Press, 2003).
39. Mabalon, *Little Manila*, 62.
40. See Allyson Tintiangco-Cubales, *Pin@y Educational Partnerships: A Filipina/o American Studies Sourcebook Series*, vols. 1 and 2 (Santa Clara, CA: Phoenix, 2007–2009).

41. Eric J. Pido, *Migrant Returns: Manila, Development, and Transnational Connectivity* (Durham, NC: Duke University Press, 2017), 14.

42. Evelyn Ibatan Rodriguez, *Celebrating Debutantes and Quinceañearas: Coming of Age in American Ethnic Communities* (Philadelphia: Temple University Press, 2013), 11.

43. The statistics, of course, do not reveal in detail the disparities between Filipinos earning different incomes or even between those in different states—for example, between the more affluent Filipinos on the West Coast and those in Hawaii. In addition, the US financial crisis that began in 2007 resulted in a series of mortgage defaults, home foreclosures, and losses of assets of Filipino families in the United States. Those who were severely affected by the crisis have considered returning to the Philippines. See Pido, *Migrant Returns*, 75–85.

44. Graziano Battistella and Maruja M. B. Asis, *Country Migration Report: The Philippines, 2013* (Makati City: International Organization for Migration, 2013), 5.

45. Steven McKay and Don Eliseo Lucero-Prisno III, "Masculinities Afloat: Filipino Seafarers and the Situational Performance of Manhood," in *Men and Masculinities in Southeast Asia*, ed. Michele Ford and Lenore Lyons (London: Routledge, 2012), 22.

46. Faier, *Intimate Encounters*, 16.

47. Constable, *Maid to Order*, 3.

48. Mariano A. Dumia, *Of Dreams, Sweat, and Tears: The Kingdom of Saudi Arabia and the Modern Filipino Heroes* (Quezon City: New Day, 2009), 58.

49. Niklas Reese, "Kitakits: Migration and Overseas Filipin@s," in *Handbook Philippines: Society, Politics, Economy, Culture*, ed. Niklas Reese and Rainer Werning (Berlin: Philippinenbüro im Asienhaus, 2013), 205.

50. Reese, "Kitakits," 205.

51. Reese, "Kitakits," 209.

52. Battistella and Asis, *Country Migration Report*, 114–118.

53. Battistella and Asis, *Country Migration Report*, 114–118.

1. Migration and the Rethinking of the Filipino Family, 1970s–2018

1. Maruja M. B. Asis, "From the Life Stories of Filipino Women: Personal and Family Agendas in Migration," *Asia Pacific Migration Journal* 11, no. 1 (2001): 74.

2. Filomeno V. Aguilar Jr. et al., *Maalwang Buhay: Family, Overseas Migration, and Cultures of Relatedness in Barangay Paraiso* (Quezon City, Ateneo de Manila University Press, 2009), 3; Estrella Dizon-Añonuevo and Augustus T. Añonuevo, eds., *Coming Home: Women, Migration, and Reintegration* (Manila: Balikabayani Foundation and Atikha Overseas Workers and Communities Initiative, 2002), 6–8 and 73–124.

3. See "Mandate," in Pearlsha Abubakar and Rochit I. Tañedo, *Mga waging kuwento ng OFW* (Manila: OWWA and Creative Collective Center, 2005), 107–124.

4. Abubakar and Tañedo, *Mga waging kuwento ng OFW*; and Liza Magtoto, Amihan Ruiz, and Totti Sanchez, *Mga waging kuwento ng OFW 2006* (Manila: Creative Collective Center and OWWA, 2006).

5. Dizon-Añonuevo and Añonuevo, *Coming Home*.

6. Parreñas, *Children of Global Migration*, 40–55.

7. Aguilar et al., *Maalwang Buhay*; Parreñas, *Children of Global Migration*; Francisco-Menchavez, *The Labor of Care*; Maria Kontos and Glenda Tibe Bonifacio, eds., *Migrant Domestic Workers and Family Life: International Perspectives* (London: Palgrave Macmillan,

2015); Dizon-Añonuevo and Añonuevo, *Coming Home*; Ma. Lourdes Arellano-Carandang, Beatrix Aileen Sison, and Christopher Carangdang, *Nawala ang Ilaw ng Tahanan: Case Studies of Families Left Behind by OFW Mothers* (Manila: Anvil, 2007); Geraldine Pratt, *Families Apart: Migrant Mothers and the Conflicts of Labor and Love* (Minneapolis: University of Minnesota Press, 2013); and Alicia Pingol, *Remaking Masculinities: Identity, Power, and Gender Dynamics in Families with Migrant Wives and Househusbands* (Quezon City: University Center for Women's Studies, University of the Philippines, 2001).

8. See, for example, Johnson and McKay, "Mediated Diasporas," 181–347; Madianou and Miller, *Migration and the New Media*; Deirdre McKay, "Sent Home: Mapping the Absent Child into Migration through Polymedia," *Global Networks* 18, no. 1 (2018): 131–150; McKay, "On the Face of Facebook"; McKay, *An Archipelago of Care*, 51–69; and Francisco-Menchavez, *The Labor of Care*.

9. Aguilar et al., *Maalwang Buhay*, 5.

10. Belen T. G. Medina, *The Filipino Family*, 2nd ed. (Quezon City: University of the Philippines Press, 2001), 17; quoted in Odine de Guzman, "Families in Transition: Gender, Migration, and the Romance of the 'Filipino Family,'" in *The Family in Flux in Southeast Asia: Institution, Ideology, Practice*, ed. Yoko Hayami et al. (Kyoto: Kyoto University Press and Silkworm Books, 2012), 390.

11. De Guzman, "Families in Transition," 390.

12. Parreñas, *Children of Global Migration*, 36.

13. De Guzman, "Families in Transition," 391.

14. Naomi Hosoda, "The Sense of Pamilya among Samarnons in the Philippines," in Hayami et al., *The Family in Flux*, 365–386.

15. Odine de Guzman argues that "while the family is central to Filipino life, the romantic conception of the 'Filipino family' as nuclear, close-knit, and conservative may not be as monolithic and dominant as the lived experiences of many Filipinos, abroad and at home, suggest" ("Families in Transition", 387); see also Parreñas, *Children of Global Migration*; Arellano-Carandang, Sison, and Carandang, *Nawala ang Ilaw ng Tahana*; and Dizon-Añonuevo and Añonuevo, *Coming Home*.

16. Parreñas, *Children of Global Migration*, 36.

17. Maria Kontos and Glenda Tibe Bonifacio, "Introduction: Domestic and Care Work of Migrant Women and the Right to Family Life," in Kontos and Bonifacio, *Migrant Domestic Workers*, 3.

18. Julia Lausch, "Reinventing Intimacy and Identity: Filipina Domestic Workers' Strategies for Coping with Family Separation in Dubai," in Kontos and Bonifacio, *Migrant Domestic Workers*, 179–187. Valerie Francisco-Menchavez coined the term "communities of care" to describe the care work between Filipina migrants who help each other and become the family away from home. See Francisco-Menchavez, *The Labor of Care*, 14.

19. Quoted in de Guzman, "Families in Transition," 395.

20. Mary Joy E. Barcelona, "My Journey to Achieve My Dreams," in *Migrants' Stories, Migrants' Voices*, ed. Corazon E. Arboleda and Carmelita G. Nuqui (Quezon City: Philippine Migrants Rights Watch, 2007), 57; and Mary Joy E. Barcelona, "Dreams That Guide My Journey," in *Moving On: Stories of DAWN Women Survivors*, ed. Carmelita G. Nuqui and Jannis T. Montañez (Manila: DAWN, 2004), 152.

21. Marites Mapa, journal, March 14, 2013.

22. Aguilar et al., *Maalwang Buhay*; Parreñas, *Children of Global Migration*. A similar point is made by Maruja M. B. Asis, "The Social Costs (and Benefits) of Migration: What Happens to Left-Behind Children and Families?," in *World Conference of OFWs: Shaping the Future of Filipino Labor Migration . . . 2004; PMRW Proceedings* (Quezon City: Philippine Migrants Rights Watch, 2004), 63–74.

23. Arellano-Carandang, Sison, and Carangdang, *Nawala ang Ilaw ng Tahanan*.

24. Stella Maris B. Baliling, "Papa," in *Migrants' Stories, Migrants' Voices 2*, ed. Carmelita G. Nuqui and Alicor L. Panao (Quezon City: Philippine Migrants Rights Watch, 2008), 72.

25. Parreñas, *Children of Global Migration*, 67–91.

26. Jarl Gamomez, "Rich Kid," in Nuqui and Panao, *Migrants' Stories, Migrants' Voices 2*, 66.

27. Gamonez, "Rich Kid," 66.

28. *Art as Reality*. Note that the children did not find it difficult to adjust because they went to Philippine schools. This is not the same for other contexts where children did not go to Philippine schools. See Nagasaka and Fresnoza-Flot, *Mobile Childhoods*; and Pratt, *Families Apart*.

29. Pratt, *Families Apart*.

30. Garcia, *Pamilya, migrasyon, disintegrasyon*.

31. Rey Ventura, *Underground in Japan* (Quezon City: Ateneo de Manila University Press, 2006); Rey Ventura, *Into the Country of Standing Men* (Quezon City: Ateneo de Manila University Press, 2007).

32. Ventura, *Into the Country of Standing Men*, 118.

33. Ventura, *Underground in Japan*, 70–71.

34. Ventura, *Underground in Japan*, 72–73.

35. Ventura, *Into the Country of Standing Men*, 119.

36. Ventura, *Into the Country of Standing Men*, 119.

37. Mai Añonuevo, interview with author, Makati City, August 1, 2014.

38. Añonuevo interview, August 1, 2014.

39. Pepper Marcelo, "Family Breakup: The Ugly Side of Migration," *Planet Philippines*, February 2007, 40.

40. Marcelo, "Family Breakup," 40.

41. Magtoto, Ruiz, and Sanchez, *Mga waging kuwento ng OFW 2006*, 107.

42. Parreñas, *Children of Global Migration*, 103–112.

43. Parreñas, *Children of Global Migration*.

44. Malu Padilla, "Women Changing Our Lives, Making HERstory: Migration Experiences of Babaylan Philippine Women's Network in Europe," in *In De Olde Worlde: Views of Filipino Migrants in Europe*, ed. Filomenita Mongaya Hoegsholm (Quezon City: Philippine Social Science Council, 2007), 85.

45. "Eighteen Years of Sacrifice" in Papias Generale Banados, *The Path to Remittance: Tales of Pains and Gains of Overseas Filipino Workers*, ed. Kalinga Seneviratne (Singapore: Global Eye Media, 2011), 51.

46. Faier, *Intimate Encounters*, 169.

47. Let-let A. Sulit, "Isang Desisyon" [A decision], in *Sa Pagyuko ng Kawayan: A Collection of Poems by Filipino Overseas Workers*, ed. Linda R. Layosa and Laura P. Luminarias (Hong Kong: AsiaPacific, 1992), 77–78.

48. Arboleda and Nuqui, *Migrants' Stories, Migrants' Voices*; and Nuqui and Panao, *Migrants' Stories, Migrants' Voices 2*.

49. "Sacrifice," in Nuqui and Panao, *Migrants' Stories, Migrants' Voices 2*, 15–22; "A Mother's Sacrifice," in Nuqui and Montañez, *Moving On*, 251–262; "Eighteen Years of Sacrifice," in Banados, *The Path to Remittance*, 50–52.

50. B. Boy, "Mag-abroad ay di biro," in Layosa and Luminarias, *Sa Pagyuko ng Kawayan*, 110.

> Kakat'wa na may sahod ka pero bulsa'y walang pilak
> Dahil lahat ng pera mo ang tungo ay sa remittance
> Kung mayroong isinananla tutubusin na kaagad
> Bukod pa ang inutang mo't sa agency ibinayad.
>
> Ilang nanay ang narito nakakuba sa trabaho
> Dahil nais na mag-aral ang anak at mapanuto
> Nag-iisang nagtitika nagtitiis ng kalbaryo
> Malas na lang pag ang mister nakaisip mag-number two.

51. Miss Thee and Abrico, "Pagtitiis at kinabukasan," *Tinig ng Marino*, November–December 2000, 38.

> Ang pamilyang mahal ang tanging nasa isip,
> Asawa't anak ng tigib din ng dalamhati . . . . . .
> . . . . . .
> Ito na ring ang nagsisilbing matibay at kalasag
> Laban sa kalungkutan ng buhay sa dagat;
> Inspirasyon din nila at pampatibay ng loob
> Upang masigurong maganda ang bukas.

52. See issues of *Tinig ng Marino*; and Layosa and Luminarias, *Sa Pagyuko ng Kawayan*.

53. Arnel Pura, poem, *Tinig ng Marino*, May–June 2000, 38.

> Sa karagatan at kalangitan
> Ngunit ano ba ito!
> Bagyong walang sabi-sabi
> Ay biglang dumating na nagsasabing
> Ikaw pala ay hindi na akin.

54. Cesar Polvorosa Jr., "Toronto Filipino Businesses, Ethnic Identity, and Place Making in the Diaspora," in *Filipinos in Canada: Disturbing Invisibility*, ed. Roland Sintos Coloma et al. (Toronto: University of Toronto Press, 2012), 194.

55. Ventura, *Into the Country of Standing Men*, 102–103.

56. Banados, *The Path to Remittance*, back cover.

57. "Eighteen Years of Sacrifice," in Banados, *The Path to Remittance*, 51.

58. Banados, *The Path to Remittance*, 52.

59. Banados, *The Path to Remittance*, vi.

60. Faier, *Intimate Encounters*, 169.

61. McKay, *Global Filipinos*, 107.

62. Leo Sicat, "I Sacrificed My Five-Year College Education to Become a Steward," in Espiritu, *Filipino American Lives*, 112.

63. Ventura, *Into the Country of Standing Men*; Arenas Felma Joy Tadios, "Managing Transnational Families: Emotional Labour and Entrepreneurial Agency among Filipino Migrant Domestics in Hong Kong" (PhD diss., City University of Hong Kong, 2015).

64. Tadios, "Managing Transnational Families," 161–164.

65. Tadios, "Managing Transnational Families," 161.

66. Raquel Delfin Padilla, "Bagong bayani o bigong bayani?," in *Sindi ng Lampara: OFW Stories*, ed. Raquel Delfin Padilla and Jovelyn Bayubay Revilla (Manila: Allibratore Enterprises, 2012), 74–75.

67. Robert de Guzman Jr., "Balikbayan Box," in Padilla and Revilla, *Sindi ng Lampara*, 168.

68. Zontini, *Transnational Families, Migration, and Gender*, 113 and 192.

69. Banados, *The Path to Remittance*, 52.

70. See issues of *Sinag*, DAWN's newsletter, January 1998–June 2010; and *Hearts Apart: Migration in the Eyes of Filipino Children* (Manila: Episcopal Commission for the Pastoral Care of Migrants and Itinerant People / Apostleship of the Sea–Manila, Scalabrini Migration Center, and Overseas Workers Welfare Administration, 2004).

71. Tzitza (pseudonym), "The Stranger," in Nuqui and Panao, *Migrants' Stories, Migrants' Voices 2*, 80.

72. Tzitza, "The Stranger," 82.

73. Tzitza, "The Stranger," 81.

74. Tzitza, "The Stranger," 81 and 83.

2. Challenging Constructions of Gender and Sexuality, 1980s–2018

1. "Kaya ang OFW na si ate o si kuya, dalawa ang asawa. Kung nasa Pinas siya, si original ang asawa. Kung nasa ibang bansa, si pangalawa naman ang itinuturing na kabiyak. Ooh la la!" Raquel Delfin Padilla, "Extra-Marital Affairs ng OFWs, Trend Daw? Ang mga naiwan, tapat din kaya?," in Padilla and Revilla, *Sindi ng Lampara*, 83.

2. "Maraming Pilipino sa Saudi, ang dami-dami, maraming may asawa rito, may asawa rin doon. Talagang doon, tukso." Nenita's story, in Garcia, *Pamilya, migrasyon, disintegrasyon*, 73.

3. Jessica Flores Napat, "Tukso, taksil, takbo," in *Masaya din, malungkot din (karanasan ng OFW)*, by Jovelyn B. Revilla (self-pub.; printed in the United States by Tatay Jobo Elizes, 2012), 102.

4. Napat, "Tukso, taksil, takbo," 99–102.

5. Papaias Generale Banados, *The Path to Remittance: Tales of Pains and Gains of Overseas Filipino Workers* (Singapore: Global Eye Media, 2011), 106–107.

6. For a discussion on the Virgin Mary as the role model for Filipino woman, see Roces, *Women's Movements and the Filipina*, 21–23.

7. Pingol, *Remaking Masculinities*; Parreñas, *Children of Global Migration*.

8. Martin F. Manalansan IV, *Global Divas: Filipino Gay Men in the Diaspora* (Quezon City: Ateneo de Manila University Press, 2006); Robert Diaz, Marissa Largo, and Fritz Pino, eds., *Diasporic Intimacies: Queer Filipinos and Canadian Imaginaries* (Chicago: Northwestern University Press, 2018); Parreñas, *Illicit Flirtations*; Sallie Yea, *Trafficking Women in Korea: Filipina Migrant Entertainers* (London: Routledge, 2015).

9. Manalansan, *Global Divas*; Diaz, Largo, and Pino, *Diasporic Intimacies*; Parreñas, *Illicit Flirtations*; Yea, *Trafficking Women in Korea*.

10. Nicole Constable, "Sexuality and Discipline among Filipino Domestic Workers in Hong Kong," *American Ethnologist* 24, no. 3 (1997): 539–558; Julian McAllister Groves and Kimberly Chang, "Romancing Resistance and Resisting Romance: Ethnography and Construction of Power in the Filipina Domestic Worker Community in Hong Kong," *Journal of Contemporary Ethnography* 28, no. 3 (1999): 235–265.

11. Manalansan, *Global Divas*.

12. Nicanor G. Tiongson, "Woman in Nineteenth Century Philippines," in *Filipino Heritage*, vol. 7, ed. Alfredo Roces (Manila: Lahing Pilipino, 1978), 1784; Maria Luisa Camagay, *Working Women of Manila in the Nineteenth Century* (Quezon City: University of the Philippines Press and University Center for Women's Studies, 1995).

13. Mina Roces, "Is the Suffragist an American Colonial Construct? Defining 'The Filipino Woman' in Colonial Philippines," in *Women's Suffrage in Asia: Gender, Nationalism and Democracy*, ed. Louise Edwards and Mina Roces (London: Routledge, 2004), 26.

14. For an in-depth discussion of Filipina feminists' engagement with Maria Clara, see Roces, "Is the Suffragist an American Colonial Construct?," 24–58; Roces, *Women's Movements and the Filipina*; and Denise Cruz, *Transpacific Femininities: The Making of the Modern Filipina* (Durham, NC: Duke University Press, 2012).

15. Cruz, *Transpacific Femininities*, 67–109.

16. Sylvia Estrada-Claudio, *Rape, Love and Sexuality: The Construction of Woman in Discourse* (Quezon City: University of the Philippines Press, 2002), 20.

17. See Roces, *Women's Movements and the Filipina*, 11; Elizabeth U. Eviota, ed., *Sex and Gender in Philippine Society* (Manila: National Commission on the Role of Filipino Women, 1994); Amaryllis Tiglao Torres, *Love in the Time of Ina Morata* (Quezon City: University Center for Women's Studies, 2002).

18. Raquel A. G. Reyes, *Love, Passion and Patriotism: Sexuality and the Philippine Propaganda Movement, 1882–1892* (Singapore: NUS Press, 2008).

19. Reyes, *Love, Passion and Patriotism*.

20. Mina Roces, "Gender, Nation and the Politics of Dress in Twentieth-Century Philippines," *Gender & History* 17, no. 2 (2005): 360.

21. Elizabeth U. Eviota, "The Social Construction of Sexuality," in Eviota, *Sex and Gender in Philippine Society*, 61.

22. Torres, *Love in the Time of Ina Morata*, 135.

23. Laurence Wai-Teng Leong, "Asian Sexuality or Singapore Exceptionalism?," *Liverpool Law Review* 33 (2012): 11.

24. Leong, "Asian Sexuality," 15.

25. Leong, "Asian Sexuality," 23.

26. Sherifa Zuhur, "Criminal Law, Women and Sexuality in the Middle East," in *Deconstructing Sexuality in the Middle East: Challenges and Discourses*, ed. Pinar Ilkkaracan (Aldershot: Ashgate, 2008), 21.

27. Zuhur, "Criminal Law," 31.

28. Pinar Ilkkaracan, "Introduction: Sexuality as a Contested Political Domain in the Middle East," in Ilkkaracan, *Deconstructing Sexuality*, 10.

29. Ilkkaracan, "Introduction," 10.

30. Lan, *Global Cinderellas*, 3, 109, 112, 167; and Brenda S. A. Yeoh and Shirlena Huang, "Negotiating Public Space: Strategies and Styles of Migrant Female Domestic Workers in Singapore," *Urban Studies* 35, no. 3 (1998): 590–594.

31. Constable, "Sexuality and Discipline," 545; and Lan, *Global Cinderellas*, 3, 109, 112, 167.

32. Asuncion Fresnoza-Flot, "The Catholic Church in the Lives of Irregular Migrant Filipinas in France: Identity Formation, Empowerment and Social Control," *Asia-Pacific Journal of Anthropology* 11, nos. 3–4 (2010): 356.

33. Madianou and Miller, *Migration and New Media*; McKay, "On the Face of Facebook"; Paragas, "Migrant Workers and Mobile Phones"; and Johnson and McKay, "Mediated Diasporas."

34. Adelle J. Esic, *Buhay Saudi ng OFW Caregiver* (self-pub.; printed in the United States by Tatay Jobo Elizes, 2013), 46 ("Bakit ngayon ka lang," which tells the story of how a caregiver who was separated from her husband who got a job in Kuwait found romance with a married Filipino man through Facebook); and 20–23 ("Mahal kita ngunit bawal" [I love you although it is forbidden], which recounts the life of two childhood friends who had married other spouses but started a romance through Facebook).

35. "A Childless 'Single Wife' Overseas," in Banados, *The Path to Remittance*, 62.

36. Banados, *The Path to Remittance*.

37. Lan, *Global Cinderellas*, 187.

38. Jovelyn Bayubay Revilla, "Kring kring, sex on phone? Aral para sa mga kababaihan," and "Kring kring, sex on phone? Hinaing ni Fred," in Padilla and Revilla, *Sindi ng Lampara*, 104–111 and 108–111.

39. Zhang Juan, "Ethnic Boundaries Redefined: The Emergence of the 'Permanent Outsiders' in Singapore" (master's thesis, National University of Singapore, 2005), 106–110.

40. Banados, *The Path to Remittance*, 62, 106–107.

41. Fresnoza-Flot, "The Catholic Church," 356–357.

42. "Damit ko na pangkatulong," in Revilla, *Masaya din*, 31–33.

43. "Sa damit ko na pangkatulong taas noo kong ipagmalaki na nakatapos kapatid ko dahil sa pagsuot ko nito na naging bahagi ng buhay ditto sa bansang dayuhan." "Damit ko na pangkatulong," in Revilla, *Masaya din*, 33.

44. "Skinny, sexy nga ba?," in Revilla, *Masaya din*, 20–22.

45. Deney Rue, "Misteryo ng Pag-iibigang Pinay at Singaporean," *Manila Press* (Singapore), 3, no. 1 (October 1995): 38–39.

46. Banados, *The Path to Remittance*, 58–63.

47. Rosanna Luz F. Valerio, "Pagtitimpi at Panggigigil: Sex and the Migrant Woman," in Dizon-Añonuevo and Añonuevo, *Coming Home*, 61.

48. Maria Thelma Noval-Jezewski, "A Simplified Map of French-Philippines: A Bird's Eye–Worm's Eye View," in Hoegsholm, *In De Olde Worlde*, 297.

49. Banados, *The Path to Remittance*.

50. "Overseas for Survival or Adventure?," in Banados, *The Path to Remittance*, 9.

51. "A Childless 'Single Wife' Overseas," in Banados, *The Path to Remittance*, 61.

52. "Private Life," *Manila Press* 2, no. 8 (April 1995): 16; "Private Life," *Manila Press* 2, no. 20 (April 1995): 21–22; "Dear Tita Lily Problem Page," *Manila Press* 2, no. 8 (April 1995): 18–19; "Dear Tita Lily Problem Page," *Manila Press* 2, no. 12: 19–20;

"Dear Tita Lily Problem Page," *Manila Press* 2, no. 12: 19–20; "True Confession," *Manila Press* 2, no. 8 (1995): 40–42.

53. Rue, "Misteryo ng Pag-iibigang Pinay," 38.
54. Rue, "Misteryo ng Pag-iibigang Pinay," 38–39.
55. Rue, "Misteryo ng Pag-iibigang Pinay," 38.
56. Rue, "Misteryo ng Pag-iibigang Pinay," 38–39.
57. Judith Lorraine S. Moreno, "When Love Speaks," in Layosa and Luminarias, *Sa Pagyuko ng Kawayan*, 82–83.
58. Layosa and Luminarias, *Sa Pagyuko ng Kawayan*.
59. Roces, *Women's Movements and the Filipina*, 121.
60. Roces, *Women's Movements and the Filipina*, 119.
61. Roces, *Women's Movements and the Filipina*, 120.
62. Nicole Constable, "Dolls, T-Birds, and Ideal Workers: The Negotiation of Filipino Identity in Hong Kong," in *Home and Hegemony: Domestic Service and Identity Politics in South and Southeast Asia*, ed. Kathleen M. Adams and Sara Dickey (Ann Arbor: University of Michigan Press, 2000), 238.
63. Amy Sim, "Lesbianism among Indonesian Women Migrants in Hong Kong," in *As Normal as Possible*, ed. Yau Ching (Hong Kong: Hong Kong University Press, 2010), 44.
64. Valerio, "Pagtitimpi at Panggigigil," 69.
65. "True Confession Ayon sa Tunay na Karanasan ni Ling Orosco Kasalukuyang DH sa Hong Kong," *Manila Press*, April 1995, 40.
66. Noval-Jezewski, "A Simplified Map," 296.
67. I have found only one memoir of homosexuality in the migrant memoirs. It is about one man's discovery of his sexuality in the migration context in Kuwait. See "It's Strange to Be What I Am in Kuwait," in Banados, *The Path to Remittance*, 64–68.
68. Banados, *The Path to Remittance*, 62.
69. Banados, *The Path to Remittance*.
70. Patrick Daly and Joel Fendelman (Directors), *Remittance*, 2015.
71. Personal communication, Jun Dulay, Metro-Manila, June 26, 2017.
72. Rue, "Misteryo ng Pag-iibigang Pinay," 38.
73. Rue, "Misteryo ng Pag-iibigang Pinay," 38.

3. Consumption and Social Change, 1980s–2018

1. Ventura, *Into the Country of Standing Men*, 101–102.
2. Ventura, *Into the Country of Standing Men*, 102–104.
3. Charito Basa, Violeta de Guzman, and Sabrina Marchetti, *International Migration and Over-Indebtedness: The Case of Filipino Workers in Italy*, International Institute for Environment and Development, Human Settlements Working Paper No. 36, Rural-Urban Interactions and Livelihood Strategies, October 2012.
4. Mirca Madianou and Daniel Miller define the balikbayan box as "the tea-chest cargo" in their book, *Migration and New Media: Transnational Families and Polymedia* (London: Routledge, 2012), 71–72.
5. For research on remittance houses, see Filomeno V. Aguilar Jr., "Labour Migration and the Ties of Relatedness: Diasporic Houses and Investments in Memory in a Rural Philippine Village," *Thesis Eleven* 98 (2009): 88–114; Aguilar et al., *Maal-*

wang Buhay; and Arnisson Andre Ortega, *Neoliberalizing Spaces in the Philippines: Suburbanization, Transnational Migration, and Dispossession* (Lanham, MD: Lexington Books, 2016). For scholarship on *balikbayan* boxes, see Jade Alburo, "Boxed In or Out? Balikbayan Boxes as Metaphors for Filipino American (Dis)Location," *Ethnologies* 27, no. 2 (2005): 137–157; Clement C. Camposano, "Enacting Embeddedness through the Transnational Traffic in Goods: The Case of Ilonggo OFWs in Hong Kong," *Review of Women's Studies* 21, no. 2 (2012): 1–28; and McKay, *Global Filipinos*.

6. Mary Hollnsteiner, "Reciprocity in Lowland Philippines," *Philippine Studies* 9, no. 3 (1961): 387–413; Frank Lynch, "Social Acceptance Reconsidered," in *Four Readings in Philippine Values*, IPC Papers No. 2, ed. Frank Lynch and Alfonso de Guzman II (Quezon City: Ateneo de Manila University Press, 1973), 1–68; and Charles Kaut, "Utang na Loob: A System of Contractual Obligation among Tagalogs," *Southwestern Journal of Anthropology* 17, no. 3 (1961): 256–272. Mirca Madianou and Daniel Miller, Migration and New Media, 71–72.

7. Verma Villanueva, interview with author, Santa Rosa, Laguna, Philippines, August 2, 2014; Gunnar M. Lamvik, "The Filipino Seafarer: A Life between Sacrifice and Shopping" (PhD diss., Norwegian University of Science and Technology, 2002), 128–133, and 185–190.

8. Lamvik, "The Filipino Seafarer."

9. Lamvik, "The Filipino Seafarer," 133.

10. Lamvik, "The Filipino Seafarer," 131.

11. Lamvik, "The Filipino Seafarer," 128–133.

12. Lorna Vea Munnecom, interview with author, Paris, November 17, 2015.

13. Villanueva interview, August 2, 2014; Munnecom interview, November 17, 2015; Rose Marie Reyes, interview with author, Milan, November 22, 2015; Maya Jezewski, interview with author, Paris, November 17, 2015; and Liza Coronado, interview with author, San Roque, Laguna, July 5, 2015.

14. Mai Añonuevo, Atikha founder and director, interview with author, Makati City, August 1, 2014.

15. Chit Balmaceda Gutierrez, "Nouveaux Riches: OFWs Join the Middle Class," *Filipinas*, August 2000, 33.

16. Gutierrez, "Nouveaux Riches," 33.

17. Sherald Salamat, "Isang malaking kahon ang pasalubong ni Papa," in Padilla and Revilla, *Sindi ng Lampara*, 189.

18. "Ang problema ay akala mo kung sino kaming mayaman. May dala akong P100,000, inutang ko pa ang iba doon, noon 1995. Maniniwala ka bang sa loob ng isa at kalahating buwan ay wala nang natira doon?" Augustus T. Añonuevo, "Reintegration, an Elusive Dream?," in Dizon-Añonuevo and Añonuevo, *Coming Home*, 131.

19. Mai Añonuevo interview, August 1, 2014.

20. Añonuevo, "Reintegration, an Elusive Dream?," 131. See also F. R. Arcinas, "Asian Migration to the Gulf Region: The Philippine Case," in *Migration to the Arab World: Experience of Returning Migrants*, ed. Godfrey Gunatilleke (Tokyo: United Nations University Press, 1991), 143–144, where Arcinas refers to this as "the proletarization of the worker in the host country and the 'bourgeoisification' of the members of his family." In his study, which focused on Filipino migrants in the Middle East, Arcinas

observed that his respondents had a tendency to flaunt their status acquisitions, highlighting the contrast between the thrifty, hardworking migrant and the dependent but materialistic family in the Philippines.

21. "Nagtitiis na parang ipis sa France para bumili ng mansion sa Pilipinas." Munnecom and Jezewski interviews, November 17, 2015.

22. Interviews with Filipino domestic workers in Milan, November 2015; Verma Villanueva, interviews with author, Padova, Italy, November 25, 2015, and Santa Rosa, Laguna, August 2, 2014.

23. Zontini, *Transnational Families*.

24. Charito Basa and Rosalud Jing de la Rosa, *Me, Us, and Them: Realities and Illusions of Filipina Domestic Workers; A Community Research Project by the Filipino Women's Council* (Rome: EU/EQUAL [ESF] and the Italian Ministry of Welfare, 2004), 11.

25. Parreñas, *Servants of Globalization*, 5.

26. Basa and de la Rosa, *Me, Us, and Them*, 12.

27. Zontini, *Transnational Families*, 13.

28. Parreñas, *Servants of Globalization*, 19.

29. Basa, de Guzman, and Marchetti, *International Migration and Over-Indebtedness*, 10.

30. Basa, de Guzman, and Marchetti, *International Migration and Over-Indebtedness*, 10.

31. Natalia Ribas, Charito Basa, and Rosalud de la Rosa, *Gender, Remittances and Development: The Case of Filipino Migration to Italy* (Santo Domingo, Dominican Republic: United Nations International Research and Training Institute for the Advancement of Women, 2008). Verma Villanueva, Welvin "Bitoy" Villanueva, and Nizer Catipon, interview with author, Padova, November 25, 2015; and Jacinta Carlos, interview with author, Milan, November 22, 2015.

32. Basa, de Guzman, and Marchetti, *International Migration and Over-Indebtedness*, 21.

33. Anja Wessels, *Home Sweet Home? Work, Life and Well-Being of Foreign Domestic Workers in Singapore* (Singapore: Humanitarian Organization for Migrant Economics, 2015), 10.

34. Wessels, *Home Sweet Home?*, 10. Another study estimated that one in six Singaporean households hired a domestic worker. See Trisha Tsui-Chuan Lin and Shirley Haiso-Li Sun, "Connection as a Form of Resisting Control: Foreign Domestic Workers' Mobile Phone Use in Singapore," *Media Asia* 37, no. 4 (2010): 183.

35. Wessels, *Home Sweet Home?*, 27. Other estimates are similar, such as S$500, cited in Chiu Yee Koh et al., "Drivers of Migration Policy Reform: The Day Off Policy for Migrant Domestic Workers in Singapore," *Global Social Policy* 17, no. 2 (2017): 196.

36. Steven C. McKay, "Filipino Sea Men: Identity and Masculinity in a Global Labor Niche," in *Asian Diasporas: New Formations, New Conceptions*, ed. Rhacel Salazar Parreñas and Lok C. D. Siu (Stanford, CA: Stanford University Press, 2007), 68.

37. "Filipino Seamen Help Prop Up Economy," *Ahoy Magazine*, January–March 1997, 8.

38. "12,000 Jobs Available to Filipino Seamen Despite Crisis This Year," GMA News Online, January 21, 2009, http://www.gmanetwork.com/news/story/145278/news/12-000-jobs-available-to-filipino-seamen-despite-crisis-this-year.

39. "Filipino Seamen Help Prop Up Economy," 8.

40. Lamvik, "The Filipino Seafarer," 131.

41. Lamvik, "The Filipino Seafarer," 113–141.

42. Lamvik, "The Filipino Seafarer," 133, and 151–152.

43. See coverage of the Paderanga-Abuid wedding, in *Tinig ng Marino*, May–June 2000, 17.

44. Advertisement for Alsomavic Cargo Ltd in the United Kingdom, *Planet Philippines*, January 2011, 20.

45. Camposano, "Enacting Embeddedness," 26; Robert de Guzman Jr., "Balikbayan Box," in Padilla and Revilla, *Sindi ng Lampara*, 170. A domestic worker in Milan revealed that her employer renovated her kitchen every five years and donated all the secondhand appliances to her, which she sent to her family in the Philippines. Jocelyn Averion Ebora, interview with author, Milan, November 22, 2015; Noeline Rivera, interview with author, Singapore, July 26, 2017.

46. Rivera interview, July 26, 2017.

47. Rivera interview, July 26, 2017.

48. Ventura, *Underground in Japan*, 68.

49. McKay, *An Archipelago of Care*, 101.

50. Personal communication, Sharon Tordesillas, regional manager of LBC, Singapore, July 26, 2017.

51. Camposano, "Enacting Embeddedness," 1–28.

52. L. Rimban, "Out of the (Balikbayan) Box," *Investigative Reporting Quarterly*, April–June 2005; and C. Mercado-Obias, "Love in a Box," *Smile Magazine*, April–May 2008, 100; both quoted in Camposano, "Enacting Embeddedness," 2.

53. McKay, *Global Filipinos*, 103.

54. Camposano, "Enacting Embeddedness," 1–28; Alburo, "Boxed In or Out?," 137–157.

55. De Guzman, "Balikbayan Box," in Padilla and Revilla, *Sindi ng Lampara*, 170.

56. Salamat, "Isang malaking kahon," in Padilla and Revilla, *Sindi ng Lampara*, 189.

57. Quoted in Alburo, "Boxed In or Out?," 148.

58. Mai Dizon-Añonuevo, "Revisiting Migrant Women's Lives: Stories of Struggles, Failures and Successes" in *Coming Home: Women, Migration, and Reintegration*, ed. Estrella Dizon-Añonuevo and Augustus T. Añonuevo (Manila: Balikabayani Foundation, Inc., and ATIKHA Overseas Workers and Communities Initiative Inc., 2002), 25.

59. McKay, *Global Filipinos*, 101–107.

60. Quoted in Marisha Maas, "Door-to-Door Cargo Agents: Cultivating and Expanding Filipino Transnational Space," in *Tales of Development: People, Power and Space*, ed. Paul Hebincks, Sef Slootweg, and Lothar Smith (Assen, The Netherlands: Royal Van Gorum B.V., 2008), 139.

61. Michael Tan, "One Day Millionaires," *Planet Philippines*, January 2008, 36.

62. Lamvik, "The Filipino Seafarer," 141.

63. Frederick Arceo, "Iba pa rin sa Pinas," *Planet Philippines*, January 2011, 7: "Kapag hindi mo nabigyan ng pasalubong ay magtatampo na yun at sisiraan ka na." See also Tadios, "Managing Transnational Families."

64. Lamvik, "The Filipino Seafarer," 141.

65. McKay, *An Archipelago of Care*, 101.

66. Divine Villanueva, "Bagahe," in Padilla and Revilla, *Sindi ng Lampara*, 187–188.

67. "Door-to-Door Boxes," in Aryo, *Nanny Tales*, 31.

68. Raquel Delfin Padilla, "Si OFW at ang Mapang-Abusong Pamilya," in Padilla and Revilla, *Sindi ng Lampara*, 30–31.
69. Marites N. Sison "Diaspora Dreams," *Filipinas*, May 2003, 55.
70. Tan, "One Day Millionaires," 36.
71. Tan, "One Day Millionaires," 36.
72. Battistella and Asis, *Country Migration Report*, 117.
73. Añonuevo, "Reintegration, an Elusive Dream?," 131; Basa, de Guzman, and Marchetti, *International Migration and Over-Indebtedness*, 21.
74. Battistella and Asis, *Country Migration Report*, 117.
75. Añonuevo, "Reintegration, an Elusive Dream?," 130–131; Basa, de Guzman, and Marchetti, *International Migration and Over-Indebtedness*, 12.
76. Gina Alunan Melgar and Estrella Dizon-Añonuevo, "Mag-Atikha Para Maka-Balikbayani: Planting the Seeds of a Comprehensive Reintegration Program for OFWs (The Atikha-Balikabayani Experience)," in Dizon-Añonuevo and Añonuevo, *Coming Home*, 173.
77. Arcinas, "Asian Migration to the Gulf Region," 137–138.
78. Mai Añonuevo interview, August 1, 2014; Augustus Añonuevo, "Reintegration, an Elusive Dream?," 131.
79. See Tadios, "Managing Transnational Families."
80. Tadios, "Managing Transnational Families," 249.
81. Battistella and Asis, *Country Migration Report*, 117.
82. Alvin Ang, Jeremaiah Opiniano, et al., "Remittance Investment Climate Analysis in Rural Hometowns (RICART): Results and Policy Implications," PowerPoint presentation for the Remittance for Development Council, circa 2014, provided to me by Rodrigo Garcia of the Commission on Filipinos Overseas; Weekley, "From Wage Labourers to Investors?," 205.
83. Ruth C. Gonzaga, "The BSP Financial Literacy Campaign (FLC): Providing Overseas Filipinos and Their Beneficiaries Practical Tools for Financial Freedom," *Bangko Sentral Review*, January 2007, 24–29.
84. Gonzaga, "The BSP Financial Literacy Campaign," 25.
85. Gonzaga, "The BSP Financial Literacy Campaign," 25.
86. Melgar and Dizon-Añonuevo, "Mag-Atikha Para Maka-Balikbayani," 170–171.
87. Melgar and Dizon-Añonuevo, "Mag-Atikha Para Maka-Balikbayani," 173.
88. PinoyWISE International, "Who We Are: Pinoy WISE Movement," accessed August 29, 2016, http://www.pinoywiseinternational.org/who-we-are/.
89. Melgar and Dizon-Añonuevo, "Mag-Atikha Para Maka-Balikbayani," 174–175.
90. Melgar and Dizon-Añonuevo, "Mag-Atikha Para Maka-Balikbayani," 182.
91. Field notes, "Family and Income Management" seminar, PinoyWISE, July 16, 2017, Singapore.
92. Mai Añonuevo interview, August 1, 2014.
93. Mai Añonuevo interview, August 1, 2014.
94. Mai Añonuevo interview, August 1, 2014; and field notes, "Family and Income Management" seminar, July 16, 2017.
95. Field notes, PinoyWISE seminar for migrant families, Malolos, Bulacan, February 27, 2019; Mai Añonuevo, interview with author, Makati City, Philippines, February 26, 2019.
96. Mai Añonuevo interview, August 1, 2014.

97. Interviews with Filipino domestic workers in Milan and Padova in 2015, and with Filipino domestic workers in Singapore, July 16, 2017.
98. Interviews with Lisa and Jesme (pseudonums), Singapore, July 16, 2017.
99. Filipino domestic workers in Milan, interview with author, November 22, 2015, and Filipino domestic workers in Padova, interview with author, November 29, 2015, and August 2018.

4. The Impact of Consumption on Businesses, 1990s–2018

1. Patricia May B. Jurilla, *Tagalog Bestsellers of the Twentieth Century: A History of the Book in the Philippines* (Quezon City: Ateneo de Manila University Press, 2008), 160–185; Georgina R. Encanto, "Savoring Romance Pinoy Style in Foreign Climes: Why Women Migrants Love Reading Tagalog Romance Novels," *Review of Women's Studies* 18, no. 1 (January–June 2008): 27–52.

2. Gemma Nemenzo, "Healthy, Fancy, Trendy: Quesada Trio Bring Filipino Tastes Mainstream," *Positively Filipino*, August 14, 2013, http://www.positivelyfilipino.com/magazine/healthy-fancy-trendy-quesada-trio-bring-filipino-tastes-to-the-mainstream?rq=healthy%2C%20fancy%20trendy; Laarni C. Almendrada, "They Mean Business: Ramar's Primo Quesada Frozen Assets," *Filipinas*, July 1997, 43–44.

3. Ethel Regis Lu, "Negotiating Transnational Belonging: The Filipino Channel, 'Global Filipinos,' and Filipino American Audiences," in *Southeast Asian Migration: People on the Move in Search of Work, Refuge and Belonging*, ed. Khatharya Um and Sofia Gaspar (Brighton: Sussex Academic Press, 2016), 114–136; Rolando B. Tolentino, "Niche Globality: Philippine Media Texts to the World," in *Popular Culture Co-Productions and Collaborations in East and Southeast Asia*, ed. Nissim Otmazgin and Eyal Ben-Ari (Singapore: NUS Press; and Kyoto: Kyoto University Press, 2013), 150–168; Roland B. Tolentino, "Globalizing National Domesticity: Female Work and Representation in Contemporary Women's Films," in *More Pinay Than We Admit: The Social Construction of the Filipina*, ed. Maria Luisa Camagay (Quezon City: Vibal Productions, 2010), 185–209; and Emily Noelle Ignacio, "'Home' and The Filipino Channel: Stabilizing Economic Security, Migration Patterns, and Diaspora through New Technologies," in *Filipino Studies: Palimpsests of Nation and Diaspora*, ed. Martin F. Manalansan IV and Augusto F. Espiritu (New York: New York University Press, 2016), 375–387.

4. Aguilar et al., *Maalwang Buhay*, 151–152; Aguilar, "Labour Migration and Ties of Relatedness," 88–114; Lieba Faier, "Affective Investments in the Manila Region: Filipino Migrants in Rural Japan and Transnational Urban Development in the Philippines," *Transactions of the Institute of British Geographers* 38, no. 3 (2013): 376–390.

5. Aguilar et al., *Maalwang Buhay*, 151–152; Aguilar, "Labour Migration and Ties of Relatedness," 88–114.

6. Pido, *Migrant Returns*, 4.

7. Pido, *Migrant Returns*, 141–142.

8. Mika Bautista (senior sales manager) and Nicole Reyes (marketing supervisor), both of Rockwell Land, interview with author, Makati City, August 13, 2014; and Phyllis Theresa C. Cruz (head of Century Properties Group's resale division), interview with author, Makati City, July 1, 2016.

9. Mynardo Macaraig, "Overseas Pinoys Fuel Real Estate Boom at Home," *Planet Philippines*, January 2011, 8 and 12.

10. For an in-depth history of the Lopez family until 2000, see Mina Roces, *Kinship Politics in Post-War Philippines: The Lopez Family, 1946–2000* (Manila: De La Salle University Press, 2001).

11. Raffy Lopez (son of Geny Lopez and CEO of ABS-CBN International), interview with author, San Francisco, December 5, 2013.

12. Tolentino, "Globalizing National Domesticity," 193.

13. Raffy Lopez interview, December 5, 2013.

14. Raffy Lopez interview, December 5, 2013.

15. "Lopez Is ABS-CBN Global's SVP-COO," *Philippine Star*, June 29, 2004, B6.

16. Raffy Lopez interview, December 5, 2013.

17. Raffy Lopez interview, December 5, 2013.

18. Raffy Lopez interview, December 5, 2013.

19. The US Census of 2010 reported that the median income of Filipina/o/x Americans was $51,668. Quoted in Rodriguez, *Celebrating Debutantes and Quinceañeras*, 11.

20. Raffy Lopez interview, December 5, 2013. TFC's rival GMA, on the other hand, was not so successful, because, although it launched a direct-to-home satellite six months before ABS-CBN International, it went bankrupt. This benefited TFC since the five hundred customers of GMA who were stuck with $2,000 worth of equipment and no programs to view became TFC's first customers.

21. Raffy Lopez interview, December 5, 2013.

22. Sheila C. Salido, "'Beamers': ABS-CBN Cashes in on the Growing Population of Filipinos in North America," *Filipinas*, September 1995, 26.

23. Antonio Katigbak, "ABS-CBN's The Filipino Channel Marks a Decade of Steady Growth," *Philippine Star*, April 11, 2004.

24. Katigbak, "ABS-CBN's The Filipino Channel."

25. Christina Mendez and Conrado Diaz Jr., "ABS-CBN Expands Reach to Japan, Italy," *Philippine Star*, April 30, 2000; ABS-CBN archives.

26. Katigbak, "ABS-CBN's The Filipino Channel."

27. Katigbak, "ABS-CBN's The Filipino Channel."

28. Jennifer B. Austria, "ABS-CBN Global Delays Listing in Singapore Bourse," *Manila Standard*, March 22, 2004, B3.

29. Raffy Lopez would prefer to have an estimate rather than the actual amount as these figures are usually held confidentially to protect the company from its rivals. With his permission, I have been allowed to state that it is over a $100 million. Raffy Lopez interview, December 5, 2013.

30. Katigbak, "ABS-CBN's The Filipino Channel"; and Raffy Lopez interview, December 5, 2013.

31. Mendez and Diaz, "ABS-CBN Expands Reach to Japan, Italy."

32. Raffy Lopez interview, December 5, 2013.

33. Raffy Lopez interview, December 5, 2013.

34. Full-page advertisement for TFC ABS-CBN, *Filipinas*, April 1999, 7.

35. Leonardo Belen, "Mabuhay OFW on Channel 21," *Manila Bulletin*, July 24, 2000, F4; and "At Last, a Show for OFWs," *Manila Times*, July 23, 2000, 3B.

36. Tolentino, "Female Work and Representation," 195.

37. Raffy Lopez interview, December 5, 2013.

38. "Anak CMMA Winner," *Philippine Star*, October 18, 2000, 53.

39. "Maalaala Mo Kaya Makes It Easy to Call Your Loved Ones in the Philippines This Valentine's Day," two-page color advertisement for ABS-CBN, *Filipinas Magazine*, February 1996, 6–7.

40. Cathy Rose A. Garcia, "ABS-CBN Global Extends Beyond Cable Business," *Today*, May 25, 2004, 13; and Raffy Lopez interview, December 5, 2013. In 2013, TFC hoped to capture the Hong Kong and Singapore domestic worker market (who live with their employers and are not able to access their own televisions without being closely watched), and seafarers who live on the ship. Raffy Lopez revealed in my interview with him that the plan was to offer them a USB stick with TFC programs on it so that they can plug it to their mobile phones and watch programs anywhere.

40. Raffy Lopez interview, December 5, 2013.

41. See full-page advertisement for TFC in *Planet Philippines*, Spoton feature section, June 2012, 34; and *Filipinas* issues from 1992 to 2010.

42. See full-page advertisement for TFC in *Planet Philippines*, June 2012, 34.

43. Jocelyn Averion Ebora, interview with author, Milan, November 22, 2015; and full-page advertisement, in *Planet Philippines*, Spoton travel supplement, January 2011, 10.

44. Ortega, *Neoliberalizing Spaces in the Philippines*, 95.

45. Macaraig, "Overseas Pinoys Fuel Real Estate Boom," 12.

46. Pido, *Migrant Returns*, 4 and 72–111.

47. Pido, *Migrant Returns*, 74.

48. Pido, *Migrant Returns*, 75.

49. "Overseas Pinoys Fuel Building Boom," *Planet Philippines*, February 2007, 22.

50. Cruz interview, July 1, 2016.

51. Ortega, *Neoliberalizing Spaces*, 97.

52. Pido, *Migrant Returns*, 85.

53. Ortega, *Neoliberalizing Spaces*, 97.

54. Bautista and Reyes interview, August 13, 2014; Cruz interview, July 1, 2016; Ortega, *Neoliberalizing Spaces*, 97–115; Pido, *Migrant Returns*, 74–106. See also advertisements in *Planet Philippines*, 2007–2008, 2011–2013.

55. Bautista and Reyes interview, August 13, 2014.

56. Rockwell full-page advertisement, *Planet Philippines*, July 2012, 9; Ayala Land full-page advertisement, *Planet Philippines*, July 2013, 27.

57. Full-page advertisement for Century Properties Mega Europe Tour, *Planet Philippines*, June 2011, 15.

58. "Overseas Pinoys Fuel Building Boom," 22.

59. Cruz interview, July 1, 2016; "Realty Firm Shows OFWs How to Be Successful Investors," *Planet Philippines*, August 2012, 20.

60. Ayala Land, "Contact Us," accessed August 8, 2016, http://www.ayalaland.com.ph/contact-us/; and Bautista and Reyes interview, August 13, 2014.

61. Robinsons Land Corporation advertisement, *Planet Philippines*, Spoton travel feature, April 2011, 5.

62. "Realty Firm Shows OFWs How to Be Successful Investors," 20.

63. Bautista and Reyes interview, August 13, 2014; *Planet Philippines*, 2007, 2008, 2011–2014; *Filipinas*, 2000–2010.

64. Bautista and Reyes interview, August 13, 2014.

65. "Century Properties European Tour 2011" full-page advertisement, *Planet Philippines*, May 2011, 11.
66. "Mega Europe Tour 2011," *Planet Philippines*, June 2011, 36, and September 2011, 15.
67. "Overseas Pinoys Fuel Building Boom," 22.
68. Overseas Pinoys Fuel Building Boom," 22.
69. Edward L. Tan, *Real Estate Buyer Profile and Behavior: Helps You Understand the Overseas Filipino Workers' Buyer Behavior* (Mandaluyong City: Miracle, 2007), 48.
70. Ortega, *Neoliberalizing Spaces*, 42.
71. Cruz interview, July 1, 2016.
72. Cruz interview, July 1, 2016.
73. Cruz interview, July 1, 2016.
74. Ortega, *Neoliberalizing Spaces*, 95–166.
75. Full-page advertisement for *Planet Philippines*, December 2007, 22–23; full-page advertisement for Ayala Land, *Planet Philippines*, September 2007, 2; advertisement for Pila Townhouses, *Planet Philippines*, September 2007, 13; advertisement for Chelsea Homes, *Planet Philippines*, September 2007, 34; full-page advertisement for Sta. Lucia Land Inc., *Planet Philippines*, June 2011, 5; full-page advertisement for Filinivest, *Planet Philippines*, June 2011, 11; and advertisement for Ayala Land, *Planet Philippines*, June 2011, 12. The search for suitable land on which to build outside the peri-urban fringe led to a new trend of converting agricultural land into real-estate projects all over the country, which produced its own problems, including the dispossession of lands owned by indigenous communities. See Ortega, *Neoliberalizing Spaces*, 243–311.
76. Bautista and Reyes interview, August 13, 2014; Cruz interview, , July 1, 2016.
77. Bautista and Reyes interview, August 13, 2014; Cruz interview, July 1, 2016.
78. Tan, *Real Estate Buyer Profile,* 46.
79. Tan, *Real Estate Buyer Profile*, 79.
80. Bautista and Reyes interview, August 13, 2014; Cruz interview, July 1, 2016; Percival V. Lacanaria II, Filinvest, Lucky Plaza, Singapore, personal communication, August 2017.
81. Pido, *Migrant Returns*, 72–111; Ortega, *Neoliberalizing Spaces*.
82. Cruz interview, July 1, 2016.
83. Bautista and Reyes interview, August 13, 2014; advertisements in *Planet Philippines*, 2007–2008, 2011–2013.
84. SM Residences advertisement, *Planet Philippines*, February 2011, 11.
85. Full-page advertisement for GA Sky Suites, *Planet Philippines*, July 2007, 5.
86. SM Residences, advertisement, *Planet Philippines*, February 2011, 11.
87. Pila Townhomes advertisement, *Planet Philippines*, September 2007, 13.
88. "A New City Soon to Rise in Cebu," *Planet Philippines*, Spoton, June 2011, 11.
89. Acqua Private Residences, Century Properties European 2011 Tour, full-page advertisement, *Planet Philippines,* May 2011, 11.
90. Simone Christ, *The Culture of Migration in the Philippines: Of Jeepneys and Balikbayan Boxes* (Berlin: Regiospectra Verlag, 2016), 173.
91. Christ, *The Culture of Migration*, 173; Roli Talampas, "Barangay Barko: Panimulang Pag-Aaral sa Buhay Panlipunan ng Marinong Pilipino," unpublished paper, October 2003.

92. "Max's Delivery in the Philippines through BDO Remit," accessed December 29, 2016, http://www.certifiedfoodies.com/2010/09/maxs-bdo-remit-delivery-ofws/.

5. Filipina/o/x Americans as Community Historians, 1980s–2018

1. Augusto Fauni Espiritu, *Five Faces of Exile: The Nation and Filipino American Intellectuals* (Stanford, CA: Stanford University Press, 2005); Rick Bonus, *Locating Filipino Americans: Ethnicity and the Cultural Politics of Space* (Philadelphia: Temple University Press, 2000); Manalansan, *Global Divas*; Yen Le Espiritu, *Home Bound*; Choy, *Empire of Care*; Gonzalves, *The Day the Dancers Stayed*; Linda España-Maram, *Creating Masculinity in Los Angeles's Little Manila: Working-Class Filipinos and Popular Cultures, 1920s–1930s* (New York: Columbia University Press, 2006); Estella Habal, *San Francisco's International Hotel: Mobilizing the Filipino American Community in the Anti-Eviction Movement* (Philadelphia: Temple University Press, 2007); Joaquin Jay Gonzalez III, *Filipino American Faith in Action: Immigration, Religion, and Civic Engagement* (New York: New York University Press, 2009); Mabalon, *Little Manila Is in the Heart*; Tiongson, Gutierrez, and Gutierrez, *Positively No Filipinos Allowed*; S. Lily Mendoza, *Between the Homeland and the Diaspora: The Politics of Theorizing Filipino and Filipino American Identities* (Manila: UST Publishing House, 2006); Lucy Mae San Pablo Burns, *Puro Arte: Filipinos on the Stages of Empire* (New York: New York University Press, 2013); Benito M. Vergara Jr., *Pinoy Capital: The Filipino Nation in Daly City* (Philadelphia: Temple University Press, 2009); Manalansan and Espiritu, *Filipino Studies*; Roderick N. Labrador, *Building Filipino Hawai'i* (Urbana: University of Illinois Press, 2015); Rick Baldoz, *The Third Asiatic Invasion: Empire and Migration in Filipino America, 1898–1946* (New York: New York University Press, 2011); Jonathan Y. Okamura, *Ethnicity and Inequality in Hawaii* (Philadelphia: Temple University Press, 2008); Fujita-Rony, *American Workers, Colonial Power*; Pido, *Migrant Returns*; Rodriguez, *Celebrating Debutantes and Quinceañeras*; Juanita Tamayo Lott, *Common Destiny: Filipino American Generations* (Lanham, MD: Rowman & Littlefield, 2006); Root, *Filipino Americans*; Leny Mendoza Strobel, *Coming Full Circle: The Process of Decolonization among Post-1965 Filipino Americans* (Quezon City: Giraffe Books, 2001); Dina C. Maramba and Rick Bonus, eds., *The "Other" Students: Filipino Americans, Education, and Power* (Charlotte, NC: Information Age Publishing, 2013).

2. Gonzalves, *The Day the Dancers Stayed*.

3. Dorothy Cordova, interview with author, Seattle, July 9, 2009; Emil de Guzman, interview with author, San Francisco, June 11, 2010; Robert Santos, interview with author, Seattle, June 5, 2010; Pio de Cano, interview with author, Seattle, July 2, 2009; and Richard Fariñas and Rosita Fariñas, interview with author, Seattle, July 8, 2009; all of these interviewees were civil rights activists.

4. Leny Mendoza Strobel, "'Born-Again Filipino': Filipino American Identity and Asian Panethnicity," *Amerasia Journal* 22, no. 2 (1996): 31–53; and Strobel, *Coming Full Circle*.

5. Strobel, *Coming Full Circle*, 98.

6. Leonard Y. Andaya, "From American-Filipino to Filipino-American," *Social Process in Hawaii* 37 (1996): 100.

7. Mendoza, *Between the Homeland and the Diaspora*, 152–154.

8. Sumi Yayashi, "Filipino Youth Drill Team: 'An Affirmation That We Have a Family,'" *International Examiner*, October 17, 1984, 5; Jacqueline Jamero, "Filipino Drill Team Goes on Tour," *International Examiner*, April 3, 1985, 3; and Fred Cordova and Dorothy Cordova, interviews with author, Seattle, July 9, 2009.

9. Office of Multicultural Student Services, FAHSOH Papers, University of Hawaii, Honolulu, circa 1982.

10. Office of Multicultural Student Services, FAHSOH Papers.

11. FANHS was conceived in 1982 but not incorporated until 1985 (Dorothy Laigo Cordova, Executive Director's Report, Conference Program, "Lure of the Salmon Song," 12th FANHS Conference, July 2008). The official FANHS website, however, identifies 1982 as the date it was founded (http://fanhs-national.org/filam/, accessed September 25, 2017). The minutes of the FANHS trustee meeting in Stockton, June 27–28, 2015, record Delano as the thirty-second and Hawaii as thirty-third chapter. In January 2021, the FANHS website boasts 38 chapters, accessed January 2021, http://fanhs-national.org/filam/chapters/.

12. FANHS, "Mission," accessed October 4, 2017, http://fanhs-national.org/filam/mission/.

13. FANHS Conference Programs for 1988, 1994, 1996, 200, Seattle, National Pinoy Archives.

14. Gonzalves, *The Day the Dancers Stayed*, 11 and 89.

15. Gonzalves, *The Day the Dancers Stayed*, 11.

16. Gonzalves, *The Day the Dancers Stayed*, 89.

17. FANHS–Hampton Roads Chapter, *In Our Uncles' Words* (San Francisco: T'Boli, 2006), 215–218.

18. Veronica Baybay Salcedo, "Introduction," in FANHS Hampton Roads Chapter, *In Our Aunties' Words*, 12.

19. Tintiangco-Cubales, *Pin@y Educational Partnerships*, vols. 1 and 2.

20. Note that I am only discussing the histories; this does not include the voluminous Filipino American fiction, theater, and visual and performing arts that also reflect on Filipino American history in various ways. In 2014, more than five hundred attended the FANHS conference in San Diego. See Leatrice B. Perez, "President's Message," *FANHS Stockton Chapter Newsletter* 20, no. 3, (July/August 2014): 2.

21. Mel LaGasca, "FANHS Museum Status Report—3rd Quarter Newsletter 2016," *FANHS Stockton Chapter Newsletter* 22, no. 4 (October 2016): 3.

22. Allan Lagasca Bergamo, "Prologue" in FANHS Hampton Roads Chapter, *In Our Aunties' Words*, 9.

23. Gonzalves, *The Day the Dancers Stayed*.

24. Fred Cordova, "The Bridge Generation and Building Bridges," presented at the Fifth National Biennial Conference of FANHS, San Francisco, August 4–6, 1994, reproduced in *FANHS Journal* 4 (1996): 13.

25. John Wehman, dir., *Filipino Americans: Discovering Their Past for Their Future*, FANHS documentary, VHS (National Video Profiles and JF Wehman Associates/MoonRae, 1994).

26. Fred Cordova, *Filipinos: Forgotten Asian Americans; A Pictorial Essay, 1763–circa 1962* (Seattle: Demonstration Program for Asian Americans, 1983); Peter Jamero, *Vanishing Filipino Americans: The Bridge Generation* (Lanham, MD: University Press of America, 2011).

27. Dorothy Laigo Cordova, "Correcting Negative Image of Filipino Americans," *Seattle Times*, August 18, 1984, in the Dorothy Cordova file held at the National Pinoy Archives in Seattle; and Mendoza, *Between the Homeland and the Diaspora*, 173.

28. Oscar Campomanes quoted in Mendoza, *Between the Homeland and the Diaspora*, 12. Asian American specialists have used similar vocabulary; see, for example, Madeline Y. Hsu, *Asian American History: A Very Short Introduction* (Oxford: Oxford University Press, 2017), 130: "Filipinos, in comparison [to other Asian Americans], lack visibility even though they are the second largest Asian American population."

29. Coloma et al., *Filipinos in Canada*.

30. Cordova, *Filipinos: Forgotten Asian Americans*; Filipino Oral History Project, *Voices: A Filipino American Oral History* (Stockton, CA: Filipino Oral History Project, 1984); Geoffrey Dunn and Mark Schwartz, dirs., *A Dollar a Day, Ten Cents a Dance: A Historic Portrait of Filipino Farmworkers in America*, documentary film (Capitola, CA: Gold Mountain Productions, 1984); Wehman, *Filipino Americans*; Marissa Aroy, dir., *Delano Manongs: Forgotten Heroes of the United Farm Workers Movement*, documentary ([New York]: Media Factory, Independent Television Service, and Center for Asian American Media, 2014); Emme Tomimbang, dir., *Mabuhay with Aloha: The Hawaii Filipino Experience, 1906–2006*, documentary ([Honolulu]: Emme, 2006); Curtis Choy, dir., *The Fall of the I-Hotel*, documentary (San Francisco: Asian Media Center, 1983).

31. Thelma Buchholdt, *Filipinos in Alaska: 1788–1958* (Anchorage: Aboriginal Press, 1996); Filipino Oral History Project, *Voices*.

32. Filipino Oral History Project, *Voices*.

33. Carlos Bulosan, *America Is in the Heart: A Personal History* (Manila: Anvil, 2006); Cordova, *Filipinos: Forgotten Asian Americans*; Filipino Oral History Project, *Voices*; Peter Jamero, *Growing Up Brown: Memoirs of a Filipino American* (Seattle: University of Washington Press, 2006): Craig Scharlin and Lilia V. Villanueva, *Philip Vera Cruz: A Personal History of Filipino Immigrants and the Farmworkers Movement* (Seattle: University of Washington Press, 2000); Virgilio Menor Felipe, *Hawai'i: A Pilipino Dream* (Honolulu: Mutual, 2002).

34. Felipe, *Hawai'i*, 19.

35. Wehman, *Filipino Americans*.

36. "Congress' House Resolution 780: A National Breakthrough," *Generations* (FANHS newsletter), November 2009, 4–5, National Pinoy Archives, Seattle.

37. Cordova, *Filipinos: Forgotten Asian Americans*; Wehman, *Filipino Americans*.

38. Oscar Campomanes quoted in Tiongson, "On Filipinos," 40.

39. Quoted in Gonzalves, *The Day the Dancers Stayed*, 140.

40. Gonzalves, *The Day the Dancers Stayed*, 123–124.

41. Benjamin J. Cayetano, *Ben: A Memoir, from Street Kid to Governor* (Honolulu: Watermark Publishing, 2009); Bob Santos, *Humbows, Not Hotdogs! Memoirs of a Savvy Asian American Activist* (Seattle: International Examiner Press, 2002).

42. Jamero, *Vanishing Filipino Americans*; and Jamero, *Growing Up Brown*.

43. FANHS Hampton Roads Chapter, *In Our Aunties' Words*; Patricia Brown, ed., *Filipinas! Voices from Daughters and Descendants of Hawaii's Plantation Era* (North Charleston, SC: CreateSpace, 2014).

44. Dorothy Cordova, personal communication, Seattle, June 2009; Scharlin and Villanueva, *Philip Vera Cruz*.

45. An anonymous informant in Filipino Oral History Project, *Voices*.

46. Santos, *Humbows, Not Hotdogs!*, 129–130.

47. FANHS chapters are proactive in involving their members in the production of histories for their various projects. There are seminars on how to "do" oral histories, how to create archives, and so on at the FANHS conferences. FANHS-Stockton's former acting president Anita Navalta Bautista invited members of FANHS to write stories about their "Filipino American experiences during the early years" or their "experiences of what it is like as a Filipina, Filipino or Mestiza growing up," and she encouraged others to interview their relatives or even collect photographs and to present them to the FANHS-Stockton chapter. I assume that other chapters did the same thing. Anita Navalta Bautista, "Write a Personal Short Story," *FANHS Stockton Chapter Newsletter* 21, no. 1 (January 2015): 2.

48. I owe this discussion of the "new history from below" to Lyons, "A New History from Below?"

49. Mamerto Calalang Canlas, interview with author, San Francisco, July 11, 2012.

50. *San Francisco Filipino Heritage Addendum to the South of Market Historic Context Statement*, prepared for the San Francisco Planning Department (San Francisco: Page & Turnbull, 2013), 36.

51. Personal communication with MC Canlas, October 25, 2017.

52. *San Francisco Filipino Heritage Addendum*, 36–37.

53. *San Francisco Filipino Heritage Addendum*, 14.

54. *San Francisco Filipino Heritage Addendum*, 7.

55. Habal, *San Francisco's International Hotel*, 10.

56. Habal, *San Francisco's International Hotel*.

57. Habal, *San Francisco's International Hotel*.

58. Manilatown Heritage Foundation website, accessed December 30, 2019, https://manilatown.org/events/#tours.

59. *San Francisco Filipino Heritage Addendum*, 18.

60. *San Francisco Filipino Heritage Addendum*, 19.

61. M. C. Canlas, *SoMa Pilipinas Studies 2000* (San Francisco: Arkipelago Books, 2002), 60.

62. *San Francisco Filipino Heritage Addendum*, 18.

63. Vergara, *Pinoy Capital*, 2.

64. Joaquin Jay Gonzales III, *Diaspora Diplomacy: Philippine Migration and Its Soft Power Influences* (Minneapolis: Mill City Press, 2012), 55.

65. Gonzales, *Diaspora Diplomacy*, 71.

66. Canlas interview, July 11, 2012.

67. Canlas, *SoMa Pilipinas Studies 2000*, 9.

68. *San Francisco Filipino Heritage Addendum*, 6.

69. Canlas interview, July 11, 2012.

70. *San Francisco Filipino Heritage Addendum*, 27–28.

71. *San Francisco Filipino Heritage Addendum*, 28.

72. Canlas, *SoMa Pilipinas Studies 2000*, 60–64.

73. Canlas interview, July 11, 2012.

74. Canlas interview, July 11, 2012.

75. Canlas interview, July 11, 2012.

76. MC Canlas, "Getting to Know SoMa Pilipinas #1: The Philippines in SoMa Pilipinas," unpublished paper, June 11, 2017, 1.

77. *San Francisco Filipino Heritage Addendum*, 28–30.

78. Canlas, *SoMa Pilipinas Studies 2000*, 74.

79. Canlas, *SoMa Pilipinas Studies 2000*, 101–102 and 198.

80. Canlas interview, July 11, 2012.

81. Canlas, *SoMa Pilipinas Studies 2000*, 196; Gonzales, *Filipino American Faith in Action*, 123.

82. Gonzales, *Filipino American Faith in Action*, 146.

83. Canlas, *SoMa Pilipinas Studies 2000*, 101–103.

84. Canlas interview, July 11, 2012; MC Canlas, "Tabi Po, Respect for Those Who Came Before: Filipinos in South of Market, San Francisco," unpublished paper.

85. Canlas, *SoMa Pilipinas Studies 2000*, 184.

86. There are several street murals in the area, including the *Filipino-American Friendship Mural* painted in 1983, on the east facade of the building at 1137–1139 Howard Street, and the seven-story mural *Lipi Ni Lapu Lapu*, which depicts the history of Filipino migration to America, on the north wall of the San Lorenzo Ruis Center. *San Francisco Filipino Heritage Addendum*, 31–36. For an article on Filipino street murals in California, see Theodore S. Gonzalves, "When the Walls Speak a Nation: Contemporary Murals and the Narration of Filipina/o America," *Journal of Asian American Studies* 1, no.1 (1998): 31–63.

87. See SoMa Map included in the SoMa self-guided tour brochure; and *San Francisco Filipino Heritage Addendum*, 32.

88. Amendment to the Whole in Committee 4/4/16, File No. 151109, Resolution No. 119-16, City and County of San Francisco, passed April 12, 2016, p. 6. Document provided to the author by Mamerto Calalang Canlas, October 2017.

89. "SOMA Pilipinas Cultural Heritage District," accessed September 25, 2017, https://www.facebook.com/SoMaPilipinas/; Mamerto Calalang Canlas, e-mail to author, September 10, 2017.

90. Canlas interview, July 11, 2012.

91. Canlas interview, July 11, 2012.

92. SoMa Pilipinas Ethnotour brochure, no date, 4.

93. Mabalon, *Little Manila Is in the Heart*, 6.

94. Dawn Mabalon et al., *Filipinos in Stockton* (Charleston, SC: Arcadia, 2008), 7; Mabalon, *Little Manila Is in the Heart*, 4–6.

95. Mabalon, *Little Manila Is in the Heart*, 62.

96. Little Manila Foundation website, accessed November 2012, http://www.littlemanila.org/about-us/; and "Remember & Reclaim: A Stockton, California, Filipino American History Calendar 2011," produced by Little Manila Foundation and Filipino American National Historical Society.

97. The organization had gone into debt and lost the land to tax forfeiture and was bought by Capital Equity Management for $64,000 at a county sale in 2015. Jeff Jardine, "A Trunk-Aided Version of Filipino History in California's Central Valley," *Modesto Bee*, January 30, 2016, http://www.modbee.com/news/local/news-columns-blogs/jeff-jardine/article57530428.html.

98. Dawn Bohulano Mabalon, "Losing Little Manila: Race and Redevelopment in Filipina/o Stockton, California," in Tiongson, Gutierrez, and Gutierrez, *Positively No Filipinos Allowed*, 89.

99. Dawn Mabalon, in *Little Manila: Filipinos in California's Heartland*, dir. Marissa Aroy, documentary, DVD (Sacramento, CA: KVIE Public Television, 2007).

100. FANHS president Terri Jamero at the FANHS 1992 conference, reported in the *Philippine Review*, August 1992, copy from the National Pinoy Archives in Seattle; same quote used in Evangeline Canonizado Buell et al., *Filipinos in the East Bay* (Charleston SC: Arcadia, 2008), 7.

101. FANHS Hampton Roads Chapter, *In Our Aunties' Words*; FANHS Hampton Roads Chapter, *In Our Uncles' Words*; Filipino Oral History Project, *Voices*; Brown, *Filipinas!*

102. "Congress' House Resolution 780."

103. Quoted in "October Is Filipino American History Month," *FANHS Stockton Chapter Newsletter* 21, no. 4, (October 2015): 3.

104. Terri Torres, Minutes of the FANHS Trustee Meeting in Stockton, June 27–28, 2015.

105. The FANHS website, accessed January 6, 2021, http://fanhs-national.org/filam/chapters/.

106. The Smithsonian exhibits were: "Through My Father's Eyes: The Filipino American Photographs of Ricardo Orceto Alvarado (1914–1976)," shown at the National Museum of American History, Washington, DC, November 21, 2002–March 31, 2003; and "Singgalot (The Ties That Bind): Filipinos in America; From Colonial Subjects to Citizens," shown at the Smithsonian's S. Dillon Ripley Center Concourse on the National Mall from May to August of 2006.

107. Flyers sent out by FANHS–Stockton Chapter, October 2016; Emma Franklin Henterly, "Our Diversity: Filipino Museum Coming to Life," *Stockton Record*, posted October 1, 2016, http://www.recordnet.com/news/20161001/our-diversity-filipino-museum-coming-to-life; Agnes Constante, "After More Than Two Decades, Filipino-American Museum Scheduled to Open," NBC News, October 5, 2016, http://www.nbcnews.com/news/asian-america/after-more-two-decades-filipino-american-museum-scheduled-open-n660191; Richard Tenaza, President's Message, *FANHS Stockton Chapter Newsletter* 22, no. 4 (October 2016): 1; and the minutes of the meetings of the FANHS–Stockton Chapter, 2015–2016.

108. City of Santa Rosa Proclamation, published in *FANHS Sonoma County*, July 2015, p. 3.

109. City of Santa Rosa Proclamation.

110. Christina Oriel, "'Larry Itliong Day' Bill Passes California State Assembly," Inquirer.net, April 18, 2015, http://globalnation.inquirer.net/120860/larry-itliong-day-bill-passes-california-state-assembly#ixzz3Xhosads.

111. "Larry Itliong & the Farm Labor Movement: An Interactive Dialogue with the Voice of Larry Itliong," October 26, 2013, San Joaquin Delta College, flyer; from the minutes of the FANHS-Stockton meetings.

112. Oriel, "'Larry Itliong Day' Bill."

113. Don Tagala, "Historical Marker Unveiled to Mark the First Filipino Settlement in the US," *BalitangAmerica*, November 12, 2019, https://balitangamerica.tv/historical-marker-unveiled-to-mark-the-first-filipino-settlement-in-the-u-s/; Maria Batayola,

"Filipino American History Month Forever Celebrates Brown Brilliance," *International Examiner*, October 17, 2019, https://iexaminer.org/filipino-american-history-month-forever-celebrates-brown-brilliance/.

114. Wehman, *Filipino Americans*; Aroy, *Little Manila*.

115. Aroy, *Delano Manongs*.

116. Mentioned in "Meet the FANHS Board Members 2015–2016," in *FANHS Sonoma County*, February 2015, p. 1.

117. Tomimbang, *Mabuhay with Aloha*.

118. Dunn and Schwartz, *A Dollar a Day*; Choy, *The Fall of the I-Hotel*.

119. Dawn Bohulano Mabalon, "Life in Little Manila: Filipinas/os in Stockton, California, 1917–1972" (Phd diss., Stanford University, 2003), 2.

120. Emma Franklin Henterly, "Little Manila Being Brought Back to Life," posted June 14, 2017, at http://www.recordnet.com/news/20170614/little-manila-being-brought-back-to-life.

121. Canlas, "Tabi Po."

122. Pelagio Valdez, post to the FANHS Stockton Chapter Facebook page, October 3, 2017.

123. Mentioned in the blog of second-generation Filipino American Peter Jamero, accessed January 7, 2018, http://www.peterjamero.net.

124. Antonio T. Tiongson Jr., "Introduction: Critical Considerations," in Tiongson, Gutierrez, and Gutierrez, *Positively No Filipinos Allowed*, 1.

6. Advocacy and Its Impacts, 1970s to circa 2000

1. Chris Cunneen and Julie Stubbs, *Gender, "Race" and International Relations: Violence against Women in Australia*, Institute of Criminology Monograph Series, no. 9 (Sydney: Institute of Criminology Monograph Series, University of Sydney, Faculty of Law, 1997), 33.

2. Linda's story, in *Buklod ng Kababaihang Filipina* (South Australia: Filipino Survivors of Family Violence, drama presentation program, December 4, 1997), 6. From the personal papers of Joan Dicka.

3. The story of Lisa's trials was given to me by Della Ipong in my interview with her. Della Ipong, interview with author, Sydney, April 27, 2014.

4. *Ngayong Aussie Ka na, Manay!* radio program, episode 4. From the personal collection of Rogelia Pe-Pua. Migrant Resource Centres were established around the country to provide settlement services for migrants.

5. Stepan Kerkyasharian, "Opening Address," in Ethnic Affairs Commission of New South Wales, *Serial Sponsorship: Perspectives for Policy Options* (Sydney: Ethnic Affairs Commission of NSW, 1992), 7.

6. Stephanie Padilla, journal, entries for January 21, 1974–May 19, 1974, Operation Manong (OM) archives, Office of Multicultural Student Services, University of Hawaii at Manoa.

7. Stephanie Padilla journal.

8. Ligaya Lindio-McGovern, *Globalization, Labor Export and Resistance: A Study of Filipino Migrant Domestic Workers in Global Cities* (London: Routledge, 2012); Stefan Rother, "Transnational Political Spaces: Political Activism of Philippine Labor Migrants in Hong Kong," in *State, Politics and Nationalism beyond Borders: Changing Dynamics*

in *Filipino Overseas Migration*, ed. Jorge V. Tigno (Quezon City: Philippine Social Science Council, 2009); 1–23; Nicole Constable, "Migrant Workers and the Many States of Protest in Hong Kong," *Critical Asian Studies* 41, no. 1 (2009): 143–164; Hsiao-Chuan Hsia, "The Making of a Transnational Grassroots Migrant Movement," *Critical Asian Studies* 41, no. 1 (2009): 113–141.

9. Melinda Tria Kerkvliet, *Unbending Cane: Pablo Manlapit, a Filipino Labor Leader in Hawaii* (Honolulu: Office of Multicultural Student Services, University of Hawaii at Manoa, 2002). For post-1970s migrant activism, see Lindio-McGovern, *Globalization*; Constable, "Migrant Workers," 143–164; and Hsia, "Transnational Grassroots Migrant Movement," 113–141.

10. See especially Lindio-McGovern, *Globalization*.

11. See, for example, Faier, *Intimate Encounters*; Glenda Tibe Bonifacio, *Pinay on the Prairies: Filipino Women and Transnational Identities* (Vancouver: University of British Columbia Press, 2013); Suzuki, "Transgressing 'Victims,'" 399–420; Nobue Suzuki, "Between Two Shores: Transnational Projects and Filipina Wives in/from Japan," *Women's Studies International Forum* 23, no. 4 (2000): 431–444; Suzuki, "Filipina-Japanese Marriages," 1–19; Suzuki, "Inside the Home," 481–506; Cleonicki Saroca, "Filipino Women, Sexual Politics, and the Gendered Discourse of the Mail Order Bride," *JIGS: Journal of Interdisciplinary Gender Studies* 2, no. 2 (1997): 89–103; Saroca, "Representing Rosalina and Annabel," 32–60; Saroca, "Filipino Women, Migration, and Violence," 75–110; Saroca, "Woman in Danger or Dangerous Woman?," 35–74; Saroca, "Violence against Migrant Filipino Women," 113–139; Desmond Cahill, *Intermarriages in International Contexts: A Study of Filipino Women Married to Australian, Japanese and Swiss Men* (Quezon City: Scalabrini Migration Centre, 1990); Elizabeth Holt, "Writing Filipina-Australian Brides: The Discourse on Filipina Brides," *Philippine Sociological Review* 44, nos. 1–4 (1996): 58–78; Kathryn Robinson, "Of Mail-Order Brides and 'Boys Own' Tales: Representations of Asian-Australian Marriages," *Feminist Review* 52 (1996): 53–68.

12. Cahill, *Intermarriages in International Contexts*; F. M. Cooke, *Australian-Filipino Marriages in the 1980s: The Myth and the Reality* (Griffith University School of Modern Asian Studies, Center for the Study of Australia-Asian Relations, Research Paper 37, 1986); J. Pendlebury, *Filipino Brides in Remote Areas*, Occasional Paper No. 5 (Darwin: Department of Social Security, 1990); C. Paredes-Maceda, "Filipino Women and Intermarriages," *Asian Migrant* 8 (1995): 109–113; C. Boer, *Are You Looking for a Filipina Wife? A Study of Filipina-Australian Marriages* (Sydney: General Synod Office, 1988).

13. Cunneen and Stubbs, *Gender, "Race" and International Relations*.

14. Holt, "Writing Filipina-Australian Brides: The Discourse on Filipina Brides," 58–78; Robinson, "Of Mail-Order Brides," 53–68; Saroca, "Filipino Women, Migration, and Violence," 75–110; Saroca, "Woman in Danger," 35–74; Saroca, "Violence against Migrant Filipino Women," 139; and Saroca, "Filipino Women, Sexual Politics," 89–103.

15. Mina Roces, "Sisterhood Is Local: Filipino Women in Mount Isa," in *Wife or Worker? Asian Marriage and Migration*, ed. Nicola Piper and Mina Roces (Boulder, CO: Rowman & Littlefield, 2003), 73–100; Michael Pinches, "Bamboo Dancers Down Under: The Filipino-Australian Intercultural Community in Western Australia," in *The Changing People: Diverse Contributions to the State of Western Australia*, ed. Raelene Wilding and Farida Tilbury (Perth: Department of the Premier and Cabinet, Office of Multicultural Interests, 2004), 284–302; Glenda Tibe Bonifacio, "Filipino Women in

Australia: Practicing Citizenship at Work, *Asian and Pacific Migration Journal* 14, no. 3 (2005): 293–326; Glenda Tibe Bonifacio, "Activism from the Margins: Filipino Marriage Migrants in Australia," *Frontiers: A Journal of Women's Studies* 30, no. 3 (2009): 142–168.

16. Kristine Aquino, in her book on Filipino experiences of racism in Australia, mentioned the activism of the CPCA and FWWP on the Filipino brides issue in one paragraph of her background chapter on the histories of the "Filipino" in Australia. See Kristine Aquino, *Racism and Resistance among the Filipino Diaspora: Everyday Anti-Racism in Australia* (London: Routledge, 2018), 28.

17. Clement Bautista, "Operation Manong Program Review," December 18, 1992, 3, OM archives.

18. Kerkvliet, *Unbending Cane*, 17 and 23.

19. Amefil R. Agbayani, "The Education of Filipinos in Hawai'i," *Social Process in Hawaii* 37 (1996): 151.

20. Labrador, *Building Filipino Hawai'i*, 5.

21. Ethel Ward, former teacher at the Farrington High School, interview with author, Honolulu, June 19, 2012.

22. Labrador, *Building Filipino Hawai'i*, 9.

23. Agbayani, "The Education of Filipinos," *Social Process in Hawaii*, 147.

24. Labrador, *Building Filipino Hawai'i*, 4.

25. Agbayani, "The Education of Filipinos," *Social Process in Hawaii*, 154; and "Education: The Filipino Dream," in *The Filipinos in Hawaii: The First 75 Years, 1906–1981* ([Honolulu]: Hawaii Filipino News Specialty Publications, [ca. 1981]), 86.

26. Labrador, *Building Filipino Hawai'i*, 2.

27. Agbayani, "The Education of Filipinos," *Social Process in Hawaii*, 154

28. "Education: The Filipino Dream," 87.

29. Labrador, *Building Filipino Hawai'i*, 2.

30. Labrador, *Building Filipino Hawai'i*, 2.

31. Labrador, *Building Filipino Hawai'i*, 2.

32. "Education: The Filipino Dream," 86.

33. Quoted in Amefil R. Agbayani, "Education of Filipinos in Hawai'i," in *Pagdiriwang 1996: Legacy and Vision of Hawaii's Filipino Americans*, ed. Jonathan Y. Okamura and Roderick N. Labrador (Honolulu: Student Equity, Excellence & Diversity and Center for Southeast Asian Studies, 1996), 14.

34. Agbayani, "Education of Filipinos in Hawai'i," in *Pagdiriwang 1996*, 14–15.

35. Agbayani, "Education of Filipinos in Hawai'i," in *Pagdiriwang 1996*, 15.

36. Adrialina B. Guerero, "A History of Operation Manong," in *Sinking Roots: Filipino American Legacy in Hawaii*, ed. Dean T. Alegado (Honolulu: Philippine Centennial Committee–Hawaii, Friends of Operation Manong, University of Hawaii at Manoa; Center for Philippine Studies, University of Hawaii at Manoa, 1998), 35–36.

37. Agbayani, "The Education of Filipinos," *Social Process in Hawaii*, 155; Operation Manong flyer information sheet, circa 1976, OM archives; Amefil Agbayani, interview with author, Honolulu, June 11, 2012.

38. Filipino Volunteers in Hawaii, "Project Proposal Operation Manong," September 15, 1972, p. 4, from the OM archives.

39. Filipino Volunteers in Hawaii, "Project Proposal Operation Manong," 6–7.

40. Clement Bautista, interview with author, Honolulu, June 18, 2012.

41. *Operation Manong, Spring 1982* (Honolulu: Department of Educational Foundations, College of Education, University of Hawaii, Manoa, 1982), 2–3.

42. *Annual Report, Operation Manong 1993–94*, 6, Office of Student Affairs, University of Hawaii at Manoa.

43. Melinda Kerkvliet, interview with author, Honolulu, June 18, 2012.

44. Kerkvliet interview, June 18, 2012.

45. Amy Agbayani, Adrialina Guerero, and Melinda Tria Kerkvliet, "Operation Manong Celebrates its 40th Anniversary on March 2012, at FilCom Center, Waipahu," *The Fil-Am Courier*, March 16–31, 2012, 4, Operation Manong flyer information sheet, circa 1976, OM archives.

46. Operation Manong flyer information sheet, circa 1976, OM archives.

47. Alan B. Ramos and Richard R. Umil, "A Look at Operation Manong: A Program Designed to Assist in the Educational and Cultural Problems Encountered by Immigrant Children," paper submitted to the College of Education Masters in Education program, December 1974, 52–53, in OM archives.

48. Farrington High School was 60 percent Filipino (Agbayani interview, June 11, 2012).

49. Ramos and Umil, "A Look at Operation Manong," 56–59.

50. Melinda Kerkvliet, memo to Manongs and Manangs, March 13, 1973, 2, in OM archives.

51. University Year for Action, Operation Manong University of Hawaii, UYA Planned Impact program, 1973, p. 4, OM archives.

52. *Operation Manong: Spring 1982*, 3.

53. *Operation Manong: Spring 1982*, 3; Ramos and Umil, "A Look at Operation Manong," 49–50.

54. *University Year for Action Progress Report*, March 20, 1974, 3, OM archives; and copies of House Resolution No. 187 and Senate Resolution No. 57, in Ramos and Umil, "A Look at Operation Manong."

55. *University Year for Action Progress Report*, July 8, 1974, 2, OM archives.

56. Agbayani interview, June 11, 2012; journal of Norma D. Sparks, February 2, 1973, 3; Kerkvliet interview, June 18, 2012.

57. Cuaresma interview, June 27, 2009.

58. Bautista interview, June 18, 2012.

59. Norma D. Sparks, journal entry, February 2, 1973, 3, OM archives.

60. Bautista interview, June 18, 2012.

61. Guerero, "A History of Operation Manong," 26.

62. Guerero, "A History of Operation Manong", 26; *Operation Manong: Spring 1982*, 1.

63. Guerero, "A History of Operation Manong," 26.

64. Operation Manong Annual Report, 1988–1989, 1–7, OM archives.

65. See *Operation Manong: Spring 1982*.

66. Agbayani, Guerero, and Kerkvliet, "Operation Manong," 6; Charlene Cuaresma, former OM tutor, interview with author, Honolulu, June 27, 2000.

67. Rosie Ramiro and Clem Bautista, "Operation Manong 40th Reunion: A Part of the History and Future of Filipinos in Hawaii," *Hawaii Filipino Chronicle News Edition*, April 14, 2002, 4, OM archives.

68. When I did my research in 2012, the sign outside the office door read "Office of Multicultural Services" with "(OM)" attached to the title in small brackets.

69. Susan Allender, "State Senate, House Proclaim Operation Manong Day," *Hawaii Filipino Chronicle News Edition*, April 19, 2012, 4, OM archives.

70. The dates of the terms of the OM directors were published in Allender, "State Senate, House Proclaim Operation Manong Day," 4.

71. William Wei, *The Asian American Movement* (Philadelphia: Temple University Press, 1995).

72. Agbayani interview, June 11, 2012.

73. Abercrombie was an OM advocate for forty years, and Cayetano was an "early OM supporter." They both attended OM's fortieth anniversary reunion celebration, and both had been in the state legislature in OM's early years. Agbayani confided in an interview: "When they were trying to cut my budget, I just called Neil Abercrombie and he telephoned the dean of the College of Education and he screamed at them and suddenly, they didn't touch us." Agbayani interview, June 11, 2012.

74. Agbayani interview, June 11, 2012.

75. Jonathan Y. Okamura, "Filipino American Access to Public Higher Education in California and Hawai'i," in Maramba and Bonus, *The "Other" Students*, 223; and Okamura, *Ethnicity and Inequality in Hawaii*, 82.

76. Operation Manong Annual Report, 1994–1995, 6, OM archives.

77. Okamura, "Filipino American Access," 222.

78. Cuaresma interview, June 27, 2009; Agbayani interview, June 11, 2012.

79. Operation Manong Annual Report, 1990–1991, 13, OM archives.

80. Bautista, "Operation Manong Program Review," 5.

81. *Operation Manong: Spring 1982*, 7.

82. *Operation Manong: Spring 1982*, 31.

83. *Operation Manong: Spring 1982*, 36–38.

84. Padilla, journal, entries for January 28, 1974, March 4, 1974, March 8, 1974, March 18, 1974, April 1, 1974, April 3, 1974, April 15, 1974, April 26. 1974, May 3, 1974, and May 6, 1974; Sparks, journal, entry for March 9, 1973; both in OM archives.

85. *Operation Manong: Spring, 1982*, 33–34.

86. Alan B. Ramos and Richard R. Umil, "A Look at Operation Manong: A Program Designed to Assist in the Educational and Cultural Problems Encountered by Immigrant Children", Paper submitted to the College of Education Masters in Education program, December 1974, 107, OM archives.

87. Agbayani interview, June 11, 2012.

88. Cuaresma interview, June 27, 2009.

89. Cuaresma interview, June 27, 2009.

90. Agbayani interview, June 11, 2012; "Proposal for the Continuation of 'Operation Manong,' at the University of Hawaii, Manoa, HB #891, SB #485" (circa 1975), p. 8, OM archives.

91. Allender, "State Senate, House Proclaim Operation Manong Day," 4; and Amefil Agbayani, e-mail message to author, December 28, 2015.

92. Theodore S. Gonzalves and Roderick N. Labrador, *Filipinos in Hawai'i* (Charleston, SC: Arcadia, 2011), 123; Agbayani interview, June 11, 2012, and e-mail message, December 28, 2015.

93. Kerkvliet interview, June 18, 2012.

94. Gonzalves and Labrador, *Filipinos in Hawai'i*, 117–126; the chapter is entitled "Amefil 'Amy' Agbayani."

95. See Labrador, *Building Filipino Hawai'i*, 29–48, esp. 30 and 120–122.
96. Cayetano, *Ben: A Memoir*, 333.
97. Labrador, *Building Filipino Hawai'i*, 98–127.
98. Labrador, *Building Filipino Hawai'i*, 102.
99. Agbayani interview, June 11, 2012.
100. Labrador, *Building Filipino Hawai'i*, 134.
101. Agbayani interview, June 11, 2012.
102. Operation Manong Annual Report, 1992–1994, 4, OM archives.

103. The OM annual report for 1994–1995 states: "FY1995 expenditures totaled $253,799.94, representing an 11.1 percent decrease over FY1994. Of this total, $137,508.00 (54.2 percent) went to regular staff salaries, $45,027.81 (17.7 percent) to student assistant salaries, $1,154.59 (0.5 percent) to casual hires, $1,342.57 (0.5 percent) for equipment purchases, and $68,745.97 (27.1 percent) to other current expenses." Operation Manong Annual Report, 1994–1995, p. 5, OM archives.

104. Agbayani, Guerero, and Kerkvliet, "Operation Manong," 5.
105. Agbayani, Guerero, and Kerkvliet, "Operation Manong," 5.
106. Solidarity Philippines Australia Network, "Violent Deaths and Disappearances of Filipino Women and Children in Australia since 1980: Summary of Data Compiled by the Centre as at 6th August 2011," CPCA website, accessed February 12, 2015, http://cpcabrisbane.org/CPCA/Deaths.htm.
107. Cunneen and Stubbs, *Gender, "Race" and International Relations*, ix, and 31.
108. Women's Coalition Against Family Violence (1994), quoted in Saroca, "Violence against Migrant Filipino Women," 117.
109. Saroca, "Violence against Migrant Filipino Women in Australia," 118; and Cunneen and Stubbs, *Gender, "Race" and International Relations*, 119.
110. Saroca, "Violence against Migrant Filipino Women in Australia," 120.
111. Rosa Droescher, former senior policy officer, Ethnic Affairs Commission of New South Wales, interview with author, Sydney, January 8, 2015.
112. Droescher interview, January 8, 2015.
113. Droescher interview, January 8, 2015.
114. Frank Galbally, *Migrant Services and Programs: Report of the Review of Post-Arrival Programs and Services for Migrants* (Canberra: Australian Government Publishing Service, 1978).

115. Galbally, *Migrant Services and Programs*, 4.
116. Galbally, *Migrant Services and Programs*, 9–10.
117. Galbally, *Migrant Services and Programs*, 12.
118. Galbally, *Migrant Services and Programs*, 70.
119. Droescher interview, January 8, 2015.
120. Droescher interview, January 8, 2015.
121. Ipong interview, Sydney, April 27, 2014.
122. Cunneen and Stubbs, *Gender, "Race" and International Relations*, 13.

123. Maria Eleanor Guanio-Bartels and Rogelia Pe-Pua, *The Development of a Radio Information Package for Filipino Women* (Sydney: Filipino Women's Working Party, 1994), 3.

124. *The People of New South Wales, 1991 Census* (Sydney: Ethnic Affairs Commission, 1993); Guanio-Bartels and Pe-Pua, *Development of a Radio Information Package*, 3.

125. Australian Bureau of Statistics, cited in Aquino, *Racism and Resistance*, 3.

126. Estrella "Lilia" McKinnon, interview with author, Wollongong, March 1, 2013.
127. Ipong interview, April 27, 2014.
128. Ipong interview, April 27, 2014.
129. Joan Dicka, interview with author, Adelaide, June 10–11, 2014.
130. Deborah Ruiz Wall, "Joan Dicka—Shortlisted for a 2009 Australian Human Rights Award," *Kasama* 24, no. 1 (2010): 1–5.
131. Concepcion "Chat" Ramilo, interview with author, Manila, August 5, 2014.
132. Pinches, "Bamboo Dancers Down Under," 295.
133. Pinches, "Bamboo Dancers Down Under," 295.
134. Deborah (Debbie) Wall, interview with author, Sydney, August 9, 2012.
135. Deborah Ruiz Wall, *Re-Imagining Australia: Voices of Indigenous Australians of Filipino Descent*, with Christine Choo (Southport, Queensland: Keeaira Press, 2016), back cover.
136. Wall interview, August 9, 2012.
137. Deborah R. Wall, "Filipino Brides: Slaves or Marriage Partners?—A Further Comment," *Australian Journal of Social Issues* 18, no. 1 (1985): 217–220.
138. Dicka interview, June 10–11, 2014; Ipong interview, April 27, 2014; McKinnon interview, March 1, 2013.
139. Dicka interview, June 10–11, 2014; Ipong interview, April 27, 2014; McKinnon interview, March 1, 2013.
140. Dicka interview, June 10–11, 2014.
141. Kym Tilbrook, "55 Filipino Women Have Sought Help: Bannon," *Advertiser* (South Australia), November 28, 1987, from the personal papers of Joan Dicka, Adelaide.
142. Ramilo interview, August 5, 2014.
143. Chat Ramilo and Rosa Droescher, *Filipino Women: Challenges and Responses (1988–1991)* (Sydney: Ethnic Affairs Commission of NSW, 1992).
144. Dicka interview, June 10–11, 2014.
145. Tilbrook, "55 Filipino Women Have Sought Help"; Dicka interview, June 10–11, 2014.
146. Hon. Diana Laidlaw, MLC, "Filipino Wives," Legislative Council, Parliament House, Adelaide, October 20, 1987, from the personal papers of Joan Dicka, Adelaide.
147. Ramilo and Droescher, *Filipino Women*, 7.
148. McKinnon interview, March 1, 2013.
149. Ramilo and Droescher, *Filipino Women*.
150. Dicka interview, June 10–11, 2014.
151. Saroca, "Woman in Danger," 35–74.
152. Saroca, "Woman in Danger," 35–74.
153. Saroca, "Woman in Danger," 48.
154. Quoted in Saroca, "Woman in Danger," 48.
155. Melba Marginson, interview with author, Melbourne, September 25, 2007; Saroca, "Woman in Danger," 53.
156. CPCA website, accessed August 10, 2015, http://cpcabrisbane.org/CPCA/.
157. CPCA website.
158. Marginson interview, September 25, 2007.
159. Melba Marginson, e-mail message to author, November 24, 2016.

160. Marginson interview, September 25, 2007; Melba Marginson, "Not for the Money," in *Breaking Through: Women, Work and Careers*, ed. Jocelynne A. Scott (Melbourne: Artemis, 1992), 115–123.

161. Marginson interview, September 25, 2007; Marginson, "Not for the Money," 120.

162. Melba Marginson, "Increasing Access for Filipina Survivors of Domestic Violence," in *Not the Same: Conference Proceedings and a Strategy on Domestic Violence and Sexual Assault for Non-English Speaking Background Women* (Brunswick, Victoria: Office of the Status of Women, 1996), 20–21.

163. Cunneen and Stubbs, *Gender, "Race": and International Relations*, 1; Rosa Droescher and Debbie Wall, interview with author, Sydney, August 2, 2012.

164. Melba Marginson, "Immigrant and Refugee Women as Victims of Crime," paper presented to the Conference on Support of Victims of Crime, "Meeting the Challenges of Diversity: Different Cultures, Different Needs," April 21, 1999, Melbourne, 2, from the personal papers of Melba Marginson, Melbourne; Marginson interview, September 25, 2007.

165. Cunneen and Stubbs, *Gender, "Race" and International Relations*, 1; Marginson interview, September 25, 2007; and Zita Antonios, Race Discrimination Commissioner, to Melba Marginson, March 16, 1995, 1, from the personal papers of Melba Marginson, Melbourne.

166. Cunneen and Stubbs, *Gender, "Race" and International Relations*, 1 and 31.

167. Nikki Barrowclough, "The Shameful Story of Australia's Serial Husbands," Good Weekend, *Sydney Morning Herald Magazine*, May 6, 1995, 46–67.

168. Elizabeth Evatt, "Serial Sponsorship and Abuse of Filipino Women in Australia," in Ethnic Affairs Commission of New South Wales, *Serial Sponsorship*, 17. "Under the Migration Regulations 1994 of the Migration Act 1958, applicants on certain Partner visas, who have experienced domestic violence after arriving in Australia and whose relationship with the sponsoring partner has broken down because of domestic violence, remain eligible for Permanent Residence if they can demonstrate that the relationship with their sponsoring partner was genuine and broke down because of domestic violence. A victim must prove that the relationship was genuine and ongoing and that domestic violence occurred in Australia." Clause 801.221 (6) of Sch 2 to the Migration Regulations 1994.

169. Evatt, "Serial Sponsorship and Abuse," 17.

170. Evatt, "Serial Sponsorship and Abuse," 17.

171. Evatt, "Serial Sponsorship and Abuse," 17.

172. Dicka interview, June 11, 2014.

173. *Marrying and Migrating . . . You Have to Work at It*, VHS video, Australia Department of Immigration and Multicultural Affairs, 1996. An information booklet published by the Department of Immigration and Multicultural Affairs, with the same title but written in the Tagalog language, was also given to prospective migrants. It was a comprehensive guide that covered issues connected with marriage migration encouraging women to think about their fiancé's past, family situation and health with a section on protection against domestic violence. *Marrying and Migration . . . You Have to Work at It* (Australia Department of Immigration and Multicultural Affairs, 1999); and Wall, "Joan Dicka," 4–5.

174. *Marrying and Migrating* (1996).

175. Marie del Rosario-Apattad and Rodrigo Garcia, Commission on Filipinos Overseas, interview with author, Manila, July 25, 2014.

176. Dicka interview, June 20, 2014; "Smoothing the Path for Migrants," *Post Migration*, June 1995, 17, from the personal papers of Joan Dicka, Adelaide.

177. "Dawn House S.A. Inc.," in *Good Practice in SAAP Services*, ed. Joanne Baulderstone and Catherine Scott (Adelaide: Flinders Institute of Public Policy and Management, Flinders University of South Australia, 1999), 107–118.

178. Jenny Clark, "For Better or Worse . . . Till Death Do Us Part . . . ?," in *The Art of Health: Using the Arts to Achieve Health* ([Adelaide]: South Australian Health Commission, 1997), 15; "Dawn House S.A. Inc.," in Baulderstone and Scott, *Good Practice in SAAP Services*, 107–118; Tahereh Ziaian, *Celebrating Our Success: Responses to Violence against Non-English Speaking Background Women*, report of the NESB Women and Violence Project ([North Adelaide]: Women's Health Statewide, 1997), app. 4, "Filipino Women and the Murray Mallee Support Group," 28–31.

179. Clark, *The Art of Health*, 15.

180. Merlinda Bobis (facilitator) and Daisy Kruizinga (project coordinator), *Writing Ten-Minute Monologue for Stage and Radio, Remembering: Stories of Eight Women* (Wollongong: Wollongong City Council Small Grants Program, 2000–2001).

181. Bobis and Kruizinga, *Writing Ten-Minute Monologue*.

182. Guanio-Bartels and Pe-Pua, *Development of a Radio Information Package*, ix.

183. Guanio-Bartels and Pe-Pua, *Development of a Radio Information Package*, 15.

184. For example, in Mudgee, Lithgow and Grafton. Guanio-Bartels and Pe-Pua, *Development of a Radio Information Package*, 16–17. The topics of the twelve episodes were: (1) "Acquiring Australian Citizenship and Sponsoring Relatives to Australia"; (2) "Acquiring Permanent Residency and Provisions for Illegal Immigrants in Australia"; (3) "Domestic Violence Provisions of the Department of Immigration"; (4) "Domestic Violence"; (5) "Legal Aid and Other Free Legal Advice and Assistance"; (6) "The Legal Implications of Marital Separation or Divorce"; (7) "Welfare Service Providers"; (8) "Making Cross-Cultural Marriages Work"; (9) "Guidelines for Survival I (Enhancing Employment Prospects and an Overview of Social Security Benefits)"; (10) "Guidelines for Survival II (Child Care, Health Care, and the Value of Establishing or Joining Support Groups)"; (11) "Dealing with Racism"; and (12) "Parenting in a Cross-Cultural Context."

185. For Filipina cultural constructions of the feminine, see Roces, *Women's Movements and the Filipina*, 31, and 35–51.

186. *Ngayong Aussie Ka na, Manay!* episode 8, "Cross-Cultural Marriage," tapes held in the private collection of Dr. Rogelia Pe-Pua.

187. *Ngayong Aussie Ka na, Manay!* episode 8.

188. *Ngayong Aussie Ka na, Manay!* episode 3, "Provisions ng Immigration Para sa Mga Biktima ng Domestic Violence," or "Domestic Violence Provisions of the Department of Immigration."

189. Ipong interview, April 27, 2014; Dicka interview, June 10–11, 2014.

190. For an account of the women's movements in the Philippines in the 1980s and 1990s, see Roces, *Women's Movements and the Filipina*.

191. John Mowatt and Deborah Wall, *Dealing with the Media: Filipino Women in Cross Cultural Marriages; A Training Manual for Community Workers* (Sydney: Filipino Women's

Working Party, Immigrant Women's Speakout Association, and the Ethnic Affairs Commission of New South Wales, 1992).

192. Droescher and Wall interview, August, 2, 2012.
193. Droescher and Wall interview, August 2, 2012.
194. McKinnon interview, March 1, 2013.
195. Wall and Droescher interview, August 2, 2012.
196. See the CPCA website and issues of its newsletter *Kasama*.
197. Ramilo interview, August 5, 2014.
198. Wall and Droescher interview, August 2, 2012.
199. McKinnon interview, March 1, 2013.
200. McKinnon interview, March 1, 2013.
201. McKinnon interview, March 1, 2013.
202. Deborah Ruiz Wall, "Reconciliation: A Process that Truly Heals," *Kasama*, 18 no. 2 (2004): 1, http://cpcabrisbane.org/Kasama/2004/V18n2/Reconciliation.htm.
203. From the plaque at the home of Estrella McKinnon.
204. McKinnon interview, March 1, 2013.
205. "Melba Marginson," Australian Centre for Leadership for Women website, accessed July 23m 2015, http://www.leadershipforwomen.com.au/transform/activism/gilliard-election-2010-campaign/melba-marginson; and Marginson, e-mail message to author, November 24, 2016.
206. Wall, "Joan Dicka," 1–5; Dicka interview, June 10–11, 2014.
207. Letter from Mrs. X to the Information Collection Unit, Department of Immigration and Citizenship, July 30, 2012, and handwritten letter of the wife of Y to the Women's Emergency Center, no date, both from the personal papers of Joan Dicka in Adelaide. The names have been withheld to protect their identities.
208. Statement by Faith (pseudonym), no date, from the personal papers of Joan Dicka in Adelaide.
209. I am indebted to Martyn Lyons for the label "writing upwards." See Martyn Lyons, "Writing Upwards: How the Weak Wrote to the Powerful," *Journal of Social History* 49, no. 2 (2015): 1–14.
210. Rogelia Pe-Pua, *Towards Full Participation in Australian Society: Report of the Workshop Series for Filipino Women and Their Families* (Wollongong: Illawarra Filipino Women's Group, 2000); Antonina Elberich, *Profile of the Filipino Community: Wollongong, Shellharbour and Kiama* (Wollongong: Illawarra Filipino Women's Group and Planning New South Wales, 2002).
211. Estrella "Lilia" McKinnon, *Filipino Youth Survey* (Figtree, NSW: Department of Immigration, Multicultural and Indigenous Affairs, 2004).
212. Wall interview, August 12, 2012.
213. Dicka interview, June 10–11, 2014.
214. Agbayani, Guerero, and Kerkvliet, "Operation Manong," 5.
215. Agbayani interview, June 11, 2012.
216. McKinnon interview, March 1, 2013.
217. McKinnon interview, March 1, 2013.
218. Dicka interview, June 10–11, 2014.
219. Ipong interview, April 27, 2014.
220. Ipong interview, April 27, 2014.
221. Droescher interview, August 12, 2012.

222. Droescher interview, August 12, 2012.
223. Ramilo, interview, August 4, 2014.
224. Droescher interview, August 12, 2012.
225. Deborah Wall, e-mail message to author, January 6, 2015. Della Ipong also described their activism as collaborative. Ipong interview, April 27, 2014.
226. Wall interview, August 2, 2012.
227. Marginson interview, September 25, 2007.
228. Ramilo interview, August 5, 2014.
229. Evatt, "Serial Sponsorship and Abuse," 14; Sue Zelinka, "Human Rights Issues in Relation to Serial Sponsorship," in Ethnic Affairs Commission of New South Wales, *Serial Sponsorship*, 20.
230. Dicka interview, June 10–11, 2014.
231. "We Fight for Our Rights," lyrics reproduced in Clark, *The Art of Health*; also reproduced in the script *Buklod ng Kababaihang Filipina*; both in the personal papers of Joan Dicka.
232. Dicka interview, June 10–11, 2014.
233. Marginson, "Increasing Access," 20.
234. Dicka interview, June 10–11, 2014; Ipong interview, April 27, 2014; Ramilo, interview with author, August 5, 2014.
235. Dicka interview, June 10–11, 2014.
236. Wall and Droescher interview, August 2, 2012

7. Migrants and the Homeland, 1986–2018

1. Nicole Curato and Jonathan Corpus Ong, "Disasters Can Lift Veils: Five Issues for Sociological Disaster Studies," *Philippine Sociological Review* 63, no. 1 (2015): 1.
2. Raffy Lopez, TFC senior vice president and chief operating officer, interview with author, San Francisco, December 5, 2013.
3. Marie del Rosario-Apattad and Rodrigo Garcia, Commission on Filipinos Overseas, interview with author, Manila, July 25, 2014.
4. Dr. Cora Francisco, PAMA founder, interview with author, Sydney, December 20, 2013.
5. Speech of James Lim, executive director of Philippine International Aid organization, at the PIA fundraising event, held at the Hyatt Embarcadero Hotel in San Francisco, Sunday, November 17, 2013.
6. Del Rosario-Apattad and Garcia interview, July 25, 2014.
7. Del Rosario-Apattad and Garcia interview, July 25, 2014.
8. Del Rosario-Apattad and Garcia interview, Manila, July 25, 2014.
9. Philippine Medical Society of Northern California website, accessed March 22, 2017, https://www.pmsnc.org/.
10. See, for example, Mark Thompson, *The Anti-Marcos Struggle: Personalistic Rule and Democratic Transition in the Philippines* (New Haven, CT: Yale University Press, 1995); and Aguilar, *Migration Revolution*, 231–244.
11. Glenda Tibe Bonifacio has devoted five pages of her book *Pinay in the Prairies* to examples of Filipina Canadian philanthropic work in the Philippines (233–238) and three pages to discussing Canadian medical missions to the Philippines (243–245).

12. L. Joyce Zapanta Mariano, "Doing Good in Filipino Diaspora: Philanthropy, Remittances, and Homeland Returns," *Journal of Asian American Studies* 20, no. 2 (2017): 219–244.

13. Maruja M. B. Asis and Fabio Baggio, eds., *Moving Out, Back and Up: International Migration and Development Prospects in the Philippines* (Quezon City: Scalabrini Migration Center, 2008); Jeremiah Opiniano, *Good News for the Poor: Diaspora Philanthropy by Filipinos* (Quezon City: Association of Foundations, 2005).

14. Executive Order No. 498, Institutionalizing the Presidential Awards for Filipino Individuals and Organizations Overseas, December 19, 1991, quoted in Mariano, "Doing Good in Filipino Diaspora," 21–22.

15. Opiniano, *Good News for the Poor*.

16. Shirleta Africa Espinosa, "Reading the Gendered Body in Filipino-Australian Diaspora Philanthropy," *Portal: Journal of Multidisciplinary International Studies* 9, no. 2 (July 2012): 1–20.

17. Francisco interview, December 20, 2013; Ophee de Vera, PAMA, interview with author, Sydney, January 20, 2014.

18. Del Rosario-Apattad and Garcia interview, July 25, 2014.

19. Anne O'Brien, *Philanthropy and Settler Colonialism* (London: Palgrave Macmillan, 2015).

20. Mona Lisa Y. Abaya, editorial, *Philippine International Aid Newsletter*, October 1986, 2.

21. Abaya, editorial, 2.

22. "PIA's Guidelines for Beneficiary Selection," *Philippine International Aid Newsletter*, October 1986, 5.

23. "New Focus Children's Projects Launched," *Philippine International Aid Newsletter*, June 1987, 1.

24. New Focus Children's Projects Launched," 1.

25. "Off the Streets–Off to School," *Philippine International Aid Newsletter*, June 1987, 1.

26. Mona Lisa Yuchengco's speech, "PIA at the Unity Conference," *PIA–The Children's Fund Newsletter* 11, no. 2 (December 1987): 10.

27. Mona Lisa Yuchengco, interview with author, San Francisco, November 25, 2013.

28. Philippine International Aid advertisements, *Filipinas*, May 1992, 29, and August 1992, 2.

29. Coratec Jimenez, "Commitment: From the Heart? Or Just from the Pocket?," *PIA–The Children's Fund Newsletter* 6, no. 1 (June 1992): 8.

30. "Off the Streets–Off to School Scholarship Program," Philippine International Aid website, accessed November 20, 2014, http://www.phil-aid.org/.

31. "Education Is a Lifetime Gift," *Filipinas*, May 1992, 28, and August 1992, 2.

32. Editorial, "Keeping the Promise," *PIA–The Children's Fund Newsletter* 6, no. 2 (December 1991): 2.

33. Cristina D. C. Pastor, "1.5 M Children Roam RP Streets," *PIA–The Children's Fund Newsletter*, Summer 1996, 1–2.

34. "New Focus Children's Projects Launched," *PIA–The Children's Fund Newsletter* 2, no. 1 (June 1987): 1.

35. "New Focus Children's Projects Launched," 1.
36. Editorial, *PIA–The Children's Fund Newsletter* 3, no. 1 (June 1988): 2.
37. "Abused Kids Need Help," *PIA–The Children's Fund Newsletter* 6, no. 2 (December 1991): 1.
38. Mona Lisa Yuchengco, e-mail message to author, March 28, 2017.
39. PIA, "About Us: Mission and History," accessed November 6, 2017, https://phil-aid.org/about-us/.
40. PIA documentary, shown at the PIA fundraising event, November 17, 2013.
41. Mona Lisa Yuchengco's speech at PIA's fundraising event, November 17, 2013.
42. PIA homepage, http://www.phil-aid.org/.
43. Ken Kashiwara, PIA homepage, http://www.phil-aid.org/.
44. "New Focus Children's Projects Launched," 1.
45. Status reports, *PIA–The Children's Fund Newsletter* 5, no. 2 (December 1990): 4.
46. Mona Lisa Yuchengco, e-mail message to author, March 28, 2017.
47. "Impact of Our Work," accessed November 21, 2014, http://www.phil-aid.org/impact-of-our-worknewsletters.html.
48. Mona Lisa Yuchengco, e-mail message to author, November 18, 2013.
49. Proposal submissions, minutes of director's meetings, PIA archives, San Francisco.
50. Father Shay Cullen, letter to Mona Lisa Yuchengco, February 2013; project proposals from Katilingban Para sa Kalambuan Inc. and the Good Shepherd Sisters, Iligan Community, 2013, PIA archives, San Francisco; and "Cebu Center Beneficiary of PIA Aid," *PIA–The Children's Fund Newsletter* 6, no. 2 (December 1989): 5.
51. "About Filipino Americans," PIA website, accessed November 21, 2014. Note: This was located on the PIA website, but since the website is updated every year the content changes, so in 2020 the headings "Filipinos" and "Filipino Americans" are no longer menitoned.
52. "Fundraisers: Holiday Double Exposure," *PIA–The Children's Fund Newsletter* (2009): 4.
53. Yuchengco interview, November 25, 2013.
54. "About Filipino Americans," PIA website.
55. "US Grants," PIA website, accessed November 21, 2014.
56. "Impact of Our Work.", PIA website, accessed November 21, 2014.
57. Sharon Nagy, "The Search for Miss Philippines Bahrain—Possibilities for Representation in Expatriate Communities," *City & Society* 20, no. 1 (2008): 79–104. My contacts in Lucky Plaza Singapore told me that there are over ten beauty contests a year held there. See also the documentary *Sunday Beauty Queen* about Filipino domestic workers in Hong Kong preparing for their participation in a beauty pageant. Baby Ruth Villarama, dir., *Sunday Beauty Queen*, documentary (TBA Studios, 2016).
58. Rodriguez, *Celebrating Debutantes and Quinceañeras*, 11.
59. Benito M. Vergara Jr., *Pinoy Capital: The Filipino Nation in Daly City* (Philadelphia: Temple University Press, 2009), 2.
60. PIA website, accessed November 21, 2014, http://www.phil-aid.org/holiday-haute-couture-xii.html.
61. Gonzalves, *The Day the Dancers Stayed*, 12.

62. Cora Francisco interview, December 20, 2013.
63. Francisco interview, December 20, 2013.
64. Bonifacio, *Pinays on the Prairies*, 244.
65. Francisco interview, December 20, 2013.
66. PAMA, "Purpose and Objectives," http://www.pama.org.au/home/goals.
67. PAMA has started to expand nationally with a branch formed in Victoria in 2013 with a membership of around thirty. Francisco interview, December 20, 2013.
68. Francisco interview, December 20, 2013.
69. Grace Maano, "2008 PAMA Medical Mission: First PAMA 'Balikbayan' Medical Mission Held at Polillo, Quezon," accessed October 17, 2016, www.pama.org.au/home/2008-medical-mission.
70. Francisco interview, December 20, 2013.
71. "History of PAMA: Timeline," http://www.pama.org.au/home/history; Mao de Vera, e-mail message to author, March 28, 2017.
72. Francisco interview, December 20, 2013.
73. Francisco interview, Sydney, December 20, 2013.
74. Francisco interview, Sydney, December 20, 2013; and Ophee de Vera and Mao de Vera, interview with author, Sydney, January 20, 2014.
75. PMSNC website, accessed March 22, 2017, https://www.pmsnc.org/history.
76. Manzel Delacruz, "Missions Possible," *Positively Filipino*, September 2, 2015, accessed March 9, 2015, http://www.positivelyfilipino.com/magazine/missions-possible.
77. Delacruz, "Missions Possible."
78. Delacruz, "Missions Possible."
79. James Espinas and Timothy Kiley, *Bloodlines: A Medical Mission to Iloilo, Philippines*, documentary (2004).
80. Quoted in Espinas and Kiley, *Bloodlines*.
81. Quoted in Espinas and Kiley, *Bloodlines*.
82. Mao de Vera interview, January 20, 2014.
83. Espinas and Kiley, *Bloodlines*.
84. Espinas and Kiley, *Bloodlines*.
85. Espinas and Kiley, *Bloodlines*.
86. de Vera interview, January 20, 2014.
87. Dr. Paul Espinas, speaking in Espinas and Kiley, *Bloodlines*.
88. Maano, "2008 PAMA Medical Mission."
89. One volunteer confessed, "I know that we are doing something over there and it is not much but we are driven to come back every year so we can help some of our co-Filipinos." Quoted in YouTube film of the 2012 PMSNC medical mission to Occidental Mindoro.
90. Francisco interview, December 20, 2013.
91. Ophee de Vera interview, January 20, 2014.
92. Quoted in the YouTube documentary of the PMSNC Medical Mission to Sarangani in 2011, PMSNC website, accessed November 21, 2014, http//www.youtube.com/watch?v=FK93ZyXHw2E&list=PL5zHrqvuoM0Z6OOcZECvzxadSoauimqe6&index=4.
93. Dr. Paul Espinas in Espinas and Kiley, *Bloodlines*.
94. Dr. Paul Espinas in Espinas and Kiley, *Bloodlines*.
95. Dr. Paul Espinas in Espinas and Kiley, *Bloodlines*.

96. Espinas and Kiley, *Bloodlines*; Francisco interview, December 20, 2013; Ophee de Vera interview, January 20, 2014.
97. Espinas and Kiley, *Bloodlines*.
98. Quoted in Espinas and Kiley, *Bloodlines*.
99. Espinas and Kiley, *Bloodlines*.
100. Espinas and Riley, *Bloodlines*.
101. Del Rosario-Apattad and Garcia interview, July 25, 2014.
102. Del Rosario-Apattad and Garcia interview, July 25, 2014.
103. Del Rosario-Apattad and Garcia interview, July 25, 2014.
104. Yuchengco interview, November 25, 2013.
105. PIA archives, San Francisco, reports from NGOs, 1990 and 2012.
106. PIA archives, San Francisco, 2012 file.
107. Speech of Mona Lisa Yuchengco, at PIA fundraising event, November 17, 2013, San Francisco.
108. "Impact of Our Work."
109. Espinas and Kiley, *Bloodlines*.
110. Espinas and Kiley, *Bloodlines*.
111. Philippine Medical Society of Northern California website, accessed November 21, 2014, http://www.pmsnc.com/pages/medicalmissions.php.
112. PMSNC website, accessed March 27, 2017, https://www.pmsnc.org/pages/medicalmissions.
113. Francisco interview, December 20, 2013.
114. Ophee de Vera interview, January 20, 2014.
115. Francisco, interview, December 20, 2013.
116. PAMA 6th Medical Mission, DVD, 2013.
117. Bonifacio, *Pinays on the Prairies*, 244; Ophee de Vera and Mao de Vera interview, January 20, 2014.
118. Mao de Vera interview, January 20, 2014.
119. Mao de Vera interview, January 20, 2014.
120. Francisco interview, December 20, 2013.
121. "History of PAMA: Merits and Citations," http://www.pama.org.au/home/history.
122. Quote in Espinas and Kiley, *Bloodlines*.
123. Quoted in Espinas and Kiley, *Bloodlines*.
124. Mao de Vera interview, January 20, 2014.
125. John Silva, Editorial, *PIA–The Children's Fund Newsletter* 6, no. 2 (December 1991): 2.
126. "PIA at the Unity Conference," *PIA–The Children's Fund Newsletter* 11, no. 2 (December 1987): 9.
127. Mona Lisa Abaya, editorial, *PIA–The Children's Fund Newsletter* 11, no. 2 (December 1987): 2.
128. Collection of children's letters held in the PIA archives, San Francisco.
129. *PIA–The Children's Fund Newsletter* (Fall 2003): 5; "Giving Back: PIA Success Stories," in Mark Tristan Ng, *Little Voices: A Photo Essay on the Children of Philippine International Aid* (San Francisco: PIA, 2010), 40–41.
130. *PIA–The Children's Fund Newsletter* (Fall 2003): 5; and "Giving Back PIA Success Stories," in Ng, *Little Voices*, 40–41.

131. "A Success Story," *PIA–The Children's Fund Newsletter* (Fall 2001): 4.
132. "A Success Story," 4.
133. Quoted in Espinas and Kiley, *Bloodlines*.
134. Dr. Paul Espinas in Espinas and Kiley, *Bloodlines*.
135. Ophee de Vera interview, January 20, 2014.
136. Anonymous volunteer in the YouTube documentary of the PMSNC Medical Missions, PMSNC website, accessed November 21, 2014, https://www.youtube.com/watch?v=LS-ykfA-yzY&list=PL5zHrqvuoM0Z6OOcZECvzxadSoauimqe6.
137. Mao de Vera interview, January 20, 2014; Francisco interview, December 20, 2014; Espinas and Kiley, *Bloodlines*.
138. Jimenez, "Commitment," 8.
139. Jimenez, "Commitment," 8.

Conclusion

1. Reynaldo Ileto, "Rizal and the Underside of Philippine History," in *Moral Order and the Question of Change: Essays on Southeast Asian Thought*, ed. David Wyatt and Alexander Woodside (New Haven, CT: Yale Southeast Asia Program Series, 1982), 274–337; and Vicente L. Rafael, "'Your Grief Is Our Gossip': Overseas Filipinos and Other Spectral Presences," *Public Culture* 9, no. 2 (1997): 267–291.
2. Bangko Sentral ng Pilipinas, quoted in Amrith, *Caring for Strangers*, 33.
3. Quoted in Ma. Jovita Zarate, "Ang Konsepto ng Bagong Bayani sa mga Naratibo ng Overseas Filipino Workers," *Malay* 20, no. 1 (2007): 104.
4. Jean Encinas-Franco, "The Language of Labor Export in Political Discourse: 'Modern-Day Heroism' and Constructions of Overseas Filipino Workers (OFWs)," *Philippine Political Science Journal* 34, no. 1 (2013): 97–112, Rafael, "Your Grief."
5. Bagong Bayani Awards 2000 program, June 16, 2000, from the personal scrapbook of Cecilia Silva.
6. Encinas-Franco, "The Language of Labor Export," 103.
7. Steven C. McKay, "Filipino Sea Men," 72; National Seafarers' Day Facebook page, accessed December 4, 2016, https://www.facebook.com/permalink.php?story_fbid=1703648233219866&id=1483107758607249.
8. National Seafarers' Day Facebook page.
9. Encinas-Franco, "The Language of Labor Export," 97.
10. Encinas-Franco, "The Language of Labor Export," 98.
11. Jean Encinas-Franco, "The Politics of Language in Labor Export: A Discourse Historical Analysis of Bagong Bayani and Overseas Employment Policies" (PhD diss., University of the Philippines, 2011).
12. Encinas-Franco, "The Politics of Language," 187–215.
13. Quoted in Zarate, "Ang Konsepto ng Bagong Bayani," 109.
14. Quoted in McKay, "Filipino Sea Men," 77.
15. Raquel Delfin Padilla, "Bagong bayani o bigong bayani?," in Delfin and Revilla, *Sindi ng Lampara*, 75.
16. "Naabot na ba namin an aming mga pangarap? . . . Ang amin bang pamilya'y buo pa rin? . . . Ang amin bang gobyerno ay nagpapahalaga sa amin? . . . Kami ba ay hindi naaabuso sa ibang bansa?" (Padilla, "Bagong bayani o bigong bayani?," 73).
17. Padilla, "Bagong bayani o bigong bayani?," 73–75.

18. Cecilia Silva, dossier for nomination for the Bagong Bayani Award, from the personal scrapbook of Cecilia Silva.

19. Cecilia Silva, curriculum vitae, from the personal scrapbook of Cecilia Silva.

20. Maria Theresa Natividad, Cecilia Silva, and Ruby Tupaz, "Associazione Donne Filippine Accomplishment Report Yr. 2010 to Yr. 2017," submitted to the Philippine Embassy, p. 1, from the personal papers of Cecilia Silva.

21. Natividad, Silva, and Tupaz, "Associazione Donne Filippine Accomplishment Report," 2–3.

22. Natividad, Silva, and Tupaz, "Associazione Donne Filippine Accomplishment Report," 2–3, and interview with members of the Associazione Donne Filippine.

23. "Join Us in Honoring the Best and the Brightest!," *Filipinas*, September 2009, 6.

24. E-mail communication from FWN member Elena Mangahas, October, 12, 2017. The books are Maria Africa Beebe and Maya Ong Escudero, eds., *Disrupt: Filipina Women; Proud, Loud, Leading without a Doubt* (San Francisco: Filipina Women's Network, 2015); Maria Africa Beebe, ed., *Disrupt 2.0: Filipina Women; Daring to Lead* (San Francisco: Filipina Women's Network, 2016); and Maria Africa Beebe, *Disrupt 3.0: Filipina Women; Rising* (San Francisco: Filipino Women's Network, 2018).

25. Interview with Mona Lisa Yuchengco, San Francisco, November 25, 2013.

26. KASAPI-Hellas website, accessed January 19, 2017, http://www.kasapi.gr.

27. In 2012 when I interviewed Joe and Debbie Valencia, founders of KASAPI-Hellas, they told me that the organization had 1,200 members.

28. Joe Valencia and Debbie Valencia, interview with author, Athens, September 11, 2012.

29. Joe Valencia, interview with author, Athens, September 11, 2012.

30. Debbie Valencia, interview with author, Athens, September 11, 2012.

31. Debbie Valencia interview, September 11, 2012.

32. Debbie Valencia interview, September 11, 2012.

33. Joe Valencia and Debbie Valencia interview, September 11, 2012.

34. Debbie Valencia interview, September 11, 2012.

35. Dean T. Alegado, "We're Here, Get Used to It!," *Filipinas*, January 2000, 18–23 and 28–29.

36. Fred Cordova, "The Browning of America," Our Story, *Filipinas*, March 1993, 11.

Bibliography

Primary Sources

Memoirs, Autobiographies, Life Stories, Community Histories

Abubakar, Pearlsha, and Rochit I. Tañado. *Mga waging kuwento ng OFW.* Manila: OWWA and Creative Collective Center, 2005.
Andaya, Leonard Y. "From American-Filipino to Filipino-American." *Social Process in Hawaii* 37 (1996): 99–111.
Arboleda, Corazon E., and Carmelita G. Nuqui, eds. *Migrants' Stories, Migrants' Voices.* Quezon City: Philippine Migrants Rights Watch, 2007.
Art as Reality: The Transition of Filipino Migrant Children in the Middle East. Muscat, Oman: Embassy of the Republic of the Philippines, Muscat, Sultanate of Oman, 2013.
Aryo, Analyn D. *Nanny Tales: Voices from the Diary of an Overseas Filipina Worker.* Benguet: ResearchMate, 2009.
Banados, Papias Generale. *The Path to Remittance: Tales of Pains and Gains of Overseas Filipino Workers.* Edited by Kalinga Seneviratne. Singapore: Global Eye Media, 2011.
Bobis, Merlinda, and Daisy Kruizinga. *Writing Ten-Minute Monologue for Stage and Radio. Remembering: Stories of Eight Women.* Wollongong: Wollongong City Council Small Grants Program, 2000–2001.
Brown, Patricia, ed. *Filipinas! Voices from Daughters and Descendants of Hawaii's Plantation Era.* North Charleston, SC: CreateSpace, 2014.
Buakan, Manuel. *I Have Lived with the American People.* Caldwell, ID: Caxton Printers, 1948.
Buchholdt, Thelma. *Filipinos in Alaska: 1788–1958.* Anchorage: Aboriginal Press, 1996.
Buell, Evangeline Canonizado, Evelyn Luluquisen, Lillian Galedo, Eleanor Hipol Luis, and Filipino American National Historical Society East Bay Chapter. *Filipinos in the East Bay.* Images of America. Charleston, SC: Arcadia, 2008.
Bulosan, Carlos. *America Is in the Heart: A Personal History.* Manila: Anvil, 2006. Originally published in 1946.
Cayaban, Ines V. *A Goodly Heritage.* Hong Kong: Gulliver Books, 1981.
Cayetano, Benjamin J. *Ben: A Memoir, from Street Kid to Governor.* Honolulu: Watermark Publishing, 2009.
Cordova, Dorothy Laigo, and the Filipino National Historical Society. *Filipinos in Puget Sound.* Images of America. Charleston, SC: Arcadia, 2009.

Cordova, Fred. "The Bridge Generation and Building Bridges." Presented at the Fifth National Biennial Conference of FANHS, San Francisco, August 4–6, 1994. Reproduced in *FANHS Journal* 4 (1996).
———. *Filipinos: Forgotten Asian Americans; A Pictorial Essay, 1763–circa 1963*. Seattle: Demonstration Project for Asian Americans, 1983.
Esic, Adelle J. *Buhay Saudi ng OFW Caregiver*. Self-published; printed in the United States by Tatay Jobo Elizes, 2013.
Espiritu, Yen Le, ed. *Filipino American Lives*. Philadelphia: Temple University Press, 1995.
FANHS [Filipino American National Historical Society] Hampton Roads Chapter. *In Our Aunties' Words: The Filipino Spirit of Hampton Roads*. San Francisco: T'Boli, 2004.
———. *In Our Uncles' Words*. San Francisco: T'Boli, 2006.
Felipe, Virgilio Menor. *Hawai'i: A Pilipino Dream*. Honolulu: Mutual, 2002.
Filipino Oral History Project. *Voices: A Filipino American Oral History*. Stockton, CA: Filipino Oral History Project, 1984.
Garcia, Fanny A. *Pamilya, migrasyon, disintegrasyon*. Quezon City: C & E Publishing for De La Salle University Press, 2012.
Gonzalves, Theodore, and Roderick N. Labrador. *Filipinos in Hawai'i*. Images of America. Charleston, SC: Arcadia, 2011.
Hearts Apart: Migration in the Eyes of Filipino Children. Manila: Episcopal Commission for the Pastoral Care of Migrants and Itinerant People / Apostleship of the Sea–Manila, Scalabrini Migration Center, and Overseas Workers Welfare Administration, 2004.
Hoegsholm, Filomenita Mongaya, ed. *In De Olde Worlde: Views of Filipino Migrants in Europe*. Quezon City: Philippine Social Science Council, 2007.
Jamero, Peter. *Growing Up Brown: Memoirs of a Filipino American*. Seattle: University of Washington Press, 2006.
———. *Vanishing Filipino Americans: The Bridge Generation*. Lanham, MD: University Press of America, 2011.
Layosa, Linda R., and Laura P. Luminarias. *Sa Pagyuko ng Kawayan: A Collection of Poems by Filipino Overseas Workers*. Hong Kong: AsiaPacific, 1992.
Mabalon, Dawn B., Rico Reyes, Stockton Chapter, Filipino American National Historical Society, and Little Manila Foundation. *Filipinos in Stockton*. Images of America. Charleston, SC: Arcadia, 2008.
Magtoto, Liza, Amihan Ruiz, and Totti Sanchez. *Mga Waging kuwento ng OFW 2006*. Manila: Creative Collective Center and OWWA, 2006.
Manlapaz, Edna Zapanta, Czarina Saloma, and Yael A. Buencamino. *Many Journeys, Many Voices: A Tribute to Filipino Overseas Workers*. Manila: Anvil, 2015.
Monrayo, Angeles. *Tomorrow's Memories: A Diary, 1924–1928*. Honolulu: University of Hawaii Press, 2004.
Montoya, Carina Monica. *Filipinos in Hollywood*. Images of America. Charleston, SC: Arcadia, 2008.
Napat, Jessica Flores. "Tukso, taksil, takbo." In *Masaya din, malungkot din (karanasan ng OFW)*, by Jovelyn B. Revilla, 99–102. Self-published, 2012.
Ng, Mark Tristan. *Little Voices: A Photo Essay on the Children of Philippine International Aid*. San Francisco: PIA, 2010.

Noval-Jezewski, Maria Thelma. "A Simplified Map of French-Philippines: A Bird's Eye–Worm's Eye View." In *In De Olde Worlde: Views of Filipino Migrants in Europe*, edited by Filomenita Mongaya Hoegsholm, 290–300. Quezon City: Philippine Social Science Council, 2007.

Nuqui, Carmelita G., and Jannis T. Montañez, eds. *Moving On: Stories of DAWN Women Survivors*. Manila: DAWN, 2004.

Nuqui, Carmelita G., and Alicor L. Panao, eds. *Migrants' Stories, Migrants' Voices 2*. Quezon City: Philippine Migrants Rights Watch, 2008.

Orpilla, Mel. *Filipinos in Vallejo*. Images of America. Charleston, SC: Arcadia, 2005.

Padilla, Malu. "Women Changing Our Lives, Making HERstory: Migration Experiences of Babaylan Philippine Women's Network in Europe." In *In De Olde Worlde: Views of Filipino Migrants in Europe*, edited by Filomenita Mongaya Hoegsholm, 83–109. Quezon City: Philippine Social Science Council, 2007.

Padilla, Raquel Delfin, and Jovelyn Bayubay Revilla, eds. *Sindi ng Lampara: OFW Stories*. Manila: Allibratore Enterprises, 2012.

Revilla, Jovelyn B. *Masaya din, malungkot din (karanasan ng OFW)*. Self-published; printed in the United States by Tatay Jobo Elizes, 2012.

Santa Clara Valley Chapter of the Filipino American National Historical Society. "Filipino American Experience: Growing Up Brown." *Filipino Journal* 3 (1993).

———. "Filipino Americans: A Patchwork in the American Quilt." *Filipino Journal* 4, no. 4 (1994–1996).

———. "Filipino Americans . . . Forever Our Legacy." *Filipino Journal* 5, no. 5 (1998–1999).

———. "Generation Insights: Reflected Memories of the Second Generation of Filipino Americans." *Filipino Journal* 2, no. 2 (1992).

———. "Lost Generation." *Filipino Journal* 1, no. 1 (1991).

Santos, Bob. *Humbows, Not Hotdogs! Memoirs of a Savvy Asian American Activist*. Seattle: International Examiner Press, 2002.

Ventura, Rey. *Into the Country of Standing Men*. Quezon City: Ateneo de Manila University Press, 2007.

———. *Underground in Japan*. Quezon City: Ateneo de Manila University Press, 1992.

Unpublished Essays

Canlas, MC. "Getting to Know SoMa Pilipinas #1: The Philippines in SoMa Pilipinas." Unpublished paper, June 11, 2017.

———. "Tabi Po, Respect for Those Who Came Before: Filipinos in South of Market, San Francisco." Unpublished paper, 2002.

Newspapers/Magazines/Newsletters

Ads and Odds (Operation Manong), from 1972; only a few issues surviving

Ahoy Magazine

FANHS Sonoma County, July 2015

Filipino American National Historical Society–Stockton, newsletters, 2013–2021

Filipino Nation, 1925–1931 (incomplete issues, Steffi San Buenaventura Papers, University of California Davis)

Kasama, 1993–2012

Filipinas, 1992–2010

Manila Press, vol. 1, no. 1, 1993, incomplete issues held at the National Library Singapore; Ten issues (vol 1, nos.1 and 3; vol 2, nos 8–12; vol 3, nos 3–4)

Operation Manong, (newsletter) from 1973; only few surviving

Philippine International Aid Newsletter, 2009–2011

Planet Philippines, 2007, 2008 (January, February, June), 2011, 2012, January–June 2013

Positively Filipino, 2012–2021

Sinag, January 1998–June 2010

Tinig ng Marino, July–August 1999, May–June and November–December 2000, July–August 2001, November–December 2002, May–June 2003, May–June 2004, January–February and November–December 2005, March–June 2006, September–December 2006, January–February 2009, and January–April 2010

Archives

ABS-CBN Archives. Benpres Building, Pasig City, Philippines.

Benny Escobido Collection. Hamilton Library, Honolulu, University of Hawaii at Manoa.

Bulolsan, Carlos. Papers. Seattle, University of Washington Library.

Dicka, Joan. Personal papers. Adelaide.

Droescher, Rosa. Personal papers. Sydney.

FIL-KNG Oral History Archives. Washington State Archives. This is a collection of transcripts of fifty-five interviews with Filipina/o/x Americans conducted in the 1970s by the Demonstration Project for Filipino Americans.

FANHS, National Pinoy Archives. Seattle.

Lakbay Dangal. Personal papers (journals). Hong Kong.

Marginson, Melba. Personal papers. Melbourne.

McKinnon, Estrella "Lilia." Personal Papers. Wollongong.

Operation Manong (OM) archives. Multicultural Student Services, University of Hawaii at Manoa.

Philippine International Aid. Papers. San Francisco.

Quezon Papers. Hamilton Library, University of Hawaii at Manoa.

San Buenaventura, Steffi. Papers. Davis, University of California-Davis.

Saroca, Cleonicki. Personal papers. Newcastle, Australia.

Silva, Cecilia. Personal scrapbook. Padova, Italy.Wood, James Earl. Collection on Filipinos in California, circa 1929–1934. San Francisco, University of California, Berkeley.

Tours

Lakbay Dangal Philippine Historical Tour of Hong Kong. April 2011.

Seattle's International District. Personal tour for author conducted by Robert Santos, July 2009.

SoMa Pilipinas Ethnotour. "Uncovering the Cultural Assets and Social Heritage of Filipinos in San Francisco," July 2010.

Stockton's Little Manila Tour. July 2012.

Museum Exhibits

Alaskero Wing Luke Asian Museum Seattle.
Carlos Bulosan Exhibit. Eastern Hotel, Seattle's International District.

Reports

Cordova, D. L. *Executive Director's Report, Conference Program, Lure of the Salmon Song*. 12th FANHS Conference. Filipino American National History Society, 2008.

Elberich, Antonina. *Profile of the Filipino Community: Wollongong, Shellharbour and Kiama*. Wollongong: Illawarra Filipino Women's Group and Planning New South Wales, 2002.

Ethnic Affairs Commission of New South Wales. *Serial Sponsorship: Perspectives for Policy Options*. Sydney: Ethnic Affairs Commission of NSW, 1992.

Galbally, Frank. *Migrant Services and Programs: Report of the Review of Post-Arrival Programs and Services for Migrants*. Canberra: Australian Government Publishing Service, 1978.

Guanio-Bartels, Maria Eleanor, and Rogelia Pe-Pua. *The Development of a Radio Information Package for Filipino Women*. Sydney: Filipino Women's Working Party, 1994.

McKinnon, Estrella "Lilia." *Filipino Youth Survey*. Figtree, NSW: Department of Immigration, Multicultural and Indigenous Affairs, 2004.

Mowatt, John, and Deborah Wall. *Dealing with the Media: Filipino Women in Cross Cultural Marriages; A Training Manual for Community Workers*. Sydney: Filipino Women's Working Party, Immigrant Women's Speakout Association, and the Ethnic Affairs Commission of New South Wales, 1992.

The People of New South Wales, 1991 Census. Sydney: Ethnic Affairs Commission, 1993.

Pe-Pua, Rogelia. *Towards Full Participation in Australian Society: Report of the Workshop Series for Filipino Women and Their Families*. Wollongong: Illawarra Filipino Women's Group, 2000.

Ramilo, Chat, and Rosa Droescher. *Filipino Women: Challenges and Responses (1988–1991)*. Sydney: Ethnic Affairs Commission of NSW, 1992.

San Francisco Filipino Heritage Addendum to the South of Market Historic Context Statement. Prepared for the San Francisco Planning Department. San Francisco: Page & Turnbull, 2013.

Wessels, Anja. *Home Sweet Home? Work, Life and Well-Being of Foreign Domestic Workers in Singapore*. Singapore: Humanitarian Organization for Migrant Economics (HOME), 2015.

Ziaian, Tahereh. *Celebrating Our Success: Responses to Violence against Non-English Speaking Background Women*. Report of the NESB Women and Violence Project, National Women's Health Program (Australia). [North Adelaide]: Women's Health Statewide, 1997.

Interviews by Author

Agbayani, Amefil. Honolulu, June 11, 2012.
Albano, Rhodora Irene, and Ellen Sana. Manila, January 28, 2008.
Añonuevo, Mai. Makati City, Philippines, August 1, 2014, and February 26, 2019.
Associacione Donne Filippine. Padova, November 28, 2015.

BIBLIOGRAPHY

Averion, Merly. Padova, November 29, 2015.
Basa, Charito. Rome, April 15, 2008.
Bautista, Anita Navalta. Stockton, California, July 10, 2012.
Bautista, Clement. Honolulu, June 18, 2012.
Bautista, Mika, and Nicole Reyes. Makati City, August 13, 2014.
Brunio, Lori. Hong Kong, April 23, 2011.
Cabais-Obra, Zita. Paris, March 4, 2008.
Cabucos, Evelyn. Hong Kong, April 24, 2011.
Camillas, Mercy, and Debbie Valencia. Athens, September 12, 2012.
Canlas, Mamerto Calalang. San Francisco, July 11, 2012.
Carlos, Jacinta. Milan, November 22, 2015.
Catipon, Nizer and Precy. Padova, November 25, 2015.
Cordova, Dorothy. Seattle, July 9, 2009.
Cordova, Fred. Seattle, July 9, 2009.
Coronado, Lisa. San Roque, Laguna, Philippines, July 5, 2015.
Cruz, Phyllis Theresa C. Makati City, July 1, 2016.
Cuaresma, Charlene. Honolulu, June 27, 2009.
de Cano, Pio. Seattle, July 2, 2009.
de Dios, Aurora Javate. Quezon City, January 26, 2008.
de Guzman, Emil. San Francisco, June 11, 2010.
de Vera, Mao. Sydney, January 20, 2014.
de Vera, Ophee. Sydney, January 20, 2014.
del Rosario-Apattad, Marie, and Rodrigo Garcia. Manila, July 25, 2014.
Dicka, Joan. Adelaide, June 10–11, 2014.
Droescher, Rosa, and Debbie Wall. Sydney, August 2, 2012.
Dulay, Jun. Manila, June 15, 2017.
Ebora, Jocelyn Averion. Milan, November 22, 2015.
Fariñas, Richard, and Rosita Fariñas. Seattle, July 8, 2009.
Fernandez, Renalin. Singapore, July 21, 2017.
Francisco, Cora. Sydney, December 20, 2013.
Gonzalez, Eddie (owner of Barrio Fiesta). Singapore, July 17, 2017.
Ipong, Della. Sydney, April 27, 2014.
Jamero, Peter. Stockton, California, July 9, 2012.
Jezewski, Maya. Paris, February 27, 2008, and November 17, 2015.
Kerkvliet, Melinda. Honolulu, June 18, 2012.
Leong, Zeny (owner Maganda Sexy Beauty Salon). Singapore, July 27, 2017.
Libao, Annabelle. Hong Kong, April 25, 2011.
Lopez, Raffy. San Francisco, December 5, 2013.
Lumibao, Wowie. Quezon City, July 23, 2010.
Malulan, Gilda, Singapore, July 24, 2017.
Marginson, Melba. Melbourne, September 25, 2007, and November 22, 2016.
McKinnon, Estrella "Lilia." Wollongong, March 1, 2013.
Mesenas, Clement (publisher, *OFW Pinoy Star Magazine*). Singapore, July 28, 2017.
Mesenas, Luz Campos (publisher, *OFW Pinoy Star Magazine*). Singapore, July 26, 2017.
Munnecom, Lorna Vea. Paris, November 17, 2015.
Patricio, Lita. Singapore, July 15, 2017.
Payoyo, Peter. Rotterdam, March 10, 2008.

Ramilo, Concepcion "Chat." Quezon City, August 4, 2014.
Reyes, Rose Marie. Milan, November 22, 2015.
Rivera, Noeline. Singapore, July 26, 2017.
Rotelo, Saturnina de los Santos ("Cute"). Singapore, July 16, 2017.
Rousset, Sally. Paris, February 26, 2008.
Santos, Robert. Seattle, June 5, 2010.
Silva, Cecilia. Padova, November 28, 2015.
Silva, Marian Laarni. Padova, August 8 and 18, 2019.
Silva, Nadine. Padova, November 27, 2015.
Talampas, Roli. Manila, January 5, 2008.
Tordesillas, Sharon (regional manager of LBC). Singapore, July 26, 2017.
Valencia, Debbie. Athens, September 11, 2012.
Valencia, Joe, Athens, September 11, 2012.
Versoza-Schepers, Maureen (AFreight manager). Singapore, July 27, 2017.
Vicente, Alpha Grace. Singapore, July 23, 2017.
Vicentia, Christine (SEA manager, Philippine National Bank). Singapore, July 26, 2017.
Villanueva, Evita May Gal. Milan, November 22, 2015.
Villanueva, Verma. Santa Rosa, Laguna, Philippines, August 2, 2014, and Padova, Italy, November 25, 2015.
Villanueva, Welvin "Bitoy." Padova, November 25, 2015.
Wall, Deborah (Debbie). Sydney, August 9, 2012.
Yuchengco, Mona Lisa, and Gemma Nemenzo. San Francisco, November 25, 2013.

Films and Radio Shows

Anak. ABS-CBN. 2000.
Bloodlines: A Medical Mission to Iloilo, Philippines. James Espinas and Timothy Kiley. Documentary. 2004.
Caregiver. ABS-CBN. 2008.
Delano Manongs: Forgotten Heroes of the United Farm Workers Movement. Marissa Aroy, dir. Documentary. [New York]: Media Factory, Independent Television Service, and Center for Asian American Media, 2014.
A Dollar a Day, Ten Cents a Dance: A Historic Portrait of Filipino Farmworkers in America. Geoffrey Dunn and and Mark Schwartz, dirs. Documentary. Capitola, CA: Gold Mountain Productions, 1984.
Dubai. Star Cinema. 2005.
Filipino Americans: Discovering Their Past for Their Future. John Wehman, dir. FANHS documentary, VHS. National Video Profiles and JF Wehman Associates/ MoonRae Production, 1994.
The Fall of the I-Hotel. Curtis Choy, dir. Documentary. San Francisco: Asian Media Center, 1983.
It Takes a Man and a Woman. Star Cinema. 2013.
Little Manila: Filipinos in California's Heartland. Marissa Aroy, dir.Documentary, DVD. Sacramento, CA: KVIE Public Television, 2007.
Mabuhay with Aloha: The Hawaii Filipino Experience, 1906–2006. Emme Tomimbang, prod. Documentary. [Honolulu]: Emme, 2006.

Marrying and Migrating to Australia: The Filipino Australian Experience. Videorecording. Canberra: Australia Department of Immigration and Ethnic Affairs, Women's Unit, 1995.
Marrying and Migrating . . . You Have to Work at It. VHS video. Canberra: Australia Department of Immigration and Multicultural Affairs, 1996.
Milan. Star Cinema. 2004.
Ngayong Aussie Ka na, Manay! Radio program, 12 episodes. Filipino Women's Working Party. 1994.
PMSNC Medical Mission to Sarangani in 2011. YouTube documentary, PMSNC website.
Remittance. Patrick Daly and Joel Fendelman (Directors), 2015.
Sunday Beauty Queen. Baby Ruth Villarama, dir. Documentary. TBA Studios, 2016.

Secondary Sources

Agbayani, Amefil R. "Education of Filipinos in Hawai'i." In *Pagdiriwang 1996: Legacy and Vision of Hawaii's Filipino Americans*, edited by Jonathan Y. Okamura and Roderick N. Labrador, 13–16. Honolulu: Student Equity, Excellence & Diversity and Center for Southeast Asian Studies, 1996.

———. "The Education of Filipinos in Hawai'i." *Social Process in Hawaii* 37 (1996): 147–160.

Aguilar, Filomeno, Jr. "Labour Migration and Ties of Relatedness: Diasporic Houses and Investments in Memory in a Rural Philippine Village." *Thesis Eleven* 98 (2009): 88–114.

———. *Migration Revolution: Philippine Nationhood and Class Relations in a Globalized Age.* Singapore and Kyoto: NUS Press in association with Kyoto University Press, 2014.

Aguilar, Filomeno, Jr., with Jose Estanley Z. Peñalosa, Tania Belen T. Liwanag, Resto S. Cruz, and Jimmy M. Melendrez. *Maalwang Buhay: Family, Overseas Migration, and Cultures of Relatedness in Barangay Paraiso.* Quezon City: Ateneo de Manila University Press, 2009.

Alburo, Jade. "Boxed In or Out? *Balikbayan* Boxes as Metaphors for Filipino American (Dis)Location." *Ethnologies* 27, no. 2 (2005): 137–157.

Amott, Teresa, and Julie Mataei. *Race, Gender and Work: A Multicultural Economic History of Women in the United States.* Boston: South End, 1991.

Amrith, Megha. *Caring for Strangers: Filipino Medical Workers in Asia.* Copenhagen: NIAS Press, 2017.

Añonuevo, Augustus T. "Reintegration, an Elusive Dream?" In *Coming Home: Women, Migration, and Reintegration*, edited by Estella Dizon-Añonueo and Augustus T. Añonuevo, 127–136. Manila: Balikabayani Foundation and Atikha Overseas Workers and Communities Initiative, 2002.

Aquino, Kristine. *Racism and Resistance among Filipino Diaspora: Everyday Anti-Racism in Australia.* London: Routledge, 2018.

Arcinas, F. R. "Asian Migration to the Gulf Region: The Philippines Case." In *Migration to the Arab World: Experience of Returning Migrants*, edited by Godfrey Gunatilleke, 103–149. Tokyo: United Nations University Press, 1991.

Arellano-Carandang, Ma. Lourdes, Beatrix Aileen Sison, and Christopher Carangdang. *Nawala ang Ilaw ng Tahanan: Case Studies of Families Left Behind by OFW Mothers.* Manila: Anvil, 2007.

Asis, Maruja M. B. "From the Life Stories of Filipino Women: Personal and Family Agendas in Migration" *Asia and Pacific Migration Journal* 11, no. 1 (2002): 67–93.

———. "The Social Costs (and Benefits) of Migration: What Happens to Left-Behind Children and Families?" In *World Conference of OFWs: Shaping the Future of Filipino Labor Migration . . . 2004; PMRW Proceedings*, 63–74. Quezon City: Philippine Migrants Rights Watch, 2004.

———. "Women Migrants Who Make a Difference." *Asian Migrant* 15, nos. 1–2 (January–June 2002): 35–36.

Asis, Maruja M. B., and Fabio Baggio, eds. *Moving Out, Back and Up: International Migration and Development Prospects in the Philippines*. Quezon City: Scalabrini Migration Center, 2008.

Baldoz, Rick. *The Third Asiatic Invasion: Empire and Migration in Filipino America, 1898–1946*. New York: New York University Press, 2011.

Basa, Charito, Violeta de Guzman, and Sabrina Marchetti. *International Migration and Over-Indebtedness: The Case of Filipino Workers in Italy*. International Institute for Environment and Development, Human Settlements Working Paper No. 36, Rural-Urban Interactions and Livelihood Strategies, October 2012.

Basa, Charito, and Rosalud Jing de la Rosa. *Me, Us, and Them: Realities and Illusions of Filipina Domestic Workers; A Community Research Project by the Filipino Women's Council*. Rome: EU/EQUAL (ESF) and the Italian Ministry of Welfare, 2004.

Battistella, Graziano, and Maruja M. B. Asis. *Country Migration Report: The Philippines, 2013*. Makati City: International Organization for Migration, 2013.

Baulderstone, Joanne, and Catherine Scott, eds. *Good Practice in SAAP Services*. Adelaide: Flinders Institute of Public Policy and Management, Flinders University of South Australia, 1999.

Beebe, Maria Africa, ed. *Disrupt 2.0: Filipina Women; Daring to Lead*. San Francisco: Filipina Women's Network, 2016.

Beebe, Maria Africa, and Maya Ong Escudero, eds. *Disrupt: Filipina Women; Proud, Loud, Leading without a Doubt*. San Francisco: Filipina Women's Network, 2015.

Benitez, Francisco. "Transnational Questing Desire in Star Cinema's *Kailangan kita* and *Milan*." *Positions: East Asia Cultures Critique* 19, no. 2 (2011): 257–280.

Boer, C. *Are You Looking for a Filipina Wife? A Study of Filipina-Australian Marriages*. Sydney: General Synod Office, 1988.

Bonifacio Glenda Tibe. "Activism from the Margins: Filipino Marriage Migrants in Australia." *Frontiers: A Journal of Women's Studies* 30, no. 3 (2009): 142–168.

———. "Filipino Women in Australia: Practicing Citizenship at Work." *Asian and Pacific Migration Journal* 14, no. 3 (2005): 293–326.

———. *Pinay on the Prairies: Filipino Women and Transnational Identities*. Vancouver: University of British Columbia Press, 2013.

Bonifacio, Glenda Tibe, and Vivienne S. M. Angeles. "Building Communities through Faith: Filipino Catholics in Philadelphia and Alberta." In *Gender, Religion, and Migration: Pathways of Integration*, edited by Glenda Tibe Bonifacio and Vivienne S. M. Angeles, 257–273. Lanham, MD: Lexington Books, 2010.

Bonus, Rick. *Locating Filipino Americans: Ethnicity and the Cultural Politics of Space.* Philadelphia: Temple University Press, 2000.

Burns, Lucy Mae San Pablo. *Puro Arte: Filipinos on the Stages of Empire.* New York: New York University Press, 2013.

Cahill, Desmond. *Intermarriages in International Contexts. A Study of Filipina Women Married to Australian, Japanese and Swiss Men.* Quezon City: Scalabrini Migration Centre, 1990.

Camagay, Maria Luisa. *Working Women of Manila in the Nineteenth Century.* Quezon City: University of the Philippines Press and University Center for Women's Studies, 1995.

Camposano, Clement C. "Enacting Embeddedness through the Transnational Traffic in Goods: The Case of Illongo OFWs in Hong Kong." *Review of Women's Studies* 21, no. 2 (2012): 1–28.

Canlas, M. C. *SoMa Pilipinas Studies 2000.* San Francisco: Arkipelago Books, 2002.

Ching, Doris, and Amefil Agbayani. *Asian Americans and Pacific Islanders in Higher Education: Research and Perspectives on Identity, Leadership, and Success.* Washington, DC: NASPA-Student Affairs Administrators in Higher Education, 2012.

Cheng, Shu-Ju Ada. *Serving the Household and the Nation: Filipino Domestics and the Politics of Identity in Taiwan.* Lanham, MD: Rowman & Littlefield, 2006.

Choy, Catherine Ceniza. *Empire of Care: Nursing and Migration in Filipino American History.* Durham, NC: Duke University Press, 2003.

Christ, Simone. *The Culture of Migration in the Philippines: Of Jeepneys and Balikbayan Boxes.* Berlin: Regiospectra Verlag, 2016.

Clark, Jenny. "For Better or Worse . . . Till Death Do Us Part . . . ?" In *The Art of Health: Using the Arts to Achieve Health.* [Adelaide]: South Australian Health Commission, 1997.

Coloma, Roland Sintos. "In Search of Filipinx Queer Histories in Canada." In *Diasporic Intimacies: Queer Filipinos and Canadian Imaginaries*, edited by Robert Diaz, Marissa Largo, and Fritz Pino, 5–22. Chicago: Northwestern University Press, 2018.

Coloma, Roland Sintos, Bonnie McElhinny, Ethel Tungohan, John Paul C. Catungal, and Lisa M. Davison, eds. *Filipinos in Canada: Disturbing Invisibility.* Toronto: University of Toronto Press, 2012.

Constable, Nicole. "Assemblages and Affect: Migrant Mothers and the Varieties of Absent Children." *Global Networks* 18, no. 1 (2018): 168–185.

———. "Dolls, T-Birds, and Ideal Workers: The Negotiation of Filipino Identity in Hong Kong." In *Home and Hegemony: Domestic Service and Identity Politics in South and Southeast Asia*, edited by Kathleen M. Adams and Sara Dickey, 221–247. Ann Arbor: University of Michigan Press, 2000.

———. *Maid to Order in Hong Kong: Stories of Filipina Workers.* Ithaca, NY: Cornell University Press, 1997.

———. "Migrant Workers and the Many States of Protest in Hong Kong." *Critical Asian Studies* 41, no. 1 (2009): 143–164.

———. *Romance on a Global Stage: Pen Pals, Virtual Ethnography, and "Mail Order" Marriages.* Berkeley: University of California Press, 2004.

———. "Sexuality and Discipline among Filipina Domestic Workers in Hong Kong." *American Ethnologist* 24, no. 3 (1997): 539–558.

Cooke, F. M. "Australian-Filipino Marriages in the 1980s: An Exploratory Study of Reasons for Marriage in the Context of Australian and Philippine Socio-Economic Conditions." Master's thesis, University of the Philippines, 1986.
———. *Australian-Filipino Marriages in the 1980s: The Myth and the Reality.* Griffith University School of Modern Asian Studies, Center for the Study of Australia-Asian Relations, Research Paper 37, 1986.
Cruz, Denise. *Transpacific Femininities: The Making of the Modern Filipina.* Durham, NC: Duke University Press, 2012.
Cunneen, Chris, and Julie Stubbs. *Gender, "Race" and International Relations: Violence against Women in Australia.* Institute of Criminology Monograph Series, no. 9. Sydney: Institute of Criminology, University of Sydney, Faculty of Law, 1997.
Curato, Nicole, and Jonathan Corpus Ong. "Disasters Can Lift Veils: Five Issues for Sociological Disaster Studies." *Philippine Sociological Review* 63, no. 1 (2015): 1–26.
de Guzman, Odine. "Families in Transition: Gender, Migration, and the Romance of the 'Filipino Family.'" In *The Family in Flux in Southeast Asia: Institution, Ideology, Practice,* edited by Yoko Hayami, Junko Koizumi, Chalidaporn Songsamphan, and Ratana Tosakul, 387–410. Kyoto: Kyoto University Press and Silkworm Books, 2012.
Diaz, Robert, Marissa Largo, and Fritz Pino, eds. *Diasporic Intimacies: Queer Filipinos and Canadian Imaginaries.* Chicago: Northwestern University Press, 2018.
Dizon-Añonuevo, Estrella, and Augustus T. Añonuevo, eds. *Coming Home: Women, Migration, and Reintegration.* Manila: Balikbayani Foundation and Atikha Overseas Workers and Communities Initiative, 2002.
Dizon-Añonuevo, Mai. "Revisiting Migrant Women's Lives: Stories of Struggles, Failures and Successes." In *Coming Home. Women, Migration, and Reintegration.* Manila: Balikbayani Foundation and Atikha Overseas Workers and Communities Initiative, 2002, 17–29.
Dumia, Mariano A. *Of Dreams, Sweat, and Tears: The Kingdom of Saudi Arabia and the Modern Filipino Heroes.* Quezon City: New Day, 2009.
"Education: The Filipino Dream." In *The Filipinos in Hawaii: The First 75 Years, 1906–1981,* 86–90. [Honolulu]: Hawaii Filipino News Specialty Publications, [ca. 1981].
Emerton, Robyn, and Carole Petersen. "Filipino Nightclub Hostesses in Hong Kong: Vulnerability to Trafficking and Other Human Rights Abuses." In *Transnational Migration and Work in Asia,* edited by Kevin Hewison and Ken Young, 126–143. London: Routledge, 2006.
Encanto, Georgina R. "Savoring Romance Pinoy Style in Foreign Climes: Why Women Migrants Love Reading Tagalog Romance Novels." *Review of Women's Studies* 18, no. 1 (January–June 2008): 27–52.
Encinas-Franco, Jean. "The Language of Labor Export in Political Discourse: 'Modern-Day Heroism' and Constructions of Overseas Filipino Workers (OFWs)." *Philippine Political Science Journal* 34, no. 1 (2013): 97–112.
———. "The Politics of Language in Labor Export: A Discourse Historical Analysis of Bagong Bayani and Overseas Employment Policies." PhD dissertation, University of the Philippines, 2011.

España-Maram, Linda. *Creating Masculinity in Los Angeles's Little Manila: Working-Class Filipinos and Popular Culture, 1920s–1950s*. New York: Columbia University Press, 2006.
Espinosa, Shirlita Africa. "Reading the Gendered Body in Filipino-Australian Diaspora Philanthropy." *Portal: Journal of Multidisciplinary International Studies* 9, no. 2 (July 2012): 1–20.
———. *Sexualized Citizenship: A Cultural History of Philippine-Australian Migration*. Singapore: Springer, 2017.
Espiritu, Augusto Fauni. *Five Faces of Exile: The Nation and Filipino American Intellectuals*. Stanford, CA: Stanford University Press, 2005.
Espiritu, Yen Le. *Home Bound: Filipino American Lives across Cultures, Communities, Countries*. Berkeley: University of California Press, 2003.
Estrada-Claudio, Sylvia. *Rape, Love and Sexuality: The Construction of Woman in Discourse*. Quezon City: University of the Philippines Press, 2002.
Eviota, Elizabeth U., ed. *Sex and Gender in Philippine Society*. Manila: National Commission on the Role of Filipino Women, 1994.
Faier, Lieba. "Affective Investments in the Manila Region: Filipino Migrants in Rural Japan and Transnational Urban Development in the Philippines." *Transactions of the Institute of British Geographers* 38, no. 3 (2013): 376–390.
———. *Intimate Encounters: Filipina Women and the Remaking of Rural Japan*. Berkeley: University of California Press, 2009.
Fajardo, Kale Bantigue. *Filipino Crosscurrents: Oceanographies of Seafaring, Masculinities, and Globalization*. Minneapolis: University of Minnesota Press, 2011.
Francisco-Menchavez, Valerie. *The Labor of Care: Filipina Migrants and Transnational Families in the Digital Age*. Urbana: University of Illinois Press, 2018.
Fresnoza-Flot, Asuncion. "The Catholic Church in the Lives of Irregular Migrant Filipinas in France: Identity Formation, Empowerment and Social Control." *Asia-Pacific Journal of Anthropology* 11, nos. 3–4 (2010): 345–361.
———. "Migration Status and Transnational Mothering: The Case of Filipino Migrants in France." *Global Networks* 9, no. 2 (2009): 252–270.
Fujita-Rony, Dorothy. *American Workers, Colonial Power: Philippine Seattle and the Transpacific West, 1919–1941*. Berkeley: University of California Press, 2003.
Gonzales, Joaquin Jay, III. *Diaspora Diplomacy: Philippine Migration and Its Soft Power Influences*. Minneapolis: Mill City Press, 2012.
———. *Filipino American Faith in Action: Immigration, Religion, and Civic Engagement*. New York: New York University Press, 2009.
Gonzalves, Theodore S. *The Day the Dancers Stayed: Performing in the Filipino/American Diaspora*. Philadelphia: Temple University Press, 2010.
———. 1998. "When the Walls Speak a Nation: Contemporary Murals and the Narration of Filipina/o America." *Journal of Asian American Studies* 1, no. 1 (1998): 31–63.
Groves, Julian McAllister, and Kimberly Chang. "Romancing Resistance and Resisting Romance: Ethnography and Construction of Power in the Filipina Domestic Worker Community in Hong Kong." *Journal of Contemporary Ethnography* 28, no. 3 (1999): 235–265.
Guerero, Adrialina B. "A History of Operation Manong." In *Sinking Roots: Filipino American Legacy in Hawaii*, edited by Dean T. Alegado, 25–29. Honolulu:

Philippine Centennial Committee–Hawaii, Friends of Operation Manong, University of Hawaii at Manoa; Center for Philippine Studies, University of Hawaii at Manoa, 1998.

Guillermo, Alice. "The Filipina OCW in Extremis." In *Geopolitics of the Visible: Essays on Philippine Film Cultures*, edited by Rolando B. Tolentino, 106–124. Quezon City: Ateneo de Manila University Press, 2000.

Habal, Estella. *San Francisco's International Hotel: Mobilizing the Filipino American Community in the Anti-Eviction Movement*. Philadelphia: Temple University Press, 2007.

Hayami, Yoko, Junko Koizumi, Chalidaporn Songsamphan, and Ratana Tosakul, eds. *The Family in Flux in Southeast Asia: Institution, Ideology, Practice*. Kyoto: Kyoto University Press and Silkworm Books, 2012.

Hewison, Kevin, and Ken Young, eds. *Transnational Migration and Work in Asia*. London: Routledge, 2006.

Hollnsteiner, Mary. "Reciprocity in Lowland Philippines." *Philippine Studies* 9, no. 3 (1961): 387–413.

Holt, Elizabeth. "Writing Filipina-Australian Brides: The Discourse on Filipina Brides." *Philippine Sociological Review* 44, nos. 1–4 (1996): 58–78.

Hosoda, Naomi. "The Sense of Pamilya among Samarnons in the Philippines." In *The Family in Flux in Southeast Asia: Institution, Ideology, Practice*, edited by Yoko Hayami, Junko Koizumi, Chalidaporn Songsamphan, and Ratana Tosakul, 365–386. Kyoto: Kyoto University Press and Silkworm Books, 2012.

Hsia, Hsiao-Chuan. "The Making of a Transnational Grassroots Migrant Movement." *Critical Asian Studies* 41, no. 1 (2009): 113–141.

Hsu, Madeline Y. *Asian American History: A Very Short Introduction*. Oxford: Oxford University Press, 2017.

Ignacio, Emily Noelle. "'Home' and The Filipino Channel: Stabilizing Economic Security, Migration Patterns, and Diaspora through New Technologies." In *Filipino Studies: Palimpsests of Nation and Diaspora*, edited by Martin F. Manalansan IV and Augusto F. Espiritu, 375–387. New York: New York University Press, 2016.

Ileto, Reynaldo. "Rizal and the Underside of Philippine History." In *Moral Order and the Question of Change: Essays on Southeast Asian Thought*, edited by David Wyatt and Alexander Woodside, 274–337. New Haven, CT: Yale University Southeast Asia Program Series, 1982.

Ilkkaracan, Pinar, ed. *Deconstructing Sexuality in the Middle East: Challenges and Discourses*. Aldershot: Ashgate, 2008.

———. "Introduction: Sexuality as a Contested Political Domain in the Middle East." In *Deconstructing Sexuality in the Middle East: Challenges and Discourses*, edited by Pinar Ilkkaracan, 1–16. Aldershot: Ashgate, 2008.

Johnson, Mark, and Deirdre McKay, eds. "Mediated Diasporas: Material Translations of the Philippines in a Globalized World." Special issue, *South East Asia Research* 19, no. 2 (June 2011).

Jurilla, Patricia May B. *Tagalog Bestsellers of the Twentieth Century: A History of the Book in the Philippines*. Quezon City: Ateneo de Manila University Press, 2008.

Kaut, Charles. "*Utang ng Loob*: A System of Contractual Obligations among Tagalogs." *Southwestern Journal of Anthropology* 17, no. 3 (1961): 256–272.

Kerkvliet, Melinda Tria. *Unbending Cane: Pablo Manlapit, a Filipino Labor Leader in Hawai'i*. Honolulu: Office of Multicultural Student Services, University of Hawaii at Manoa, 2002.

Koh, Chiu Yee, Charmian Goh, Kellyn Wee, and Brenda S. A. Yeoh. "Drivers of Migration Policy Reform: The Day Off Policy for Migrant Domestic Workers in Singapore." *Global Social Policy* 17, no. 2 (2017): 188–205.

Kontos, Maria, and Glenda Tibe Bonifacio. "Introduction: Domestic and Care Work of Migrant Women and the Right to Family Life." In *Migrant Domestic Workers and Family Life: International Perspectives*, edited by Maria Kontos and Glenda Tibe Bonifacio, 1–24. London: Palgrave Macmillan, 2015.

———, eds. *Migrant Domestic Workers and Family Life: International Perspectives*. London: Palgrave Macmillan, 2015.

Labrador, Roderick N. *Building Filipino Hawai'i*. Urbana: University of Illinois Press, 2015.

Lamvik, Gunnar. "The Filipino Seafarer: A Life between Sacrifice and Shopping." PhD dissertation, Norwegian University of Science and Technology, 2002.

Lan, Pei-Chia. *Global Cinderellas: Migrant Domestics and Newly Rich Employers in Taiwan*. Durham, NC: Duke University Press, 2006.

Lausch, Julia. "Reinventing Intimacy and Identity: Filipina Domestic Workers' Strategies for Coping with Family Separation in Dubai." In *Migrant Domestic Workers and Family Life: International Perspectives*, edited by Maria Kontos and Glenda Tibe Bonifacio, 165–188. London: Palgrave Macmillan, 2015.

Leong, Laurence Wai-Teng. "Asian Sexuality or Singapore Exceptionalism?" *Liverpool Law Review* 33 (2012): 11–26.

Lin, Trisha Tsui-Chuan, and Shirley Haiso-Li Sun. "Connection as a Form of Resisting Control: Foreign Domestic Workers' Mobile Phone Use in Singapore." *Media Asia* 37, no. 4 (2010): 183–214.

Lindio-McGovern, Ligaya. *Globalization, Labor Export and Resistance: A Study of Filipino Migrant Domestic Workers in Global Cities*. London: Routledge, 2012.

Lott, Juanita Tamayo. *Common Destiny: Filipino American Generations*. Lanham, MD: Rowman & Littlefield, 2006.

Lu, Ethel Regis. "Mediating Global Filipinos: The Filipino Channel and the Filipino Diaspora." PhD dissertation, University of California, Berkeley, 2013.

———. "Negotiating Transnational Belonging: The Filipino Chanel, 'Global Filipinos,' and Filipino American Audiences." In *Southeast Asian Migration: People on the Move in Search of Work, Refuge and Belonging*, edited by Khatharya Um and Sofia Gaspar, 114–136. Brighton: Sussex Academic Press.

Lynch, Frank. "Social Acceptance Reconsidered." In *Four Readings in Philippine Values*, IPC Papers No. 2, edited by Frank Lynch and Alfonso de Guzman II, 1–68. Quezon City: Ateneo de Manila University Press, 1973.

Lyons, Martyn. "A New History from Below? The Writing Culture of Ordinary People in Europe." *History Australia* 7, no. 3 (2010): 59.1–59.9.

———. "Writing Upwards: How the Weak Wrote to the Powerful." *Journal of Social History* 29, no. 2 (2015): 1–14.

Maas, Marisha. "Door-to-Door Cargo Agents: Cultivating and Expanding Filipino Transnational Space." In *Tales of Development: People, Power and Space*, edited by Paul Hebinck, Sef Slootweg, and Lothar Smith, 135–146. Assen, The Netherlands: Royal Van Gorum B.V., 2008.

Mabalon, Dawn Bohulano. "Life in Little Manila: Filipinas/os in Stockton, California, 1917–1972." PhD dissertation, Stanford University, 2003.

———. *Little Manila Is in the Heart: The Making of the Filipina/o American Community in Stockton, California*. Durham, NC: Duke University Press, 2013.

———. "Losing Little Manila: Race and Redevelopment in Filipina/o Stockton, California." In *Positively No Filipinos Allowed: Building Communities and Discourse*, edited by Antonio T. Tiongson Jr., Edgardo V. Gutierrez, and Ricardo V. Gutierrez, 73–89. Philadelphia: Temple University Press, 2006.

Madianou, Mirca, and Daniel Miller. *Migration and New Media: Transnational Families and Polymedia*. London: Routledge, 2012.

Manalansan, Martin F., IV. *Global Divas: Filipino Gay Men in the Diaspora*. Quezon City: Ateneo de Manila University Press, 2003.

Manalansan, Martin F., IV, and Augusto F. Espiritu, eds. *Filipino Studies: Palimpsests of Nation and Diaspora*. New York: New York University Press, 2016.

Maramba, Dina C., and Rick Bonus, eds. *The "Other" Students: Filipino Americans, Education, and Power*. Charlotte, NC: Information Age Publishing, 2013.

Marginson, Melba. "Increasing Access for Filipina Survivors of Domestic Violence." In *Not the Same: Conference Proceedings and a Strategy on Domestic Violence and Sexual Assault for Non-English Speaking Background Women*, 20–21. Brunswick, Victoria: Office of the Status of Women, 1996.

———. "Not for the Money." In *Breaking Through: Women, Work and Careers*, edited by Jocelynne A. Scott, 115–123. Melbourne: Artemis, 1992.

Margold, Jane. "Narratives of Masculinity and Transnational Migration: Filipino Workers in the Middle East." In *Bewitching Women, Pious Men*, edited by Aihwa Ong and Michael Peletz, 274–298, Berkeley: University of California Press, 1995.

———. "Narratives of Masculinity and Transnational Migration: Filipino Workers in the Middle East." In *Filipinos in Global Migrations: At Home in the World?*, edited by Filomeno Aguilar Jr., 209–236. Quezon City: Philippine Migration Research Nework and Philippine Social Science Research Council, 2002.

Mariano, L. Joyce Zapanta. "Doing Good in Filipino Diaspora: Philanthropy, Remittances, and Homeland Returns." *Journal of Asian American Studies* 20, no. 2 (2017): 219–244.

McKay, Benjamin. "The Politics of Mirrored Metaphors: Flor Contemplacion and The Maid." *Positions: East Asia Cultures Critique* 19, no. 2 (Fall 2011): 463–498.

McKay, Deirdre. *An Archipelago of Care: Filipino Migrants and Global Networks*. Bloomington: University of Indiana Press, 2016.

———. *Global Filipinos: Migrants' Lives in the Virtual Village*. Bloomington: Indiana University Press, 2012.

———. "On the Face of Facebook: Historical Images and Personhood in Filipino Social Networking." *History and Anthropology* 21, no. 4 (2010): 483–502.

———. "'Sending Dollars Shows Feeling': Emotions and Economies in Filipino Migration." *Mobilities* 2, no. 2 (July 2007): 175–194.

———. "Sent Home: Mapping the Absent Child into Migration through Polymedia." *Global Networks* 18, no. 1 (2018): 133–150.

McKay, Steven C. "Filipino Sea Men: Identity and Masculinity in a Global Labor Niche." In *Asian Diasporas: New Formations, New Conceptions*, edited by Rhacel S. Parreñas and Lok C. D. Siu, 63–83. Stanford, CA: Stanford University Press, 2007.

McKay, Steven, and Don Eliseo Lucero-Prismo III. "Masculinities Afloat: Filipino Seafarers and the Situational Performance of Manhood." In *Men and Masculinities in Southeast Asia*, edited by Michele Ford and Lenore Lyons, 20–37. London: Routledge, 2012.

Medina, Belen T. G. *The Filipino Family*. 2nd ed. Quezon City: University of the Philippines Press, 2001.

Melgar, Gina Alunan, and Estrella Dizon-Añonuevo. "Mag-Atikha Para Maka-Balikabayani: Planting the Seeds of a Comprehensive Reintegration Program for OFWs (The Atikha-Balikabayani Experience)." In *Coming Home: Women, Migration, and Reintegration*, edited by Estrella Dizon-Añonuevo and Augustus T. Añonuevo, 169–183. Manila: Balikabayani Foundation and Atikha Overseas Workers and Communities Initiative, 2002.

Mendoza, S. Lily. *Between the Homeland and the Diaspora: The Politics of Theorizing Filipino and Filipino American Identities*. Manila: UST Publishing House, 2002.

Nagasaka, Itaru, and Asuncion Fresnoza-Flot, eds. *Mobile Childhoods in Filipino Transnational Families: Migrant Children with Similar Roots in Different Routes*. Houndmills, Basingstoke: Palgrave Macmillan, 2015.

O'Brien, Anne. *Philanthropy and Settler Colonialism*. London: Palgrave Macmillan, 2015.

Okamura, Jonathan Y. *Ethnicity and Inequality in Hawaii*. Philadelphia: Temple University Press, 2008.

———. "Filipino American Access to Public Higher Education in California and Hawai'i." In *The "Other" Students: Filipino Americans, Education, and Power*, edited by Dina C. Maramba and Rick Bonus, 213–235. Charlotte, NC: Information Age Publishing, 2013.

Operation Manong, Spring 1982. Honolulu: Department of Educational Foundations, College of Education, University of Hawaii at Manoa, 1982.

Opiniano, Jeremiah. *Good News for the Poor: Diaspora Philanthropy by Filipinos*. Quezon City: Association of Foundations, 2005.

Ortega, Arnisson Andre. *Neoliberalizing Spaces in the Philippines: Suburbanization, Transnational Migration, and Dispossession*. Lanham, MD: Lexington Books, 2016.

Paragas, Fernando. "Migrant Workers and Mobile Phones: Technological, Temporal and Spatial Simultaneity." In *The Reconstruction of Space and Time: Mobile Communication Practices*, edited by Rich Ling and Scott W. Campbell, 39–65. New Brunswick, NJ: Transaction, 2010.

Paredes-Maceda, C. "Filipino Women and Intermarriages." *Asian Migrant* 8 (1995): 109–113.

Parreñas, Rhacel Salazar. *Children of Global Migration: Transnational Families and Gendered Woes*. Stanford, CA: Stanford University Press, 2005.

———. *The Force of Domesticity: Filipina Migrants and Globalization*. New York: New York University Press, 2008.

———. *Illicit Flirtations: Labor, Migration, and Sex Trafficking in Tokyo*. Stanford, CA: Stanford University Press, 2011.

———. "Mothering from a Distance: Emotions, Gender and Intergenerational Relations in Filipino Transnational Families." *Feminist Studies* 27, no. 2 (2001): 361–390.

———. *Servants of Globalization: Women, Migration, and Domestic Work*. Stanford, CA: Stanford University Press, 2001.

Pendlebury, J. *Filipino Brides in Remote Areas*. Occasional Paper No. 5. Darwin: Department of Social Security, 1990.

Pido, Eric J. *Migrant Returns: Manila, Development, and Transnational Connectivity*. Durham, NC: Duke University Press, 2017.

Pinches, Michael. "Bamboo Dancers Down Under: The Filipino-Australian Intercultural Community in Western Australia." In *The Changing People: Diverse Contributions to the State of Western Australia*, edited by Raelene Wilding and Farida Tilbury, 284–302. Perth: Department of the Premier and Cabinet, Office of Multicultural Interests, 2004.

Pingol, Alicia. *Remaking Masculinities: Identity, Power, and Gender Dynamics in Families with Migrant Wives and Househusbands*. Quezon City: University Center for Women's Studies, University of the Philippines, 2001.

Pisares, Elizabeth H. "The Social-Invisibility Narrative in Filipino-American Feature Films." *Positions: East Asia Cultures Critique* 19, no. 2 (Fall 2011): 421–437.

Polvorosa, Cesar, Jr. "Toronto Filipino Businesses, Ethnic Identity, and Place Making in the Diaspora." In *Filipinos in Canada: Disturbing Invisibility*, edited by Roland Sintos Coloma, Bonnie McElhinny, Ethel Tungohan, John Paul C. Catungal, and Lisa M. Davison, 181–200. Toronto: University of Toronto Press, 2012.

Pratt, Geraldine. *Families Apart: Migrant Mothers and the Conflicts of Labor and Love*. Minneapolis: University of Minnesota Press, 2012.

Rafael, Vicente L. "'Your Grief Is Our Gossip': Overseas Filipinos and Other Spectral Presences." *Public Culture* 9, no. 2 (1997): 267–291.

Raymundo, Sarah. "In the Womb of the Global Economy: *Anak* and the Construction of Transnational Imaginaries." *Positions: East Asia Cultures Critique* 19, no. 2 (Fall 2011): 551–579.

Reese, Niklas. "Kitakits: Migration and Overseas Filipin@s." In *Handbook Philippines: Society, Politics, Economy, Culture*, edited by Niklas Reese and Rainer Werning, 205–216. Berlin: Philippinenbüro im Asienhaus, 2013.

Reyes, Raquel A. G. "Gender and Sexuality in Southeast Asian History." In *Routledge Handbook of Southeast Asian History*, edited by Norman G. Owen, 246–257. London: Routledge, 2014.

———. *Love, Passion and Patriotism: Sexuality and the Philippine Propaganda Movement, 1882–1892*. Singapore: NUS Press, 2008.

Ribas, Natalia, Charito Basa, and Rosalud de la Rosa. *Gender, Remittances and Development: The Case of Filipino Migration to Italy*. Santo Domingo, Dominican Republic: United Nations International Research and Training Institute for the Advancement of Women, 2008.

Ribas-Mateos, Natalia, and Charito Basa. *How Filipino Immigrants in Italy Send Money Back Home: The Role of Cross-Border Remittances in the Global Economy*. Lewiston, NY: Edwin Mellen Press 2013.

Robinson, Kathryn. "Of Mail-Order Brides and 'Boys Own' Tales: Representations of Asian- Australian Marriages." *Feminist Review* 5 (1996): 53–68.

Roces, Mina. "Gender, Nation and the Politics of Dress in Twentieth-Century Philippines." *Gender & History* 17, no. 2 (2005): 354–377.
——. "Is the Suffragist an American Colonial Construct? Defining 'The Filipino Woman' in Colonial Philippines." In *Women's Suffrage in Asia: Gender, Nationalism and Democracy*, edited by Louise Edwards and Mina Roces, 24–58. London: Routledge, 2004.
——. *Kinship Politics in Post-War Philippines: The Lopez Family, 1846–2000*. Manila: De La Salle University Press, 2001.
——. "Sisterhood Is Local: Filipino Women in Mount Isa." In *Wife or Worker? Asian Marriage and Migration*, edited by Nicola Piper and Mina Roces, 73–100. Boulder, CO: Rowman & Littlefield, 2003.
——. *Women's Movements and the Filipina, 1986–2008*. Honolulu: University of Hawaii Press, 2012.
Rodriguez, Evelyn Ibatan. *Celebrating Debutantes and Quinceañeras: Coming of Age in American Ethnic Communities*. Philadelphia: Temple University Press, 2013.
Rodriguez, Robin Magalit. *Migrants for Export: How the Philippine State Brokers Labor to the World*. Minneapolis: University of Minnesota Press, 2010.
Root, Maria P. P., ed. *Filipino Americans: Transformation and Identity*. London: Sage, 1997.
Rother, Stefan. "Transnational Political Spaces: Political Activism of Philippine Labor Migrants in Hong Kong." In *State, Politics and Nationalism beyond Borders: Changing Dynamics in Filipino Overseas Migration*, edited by Jorge V. Tigno, 1–23. Quezon City: Philippine Social Science Council, 2009.
Saroca, Cleonicki. "Filipino Women, Migration, and Violence in Australia: Lived Reality and Media Image." *Kasarinlan: Philippine Journal of Third World Studies* 1, no. 1 (2006): 75–110.
——. "Filipino Women, Sexual Politics, and the Gendered Discourse of the Mail Order Bride." *JIGS: Journal of Interdisciplinary Gender Studies* 2, no. 2 (1997): 89–103.
——. "Representing Rosalina and Annabel: Filipino Women, Violence, Media Representation, and Contested Realities." *Kasarinlan* 22, no. 1 (2007): 32–60.
——. "Violence against Migrant Filipino Women in Australia: Making Men's Behavior Visible." *Review of Women's Studies* 15, no. 2 (2005): 113–139.
——. "Woman in Danger or Dangerous Woman? Contesting Images of Filipina Victims of Domestic Homicide in Australia." *Asian Journal of Women's Studies* 12, no. 3 (2006): 35–74.
Scharlin, Craig, and Lilia V. Villanueva. *Philip Vera Cruz: A Personal History of Filipino Immigrants and the Farmworkers Movement*. Seattle: University of Washington Press, 2000.
Sim, Amy. "Lesbianism among Indonesian Women Migrants in Hong Kong." In *As Normal as Possible*, edited by Yau Ching, 37–50. Hong Kong: Hong Kong University Press, 2010.
Strobel, Leny Mendoza. "'Born-Again Filipino': Filipino American Identity and Asian Panethnicity." *Amerasia Journal* 22, no. 2 (1996): 31–53.
——. *Coming Full Circle: The Process of Decolonization among Post-1965 Filipino Americans*. Quezon City: Giraffe Books, 2001.

Suzuki, Nobue. "Between Two Shores: Transnational Projects and Filipina Wives in/from Japan." *Women's Studies International Forum* 23, no. 4 (2000): 431–444.
———. "Filipina-Japanese Marriages: Intimate Relationships Located in the Space between the Colonial, Global and National." *Journal of Comparative Family History* 24 (2010): 1–19.
———. "Inside the Home: Power and Negotiation in Filipina-Japanese Marriages." *Women's Studies: An Interdisciplinary Journal* 33, no. 4 (2003): 481–506.
———. "'Japayuki,' or Spectacles for the Transnational Middle Class." *Positions: East Asia Cultures Critique* 19, no. 2 (Fall 2011): 439–462.
———. "Transgressing 'Victims': Reading Narratives of 'Filipina Brides' in Japan." *Critical Asian Studies* 35, no. 3 (2003): 399–420.
Tadios, Arenas Felma Joy. "Managing Transnational Families: Emotional Labour and Entrepreneurial Agency among Filipino Migrant Domestics in Hong Kong." PhD dissertation, City University of Hong Kong, 2015.
Talampas, Roli. "Barangay Barko: Panimulang Pag-Aaral sa Buhay Panlipunan ng Marinong Pilipino." Unpublished paper, October 2003.
Tan, Edward L. *Real Estate Buyer Profile and Behavior: Helps You Understand the Overseas Filipino Workers' Buyer Behavior*. Mandaluyong City: Miracle, 2007.
Thompson, Mark. *The Anti-Marcos Struggle: Personalistic Rule and Democratic Transition in the Philippines*. New Haven, CT: Yale University Press, 1995.
Tintiangco-Cubales, Allyson. *Pin@y Educational Partnerships: A Filipina/o American Studies Sourcebook Series*. Vol. 1, *Philippine and Filipina/o American History*; and vol. 2, *Filipina/o American Identities, Activism and Service*. Santa Clara, CA: Phoenix, 2007–2009.
Tiongson, Antonio T., Jr. "Introduction: Critical Considerations." In *Positively No Filipinos Allowed: Building Communities and Discourse*, edited by Antonio T. Tiongson, Edgardo V. Gutierrez, and Ricardo V. Gutierrez, 1–14. Philadelphia: Temple University Press, 2006.
———. "On Filipinos, Filipino Americans, and U.S. Imperialism: Interview with Oscar V. Campomanes." In *Positively No Filipinos Allowed: Building Communities and Discourse*, edited by Antonio T. Tiongson, Edgardo V. Gutierrez, and Ricardo V. Gutierrez, 26–42. Philadelphia: Temple University Press, 2006.
———. "Reflections on the Trajectory of Filipino/a American Studies: Interview with Rick Bonus." In *Positively No Filipinos Allowed: Building Communities and Discourse*, edited by Antonio T. Tiongson, Edgardo V. Gutierrez, and Ricardo V. Gutierrez, 162–171. Philadelphia: Temple University Press, 2006.
Tiongson, Antonio T., Jr., Edgardo V. Gutierrez, and Ricardo V. Gutierrez, eds. *Positively No Filipinos Allowed: Building Communities and Discourse*. Philadelphia: Temple University Press, 2006.
Tiongson, Nicanor G. "Woman in Nineteenth Century Philippines." In *Filipino Heritage*, vol. 7, edited by Alfredo Roces, 1780–1787. Manila: Lahing Pilipino, 1978.
Tolentino, Rolando B. "Globalizing National Domesticity: Female Work and Representation in Contemporary Women's Films." In *More Pinay Than We Admit: The Social Construction of the Filipina*, edited by Maria Luisa T. Camagay, 185–209. Quezon City: Vibal Foundation, 2010.

———. "Niche Globality: Philippine Media Texts to the World." In *Popular Culture Co-Productions and Collaborations in East and Southeast Asia*, edited by Nissim Otmazgin and Eyal Ben-Ari, 150–168. Singapore: NUS Press; and Kyoto: Kyoto University Press, 2013.

———, ed. "Vaginal Economy: Cinema and Sexuality in the Post-Marcos, Post-Brocka Philippines." Special issue, *Positions: East Asia Cultures Critique* 19, no. 2 (Fall 2011).

Torres, Amaryllis Tiglao. *Love in the Time of Ina Morata*. Quezon City: University Center for Women's Studies, 2002.

Tyner, James. *The Philippines: Mobilities, Identities, Globalization*. London: Routledge, 2009.

Uy-Tioco, Cecilia. "Overseas Filipino Workers and Text Messaging: Reinventing Transnational Mothering." *Continuum* 21, no. 2 (2007): 253–265.

Valerio, Rosanna Luz F. "Pagtitimpi at Panggigigil: Sex and the Migrant Woman." In *Coming Home: Women, Migration, and Reintegration*, edited by Estrella Dizon-Añonuevo and Augustus T. Añonuevo, 60–69. Manila: Balikabayani Foundation and Athikha Overseas Workers and Communities Initiative, 2002.

Vergara, Benito M., Jr. *Pinoy Capital: The Filipino Nation in Daly City*. Philadelphia: Temple University Press, 2009.

Wall, Deborah R. "Filipino Brides: Slaves or Marriage Partners?—A Further Comment." *Australian Journal of Social Issues* 18, no. 1 (1985): 217–220.

———. *Re-Imagining Australia: Voices of Indigenous Australians of Filipino Descent*. With Christine Choo. Southport, Queensland: Keeaira Press, 2016.

Weekley, Kathleen. "From Wage Labourers to Investors? Filipina Migrant Domestic Workers and Popular Capitalism." In *Transnational Migration and Work in Asia*, edited by Kevin Hewison and Ken Young, 193–212. London: Routledge, 2006.

Wei, William. *The Asian American Movement*. Philadelphia: Temple University Press, 1995.

Yea, Sallie. *Trafficking Women in Korea: Filipino Migrant Entertainers*. London: Routledge, 2015.

Yeoh, Brenda S. A., and Shirlena Huang. "Negotiating Public Space: Strategies and Styles of Migrant Female Domestic Workers in Singapore." *Urban Studies* 35, no. 3 (1998): 583–602.

Zhang Juan. "Ethnic Boundaries Redefined: The Emergence of the 'Permanent Outsiders' in Singapore." Master's thesis, National University of Singapore, 2005.

Zontini, Elisabetta. *Transnational Families, Migration, and Gender: Moroccan and Filipino Women in Bologna and Barcelona*. New York: Berghahn Books, 2010.

Zuhur, Sherifa. "Criminal Law, Women and Sexuality in the Middle East." In *Deconstructing Sexuality in the Middle East: Challenges and Discourses*, edited by Pinar Ilkkaracan, 17–40. Aldershot: Ashgate, 2008.

Zulueta, Joanna O., ed. *Thinking beyond the State: Migration, Integration, and Citizenship in Japan and the Philippines*. Brighton: Sussex Academic Press, 2018.

INDEX

Page numbers in *italics* refer to figures.

Abercrombie, Neil, 127, 147, 213n73
ABS-CBN enterprises, 78–81, 85, 158. *See also* Filipino Channel (TFC)
abuse: of children, 155–156; by employers, 118; human rights discourse on, 146; NGO assistance in cases of, 25. *See also* domestic violence
academic historians, 92–93
activism, 114–147; class status and, 115; cultural, 90, 92, 93, 101, 102; exploited workers and, 2; financial literacy and, 73; funding challenges in, 146; government allies for, 118, 131, 140, 144–147; human rights discourse in, 144, 146–147, 156; minority youth education and, 116–119, 121–130; redevelopment projects and, 104; social, 38, 91, 93, 102; transethnic trends in, 143. *See also* domestic violence; nongovernmental organizations (NGOs)
adolescents. *See* children and adolescents
adultery. *See* infidelity
advocacy. *See* activism
affirmative action initiatives, 93, 127, 147
Agbayani, Amefil "Amy," 120, 122, 123, 126–130, 145, 147, 213n73
agents of change, 1–9, 74, 101, 131, 152, 173
Aguilar, Filomeno, Jr., 6, 23, 27, 77, 185n18
Agyekum, Edward, 164
Alaska, Filipino migrants in, 15, 91, 92, 97
Alburo, Jade, 66
Alegado, Dean, 182
Alejo, Ning, 145
Almedilla, Joan, 160
Almosara, Maria Dolores, 170
Andaya, Leonard, 94
Añonuevo, Mai, 30–31, 72, 73
Antigua, Mary Marcia, 157
anti-miscegenation laws, 89, 97
Aquino, Corazon, 174

Aquino, Melchora, 105
Arceo, Frederick, 68
Arcinas, F. R., 70, 195–196n20
Aroy, Marissa, 108–109
Asis, Maruja M. B., 21
Atikha, 30, 37, 52, 60, 69–74
Australia: ABS-CBN programming in, 80; diasporic philanthropy in, 151, 152, 171; Ethnic Affairs Commission of, 120, 133, 135–137, 142, 144–146; marriage migrants in, 16, 114–116, 119, 130, 134, 137–142; medical missions from, 148, 151–153, 162–165, 168–169; Migrant Resource Centres, 116, 120, 131, 133–137, 142, 145–146, 209n4. *See also* Centre for Philippine Concerns–Australia (CPCA); domestic violence; Filipino Women's Working Party (FWWP)

bagong bayani (new heroes), 6, 11, 12, 174–178
balikbayan boxes, 59, 62, 65–67, 81, 180
Banados, Papias Generale, 35, 40–41
banking services, 22, 60, 70, 71, 75, 85
Baraquio, Angela Perez, 129
Barcelona, Mary Joy, 25–26
Basa, Charito, 63
Bates, Dolly, 135, 145
Batula, Cynthia, 171
Bautista, Anita Navalta, 108, 206n47
Bautista, Clement, 120, 127, 145
Bautista, Mika, 82
biases. *See* discrimination; stereotypes
bilingual education, 122, 125
Bobis, Merlinda, 141
Bongcodin, Generosa "Gene," 138
Bonipasyo, Lilo, 98
Bonus, Rick, 13
Borayuga, Artemio, 116
Borja, Mario, 104–105

247

248 INDEX

bridge generation, 14, 96–97, 99
Brown, Patricia, 100
Buklod theater group, 140–141, 146–147
Bulosan, Carlos, 98, 110

Cabahug, Enrique J., Jr., 168–169
Cabais, Zita, 1–2
California: agricultural workers in, 15, 89, 97; ethnotours in, 102–109; Filipinotowns in, 101–103; medical missions from, 150, 153, 164–169, 171; state curriculum in, 110–111
Campomanes, Oscar, 12–13, 97, 98
Camposano, Clement, 66
Canlas, Mamerto Calalang "MC," 102–107
Caritas Manila, 154, 155, 157
Catholic Church: on feminine ideal, 42, 43; on marriage, 24; moral surveillance by, 46–47; philanthropic partnerships with, 157; on sex and sexuality, 30, 41, 52
Cayetano, Benjamin J., 99, 127, 129, 213n73
celibacy, 46, 52, 53
Centre for Philippine Concerns–Australia (CPCA): achievements of, 118, 145; archival sources from, 120; establishment of, 138; objectives of, 117, 138–139, 143; spousal homicide data from, 130
CFO (Commission on Filipinos Overseas), 70, 120, 140, 148–151
charitable works. *See* philanthropy
children and adolescents: abuse of, 155–156; deaf and hearing-impaired, 156, 158, 160, 167; interethnic, 37–38; medical mission services for, 164–166; migrant archive accounts by, 8–9; philanthropic programs for, 154–158, 160, 167, 169–170; in prostitution, 154, 156, 157; reception for returned migrant parents, 4–5, 28; sex trafficking of, 156, 157; in transnational families, 22, 27–30. *See also* education; families; motherhood
Ching, Doris, 130
Chirac, Bernadette, 2
civil rights movement, 15, 93, 127, 144, 179
class: activism and, 115; consumption and, 58, 59, 62, 74, 79–80; diasporic philanthropy and, 152, 161; diversity among migrants, 10, 16; in transnational context, 10, 59, 62
Commission on Filipinos Overseas (CFO), 70, 120, 140, 148–151
communities of care, 25, 188n18

community histories, 89–113; achievements resulting from, 109–112; activist agenda of, 91–93, 101; androcentric nature of, 100; crisis discourse and, 96–97, 108; criticisms of, 98–100; discrimination in, 89, 97–98, 100; heritage sites and, 101–109; heroic narrative in, 90, 91, 98, 109, 112–113; as histories from below, 9, 91, 92, 101, 106; language used in, 92; origins and growth of, 94–96; as perpetual anthologies, 9, 96; use of term, 92–93. *See also* migrant archives
condominiums, 78, 81–84, 86
conspicuous consumption, 58, 69–72, 74
consumption, 57–86; *balikbayan* boxes and, 59, 62, 65–67, 81, 180; businesses impacted by, 3, 7, 76–86; class status and, 58, 59, 62, 74, 79–80; conspicuous, 58, 69–72, 74; debt resulting from, 58, 69, 72, 74; directing migrant practices of, 70–75; as love, 58, 60–61, 65–68, 71–75; in media sector, 76–81, 85–86; purchasing power and, 76–78, 85; in real-estate sector, 76–78, 81–86; reciprocity norms and, 3, 10, 59–60; remittances and, 62–64, 69
Cordova, Dorothy, 94, 95, 97, 99–100
Cordova, Fred, 13, 94–96, 98–100, 182
CPCA. *See* Centre for Philippine Concerns–Australia (CPCA)
cross-cultural marriages, 7, 114–115, 130–131, 138–142
Cruz, Phyllis Theresa, 82
Cuaresma, Charlene, 120, 128–129
Cullen, Shay, 157
cultural activism, 90, 92, 93, 101, 102
cultural preservation areas, 101–109

DAWN (Development Action Women's Network), 25–26, 37–38
Dawn House S.A. Inc., 140–141
deaf children, 156, 158, 160, 167
debt, 32–33, 58, 69, 72, 74
de Guzman, Emil, 160
de Guzman, Odine, 23–25, 188n15
de Guzman, Robert, 36
de Guzman, Violeta, 63
de Juan, Jaypy, 169–170
de la Cruz, Policarpio Pete, 89, 90, *90*
Delvo, Dillon, 107
Development Action Women's Network (DAWN), 25–26, 37–38
de Vera, Mao, 165, 168
de Vera, Ophee, 165, 166, 168

diasporic philanthropy, 149–152, 160–161, 167, 170–171, 178
Dicka, Joan, 120, 135, 136–137, 138, 140–141, 143–147
discrimination: anti-miscegenation laws, 89, 97; in community histories, 89, 97–98, 100; in heroic narrative, 8, 91; interethnic children and, 37–38. *See also* stereotypes
divorce, 21, 24, 39, 47, 49, 51, 138
Dizon-Añonuevo, Mai, 71
domestic violence, 130–146; forms of, 132, 136–137, 142; government allies in fight against, 131, 140; heroic narrative and, 119; history of advocacy for victims of, 134–137; homicides related to, 129, 130, 132, 138, 139; legislation for victims of, 116, 137–140, 216n169; in migration context, 114–115; shame associated with, 120, 132; support services for, 140–144; welfare workers and, 131, 141, 145–146
domestic workers: class status of, 10, 59, 62; consumption habits of, 63, 65, 68, 73, 76; exploitation of, 1–2; family challenges for, 5; infidelity by, 40–41, 48–54; as investors, 78; lesbianism among, 51–52; moral surveillance of, 46–47; placement fees for, 34; salaries of, 1, 32, 63; stereotypes regarding, 42; as tourist guides, 26
Domingo, Silme, 97
Draves, Victoria Manalo, 105
Droescher, Rosa, 120, 137, 146, 147
Duyugan, Virgil, 97
Dwyer, Dianne, 158

economy: banking services, 22, 60, 70, 71, 75, 85; media sector, 76–81, 85–86, 148, 158; philanthropy in development of, 150; real-estate market, 76–78, 81–86; remittances, impact on, 6, 17, 174. *See also* consumption
education: bilingual, 122, 125; Filipina/o/x American studies, 96, 110–112; financial, 70–72, 75; human rights discourse on, 146; of minority youth, 116–119, 121–130; at private schools, 59, 62; remittances going toward, 31, 62, 69; scholarships for, 3, 126, 130, 153–159, 167, 170
emigration. *See* migration
Encinas-Franco, Jean, 174, 175
entertainers, 16, 25–26, 37, 42, 118
Espana, Jonathan, 169
Espinas, Paul, 166, 170
Espinosa, Shirlita, 151

Estrada-Claudio, Sylvia, 44
Ethnic Affairs Commission (Australia), 120, 133, 135–137, 142, 144–146
ethnic discrimination. *See* discrimination
ethnic identity: awareness of, 126; families and, 37–38; of Filipina/o/x Americans, 93–94, 96; sexuality and, 42, 47–48
ethnic pride, 11–12, 95, 109, 113, 150
ethnotours, 14, 91, 102–109
Evatt, Elizabeth, 146
Everly, Hugh, 130
Eviota, Elizabeth, 44
exploitation: of children, 155–156; by family members, 34–37; in heroic narrative, 91; human rights discourse on, 146; of migrant workers, 1–2, 118, 175; NGO assistance in cases of, 25
extramarital affairs. *See* infidelity

FAHSOH (Filipino American Historical Society of Hawaii), 94–95, 112, 113
Faier, Lieba, 77
families, 21–38; critiques by migrants, 24, 31–37; cultural constructions of, 3, 5, 23; ethnic identity and, 37–38; in hegemonic discourses, 23–24; in heroic narrative, 21; idealized, 21–24, 37, 51, 188n15; intervention seminars for, 72–73; NGOs as, 24–26, 27; refashioning membership in, 24–31; social costs of migration on, 21, 22; technology for connection with, 7, 22–23, 47; transnational, 22, 27–31. *See also* children and adolescents; marriage
FANHS. *See* Filipino American National Historical Society
Felipe, Virgilio Menor, 98
feminine ideal, 5, 40, 42–44, 141–142
filial piety, 21, 24, 59
Filipina/o/x Americans: bridge generation of, 14, 96–97, 99; in civil rights movement, 15, 93; class status of, 10, 16, 79–80, 161; consumption habits of, 76; ethnic pride among, 11–12, 95, 109, 113; identity formation among, 93–94, 96; investment in Philippine property, 81–84; *manong* generation of, 15, 16, 111, 113, 123–124; as marriage migrants, 17; median income of, 161, 200n19; philanthropy of, 148, 150–152, 156; Pilipino Cultural Nights for, 9, 93–96, 99, 112, 161; use of term, 12–13, 186n33. *See also* community histories
Filipinas (magazine), 11–12, 64, 78, 81, 83, 153, 155, 179

INDEX

Filipina Women's Network (FWN), 160, 179
Filipino American Historical Society of Hawaii (FAHSOH), 94–95, 112, 113
Filipino American History Month, 98, 109–111
Filipino American National Historical Society (FANHS): achievement awards from, 179; archival sources from, 9, 91; conferences held by, 91, 92, 95, 206n47; documentaries produced by, 96, 98, 111; founders of, 13, 97, 99–100, 182; history and growth of, 92, 95, 110, 113, 204n11; lobbying efforts of, 98, 108–112; museum operated by, 9, 96, 110
Filipino Channel (TFC), 76–81, 83, 85–86, 148, 158, 200n20, 201n40
Filipino migrants: as activists. (*see* activism); as agents of change, 1–9, 74, 101, 131, 152, 173; as *bagong bayani* (new heroes), 6, 11, 12, 174–178; class differences among, 10, 16; as consumers. (*see* consumption); discrimination against. (*see* discrimination); as entertainers, 16, 25–26, 37, 42, 118; ethnic pride among, 11–12, 95, 109, 113, 150; exploitation of. (*see* exploitation); family life of. (*see* families); as historians. (*see* historians); as investors, 70–74, 77–78, 81–86; liminal status of, 6, 86, 173, 182; as martyrs, 5–6, 11–12, 31, 62, 174, 179; migration history of, 15–17, 98–99; motivations for migration, 3, 21, 30, 31; personal transformations of, 2–3, 26; as philanthropists. (*see* philanthropy); remittances from. (*see* remittances); role models for, 105, 128, 172, 179–180; undocumented, 1–2, 10, 16, 29–30, 57, 65, 68. *See also* domestic workers; marriage migrants; seafarers
Filipinotowns, 85, 101–103
Filipino Women's Working Party (FWWP): achievements of, 115, 118, 142, 145; archival sources from, 120; community response to, 147; decline of, 142–143; establishment of, 137; funding for, 146; lobbying efforts of, 140; objectives of, 117, 142; radio programs produced by, 141
Filipino Youth Activities (FYA), 94
financial literacy, 14, 37, 60, 64–65, 70–75, 85, 178
Flores, May Jane, 25
Forman, Sheila, 123, 145
France, Filipino migrants in, 1–2, 46–47, 49, 52, 53, 61–62

Francisco, Cora, 162, 163, 166
Francisco-Menchavez, Valerie, 188n18
fundraising, 82, 130, 148–149, 152–153, 158–164, 170
FWN (Filipina Women's Network), 160, 179
FWWP. *See* Filipino Women's Working Party
FYA (Filipino Youth Activities), 94

gender, 39–54; in community histories, 100; cultural constructions of, 3, 7, 41–46, 141–142; infidelity and, 29–31, 39–41, 44, 48–54; norms related to, 40, 42; in overseas context, 45–46; transgression of gender ideals, 48–54. *See also* men; women
Gonzalez, N. V. M., 94
Gonzalves, Theodore S., 93, 95, 96, 99, 161
Graulty, Rey, 130

Habal, Estella, 102
Haiyan (Yolanda), Typhoon (2013), 148–149, 152, 178
Hawaii: community histories from, 100, 112; education of minority youth in, 116–119, 121–130; Filipino population of, 114, 121–122; plantation workers in, 15, 97, 98, 121. *See also* Operation Manong (OM)
hearing-impaired children, 156, 158, 160, 167
Hee, Clayton, 130
heritage sites, 101–109
Hernandez, Jessica, 108
Hernando, Mariano, 128
heroic narrative of migration: characteristics of, 11–12; in community histories, 90, 91, 98, 109, 112–113; discrimination in, 8, 91; domestic violence and, 119; families as element of, 21; in migrant archive accounts, 9; philanthropy in, 161–162, 171–172; role models in, 179–180
historians: academic vs. community, 92–93; social memory influenced by, 7, 90, 91; training for, 95, 101. *See also* community histories; migrant archives
HOME (Humanitarian Organization for Migration Economics), 2, 14
Hong Kong, Filipino migrants in, 4–5, 16, 32–33, 51–54, 68–72, 151
Hosoda, Naomi, 24
housing market, 76–78, 81–86
Humanitarian Organization for Migration Economics (HOME), 2, 14
human rights, 6, 11, 136, 143–147, 156, 180
Hunt, Dee, 145

identity. *See* ethnic identity
Ileto, Reynaldo, 174
immigration. *See* migration
infidelity, 29–31, 33, 39–41, 44, 48–54
International Hotel (San Francisco), 102–103, 112
interracial romances, 40–41, 43, 49–50, 54
investors, 70–74, 77–78, 81–86
Ipong, Della, 135, 137, 145–147
Isanan, Laarni, 169, 170
Italy, Filipino migrants in, 10, 52, 61–63, 72, 73, 177–178
Itliong, Larry, 97, 110, 111

Jamero, Peter, 99
Jamero, Terri, 109
Japan, Filipino migrants in, 16, 25, 29–30, 32, 57, 65, 80
Jimenez, Coratec, 171

Kashiwara, Ken, 156
Kerkvliet, Melinda, 120, 123, 124, 127, 129, 145

Labrador, Roderick, 129
LaCuesta, Lloyd, 158, 159
Lakbay Dangal, 26, 27
Lamvik, Gunnar, 61, 64, 68
Leong, Laurence Wai-Teng, 45
lesbianism, 45, 51–52
liminality, 6, 86, 173, 182
literacy, financial, 14, 37, 60, 64–65, 70–75, 85, 178
Little Manila Foundation, 93, 102, 107–109, 111–112
Lopez family business empire, 79–80, 82
love, consumption as, 58, 60–61, 65–68, 71–75

Maano, Grace, 165
Mabalon, Dawn, 107–109, 111
Macabenta, Greg, 11, 160
Macapagal, Gloria, 174
Machado, Colette, 129
Managan, Arnold, 128
Manahan, Joey, 129
Mananzan, Mary John, 180
Mangahas, Elena, 108
Manilatown Heritage Foundation, 91, 93, 101–103, 112
Manlapit, Pablo, 97, 99
manong generation, 15, 16, 111, 113, 123–124
Mapa, Marites, 26, 27
Marchetti, Sabrina, 63

Marcos, Ferdinand, 7, 16, 79, 131, 136, 139, 154
Marginson, Melba, 120, 136, 138–139, 143, 145, 146
Mariano, Joyce, 150
marriage: Catholic Church on, 24; cross-cultural, 7, 114–115, 130–131, 138–142; infidelity in, 29–31, 33, 39–41, 44, 48–54; in transnational families, 22. *See also* divorce; marriage migrants
marriage migrants: prevalence of, 16–17, 114, 115, 134; in rural and remote areas, 7, 134; serial sponsorship of, 116, 130, 137–140; stereotypes regarding, 119; support services for, 139–142, 216n173. *See also* domestic violence
martyr migrants, 5–6, 11–12, 31, 62, 174, 179
masculine ideal, 44–45
Masian, Sennie, 137
McKay, Deirdre, 35, 66, 68
McKay, Stephen, 16, 176
McKinnon, Estrella "Lilia," 120, 134, 138, 143–145
media sector, 76–81, 85–86, 148, 158
medical missions, 148–153, 162–171
Medina, Belen, 23
men: breadwinner role of, 42, 44; in community histories, 100; infidelity by, 29–31, 40, 44, 50, 53; masculine ideal for, 44–45. *See also* gender
Mendoza, Lily, 97
Middle East, Filipino migrants in, 28, 45–46, 53, 80, 195–96n20
migrant archives: on consumption, 62, 64; on exploitation, 1–2; family critiques in, 36–37; languages used in, 8–9; philanthropy in, 153; platforms utilized for, 8–9, 14; sex and sexuality in, 42, 53; use of term, 8, 14. *See also* community histories
Migrant Resource Centres (Australia), 116, 120, 131, 133–137, 142, 145–146, 209n4
migration: motivations for, 3, 21, 30, 31; social costs of, 6, 7, 21, 22; transnational context of, 10, 59. *See also* Filipino migrants; heroic narrative of migration; migrant archives
Monrayo, Angeles, 99
moral surveillance, 46–47
Moss, Irene, 139, 146
motherhood, 5, 22, 31, 42. *See also* children and adolescents
Munnecom, Lorna Vea, 61
Munting Nayon day-care center, 180–182

INDEX

Napat, Jessica Flores, 40
Nicolas, Violeta, 175–176
nongovernmental organizations (NGOs): *bagong bayani* discourse used by, 175; combative position of, 118; as families, 24–26, 27; financial literacy seminars by, 14, 37, 60, 64–65, 70–75; fundraising for, 152; migrant involvement with, 2, 5; philanthropic partnerships with, 157; remittance advice from, 37; on social costs of migration, 7, 22. *See also* activism; *specific NGOs*
Novel-Jezewski, Maria Thelma, 62

Obama, Barack, 110
O'Brien, Anne, 152
Oliverio, Rodolfo, 78
Operation Manong (OM), 122–130; achievements of, 115, 118, 127–129, 145; archival sources from, 120; community response to, 147; curriculum development by, 126; funding for, 125, 126, 130, 145; higher education initiatives, 125–127; human rights discourse utilized by, 146; name selection for, 123–124; objectives of, 117, 122–123; populations targeted by, 122–123, 125, 126; volunteers with, 116–117, 123–125
Opiniano, Jeremiah, 151
Orientalist stereotypes, 119, 132
Ortega, Arnisson Andre, 82, 84
Overseas Workers Welfare Administration (OWWA), 22, 31, 70, 175–176

Padilla, Malu, 31–32
Padilla, Nestor, 83
Padilla, Raquel Delfin, 36, 68, 176
Padilla, Stephanie, 116–117, 128
Paglinawan, Faustino, 157
PAMA (Philippine Australian Medical Association), 148, 153, 162–165, 168–170, 222n67
Parreñas, Rhacel, 22, 27–28
Pas, Asuisui, 116
Pascao, Clemen, 170
Pascual, Piolo, 83
PATH (Philippine-American Tour of History), 106–107
PCNs (Pilipino Cultural Nights), 9, 93–96, 99, 112, 161
pensionados (government scholars), 15, 98
People Power Revolution, 150, 153–154
Pe-Pua, Rogelia, 142

perpetual anthologies, 9, 96
philanthropy, 148–172; children as targets of, 154–158, 160, 167, 169–170; diasporic, 149–152, 160–161, 167, 170–171, 178; economic development and, 150; fundraising and, 82, 130, 148–149, 152–153, 158–164, 170; in heroic narrative, 161–162, 171–172; medical missions and, 148–153, 162–171; social change through, 3, 7, 149–150, 170–171; transnational partnerships in, 149, 151–153, 156–157, 162
Philippine-American Tour of History (PATH), 106–107
Philippine Australian Medical Association (PAMA), 148, 153, 162–165, 168–170, 222n67
Philippine International Aid (PIA), 152–162; appeals to donors, 155–156, 169, 170; beneficiary selection, 152, 154–155; establishment of, 153–154; fundraising events for, 82, 153, 156, 158–162; scholarships awarded by, 153–159, 167, 170; transnational partnerships in, 152–153, 156–157; transparency of, 153, 157
Philippine Medical Society of Northern California (PMSNC), 150, 153, 164–169, 171
Philippine Overseas Employment Administration (POEA), 31, 174
Philippines: Catholicism in, 24, 30, 41–43; colonization of, 15, 43–44; economic impact of remittances on, 6, 17, 174; gender and sexuality in, 3, 7, 41–45; government-led migration efforts, 16, 22, 175; idealized families in, 21–24, 37, 51, 188n15; martial law in, 79, 131, 136, 150; medical missions to, 148–153, 162–171; People Power Revolution in, 150, 153–154; typhoons in, 25, 148–49, 152, 178. *See also* Filipino migrants; Tagalog language
PIA. *See* Philippine International Aid
Pido, Eric, 77–78, 82, 84
Pilipino Cultural Nights (PCNs), 9, 93–96, 99, 112, 161
PinoyWISE, 14, 37, 65, 71–73
Planet Philippines (magazine), 64, 78, 81, 83, 85
PMSNC (Philippine Medical Society of Northern California), 150, 153, 164–169, 171
POEA (Philippine Overseas Employment Administration), 31, 174

INDEX

Positively Filipino (online newspaper), 9, 12, 113, 179
poverty, 16, 89, 98, 149, 155–158, 161
Pratt, Geraldine, 28
prejudice. *See* discrimination; stereotypes
pride, ethnic, 11–12, 95, 109, 113, 150
prostitution, 26, 132, 154, 156, 157
Pura, Arnel, 33
purchasing power, 76–78, 85

Quesada, Ramon, 76

racial discrimination. *See* discrimination
Rafael, Vicente, 174
Ramilo, Concepción "Chat," 120, 135–137, 143, 146
Ramos, Barge, 158, 159
Rapinsky, Emilie, 145
real-estate market, 76–78, 81–86
Rebollos, Eloina Reyes, 69
reciprocity norms, 3, 10, 59–60
religion. *See* Catholic Church
remittances: ABS-CBN remittance services, 81; banking transformed by, 85; consumption habits of, 62–64, 69; economic impact of, 6, 17, 174; family exploitation of, 34–37; sacrifices in provision of, 31–34; from seafarers, 64, 176; transnational family life and, 29, 30
Reyes, Raquel, 44
Reyes, Robert, 26
Rizal, Jose, 43, 104, 105, 174
Roman Catholic Church. *See* Catholic Church
Root, Maria, 13, 186n33
Rotelo, Nina "Cute," 2
Rue, Deney, 54
Ruiz, Jocelyn, 175–176

Sakima, Akira, 130
Salamat, Sherald, 61, 66
Sana, Ellene, 31
Santos, Aida, 51
Santos, Robert "Uncle Bob," 91, 99–101, 112
Sato, Josephine Nene, 166
Saudi Arabia, Filipino migrants in, 4, 16, 28, 40, 83
Sawyer, John, 110
Schembri, Charles, 138
scholarships, 3, 126, 130, 153–159, 167, 170
schooling. *See* education
seafarers: career advancement, 31; class status of, 59; consumption habits of, 61, 62, 64, 68; family challenges for, 33; as investors, 78, 83, 84; national recognition of, 175; percentage of Filipinos in global workforce, 16, 64; remittance requirements, 64, 176
Serapio, Maria, 76
serial sponsorship of marriage migrants, 116, 130, 137–140
Serrano, Manuel, 81
sex and sexuality, 39–54; Catholic Church on, 30, 41, 52; celibacy, 46, 52, 53; cultural constructions of, 3, 7, 41–46, 141–142; ethnic identity and, 42, 47–48; infidelity, 29–31, 33, 39–41, 44, 48–54; interracial romances, 40–41, 43, 49–50, 54; lesbianism, 45, 51–52; moral surveillance of, 46–47; in overseas context, 45–46; prostitution, 26, 132, 154, 156, 157; resistance to rules of, 47–54; trafficking, 142, 156, 157; in transnational families, 29–31. *See also* gender; men; women
Sicat, Leo, 35–36
Silva, Cecilia, 177–178
Silva, John, 169
Silva, Marian Laarni, 177
Sim, Amy, 52
Singapore, Filipino migrants in, 2, 32, 40–41, 45–54, 63–67, 72–73
social activism, 38, 91, 93, 102
social costs of migration, 6, 7, 21, 22
SoMa Pilipinas Ethnotour, 102–107
Spain, Philippines as colony of, 43, 44
Sparks, Norma D., 125, 128
spending habits. *See* consumption
spousal migration. *See* marriage migrants
stereotypes: in community histories, 100; dismantling of, 12, 43, 112–113, 180; of domestic workers, 42; of ethnic minority students, 122, 124, 128; of marriage migrants, 119; of martyr migrants, 6; Orientalist, 119, 132. *See also* discrimination
Strobel, Leny, 94
Sulit, Let-let A., 32

Tacardon, Myrna, 154, 155
Tadios, Joy, 70
Tagalog language: film industry in, 1, 6; financial literacy seminars in, 72; migrant archives and, 8–9; poetry in, 32–33; radio programs in, 141; romance novels in, 76
Tan, Bridget, 2
technology, family connections through, 7, 22–23, 47

INDEX

TFC (Filipino Channel), 76–81, 83, 85–86, 148, 158, 200n20, 201n40
Tiongson, Antonio T., 113
Tomimbang, Emme, 127, 128
Torres, Amaryllis, 44
trafficking, sex, 142, 156, 157
transnational families, 22, 27–31
transnational motherhood, 22
Treñas, Jerry, 169
typhoons, 25, 148–149, 152

Umil, Richard R., 128
undocumented workers, 1–2, 10, 16, 29–30, 57, 65, 68
United States: ABS-CBN programming in, 79–80; civil rights movement in, 15, 93, 127, 144, 179; diasporic philanthropy in, 150–152, 160–161, 171; Filipino American History Month in, 98, 109–111; financial crisis in (2007), 82, 187n43; history of migration to, 7, 15–16, 98–99; Philippines as colony of, 15, 43–44. *See also* Filipina/o/x Americans; *specific states*

Valencia, Joe and Debbie, 181
Velasco, Pete, 97
Ventura, Rey, 29–30, 34, 57–58, 65
Vera Cruz, Philip, 97, 99, 111
Verzon, Amadeo, 128

Verzon, Johnny, 127, 128
Viernes, Gene, 97
Viernes, Milagros, 164
Villanueva, Divine, 68
violence. *See* abuse; domestic violence

Wall, Deborah Ruiz, 120, 136, 137, 143, 145–147
Ward, Ethel, 120
Weekley, Kathleen, 70
Wehman, John, 98
women: in community histories, 100; empowerment of, 140–144; feminine ideal for, 5, 40, 42–44, 141–142; infidelity by, 39–41, 48–54; moral surveillance of, 46–47; sex trafficking of, 142, 156, 157; sexual agency of, 41, 42, 46, 50–51. *See also* domestic violence; gender; marriage migrants; motherhood

Yolanda (Haiyan), Typhoon (2013), 148–149, 152, 178
youth. *See* children and adolescents
Yuchengco, Mona Lisa, 154–158, 160, 169, 179

Zarate, Maria Jovita, 175
Zelinka, Sue, 146
Zontini, Elisabeth, 36
Zuhur, Sherifa, 45

www.ingramcontent.com/pod-product-compliance
Lightning Source LLC
Chambersburg PA
CBHW021853230426
43671CB00006B/372